THE PLACE OF JUDAISM IN PHILO'S THOUGHT

Israel, Jews, and Proselytes

Program in Judaic Studies
Brown University
BROWN JUDAIC STUDIES

Edited by
Shaye J. D. Cohen and Calvin Goldscheider

Editor for *Studia Philonica*
Shaye J. D. Cohen

Number 290
Studia Philonica Monographs 2

The Place of Judaism in Philo's Thought
Israel, Jews, and Proselytes

by
Ellen Birnbaum

THE PLACE OF JUDAISM IN PHILO'S THOUGHT

Israel, Jews, and Proselytes

by

Ellen Birnbaum

Scholars Press
Atlanta, Georgia

THE PLACE OF JUDAISM IN PHILO'S THOUGHT

Israel, Jews, and Proselytes

by
Ellen Birnbaum

Published with the assistance of the
Louis and Minna Epstein Fund of the
American Academy for Jewish Research

Library of Congress Cataloging-in-Publication Data
Birnbaum, Ellen.
    The place of Judaism in Philo's thought : Israel, Jews, and proselytes /
by Ellen Birnbaum.
        p.   cm. — (Studia Philonica monographs) (Brown Judaic studies ;
no. 290)
    Includes bibliographical references and index.
    ISBN 0-7885-0182-8 (cloth : alk. paper)
    1. Philo, of Alexandria—Views on Jewish identity. 2. Jews—
Identity—History of doctrines. I. Title. II. Series.
III. Series : Brown Judaic studies ; no. 290.
B689.Z7B56 1996
296.3'092—dc20   96-26263
                                            CIP

Printed in the United States of America
on acid-free paper

STUDIA PHILONICA MONOGRAPHS

STUDIES IN HELLENISTIC JUDAISM

EDITOR
David M. Hay, *Coe College, Cedar Rapids*

ADVISORY BOARD

Like *The Studia Philonica Annual*, the Studia Philonica Monographs series accepts monographs in the area of Hellenistic Judaism, with special emphasis on Philo and his *Umwelt*. Proposals for books to be published in the Monograph series should be sent to Prof. David M. Hay, Coe College, Cedar Rapids, IA 52402, U.S.A.

Article-length contributions should be sent to the Editor of *The Studia Philonica Annual,* Prof. David T. Runia, Rijnsburgerweg 116, 2333 AE Leiden, The Netherlands. Books for review in the Annual should be sent to the Book Review Editor, Prof. Gregory E. Sterling, Dept. of Theology, University of Notre Dame, Notre Dame, IN 46556, U.S.A.

To

MY PARENTS,
RUTH AND MILTON BIRNBAUM,

AND

MY HUSBAND,
DONALD ALTSCHILLER

CONTENTS

ACKNOWLEDGMENTS

This book, a lightly revised version of my doctoral dissertation (Columbia University, 1992), has followed a long path from its inception to its publication, and I am pleased to acknowledge with much appreciation the many people who have contributed to and been part of the journey.

Over the years, I have benefitted considerably from the scholarship and collegiality of the Philo of Alexandria Group in the Society of Biblical Literature. It is with gratitude and pleasure that I now publish this study in the new Studia Philonica Monographs subseries of Brown Judaic Studies. I wish to thank David M. Hay, Editor of this subseries, for his guidance, support, and encouragement. My appreciation also goes to Alan Mendelson and David Winston for their many constructive comments and suggestions and to Shaye J. D. Cohen, an Editor of Brown Judaic Studies, for his assistance. I am also grateful to the American Academy for Jewish Research for awarding me a grant to help defray publication expenses.

As my dissertation evolved into this book, I received invaluable support from a number of individuals. Michael Carasik carefully read through the dissertation and offered me much worthwhile advice about how I might revise it. D. Lowell White spared me a great deal of time and effort by his work on the indices. David T. Runia and Gonni Runia-Deenick helped smooth the path to publication in several ways. I am especially indebted to Gonni Runia-Deenick for her fine expertise in preparing the camera-ready copy of this book. She has generously accommodated my requests for late changes and my very specific preferences on even the smallest details. I wish also to thank David T. Runia, who was a gracious consultant on matters that ranged from positioning subheads to locating philosophical references about seeing God.

Patricia Benfari Tucker of the Office for Sponsored Research at Harvard University kindly permitted me to adjust my schedule as my academic activities required and allowed me to produce my work on office equipment. I am grateful to her, Patrice A. Carroll, Carol Salway, and all the other staff members at OSR, who provided a supportive and congenial community during my solitary academic pursuits.

James Dunkly, whom I met when he was Director of Libraries at Episcopal Divinity School and Weston School of Theology, has notably enhanced my awareness of scholarly resources in general and Philonic scholarship in particular. He readily lent an ear and was a continual source of encouragement and assistance. I also wish to express warm thanks to the following people who listened, helped in specific ways, or generally shared with me their learning and experience: Dorothy Africa, Bradley Clompus, Scott Cook, Julie Duncan, Gary Finder, Hayim Goldgraber, Kenneth H. Green, Sharon Green, Margaret Hutaff, Shulamit Kahn, James L. Kugel, Sherry Leffert, Jon D. Levenson, Diana Lobel, Pamela Marshall, Jean Rittmueller, Steven Ronner, Joel Rosenberg, Thomas H. Tobin, Sze-kar Wan, Elliot Wolfson, Dvora Yanow, and Gerald Zuriff.

I am particularly grateful to Prof. Alan Segal, who willingly agreed to become my advisor at Columbia University when I was already a student *in absentia*. His assistance and flexibility helped ease the difficulties posed by my long-distance residence. He encouraged me to participate in the Columbia community even from afar, showed enthusiasm for my project, and offered many helpful comments and suggestions for clarifying my ideas and improving my presentation. I am also indebted to Prof. Arthur Hyman for his astute remarks and observations about my work in progress. Thanks are due as well to other members of my dissertation defense committee—Profs. David Weiss Halivni, Robert Somerville, and Michael Stanislawski.

With deepest appreciation, I wish to acknowledge Prof. John Strugnell, who has watched the evolution of this book from its beginnings and who has enriched my education in many ways. A professor at Harvard University with no official obligations toward me, he generously helped facilitate my progress before the dissertation, offered direction as I defined my topic, and invested many hours and much care in reading my work and discussing it with me. Most important, from the first, he guided and stood by me, providing ample time and room so that I might learn and grow at my own pace and pursue my curiosity where it would lead. I am very grateful for and have especially benefitted from his expert instruction, which was finely tuned to my needs and abilities and which respected and fostered independence of mind.

Last, but hardly least, I wish to express loving gratitude to my husband, Donald Altschiller, and my parents, Ruth and Milton Birnbaum, for their help, encouragement, and confidence in me. My parents—professors of Judaic studies and English literature, respectively—are also my teachers. From their example, I have acquired a love of learning, which has inspired and vitalized my work on this book and which continues to inspire my other endeavors. I am also grateful to my mother for reading drafts of this work so carefully and to both my parents for nurturing my interests and contributing to my scholarly pursuits their own learned perspectives.

During the past few years, Philo, the book, and their several attendant issues have subtly become members of my household. My husband accepted these with forbearance and a wonderful sense of humor, sparing me from ponderousness by making me laugh when things seemed most difficult. A writer and professional librarian with a remarkable ability to locate information, he offered editorial advice and bibliographic assistance, keeping me informed about a wide variety of items. As the seasons of this book evolved, he patiently tolerated my numerous and sundry preoccupations. Above all, his constant support through many vicissitudes has sustained me from the beginning of this project to its fulfillment.

Cambridge, Massachusetts

June 1996

A Note to the Reader

In this book, I explore how Philo balances his particular Jewish loyalties and his universal spiritual strivings. My inquiry has involved careful studies of Philonic vocabulary and interpretation, and I hope the specialist will find my presentation of these studies to be useful. Because these studies have implications for issues beyond Philo, as I suggest at the end of this Note, I also hope the interested non-specialist will not be deterred by foreign words and exegetical analyses. Below is information—intended to help both kinds of readers—about stylistic matters, texts, translations, and features of Philo's writings.

1. To make the material more accessible, I have translated all Greek and Hebrew terms and, in the Index of Greek Terms, I have transliterated the most significant Greek words and expressions. In most chapters with detailed examination of Philonic terms and passages, I offer summaries—generally organized according to the different series of writings by Philo, as described further below and in the Introduction.

2. Translations of Philo's writings are from The Loeb Classical Library (LCL), except when otherwise indicated. Occasionally, I have replaced portions of the LCL translation with a translation of my own, which is included within brackets in the excerpt from LCL. In rare instances in which manuscript variations—recorded in the Cohn-Wendland edition of Philo—are particularly relevant, I have listed these in the notes.

Bible translations are from the Revised Standard Version (RSV) (1952), except when the Greek Bible, which Philo uses, differs significantly from the Hebrew text, upon which the RSV is based. In these cases, I have either modified the RSV translation to reflect the Greek and included my modification within brackets, or I have provided my own translations based upon the Greek. For the Greek Bible, I have used Alfred Rahlfs's edition of the Septuagint. When Philo's Biblical quotations differ from this text, I cite the differences in the notes. Full bibliographic information about the editions of LCL, Cohn-Wendland, and Rahlfs can be found in the Bibliography.

3. Besides including my own adaptations to translations from LCL or RSV, brackets may simply indicate words inserted for clarity or may contain alternative Greek articles and endings for words that can be either

masculine or neuter. The function of the brackets should be evident in each case.

4. Initial citations to all works are provided in full in the notes and thereafter in shortened form. Abbreviations of Philonic treatises and other works are listed immediately after this Note; in some cases, abbreviations of non-Philonic works differ from those listed in *The Studia Philonica Annual*. All references in this book to LCL are to the LCL edition of Philo's works only and not to the works of any other author. When a list of Philonic passages includes numbers in parentheses after certain passages, these numbers indicate how many times a word or expression occurs in those passages.

5. I frequently mention Philo's three exegetical series—the Allegory, the Exposition, and Questions and Answers on Genesis and Exodus (QGE). The Allegory and the Exposition are also known by longer titles as The Allegorical Commentary or The Allegory of the Law, and The Exposition of the Law. Besides these three exegetical series, I refer to several miscellaneous treatises as non-exegetical works. Although these so-called non-exegetical treatises may include some Biblical interpretation, they are not primarily commentaries on the Bible.

6. The List of Abbreviations that follows this Note also shows the series or category to which each treatise belongs. In the LCL edition, Allegory treatises can be found in vols. 1-5, and Exposition treatises in vols. 6-8, with the exception of the Exposition treatise *Opif.*, which is at the beginning of vol. 1. QGE is published in two supplementary volumes. The other works—except for *Anim.* and *Deo,* which survive chiefly in Armenian and not in Greek—are in vols. 9 and 10. Each LCL volume has a list of treatises, showing the order in which they are presented and the volumes into which they are divided in this edition.

7. Because Philo's etymology of "Israel" is centrally important to this study, the following clarifications are in order. When I speak of Philo's etymology of "Israel," I am referring to the expression he uses both to explain the meaning of the word "Israel" and to describe the entity "Israel."

Philo uses the etymology with and without definite articles. When he explains the meaning of the word "Israel," he gives the etymology as ὁρῶν θεόν, without definite articles. In describing the entity "Israel," however, he does use a definite article with ὁρῶν and sometimes with θεόν. θεός, or God, takes a masculine article. The participle ὁρῶν, however, can be either masculine (m.) or neuter (n.), so that Philo may describe "Israel" as ὁ – or τὸ – ὁρῶν [τὸν] θεόν. Although Philo generally uses a masculine article with ὁρῶν, he also uses the neuter article at least once; and when ὁρῶν appears with the article in the genitive case, one cannot determine the gender of these words. Whether or not τόν appears before θεόν does not affect the translation.

I have translated this etymology most often as "[the] one who (m.) sees God" or "[the] one that (n.) sees God," using the definite article in English when Philo uses it before the Greek participle. When the gender is ambiguous but not relevant to the discussion, I have used these translations interchangeably. To convey the ambiguity of the gender when this ambiguity *is* relevant, I use the translation "one that sees God." After the first few occurrences of these translations in this book, I generally provide them without quotation marks. Various modern scholars, some of whom I quote in this book, have rendered the etymology ὁρῶν θεόν as "seeing God," translating the participle ὁρῶν as a gerund. I myself, however, do not use this translation; instead I render the participle ὁρῶν, with its number and gender, as "one who sees" or "one that sees."

Philo's etymology of "Israel" is significant precisely because it opens the way for him to redefine this entity beyond a specific ethnic group. His treatment of other themes such as the covenant and the chosen people also reflects a spiritual vision that reaches beyond a particular nation. Though I have focused solely upon Philo, the topics covered in this book shed light upon much broader questions, to which I hope these Philonic studies will contribute. Among the broader questions are how the meaning of "Israel" evolves in Jewish and Christian thought, what significance the covenant holds in the history of Judaism, how a pre-rabbinic—or non-rabbinic— Jew might understand the role of his people in relation to God and to other peoples, and how in antiquity an individual committed to a specific tradition might negotiate between the particular and the universal. Should the reader recognize other issues to which these Philonic studies might apply, so much the better.

ABBREVIATIONS

Philonic Works

Abbreviations for Philonic works are listed alphabetically. The following letters in the right-hand column indicate the series or category to which each treatise belongs, as it is discussed in this book: A (Allegory), E (Exposition), M (miscellaneous), N (non-exegetical), and Q (Questions and Answers on Genesis and Exodus).

Abr.	*De Abrahamo*	E
Aet.	*De Aeternitate Mundi*	N
Agr.	*De Agricultura*	A
Anim.	*De Animalibus*	N
Cher.	*De Cherubim*	A
Conf.	*De Confusione Linguarum*	A
Congr.	*De Congressu Quaerendae Eruditionis Gratia*	A
Contempl.	*De Vita Contemplativa*	N
Decal.	*De Decalogo*	E
Deo	*De Deo*	M
Det.	*Quod Deterius Potiori Insidiari Solet*	A
Deus	*Quod Deus Immutabilis Sit*	A
Ebr.	*De Ebrietate*	A
Flacc.	*In Flaccum*	N
Fug.	*De Fuga et Inventione*	A
Gig.	*De Gigantibus*	A
Her.	*Quis Rerum Divinarum Heres Sit*	A
Hypoth.	*Hypothetica (Apologia pro Iudaeis)*	N
Ios.	*De Iosepho*	E
Leg. 1-3	*Legum Allegoriae* I-III	A
Legat.	*De Legatione ad Gaium*	N
Migr.	*De Migratione Abrahami*	A
Mos. 1-2	*De Vita Mosis* I-II	E
Mut.	*De Mutatione Nominum*	A
Opif.	*De Opificio Mundi*	E
Plant.	*De Plantatione*	A
Post.	*De Posteritate Caini*	A

Praem.	*De Praemiis et Poenis*	E
Prob.	*Quod Omnis Probus Liber Sit*	N
Prov.	*De Providentia*	N
QE 1-2	*Quaestiones et Solutiones in Exodum* I-II	Q
QG 1-4	*Quaestiones et Solutiones in Genesim* I-IV	Q
QGE	Questions and Answers on Genesis and Exodus	
Sacr.	*De Sacrificiis Abelis et Caini*	A
Sobr.	*De Sobrietate*	A
Somn. 1-2	*De Somniis* I-II	A
Spec. 1-4	*De Specialibus Legibus* I-IV	E
Virt.	*De Virtutibus*	E

OTHER WORKS

ANRW	*Aufstieg und Niedergang der romischen Welt*
BT	Babylonian Talmud
CRINT	Compendia Rerum Iudaicarum ad Novum Testamentum
HTR	*Harvard Theological Review*
JBL	*Journal of Biblical Literature*
JTS	*Journal of Theological Studies*
LCL	The Loeb Classical Library
LXX	Septuagint
OPA	*Les oeuvres de Philon d'Alexandrie*
OTP	*Old Testament Pseudepigrapha*
PJ	*Prayer of Joseph*
SBL	Society of Biblical Literature
SP	*Studia Philonica*
SPhA	*The Studia Philonica Annual*
TDNT	*Theological Dictionary of the New Testament*
TLG	Thesaurus Linguae Graecae

Introduction

From Biblical times and indeed throughout the history of Judaism, one can trace a persistent tension between particularism and universalism. To be sure, one can define these terms differently and examine the tensions between them within different contexts. In Jewish history, however, one might well argue that in one way or another, the two opposing tendencies derive from a fundamental belief established at the very beginning of the Hebrew Scriptures, in the Book of Genesis. This is the belief that the Creator and Father of the entire universe is also the particular, national God of Abraham, Isaac, Jacob, and their descendant people, Israel.

The identification of Israel's national God with the God of all creation can and does raise several questions for Jews and non-Jews alike. To what extent, for example, are Jews—who worship the universal Creator in a particular way—different from or the same as every other nation? If indeed the God of the Jews is also God of the universe, must one worship Him only in the Jewish way? Is it not simply enough to believe—as many non-Jewish philosophers do—that He exists? And if this belief is enough, why be a Jew?

In the centuries following the conquests of Alexander the Great (334–323 B.C.E.), the intermingling of local cultures with the Hellenic way of life introduced by Alexander and his successors brought these issues into sharper focus for Judean Jews as well as those in the diaspora. At issue was how to preserve their unique Jewish heritage while participating in the international Hellenistic culture whose very hallmark was the blend of Hellenic and local influences. Could one be a cosmopolitan—a citizen of the world—and a disciple of Moses at the same time? And if so, how?

If one were seeking to pose these various questions—which continue to inspire debate in our own times—to a Jew living in antiquity, one could hardly find a more apt partner in conversation than Philo of Alexandria (ca. 20 B.C.E.–50 C.E.). As a resident of this thriving cultural center during the first century C.E., he is an excellent witness to the forceful encounter between Jewish and Greek values, beliefs, and practices. He has left us, moreover, with a fairly generous record of his ideas.

Any reader of Philo can hardly fail to notice that he is extremely devoted to the Jewish people and their Scriptures, beliefs, and practices. Indeed most of his works are Biblical commentaries, in which he expounds upon the writings of utmost importance to Jews and also explains their way of life. Philo's dedication to his people, moreover, extends beyond study and writing to political involvement, as exemplified by his participation in a delegation to the Emperor Caligula to plead on behalf of his suffering compatriots.

Besides this commitment to his people and their religion, however, Philo seems equally devoted to philosophical and spiritual pursuits which might be shared by any likeminded persons, whether Jewish or not. To be sure, Philo's works are a rich and complex weave of Jewish and Greek strands of thought. Not only does he use and criticize concepts and vocabulary from a variety of contemporary philosophical currents, but even his characteristic method of interpreting Scripture as allegory reflects the influence of his surrounding philosophical culture. The tensions in Philo's thought, however, derive not just from his blending of Jewish and Hellenistic cultural elements, they also spring from his explicitly universal interpretations for the very particular details of Scripture. Frequently, for example, he portrays individuals like Abraham and Moses as wise or good men in general instead of as specific historical figures, and his allegorical interpretations transform individuals and nations into souls or characteristics of the soul.

While no one, then, would question Philo's steadfast commitment to the Jews and their religion, his tendencies toward universalism and individualism are marked enough to undermine or at least pose a challenge to this commitment. He himself, however, rarely acknowledges or addresses this potential challenge directly.

Although scholars have long debated the extent to which Philo is influenced by Greek or Jewish sources, no one has thoroughly examined the tension in his thinking between particularism and universalism. For years, writers have argued about whether Philo is more fundamentally Greek or Jewish, comparing his writings with other manifestations of Judaism, various philosophical schools, pagan mystery cults, Gnosticism, and Christianity. Scholars have also examined Philo as—among other things—a philosopher, a mystic, a Jew, a Biblical interpreter, and a rhetorician. Without a doubt, these approaches have contributed impressively to understanding the writings of this first-century Alexandrian Jew. While recognizing his manifold dimensions, however, the authors of these various studies address only tangentially the basic question of how Philo himself evaluates his Jewish identity in relation to other elements in his thought.

In 1971, Samuel Sandmel published a work whose title epitomizes one of the approaches just described; it is called *Philo's Place in Judaism*.[1]

---

[1] Samuel Sandmel, *Philo's Place in Judaism: A Study of Conceptions of Abraham in Jewish Literature*, augmented ed. (New York: Ktav, 1971).

Sandmel compares portrayals of Abraham in Philonic works with those found in rabbinic literature and concludes that Philo represents a Judaism quite different from that of the Rabbis. The title of the present study, "The Place of Judaism in Philo's Thought," is a deliberate reworking of Sandmel's title. The shift in words is meant to signal the shift in focus from the question of whether Philo is more fundamentally a Greek or a Jew and from the comparison of his Judaism with other manifestations to the question of how he himself assesses the significance of being a Jew. At the outset, however, we should note that Philo himself never uses the term "Judaism"—though it was in use during his time[2]—nor shall I speculate about how he might define this phenomenon. Instead I shall address the question of why and how it is important to him.

Particularism and Universalism

Although this study pertains directly to tensions between particularism and universalism in Philo's thought, I shall use these terms with caution. For one thing, Philo himself does not use these words, even though his writings may display particularist or universalist concerns. Second, and perhaps more important, the two terms have quite varied meanings even for those of us who do use them.

Indeed "particularism" and "universalism" are imprecise, and each word has several definitions. The *Oxford English Dictionary* (2nd ed.), for example, offers a theological definition and two somewhat general ones for both words. According to the theological definitions, particularism is "the doctrine of particular election or particular redemption; the dogma that Divine grace is provided for or offered to a selected part, not the whole, of the human race." Universalism, in contrast, represents "the doctrine of universal salvation or redemption"; presumably, that is the belief that salvation or redemption is equally available to all humanity.

According to the more general definitions, particularism denotes "exclusive attachment or devotion to one's particular party, sect, nation, etc.," while universalism is "the fact or condition of being universal in character or scope." Finally, according to another general definition, particularism is "exclusive attention to a particular subject, specialism," while universalism denotes "the fact or quality of being concerned with or interested in all or a great variety of subjects."

---

[2] The Greek term Ἰουδαϊσμός first appears in 2 Maccabees (2:21, 8:1, 14:38). It is also found in 4 Macc. 4:26 and Gal. 1:13–14. See Yehoshua Amir, "The Term Ἰουδαϊσμός : A Study in Jewish-Hellenistic Self-Identification," *Immanuel* 14 (1982): 34–41.

Because these two terms can be understood so differently, one can present tensions between particularism and universalism in various ways. In Philo's works alone, for example, one might focus upon a figure like Moses and examine his significance to Philo as a national leader and lawgiver or as a spiritual exemplar for all. Or, one might consider Philo's attitudes toward the special laws of Moses and the laws of nature or toward messianic expectation as a national or universal ideal.[3]

The first two topics, Philo's attitude toward Moses and toward different kinds of laws, illustrate a more general understanding of particularism and universalism, namely, exclusive interest in a particular group versus concern for all humanity. Insofar as one emphasizes divine authority behind the laws of Moses, a study of Philo's attitudes toward the different kinds of laws may also involve a theological understanding of the terms, since one may ask whether or not the Mosaic laws are divinely ordained for one group as opposed to all groups. Finally, the last topic—messianic expectation—suggests the theological definition of particularism and universalism because this issue touches upon whether divine redemption extends to all people or only to some.

In this study, I shall concentrate upon two kinds of relationships to God and offer a theological definition of universalism and particularism within this context. My primary focus will not be upon these terms and their definitions, however, but rather upon certain related questions. Specifically, I am interested in 1) the philosophical quest to "see God" or

---

[3] Examples of studies on these topics include the following: *Moses*: Yehoshua Amir, "Mose als Verfasser der Tora bei Philon," *Die hellenistische Gestalt des Judentums bei Philon von Alexandrien*, Forschungen zum jüdisch-christlichen Dialog, ed. Yehuda Aschkenasy and Heinz Kremers, no. 5 (Neukirchen-Vluyn: Neukirchener Verlag, 1983), 77–106; Erwin R. Goodenough, *By Light, Light: The Mystic Gospel of Hellenistic Judaism* (New Haven: Yale University Press, 1935), 180–234; Burton L. Mack, "Imitatio Mosis: Patterns of Cosmology and Soteriology in the Hellenistic Synagogue," *Studia Philonica* (*SP*) 1 (1972): 27–55; *Natural Laws and Mosaic Laws*: André Myre, "La loi de la nature et la loi mosaïque selon Philon d'Alexandrie, *Science et Esprit* 28 (1976): 163–81; Valentin Nikiprowetzky, *Le commentaire de l'Écriture chez Philon d'Alexandrie: Son caractère et sa portée; Observations philologiques*, Arbeiten zur Literatur und Geschichte des hellenistischen Judentums, ed. K. H. Rengstorf et al., no. 11 (Leiden: E. J. Brill, 1977), 117–55; Harry A. Wolfson, *Philo: Foundations of Religious Philosophy in Judaism, Christianity, and Islam* (Cambridge: Harvard University Press, 1975, repr. 1982), 2:165–438; *Messianic Expectation*: Peder Borgen, "'There Shall Come Forth a Man': Reflections on Messianic Ideas in Philo," *The Messiah: Developments in Earliest Judaism and Christianity*, ed. James H. Charlesworth (Minneapolis: Fortress Press, 1992), 341–61; Ferdinand Dexinger, "Ein 'messianisches Szenarium' als Gemeingut des Judentums in nach-herodianischer Zeit?" *Kairos* 17 (1975): 249–78, esp. 250–55; Richard D. Hecht, "Philo and Messiah," *Judaisms and Their Messiahs at the Turn of the Christian Era*, ed. Jacob Neusner et al. (Cambridge: Cambridge University Press, 1987), 139–68.

the goal of seeing Him and 2) the covenant between God and Biblical Israel—and, by extension, its Jewish descendants. My chief concerns will be: Does Philo believe that all people can participate in these relationships or that only some people can participate? If only some can participate, then must they be Jews? If not, then what are the requirements?

Within this framework, universalism will represent the position that anyone can participate in either of the two relationships with God, whereas particularism will represent the position that only Jews can participate in these relationships. At the conclusion of this investigation, I shall further amplify and refine these observations.

Considered together, the quest to see God or the goal of seeing Him and the covenant between Israel and God described in the Bible have potentially conflicting aspects. A closer look at each relationship highlights just what these aspects are.

For Philo, "seeing God" is the height of human happiness. His ideas about this experience are strongly influenced by Greek philosophical— and, especially, Platonic—notions. Since Philo is not consistent about what it means to see God, we cannot always distinguish between the quest to see Him and its fulfillment. I shall therefore speak of seeing God as both a quest and a goal. I shall also use the word "mystical" to describe this quest or goal, understanding mysticism loosely as the impulse to have a direct, i.e., unmediated, experience of God, who is transcendent and immaterial. This definition sidesteps such issues as whether the experience is intellectual or ecstatic or both and whether "direct experience" implies mere perception of or actual union with God. I shall, however, address these issues as they pertain to Philo's thought in the course of this study.

Several features of the quest to see or the goal of seeing God are particularly relevant to our discussion. First, this quest or goal is contemporary to one's lifetime in that one begins the quest or achieves the goal only during the span of one's life. Related to this observation is that seeing God can be characterized as an achievement or an ability, which may be either innate or acquired. In addition, the quest to see or goal of seeing God may theoretically be considered universal since anyone—Jew or non-Jew—may strive to see Him. Highlighting this feature is that Philo rarely if ever speaks of the quest in explicitly Jewish terms.[4] Finally, while any

---

[4] By "explicitly Jewish terms," I mean explicit use of the word Ἰουδαῖος (Jew) or Ἰουδαϊκός (Jewish). Thus, although Philo uses the expression "disciple of Moses" (γνώριμος, ὁμιλητής, or φοιτητὴς Μωυσέως) (*Det.* 86; *Post.* 12; *Conf.* 39; *Her.* 81; *Mos.* 2.205; *Spec.* 1.319, 345; *Spec.* 2.88, 256; *Contempl.* 63; *Hypoth.* 11.1; cf. *Deus* 120), one could argue that such a disciple need not necessarily be a Jew. Philo also uses "Israel" (Ἰσραήλ) to describe spiritual seekers. The ambiguity of this term is amply discussed below and throughout this study.

or all people may pursue this goal, the very nature of the pursuit is separate and individual, since Philo describes seeing God as an internal experience—a function of the mind or soul. Thus, although he speaks of the collective race or class that can see—the ὁρατικὸν γένος—he speaks enough about individual people, minds, and souls that see God to lend the experience a decidedly individualistic dimension.

Besides embracing this mystical approach to God, Philo is also heir to Biblical claims that God chose the nation Israel to join Him in a covenant and be His special people. This theme is expressed throughout the Bible, beginning in the Book of Genesis, in which God establishes His covenant with the patriarchs Abraham, Isaac, and Jacob and declares His intentions to be God to their descendants. In the Book of Exodus, God proclaims their descendant nation, Israel, to be His own special people, and He establishes His covenant with them. This relationship serves as the foundation for the entire, subsequent history of Biblical Israel.

In contrast to Philo's discussion of seeing God, the Biblical description of God's relationship with Israel can be characterized as historical, though also ongoing; inherited; corporate, though also individual; and exclusive. Since God established His covenant with Israel at a specific point in the past, the relationship has a historical dimension, and members of the nation inherit the relationship through tradition. Although each person individually is part of the covenant, the relationship also has a corporate dimension because God established it simultaneously with the entire nation. Finally, the covenant is exclusive because it was established only with Israel as opposed to any and all other peoples.

When these two relationships with God, then—i.e., the quest to see or the goal of seeing Him and the covenant between Him and Biblical Israel—are juxtaposed or brought together in some way, as they are in Philo's thought, a tension arises between the conflicting qualities of each: the quality of being contemporary to one's life versus historical; innate or acquired versus inherited; individual versus corporate; and most important, perhaps, universal versus exclusive. As we examine where Philo lies between the poles of particularism and universalism, it will be useful to keep these component tensions in mind.

Other Scholarly Approaches

Many scholars acknowledge the kinds of tensions just described, whether they use terms like particularism, universalism, nationalism, individualism, Judaism, mysticism, or as one writer suggests, religion and religiosity.[5] Although some authors may depict these tensions with sensitivity, they generally address them only in passing.

Since we shall be considering Philo's discussion of the quest to see or goal of seeing God, his attitude toward the relationship between God and Biblical Israel, and his evaluation of the significance of being a Jew, of special interest are those works which closely examine these topics and the possible relationship among them. To sample the range of approaches, I shall briefly review works which concentrate either upon Philo's attitude toward Jews and Jewish tradition or upon his depiction of a spiritual quest.[6] Although I am focusing specifically upon the quest for a vision of God, Philo speaks about the quest for God in different ways, variously calling it a quest for knowledge, reverence, or vision of God, or simply a quest for God Himself.

Noteworthy among those who investigate Philo's attitude toward Jews and Jewish tradition are Annie Jaubert, Alan Mendelson, and Yehoshua Amir. While these writers look at Philo's treatment of Judaism from different perspectives, in one way or another, each of them acknowledges and addresses the tensions we have been discussing.

Jaubert's consideration of Philo comprises a rather lengthy chapter in a much longer study entitled *La notion d'Alliance dans le judaïsme aux abords de*

---

[5] Samuel Sandmel distinguishes between Philo's religion and religiosity in *Philo of Alexandria: An Introduction* (New York: Oxford University Press, 1979), 82–83. He defines religiosity as "the tone and character of the carrying out of the religion on the part of differing personalities within the tradition." While Philo's "religion" is Judaism, which is also the religion of the Rabbis, Sandmel notes that Philo's religiosity is quite different from theirs. He writes, "One clue to the distinction in religiosity is the place of the Laws of Moses. In Rabbinic Judaism the Laws are an end in themselves; in Philo they are a means to what he conceives as a greater end. There is no echo I know of in Rabbinic literature of the central goal in Philo's Judaism, that of mystic communion with the Godhead" (83).

[6] One could also select several noteworthy studies which incorporate both aspects of Philo—as a Jew and a spiritual seeker—but generally, these broader studies do not focus primarily upon these two aspects. An exception is Émile Bréhier's *Les idées philosophiques et religieuses de Philon d'Alexandrie*, 2nd ed., Études de Philosophie Mediévale, ed. Étienne Gilson, no. 8 (Paris: J. Vrin, 1925). Bréhier provides a balanced picture of Philo's Jewish and spiritual sides, keeping them, however, quite separate. Three other works which also present Philo's mystical and Jewish dimensions with sensitivity are Erwin R. Goodenough, *An Introduction to Philo Judaeus*, Brown Classics in Judaica, ed. Jacob Neusner (Oxford: Basil Blackwell, 1962; repr. Lanham, Maryland: University Press of America, 1986); Hans Lewy, "Introduction," "Philo: Selections," *Three Jewish Philosophers* (New York: Harper & Row, 1965), 7–25; and Sandmel, *Philo of Alexandria*. Goodenough's *Introduction to Philo Judaeus* presents a more balanced view than his *By Light, Light*, which is discussed later in the Introduction. In his monumental study of Philo, Harry Wolfson does not develop Philo's mystical side at all. For Wolfson's discussion of seeing God, see *Philo*, 2:83–93.

l'ère chrétienne.[7] Jaubert examines how Philo deals with such Biblical themes as election and messianism, the law, the idea of a priestly people, and the notion of "Israel." Finally, she reviews his various ways of using the word for covenant, διαθήκη. Although she recognizes that Philo values the internal relationship to God above all else, Jaubert concludes nonetheless that he never denies any of the prerogatives of Israel.[8]

In contrast with Jaubert, Alan Mendelson, in his book *Philo's Jewish Identity*,[9] presents both a phenomenological and a social analysis. First Mendelson describes Philo's beliefs and practices in two sections called "Orthodoxy" and "Orthopraxy," respectively. He then considers Philo's works in context of the social realities of his time by exploring Philo's reflections about his Jewish and non-Jewish environment, his apologetic statements in relation to anti-Jewish polemics, and, in turn, Philo's own polemics against non-Jewish beliefs and practices.

It is when he looks at Philo's polemics in relation to his non-Jewish neighbors that Mendelson most clearly addresses the kinds of tensions we have been discussing. Mendelson, however, places these tensions squarely in the social arena rather than confining them to the realm of thought, as Jaubert does. From this perspective, he emphasizes the particularist side of Philo, noting that Philo presents the Jews as spiritually superior to other nations. Mendelson concludes his book emphasizing this particularist attitude. He writes, "Philo's sense of spiritual superiority may have helped to preserve the Alexandrian Jews' religious identity. But, as in other times and places, the Jews of Alexandria paid a heavy price for this sense of themselves."[10]

Finally, we shall consider an extended essay by Yehoshua Amir called "Philon und die jüdische Wirklichkeit seiner Zeit," the first in a collection of essays entitled *Die hellenistische Gestalt des Judentums bei Philon von Alexandrien.*[11] In this opening essay, Amir explores Philo's treatment of Biblical themes, aspects of his Judaism, and related social phenomena. To

---

[7] Annie Jaubert, *La notion d'Alliance dans le judaïsme aux abords de l'ère chrétienne*, Patristica Sorbonensia, no. 6 (Paris: Éditions du Seuil, 1963), 375–442.

[8] The reader may notice that some of these prerogatives are accorded to Israel in the Bible, and some derive from Philo's own interpretations.

[9] Alan Mendelson, *Philo's Jewish Identity*, Brown Judaic Studies, ed. Jacob Neusner et al., no. 161 (Atlanta: Scholars Press, 1988). In another study, Mendelson explores the spiritual quest in Philo's works; see his *Secular Education in Philo of Alexandria*, Monographs of the Hebrew Union College, no. 7 (Cincinnati: Hebrew Union College Press, 1982).

[10] *Philo's Jewish Identity*, 138. Although he does not elaborate upon this innuendo, presumably Mendelson means that the Jewish sense of superiority has engendered anti-Jewish feelings and behavior, in Alexandria and elsewhere.

[11] Yehoshua Amir, "Philon und die jüdische Wirklichkeit seiner Zeit," *Die hellenistische Gestalt*, 3–51.

a certain extent, then, he brings together the perspectives of Biblical motifs presented by Jaubert and religious phenomena and social reality presented by Mendelson. Amir includes sections dealing, for example, with Philo's attitude toward the Levites, messianic expectation, commandments of the Torah, motherland and diaspora, the Jewish people, proselytes, and the Therapeutae. Many of these topics directly pertain to the theme of particularism and universalism—in both a theological and a general sense—and Amir argues that Philo presents a universalized version of Judaism through his spiritualizing interpretations. In this essay and, in fact, throughout the book, Amir is keenly aware of the tensions in Philo's thought between particularism and universalism, always placing him closer to the universalist pole.[12]

When one turns to works that describe a spiritual quest in Philo's writings, what is especially striking is how little discussion is devoted to the topics mentioned above, even though these works recognize and indeed emphasize to different degrees that the spiritual quest in Philo is a Jewish one. Common to all the writers considered below is that they understand the central element in Philo's religion to be a quest with a goal. While the abovementioned authors on Jewish aspects of Philo may acknowledge this quest and goal, they do not make these central.

Here I shall briefly mention Erwin R. Goodenough's *By Light, Light,* Walther Völker's *Fortschritt und Vollendung bei Philo von Alexandrien,* and David Winston's *Logos and Mystical Theology in Philo of Alexandria.*[13] In *By Light, Light* and elsewhere, Goodenough argues that Philo's Judaism is actually a mystery religion which offers a "distinctly non-Jewish type of salvation," whereby "the spirit [is] released from the flesh in order to return to its spiritual source in God."[14] His chapters cover, among other things, "The God of the Mystery," "The Higher Law," "The Torah," and various figures who represent different aspects of the mystery or different types of seekers: Aaron; Enos, Enoch, Noah, and Abraham; Isaac and Jacob; and Moses. Although the themes and figures he mentions are

---

[12] Amir has consistently shown an interest in these tensions in Philo's thought, beginning with his dissertation, whose theme is related to the present study. Written under the name Hermann Neumark, it is entitled *Die Verwendung griechischer und jüdischer Motive in den Gedanken Philons über die Stellung Gottes zu seinen Freunden* (Würzburg, 1937). Some of Amir's other studies are cited in nn. 2, 3, 30, and 33.
[13] Goodenough, *By Light, Light* (see n. 3); Walther Völker, *Fortschritt und Vollendung bei Philo von Alexandrien: Eine Studie zur Geschichte der Frömmigkeit,* Texte und Untersuchungen zur Geschichte der altchristlichen Literatur 49:1 (Leipzig: J. C. Hinrichs, 1938); David Winston, *Logos and Mystical Theology in Philo of Alexandria* (Cincinnati: Hebrew Union College Press, 1985).
[14] Goodenough, *By Light, Light,* 254; idem, *Introduction to Philo Judaeus,* 14; cf. *By Light, Light,* 7.

Biblical, their chief significance lies not in their historical reality but in their role in Philo's Jewish mystery. Goodenough, however, does not see a tension between Philo's Jewish and mystical sides. Emphasizing that Philo's mystery is thoroughly Jewish, he presents his Judaism as completely transformed by the mystical quest. As Goodenough writes elsewhere, he believes that Philo is "not going out of Judaism but only deeper into it."[15]

Walther Völker repudiates the idea that Philo himself could experience mystical vision, maintaining that this experience is possible only through belief in Christianity. Instead he claims Philo uses mystical and philosophical language to serve as mere "window-dressing" for his exegetical insights, not to describe real ecstatic experience.[16] Apart from the polemical issue of whether or not Philo's language reflects his own genuine experience, Völker outlines a schema of progress and perfection, which can easily be understood as a universal pursuit in that it might be undertaken by anyone, whether Jewish or not. Völker describes different aspects of the battle against the senses, the passions, and the world. He then discusses various paths to perfection—via learning, practice, and belief—and their different stages. Finally, Völker focuses upon the endpoints of these various paths—the virtuous life, vision of God, and portrayal of the τέλειος, or perfect man.

Because he argues that Philo's depictions of ecstasy are drawn from his Greek philosophical hermeneutic and do not reflect his own firsthand experience, Völker's assessment of Philo's spirituality is completely opposite to that of Goodenough.[17] Obviously, Völker's definition of mysticism as possible only through Christianity precludes the opinion that Philo could be a true mystic. Ironically, though, like Goodenough, Völker too sees no conflict between Philo's Judaism and his spirituality.[18] Whereas Goodenough, however, understands Philo's Judaism to be completely integrated with his mysticism, Völker rejects the genuineness of Philo's mysticism entirely.

David Winston is another writer who discusses the spiritual quest in Philo, emphasizing its Greek philosophical aspects. Winston devotes chapters to "Philo's Logos Doctrine Against Its Platonic Background," "The Psyche and Its Extra-Terrestrial Life in Philo's Anthropology," and "Philo's Mystical Theology." He notes that for Philo, "man's goal and ultimate

---

15 Goodenough, *Introduction to Philo Judaeus*, 153.
16 See, e.g., Völker, *Fortschritt und Vollendung*, xii, 287, 300, 313–17.
17 See Goodenough's review of Völker's book, "Problems of Method in Studying Philo Judaeus," *Journal of Biblical Literature* (*JBL*) 58 (1939): 51–58, and his remarks about Völker in his *Introduction to Philo Judaeus*, 14–16.
18 See, e.g., Völker, *Fortschritt und Vollendung*, 297.

bliss lie in the knowledge or vision of God."[19] In his concluding remarks, Winston addresses the tension between nationalism and universalism in the context of Philo's eschatological hopes. He comments as follows:

> Everything said of the Jewish nation in Lev. 26:12 and Deut. 28:13 is transferred by Philo to the human mind, and in direct contrast to that verse God is designated by Philo not as the God of Israel, but of all people (*Praem.* 158–61). Still, enough of the earthly sphere remains in Philo's messianic vision to reveal the inner tensions in his thought between nationalism and universalism, the mystical and the this-worldly.[20]

It is interesting that, of these six authors who focus upon Philo either as a Jew or as a spiritual seeker, only Alan Mendelson emphasizes Philo's particularism over and above any universalist tendencies. From Mendelson's perspective, the chief tension in Philo's works lies not between two sides of Philo himself but between Philo and his non-Jewish environment. The other authors pay due attention to Philo's particular and universal sides—whether they recognize a tension between these forces— like Jaubert, Amir, and Winston—or deny a tension by viewing Philo's Jewish and mystical sides as wholly integrated (Goodenough) or completely separate (Völker).

Mendelson, however, believes that any universalist tendencies Philo may have are overshadowed by his sense of Jewish identity. Mendelson comments, "Even as Philo proclaims the openness of the Jews to other peoples, we can detect a counter-current of exclusiveness which undermines the very concept he espouses."[21] Perhaps at the conclusion of this investigation, we shall be better able to evaluate Mendelson's singular position.

Approach of the Present Study

In contrast to the various approaches outlined above, in this study I shall focus upon both aspects of Philo as Jew and spiritual seeker in order to examine how he does or does not address the possible tensions between these aspects. Happily, Philo himself provides us with a term that combines the two aspects in one. This term is "Israel."

As Philo frequently explains, according to its etymology, "Israel" means "one that sees God" (ὁρῶν θεόν). We have noted that for Philo, seeing God represents the height of human happiness and that, in and of itself, seeing God may be considered universal since anyone—regardless of birth—may pursue this quest or goal. At the same time, however,

---

[19] Winston, *Logos and Mystical Theology*, 54.
[20] Ibid., 58.
[21] Mendelson, *Philo's Jewish Identity*, 113.

"Israel" is also the name used in the Bible for the nation of Philo's ancestors and for the Jews themselves before and during his time. Moreover, according to the Bible, Israel is the nation that God selects to be His own people and to serve Him in a covenantal relationship. In Philo's writings, then—both in his interpretations and in quotations of Biblical texts—"Israel" may potentially represent one who sees God, the Biblical nation and its Jewish descendants, or both.

Philo's blend of associations to "Israel" gives rise to a series of questions. Does he equate "Israel" only with the historical Biblical nation and its Jewish descendants? If so, does he think that only they can see God? Moreover, does he believe that the relationship between God and Israel as it is described in the Bible automatically applies to his own Jewish contemporaries? Conversely, does he redefine Israel to mean only those who see God, regardless of their ancestry? If so, then how does Philo regard the Biblical account of God's election of Israel? And what relationship does Philo's understanding of Israel as "the one that sees God" have with Biblical Israel or with any contemporary social group, particularly his fellow Jews?

Because of the ambiguities that result from the way Philo understands "Israel," a key question in this study is how he uses the terms "Israel" and "Jew" in relation to each other. Indeed my pivotal argument is that one may in fact distinguish in his work between "Israel," a rather loosely defined entity that sees God, and the Jews, the real nation that believes in and worships God. Accordingly, "Israel" is not a clearly recognizable social group but instead may be similar to what we speak of today as an "intellectual elite." In contrast, the Jews are a social, ethnic, and political community whose members—by birth or choice—are easily identified.[22] Although "Israel" and the Jews may overlap or indeed be the same, Philo discusses them as two distinct entities.

To support this argument, I offer and shall elaborate upon the following observations:

1. *Philo generally speaks about "Israel" and the Jews in different series of works, which are probably intended for different, though perhaps overlapping, audiences.* The terms "Israel" and "Jew," in fact, appear together only once, in

---

[22] Here and throughout this investigation, I speak of the Jewish nation or the Jewish people as "real" in the sense that they are a recognized social, ethnic, or political group. This is not to imply that "Israel" is not a "real" group, but rather that its membership is not readily identified. Also, in describing the Jews as clearly identifiable, I am sidestepping the controversy about who was a Jew in antiquity. Philo himself seems to use the terms "Jew" and "proselyte" without ambiguity even though he does not define them precisely. In contrast, his use of "Israel" appears to be deliberately ambiguous.

the political treatise *Legat*. No other treatise—either exegetical or non-exegetical—mentions both "Israel" and the Jews in the same individual work.

2. *To describe "Israel" and the Jews as collectivities, Philo uses different words with different connotations.* While his terms for the Jews denote a people or nation—whether they are defined by birth or shared laws—Philo's term for "Israel" (γένος) has a range of meanings that include but go beyond the idea of a group determined by common origins. Accordingly, "Israel" may also be a class defined by shared characteristics or a nebulous ideal.

3. *Philo describes the relationship between God and each entity in different ways.* "Israel" is primarily associated with seeing God, while the Jews are depicted as the people that believe in and worship Him through specific laws and customs.

4. *"Membership requirements" for belonging to "Israel" and the Jews appear to be different.* Although Philo does not address this issue directly, one can speculate that membership in "Israel" depends upon spiritual capability, while membership in the Jewish nation requires one a) to abandon false beliefs and worship to adopt belief in and worship of the one God and b) to leave behind one's family and friends to join a new community.

Besides maintaining that Philo distinguishes between "Israel" and the Jews, I shall also argue that he presents a potentially universalist vision of both entities. Because it represents the ideal of seeing God, "Israel" could theoretically encompass some or all Jews and perhaps some non-Jews—whoever is able to see God. Similarly, as the nation that believes in and worships God, the Jews stand ready to embrace all people—regardless of birth—who choose to serve the one God along with them, i.e., proselytes. We shall consider Philo's potential universalism further in the conclusions.

It is worth noting that in Philo's time—the first part of the first century C.E.—Judaism was the only monotheistic religion. Philo gives no evidence of knowing about the beginnings of Christianity. While philosophers may have believed in one God or one transcendent Being, Judaism was the only religion that brought together belief in and worship of this Being, the Creator of all the universe and personal God of the Jews. Philo's openness to and eagerness for proselytes to join the Jewish people is, to some extent, characteristic of other varieties of Judaism in this period as well.

The arguments outlined above and their implications for how Philo evaluates the importance of being a Jew are set forth in six chapters. Chapter One lays the groundwork by carefully surveying how Philo uses certain vocabulary pertaining to "Israel" and the Jews. Chapter Two addresses what he means by "Israel," how he derives its etymology, and how he understands the experience of seeing God. Chapter Three explores who Philo believes can see God. Chapter Four takes up whether or not Philo affirms God's relationship with Israel as the Bible presents it and whether or not this relationship automatically applies to all Jews. Finally, in Chapters Five and Six respectively, I examine the relationship to God— first, of one who is a Jew and then, of one who becomes a Jew.

Before we proceed, a comment about terminology is in order. Since "Israel" has both a literal and a symbolic meaning, for the sake of clarity, when speaking about "Israel" as the nation mentioned in the Bible, I use the expressions "Biblical Israel" or "historical Israel." Either of these expressions denotes the real nation that existed during Biblical times. When "Israel" refers both to the Biblical nation and its Jewish descendants—up to and/or during Philo's time—I say so explicitly. When "Israel" denotes an entity that sees God, and it is unclear whether this term also denotes the Biblical nation and/or its Jewish descendants, I refer simply to "Israel," and the quotation marks indicate the ambiguity of the referent, i.e., the specific social group or entity that "Israel" is meant to represent.

Since Philo uses the word "Jew" to refer to the Biblical nation and also to its Jewish descendants up to his own day, whenever possible, I indicate whether he is speaking of the nation in the past, in his present, or both. If further refinements to these various usages are necessary, these will be made in the appropriate contexts.

Method

In 1939, E. R. Goodenough noted that in advancing a particular interpretation of Philo, any scholar must necessarily select certain Philonic passages, and each scholar's selection is bound to be influenced by preconceived and often implicit premises. Since selectivity is unavoidable, he argued, it is essential for scholars to make explicit their criteria of selection and their unspoken assumptions. As Goodenough emphasized, "The first consideration in studying Philo must be that of method."[23]

More than half a century later, Goodenough's observation still holds true.[24] To be sure, even today scholars base studies upon selected Philonic passages, offering no explanation of how they identify these passages or why they regard them as more significant than others. Also crucial is how one goes about interpreting these passages. In strong agreement that

---

[23] Goodenough, "Problems of Method," 58.
[24] See, e.g., Borgen's opening statement in his 1992 study "'There Shall Come Forth a Man'" (341): "The problem of method is a critical issue in Philonic studies."

methodological issues are of paramount importance in studying Philo, I
purposely devote ample attention to these issues throughout this investigation.[25]

Simply stated, my method combines word studies and exegetical
analyses, based upon virtually all of Philo's extant works. To a great extent,
this approach agrees with guidelines suggested by David T. Runia in an
article entitled "How To Read Philo."[26] Runia suggests that to tackle any
problem in Philo, a researcher must begin by considering all the relevant
passages and then analyze these passages keeping in mind several factors,
listed further below.

To identify all the relevant passages for this study, I have relied upon
word searches, verse searches, and a careful reading through Philo's
works.[27] I then analyze these passages, guided by several considerations,
most of which Runia mentions. He notes that in reading Philo, one must

1) Take into account the immediate exegetical context of each
    passage—that is, identify what Biblical verses are being inter-
    preted—and the thematic context—i.e., the themes discussed in
    sections and the whole of the treatise;

2) Establish the exegetical problem that gives rise to the inter-
    pretation; and

3) Attempt to understand the ideas which Philo uses in his
    interpretation and to show how these ideas are used to interpret the
    passage.

---

[25] As Goodenough wrote, "It seems much safer to keep the process in the conscious ...
As men we must proceed in this way whether we like it or not" ("Problems of
Method," 56). I am assuming Goodenough would hold women to the same standards!
[26] David T. Runia, "How to Read Philo," *Nederlands Theologisch Tijdschrift* 40 (1986):
185–98 (reprinted as the second entry in idem, *Exegesis and Philosophy: Studies on Philo of
Alexandria*, Variorum Collected Studies [Hampshire, Great Britain: Variorum, 1990]).
[27] Word studies for works in *Philo*, trans. F. H. Colson and G. H. Whitaker, vols. 1–
10, The Loeb Classical Library (LCL) (Cambridge: Harvard University Press, 1929–62),
except for *Prov.*, are based upon Günter Mayer, *Index Philoneus* (Berlin: de Gruyter,
1974) and the Thesaurus Linguae Graecae (TLG) database on IBYCUS (see David T.
Runia, "How to Search Philo," *The Studia Philonica Annual* [*SPhA*] 2 [1990]: 106–39). For
the fragmentary Questions and Answers on Genesis and Exodus (QGE), which
survives chiefly in Armenian, word studies are based upon the English translation
and Index prepared by Ralph Marcus in LCL, 2 supps. (Cambridge: Harvard
University Press, 1953, repr. 1970 and 1979). Word studies do not include fragments
or *Anim.*, *Deo*, and *Prov.*—three works surviving chiefly in Armenian, whose contents
are not central to this investigation. Biblical verse searches are based upon the Index
biblique in *Biblia Patristica: Supplément, Philon d'Alexandrie* (Paris: Éditions du Centre
National de la Recherche Scientifique, 1982).

To these I have added two more factors, namely, the need to

4) Be aware of the possibility that Philo may be adapting his presentation to suit a particular audience or literary genre; and
5) Recognize that some of Philo's interpretations may derive from traditional Jewish exegesis.

Although I am not providing any immediate illustrations of this method for reading Philo, I hope that the numerous analyses in the text of this work will serve as fitting, concrete examples.

Assumptions

Informing my approach are several key assumptions about Philo and his enterprise. Detailed below, these assumptions pertain to Philo's role as an exegete, his audience(s) and the aims of his various works, his intellectual background, and his ambiguity and silence on certain issues.

1. Philo as an Exegete

Most of the Philonic writings discussed in this study are exegetical, and I am proceeding on the assumption that Philo is first and foremost an interpreter of Scripture instead of a philosopher, as many scholars have argued.[28] To be sure, Philo's philosophical interests run deep and one might indeed characterize most of his exegesis as philosophical. In viewing him primarily as a Scriptural interpreter rather than a philosopher, however, I am assuming that he uses philosophical notions to explicate the Bible rather than using the Bible as a springboard to present some kind of unified philosophy. Whatever philosophical notions can be abstracted from his works, these are used to explain Scripture rather than to set forth a systematic way of thinking or a definitive statement about individual concepts.

As many scholars have observed, a major theme or hermeneutic in Philo's interpretations is the journey of the soul,[29] and to describe this journey Philo most certainly uses language and ideas from his surrounding culture, as we shall see. The methodological implication of the assumption that Philo is primarily an exegete, however, is that passages must always be considered in their exegetical context, i.e., in relation to the verse(s) they are discussing. Thus, I shall generally be more concerned to identify the exegetical function of Philo's language and ideas than their sources.

---

[28] On Philo as an exegete, see Nikiprowetzky, *Le commentaire de l'Écriture*, esp. 170–242.
[29] See, e.g., Goodenough, *By Light, Light*, 235–64; Nikiprowetzky, *Le commentaire de l'Écriture*, 239; Sandmel, *Philo of Alexandria*, 83–88.

Whether or not Philo knew Hebrew—and it appears unlikely that he knew it well if at all—his interpretations are based upon the Greek Bible or Septuagint (LXX).[30] As to the literal meaning of the Greek Bible, he does not maintain a consistent position. Sometimes Philo affirms this meaning, sometimes he rejects it, and sometimes he simply provides a symbolic interpretation of the text without commenting upon its literal sense at all.[31] One can also observe differences among his various works in the way he approaches the literal sense of Scripture.

It should quickly be noted, however, that Philo's use of the term "literal" itself is inconsistent and somewhat equivocal.[32] For example, in the Exposition, one of his three exegetical series, what he considers "literal" is often in fact a reworking of the text, which may elaborate upon or even omit certain details. In his two other exegetical series, discussed below, Philo may have somewhat different understandings of the term "literal." Regardless of the different ways in which he may conceive of or deal with the literal meaning of Scripture, Philo nonetheless understands the authority behind the text to be ultimately divine, viewing the Bible as a cooperative venture, as it were, between God and his prophet Moses.[33]

2. *Philo's Audience(s) and Aims*

A second and rather important assumption for my argument is that Philo's various works are directed toward different, though perhaps overlapping, audiences and are composed with different aims. Although I have considered all Philo's extant works for this study, I am chiefly concerned with those in which he discusses seeing God and especially

---

[30] For a good overview of the debate about whether or not Philo knew Hebrew, see Nikiprowetzky, *Le commentaire de l'Écriture*, 50–96. See also "The Source of Philo's Etymologies," below in Chapter Two. On Philo's use of the Greek Bible, see Yehoshua Amir, "Authority and Interpretation of Scripture in the Writings of Philo," *Mikra: Text, Translation, Reading and Interpretation of the Hebrew Bible in Ancient Judaism and Early Christianity*, ed. Martin Jay Mulder, Compendia Rerum Iudaicarum ad Novum Testamentum (CRINT), sec. 2, vol. 1 (Assen/Maastricht: Van Gorcum, 1988), 440–44; and Peder Borgen, "Philo of Alexandria: A Critical and Synthetical Survey of Research since World War II," *Aufstieg und Niedergang der römischen Welt* (*ANRW*): *Geschichte und Kultur Roms im Spiegel der neueren Forschung*, 2.21.1: *Religion (Hellenistisches Judentum in römischer Zeit: Philon und Josephus)*, ed. Wolfgang Haase (Berlin: de Gruyter, 1984), 121–23.

[31] See Montgomery J. Shroyer, "Alexandrian Jewish Literalists," *JBL* 55 (1936): 261–84; Wolfson, *Philo* 1:120–31.

[32] See Burton L. Mack, "Philo Judaeus and Exegetical Traditions in Alexandria," *ANRW*, 2.21.1:258–59 and 261–62.

[33] *Det.* 13; *Mos.* 2.11, 34; *Decal.* 18–19; *Praem.* 1–2; *Prob.* 80. See also Yehoshua Amir, "Philo and the Bible," *SP* 2 (1973): 1–8; idem, "Authority and Interpretation," 421–53; idem, "Mose als Verfasser der Tora," 77–106.

those in which he mentions "Israel" and the Jews, whether in the past or present, explicitly by name or implicitly without name. My focus, therefore, is upon all Philo's exegetical writings, which fall into three series— the Allegory, the Exposition, and Questions and Answers on Genesis and Exodus (QGE). Among the non-exegetical writings, the most relevant are Philo's two political treatises, *Flacc.* and *Legat.*, in which he recounts the political travails of his Jewish contemporaries; the fragmentary *Apology for the Jews* (*Hypoth.*), in which he refers to the Biblical nation, his Jewish contemporaries, and the Essene sect; and *Contempl.*, in which Philo describes the life of the Therapeutae (another contemporary sect) and briefly mentions the Biblical nation.

Much has been written concerning the question of Philo's intended readership(s) and aims.[34] He himself, however, rarely tells us whom he is addressing.[35] Nonetheless, certain characteristics of his writings suggest that they are composed with different purposes for individuals who differ in their spiritual sensibilities and in their familiarity with Jewish beliefs, practices, and people. At best one can only attempt to make intelligent guesses about who these various readers are and what Philo's aims might be. With this caution in mind, I offer the following observations and reflections about his works.

The Allegory presupposes an audience with a sophisticated knowledge of both Scripture and philosophy. This series consists of treatises that, for the most part, provide a running commentary on the Bible. Usually these treatises begin with a quotation from Scripture and then set forth a sequence of interpretations on individual sections or words in the verse, frequently incorporating secondary texts and interpretations. While passages from Genesis serve as the bases of these treatises, in the course of each work Philo quotes from other parts of the Bible, predominantly from

---

[34] In his basic study, which is still cited, M. L. Massebieau classifies and discusses the purposes of Philo's different writings in "Le classement des oeuvres de Philon," *Bibliothèque de l'École des Hautes Études: Sciences religieuses* 1 (1889): 1–91. For references to subsequent scholarship on these questions, see Jenny Morris, "The Jewish Philosopher Philo" in Emil Schürer, *The History of the Jewish People in the Age of Jesus Christ (175 B.C.–A.D. 135)*, rev. and ed. Geza Vermes et al. (Edinburgh: T. & T. Clark, 1987), 3:2:809–89. Regarding the Allegory and the Exposition, see Erwin R. Goodenough, "Philo's Exposition of the Law and His De Vita Mosis," *Harvard Theological Review* (*HTR*) 26 (1933): 109–25; Nikiprowetzky, *Le commentaire de l'Écriture*, 192–202; idem, "Brève note sur le *Commentaire Allégorique* et l'*Exposition de la Loi* chez Philon d'Alexandrie," *Mélanges bibliques et orientaux en l'honneur de M. Mathias Delcor*, ed. André Caquot et al. (Kevelaer: Butzon & Bercker, 1985), 321–29. On Philo's political treatises, *Flacc.* and *Legat.*, see also Erwin R. Goodenough, *The Politics of Philo Judaeus: Practice and Theory* (New Haven: Yale University Press, 1938), 9–13, 19.

[35] In *Mos.* 1.1, Philo states that he wishes to present the story of Moses to "those who are worthy not to be ignorant" of it (my translation).

the Pentateuch. Occasionally, he explicitly rejects the literal sense of Scripture or explicitly favors allegorical interpretations over others.[36] A dominant concern of these allegorical exegeses is the journey of the soul, its struggle against the passions, and its quest for God. Most likely, Philo's readers in this series are Jews like himself, who may look to the Allegory as a guide to reading the Bible so that it will reveal to them its secrets about the soul's quest.

Philo's audience in QGE is probably also quite knowledgeable about Scripture and philosophy, but this series—which includes a broader spectrum of interpretations than the Allegory—may be intended for a wider Jewish audience. In contrast to the treatises of the Allegory, QGE is written atomistically, presenting separate questions and answers on individual verses or parts of verses. Frequently Philo juxtaposes literal and symbolic interpretations without commenting about their relative merits. Indeed the answers in this series often include without criticism a wider variety of exegeses than we find in the Allegory for each verse.[37] QGE may therefore be intended as a collation or digest of interpretations reflecting the opinions of a broader community of Alexandrian Jews than just those who share Philo's interest in allegory and the journey of the soul. Perhaps, in fact, QGE may function as a sourcebook or even a textbook for this broader Alexandrian Jewish community.[38]

Unlike the Allegory and QGE, Philo's other exegetical series, the Exposition, does not necessarily assume any familiarity with Scripture at all. Instead this collection of treatises—which cover Biblical themes and figures, like Creation, Abraham, Moses, or the Decalogue[39]—might serve equally well for people at different levels of knowledge about the Bible.[40]

---

[36] See, e.g., *Leg.* 1.43 on Gen. 2:8 (cf. *QG* 1.6, in which Philo does not reject the literal meaning of the verse); *Leg.* 2.19; *Agr.* 96–97; *Plant.* 32. See also Shroyer, "Alexandrian Jewish Literalists," 271–79.
[37] David M. Hay, "References to Other Exegetes in Philo's *Quaestiones*," *Both Literal and Allegorical: Studies in Philo of Alexandria's* Questions and Answers on Genesis and Exodus, ed. David M. Hay, Brown Judaic Studies, ed. Ernest S. Frerichs et al., no. 232 (Atlanta: Scholars Press, 1991), 81–97.
[38] Cf. Gregory E. Sterling, "Philo's *Quaestiones*: Prolegomena or Afterthought?" *Both Literal and Allegorical*, ed. David M. Hay, 99–123; and Sze-kar Wan, "Philo's *Quaestiones et solutiones in Genesim et in Exodum*: A Synoptic Approach" (Th.D. diss., Harvard University, 1992).
[39] Other treatises deal with Joseph, Special Laws, Virtues, and Rewards and Punishments. Writings on Isaac and Jacob mentioned in *Ios.* 1 are lost. Scholars have debated how the treatises on Moses are related to the Exposition as a whole. Goodenough ("Philo's Exposition of the Law") has suggested that these treatises are separate from the Exposition. If he were correct, however, the narrative in the Exposition would have an unaccountable gap between the life of Joseph and the Decalogue (see F. H. Colson, "Introduction," *Philo*, LCL, 6:xiv–xvi).
[40] Typically, Philo presents the material as a rewritten Bible, occasionally inter-

In addition, since Philo resorts much less frequently to allegorical exegesis and since his discussions are, in some ways, less philosophically
complex than those in his other Biblical commentaries, he may also be
addressing people with a varied range of familiarity with philosophy.[41]
More to the point, Philo's occasional exhortations about disloyal Jews,
apologetic remarks defending the Jews and their practices, and welcoming attitude toward proselytes suggest that the Exposition is probably aimed
primarily at Jews and non-Jews—whether hostile or friendly—who know
little about Jewish beliefs and practices. Philo may have several aims in
mind here: to reclaim the alienated Jews, educate the less knowledgeable
ones, assuage non-Jews who may be hostile, and appeal to those who
might be interested.

Among the non-exegetical writings, in the historical or political
treatises *Flacc.* and *Legat.*, Philo's apparent purpose is to demonstrate that
God watches over the Jews especially when they are in trouble.[42] Both
treatises recount the sufferings of the Jews—particularly the Alexandrian
Jews—in the latter part of the fourth decade C.E. In *Flacc.*, which also tells
of the prefect Flaccus's own subsequent travails, Philo has none other than
Flaccus himself declare that he is being punished by the God of the Jews
(*Flacc.* 170). Since we do not have the final part of *Legat.*, we cannot know
for sure how it ends. In the introductory section (*Legat.* 1–7), however,
Philo stresses that God extends providence toward all people, especially
toward the Jews. One might expect therefore that the ending of this treatise
describes precisely how God delivers His people.[43]

---

spersing his "literal" retellings with symbolic interpretations. For symbolic interpretations of narrative parts of the Bible, see, e.g., *Abr.* 68, 99, 119, 200; *Ios.* 28, 125; for
symbolic interpretations of the non-narrative, legal parts of the Bible, see, e.g., *Spec.*
1.327, *Spec.* 2.29, et al.

[41] An exception to this observation is the treatise *Opif.*, which Goodenough regards as
Philo's "most difficult treatise" (*Introduction to Philo Judaeus*, 35). This work is con-
sidered part of the Exposition but is found in manuscripts at the beginning of the
Allegory. It has been suggested that the treatise may serve as an introduction to both
series. See Morris, "The Jewish Philosopher Philo," 832, 844–45; Nikiprowetzky, *Le
commentaire de l'Écriture*, 197–200. On the lower frequency of allegorical exegesis in the
Exposition, see, e.g., Thomas H. Tobin, "Tradition and Interpretation in Philo's
Portrait of the Patriarch Joseph," *Society of Biblical Literature [SBL] 1986 Seminar Papers*,
SBL Seminar Papers Series, ed. Kent Harold Richards, no. 25 (Atlanta: Scholars
Press, 1986), 272.

[42] *Flacc.*, in particular, may reflect a genre of literature whose theme is expressed in
the title of a later work, *De Mortibus Persecutorum*. This literature tries to demonstrate
that the oppressors of the righteous or those who believe in God are eventually
punished themselves. See Morris, "The Jewish Philosopher Philo," 861. See also
Lactantius, *De Mortibus Persecutorum*, ed. J. L. Creed (Oxford: Oxford University Press,
1984), xxxv–xli.

[43] Morris, "The Jewish Philosopher Philo," 860–62; E. Mary Smallwood, ed., *Philonis*

These two historical or political works, *Flacc.* and *Legat.*, may be directed toward both Jews and non-Jews, regardless of their familiarity with the Bible or their religious sensibilities. By emphasizing divine providence in both these treatises, Philo may, on the one hand, wish to bolster the spirits of his fellow Jews during a time of suffering; on the other hand, he may also wish to sound a warning to Gentiles to stop their maltreatment of his people.

Two remaining works pertain to this study in only a minor way. The *Hypothetica*, written in defense of the Jews, is most likely intended for non-Jews, although Philo may also be addressing Jewish readers. As with other apologetic literature, it is hard to determine whether the audience is the author's own people or hostile outsiders.[44] *Hypoth.* briefly recounts the Biblical nation's exodus from Egypt and settlement in Canaan, reviews some of the Jewish laws, and describes the Essene sect.

Finally, in *Contempl.*, Philo sympathetically presents the Therapeutae, describing their beliefs, practices, and allegorical method of interpreting Scripture. This work may be written to impress Jews as well as non-Jews with the ways of this sect. Philo compares, for example, the modest banquets of the Therapeutae to Greek banquets and to philosophical symposia discussed by Xenophon and Plato, admiring the frugal and continent ways of the sect and deploring the sensual excess and frivolity of the other banquets.

3. *Philo's Intellectual Background*

My third assumption about Philo and his enterprise pertains to his intellectual antecedents. Indeed, although I focus almost exclusively upon his own writings, I most certainly do not mean to imply that Philo is uninfluenced by outside sources. Many of those works alluded to earlier —the ones which study where Philo stands in relation to other philosophical and religious traditions—show quite convincingly that he is part of a long history of philosophical thought and Jewish exegesis.

The Alexandrian intellectual milieu from which Philo draws is quite complex, consisting of different philosophical trends, pagan mystery cults, and Jewish exegetical traditions. In keeping with my understanding of Philo primarily as a Biblical interpreter instead of a philosopher, I believe that he draws from a variety of contemporary philosophical currents rather than serving as the representative of any single school of thought, although he is perhaps most influenced by Platonism. Thus Philo is exposed to, selects from, and criticizes ideas from Platonic, Stoic,

Alexandrini: Legatio ad Gaium, 2nd ed. (Leiden: E. J. Brill, 1970), 40–43 and 324, n. 373.
[44]   Victor Tcherikover, "Jewish Apologetic Literature," *Eos* 48/3 (1956): 169–93.

Epicurean, Pythagorean, Peripatetic, and Sceptical thought.[45] The influence of philosophy, moreover, extends beyond intellectual content to
method; by the first century C.E., allegorical interpretation was a well-
known approach used by Greek commentators on Homer.[46]

In Philo's time, of course, many of the various positions named above
had already intermingled. Scholars have described a school of Middle
Platonism characterized, among other things, by the belief in a transcendent God, aspiration to assimilate to God, and interest in numerology.
Philo's exact relation to the Middle Platonists is still debated, but he is
certainly a sympathetic witness to many of their ideas and concerns.[47]

Another question that has sparked some debate in Philonic studies is
how he might have been influenced by mystery cults. Some scholars
have so emphasized the importance of these cults for understanding Philo
that they believe he himself practiced a Jewish form of mystery. Of the
wide array of these cults, however, some precede Philo by several
centuries. With their emphasis on secrecy, initiation, and transformation,
they have offered a rich metaphorical vocabulary to philosophers at least

---

[45] H. Chadwick, "Philo," *The Cambridge History of Later Greek and Early Medieval Philo-
sophy*, ed. A. H. Armstrong (Cambridge: Cambridge University Press, 1970), 137–57;
Thomas H. Tobin, *The Creation of Man: Philo and the History of Interpretation*, Catholic
Biblical Quarterly Monograph Series, no. 14 (Washington D.C.: The Catholic
Biblical Association of America, 1983), 10–19; Wolfson, *Philo* 1:107–13.

[46] Félix Buffière, *Les mythes d'Homère et la pensée grecque* (Paris: Société d'Édition "Les
Belles Lettres," 1956); David Dawson, *Allegorical Readers and Cultural Revision in Ancient
Alexandria* (Berkeley: University of California Press, 1992), esp. 1–126; Robert Lamberton and John J. Keaney, eds., *Homer's Ancient Readers: The Hermeneutics of Greek Epic's
Earliest Exegetes* (Princeton: Princeton University Press, 1992); Jean Pépin, *Mythe et
allégorie: les origines grecques et les contestations judéo-chrétiennes*, rev. ed. (Paris: Études
augustiniennes, 1976); David Winston, "Introduction," *Philo of Alexandria: The Contemplative Life, The Giants, and Selections*, with a Preface by John Dillon, The Classics of
Western Spirituality (New York: Paulist Press, 1981), 4–6.

[47] John Dillon, *The Middle Platonists, 80 B.C. to A.D. 220* (Ithaca: Cornell University
Press, 1977), 135–83; idem, "Self-Definition in Later Platonism," *Jewish and Christian
Self-Definition*, vol. 3: *Self-Definition in the Greco-Roman World*, ed. Ben F. Meyer and E. P.
Sanders (Philadelphia: Fortress Press, 1982), 60–75; David T. Runia, *Philo of Alexandria
and the* Timaeus *of Plato*, Philosophia Antiqua, ed. W. J. Verdenius and J. C. M. van
Winden, vol. 44 (Leiden: E. J. Brill, 1986), 505–19; Tobin, *The Creation of Man*, 11–19;
Antonie Wlosok, *Laktanz und die philosophische Gnosis: Untersuchungen zu Geschichte und
Terminologie der gnostischen Erlösungsvorstellung*, Abhandlung der Heidelberger Akade-
mie der Wissenschaften, Philosophisch-historische Klasse, no. 2 (Heidelberg: Carl
Winter, Universitätsverlag, 1960), 50–60. More recently, the relationship between
Philo and Middle Platonism was debated in a special section of *SPhA* 5 (1993): 95–155.
The contents are as follows: G. E. Sterling, "Platonizing Moses: Philo and Middle
Platonism" (96–111); D. T. Runia, "Was Philo a Middle Platonist? a Difficult
Question Revisited" (112–40); D. Winston, "Response to Runia and Sterling" (141–46);
T. H. Tobin, "Was Philo a Middle Platonist? Some suggestions" (147–50); J. Dillon,
"A Response to Runia and Sterling" (151–55).

as far back as Plato. Since we have no conclusive evidence of a Jewish mystery, and since the use of mystery language without the practice of mystery rites was by Philo's day a time-honored tradition in philosophy, I assume that he uses mystery vocabulary only as a metaphor to describe the soul's quest for God and, quite possibly, his own religious experience.[48]

Besides this rich background of Greek philosophy and pagan mystery language, Philo's work also relies upon Jewish exegesis that developed well before him.[49] Here the difficulty presented by the paucity of sources can hardly be overstated. Nonetheless, beginning with the Septuagint, one can trace in Alexandrian Jewish works themes, tendencies, and traditions —described below—which are exhibited in full development in the writings of Philo.[50]

---

[48] In *By Light, Light*, Goodenough gives fullest expression to the view that Philo's Judaism is a mystery religion. For a review of his position and those of his predecessors, see G. Lease, "Jewish Mystery Cults Since Goodenough," *ANRW*, 2.20.2: *Religion (Hellenistisches Judentum in römischer Zeit: Allgemeines)*, ed. Wolfgang Haase (Berlin: de Gruyter, 1987), 858–80. See also Chadwick, "Philo," 152–54. For a useful perspective on mystery cults in general, see Walter Burkert, *Ancient Mystery Cults* (Cambridge: Harvard University Press, 1987). On Philo's use of mystery language as metaphor, see ibid., 45, 67, 80, and 92.

[49] This point of view has been expanded upon in various ways by Richard Goulet, *La philosophie de Moïse: essai de reconstitution d'un commentaire philosophique préphilonien du Pentateuque*, Histoire des doctrines de l'antiquité classique, no. 11 (Paris: Librairie Philosophique J. Vrin, 1987) (see also the review of this book by David T. Runia in *Journal of Theological Studies [JTS]* 40 [1989]: 588–602, reprinted as the seventh entry in idem, *Exegesis and Philosophy*); Robert G. Hamerton-Kelly, "Sources and Traditions in Philo Judaeus: Prolegomena to an Analysis of His Writings," *SP* 1 (1972): 3–26; Tobin, *The Creation of Man*; and Burton L. Mack in the following works: "Exegetical Traditions in Alexandrian Judaism: A Program for the Analysis of the Philonic Corpus," *SP* 3 (1974–75): 71–112; *Logos und Sophia: Untersuchungen zur Weisheittheologie im hellenistischen Judentum*, Studien zur Umwelt des Neuen Testaments, vol. 10, ed. Karl Georg Kuhn (Göttingen: Vandenhoeck & Ruprecht, 1973); "Philo Judaeus and Exegetical Traditions," 227–71; and "Weisheit und Allegorie bei Philo von Alexandrien: Untersuchungen zur Traktat *De Congressu eruditionis*," *SP* 5 (1978): 57–105. For a recent exploration of the relationship between Philo's works and Palestinian traditions, see Naomi G. Cohen, *Philo Judaeus: His Universe of Discourse*, Beiträge zur Erforschung des Alten Testaments und des antiken Judentums, ed. Matthias Augustin and Michael Mach, vol. 24 (Frankfurt am Main: Peter Lang, 1995).

[50] On Philo's predecessors in general, see Peter Dalbert, *Die Theologie der hellenistisch-jüdischen Missions-Literatur unter Ausschluss von Philo und Josephus*, Theologische Forschung, no. 4 (Hamburg: Herbert Reich Evangelischen Verlag, 1954); James Drummond, *Philo Judaeus; or, The Jewish Alexandrian Philosophy in Its Development and Completion* (London: Williams and Norgate, 1888), 1:131–255; P. M. Fraser, *Ptolemaic Alexandria* (Oxford: Clarendon Press, 1972, repr. 1984), 2:687–716. On Philo and individual writers, see also Peder Borgen, "Aristobulus and Philo," *Philo, John and Paul: New Perspectives on Judaism and Early Christianity* (Atlanta: Scholars Press, 1987), 7–16; Carl A. Holladay, *Fragments from Hellenistic Jewish Authors*, vol. 3: *Aristobulus*, SBL Texts and Translations 39; Pseudepigrapha Series 13, ed. Martha Himmelfarb (Atlanta: Scholars

The Pentateuch of the Septuagint, for example, dating from the third century B.C.E., already shows a sensitivity in its translations to descriptions of God in the Hebrew Bible that are anthropomorphic and anthropopathic. The fragmentary evidence from Aristobulus, who probably lived in the mid-second century B.C.E., includes allegorical interpretations similarly concerned with anthropomorphisms. His writings also contain discussion of the Sabbath, highlighting the significance of the number seven, a theme upon which Philo expounds as well. In general, the fragments from Aristobulus reflect an effort to reconcile Jewish tradition with Greek philosophy.

In the Letter of Aristeas, whose dating is more uncertain (250 B.C.E. to the first century C.E.), we find rationalizations of Jewish laws through symbolic interpretations (sections 144–67), similar to interpretations in Philo. The Letter also rejects idolatry and polytheism (134–38) and conveys the awareness of presenting Judaism to a Gentile audience by emphasizing, among other things, God's concern for all humanity, not just the Jews (187–292, passim). Finally, the Wisdom of Solomon—which, though its dating is debated, may be contemporary to Philo[51]—also denounces idolatry and polytheism (chapter 13) and mentions reflection upon creation as a means to discover God. A passing reference to the high priest's robe (18:24) suggests familiarity with a more elaborate allegory found in both Josephus and Philo.

In addition to the scattered evidence from these Alexandrian Jewish sources, Philo himself frequently refers to other exegetes and their interpretations.[52] Even when he does not refer explicitly to others, the level of sophistication of some of his exegeses and his implicit assumption that certain associations are understood without needing further explanation can only suggest that these various interpretations are based upon earlier, well-known traditions. Prominent among these interpretations are the numerous etymologies that appear throughout his work. Most relevant for our purposes is the etymology for "Israel" as "one that sees God," or ὁρῶν θεόν.

Given the complexity of Philo's background, one can hardly escape the

---

Press, 1995); Nikolaus Walter, *Der Thoraausleger Aristobulos: Untersuchungen zu seinen Fragmenten und zu pseudepigraphischen Resten der jüdische-hellenistischen Literatur,* Texte und Untersuchungen zur Geschichte der altchristlichen Literatur, vol. 86 (Berlin: Akademie Verlag, 1964), esp. 58–86 and 141–49; David Winston, ed., *The Wisdom of Solomon,* vol. 43 of *The Anchor Bible,* ed. William Foxwell Albright and David Noel Freedman (Garden City, N.Y.: Doubleday, 1979), 59–63.

[51] See Winston, *The Wisdom of Solomon,* 20–25.

[52] David M. Hay, "Philo's References to Other Allegorists," *SP* 6 (1979–80): 41–75; idem, "References to Other Exegetes"; Shroyer, "Alexandrian Jewish Literalists"; Wolfson, *Philo,* 1:55–73.

conclusion that much of his work is deeply influenced by those who came before him. Indeed so much does Philo fit into a history of philosophical and Jewish traditions, that his positions on the very issues of this study are probably affected by his predecessors. Certainly Philo's notions about seeing God are influenced by Greek—and, especially, Platonic—philosophy. Moreover, the etymology linking "Israel" with seeing God derives in all likelihood from earlier Jewish exegesis. Similarly, some of Philo's interpretations about the relationship between God and Israel as described in the Bible may also be inherited from his Jewish predecessors.

While recognizing the inevitability of these various influences, I nonetheless assume that the evidence presented herein still does represent Philo's own view. The questions posed in this study, after all, are quite complex. Even if we could identify all the earlier traditions found in his work, to determine Philo's position on these matters certainly requires us to consider more than simply individual strands of thought or specific interpretations. It also requires that we consider how all the various elements are or are not brought together in his work. Moreover, if Philo does in fact have a rich banquet of ideas and traditions from which to choose, he most assuredly selects and highlights the ones he prefers.

4. *Ambiguity and Other Features in Philo's Work*

Reflections like these bring me to my fourth assumption, namely, that what Philo does and does not discuss is significant for this investigation but, ultimately, one cannot determine the nature of its significance to Philo himself. To be sure, it is always somewhat risky to study issues which an author himself—in this case Philo—does not explicitly address. For example, Philo nowhere tells us that Jews and only Jews can see God, that non-Jews can see God, or that "Israel" is a code word for those who can see God and may include all Jews, some Jews, or even non-Jews. Nor does he take an explicit stand on the implications for his Jewish contemporaries of the Biblical teaching that God chose Israel. Last, and perhaps most important, Philo never addresses why he believes an individual should be a Jew rather than, say, a Gentile philosopher.

Perhaps Philo's contemporary readers did know exactly what he meant by "Israel," did understand the relationship between being a Jew and seeing God, were familiar with his position on the covenant described in the Bible, and did understand why he considered it important to be a Jew. If so, they undoubtedly knew these things not from Philo's writings but from their shared environment in which these issues were perhaps taken for granted. We who come to Philo centuries later, however, cannot but be struck by the rich ambiguity of his discussions and his silence about certain issues. Indeed, so striking are these qualities that it is hard not to regard them as significant. They are significant, though, precisely because our questions pertain to the very issues about which he is ambiguous or silent—i.e., the exact meaning of "Israel," the relationship between being a Jew and seeing God, the relevance for his Jewish contemporaries of the covenant described in the Bible, and the importance of being a Jew. Since Philo himself never addresses these issues directly, we cannot determine whether or not or to what extent they are significant to him.

With these considerations in mind, I note below four features of Philo's discussion, evaluate their significance for this study, and speculate about why these features occur. I cannot, however, ultimately explain them.

First, Philo uses words with several meanings which cannot always be clearly separated so that his precise understanding eludes us. Second, with one exception—the non-exegetical treatise *Legat.*—Philo uses the terms "Israel" and "Jew" in separate writings. Third, in his Exposition treatises on Moses, he never uses the word "Israel" to describe the Biblical nation. Fourth and finally, Philo offers symbolic interpretations of Biblical passages without explicitly affirming the literal sense of these passages so that we cannot know whether he accepts or rejects their literal meaning. These four observations merit some elaboration.

As to the first, a certain ambiguity arises because Philo uses words—like "Israel" and γένος—that carry different senses which may operate at once. "Israel," he explains, means "one that sees God." "Israel," however, is also the name of the Biblical nation. When Philo uses this term, then, does he mean the one that sees God, the Biblical nation—expanded perhaps to include its Jewish descendants—or both?

Another polysemous word that Philo uses is γένος. This word can signify a race determined by birth; a class defined by acquired characteristics; an abstract nature or kind; a genus—i.e., a collective class—as opposed to individual species; or an idea in the intelligible as opposed to the sensible world. The many meanings of γένος are pertinent because Philo uses this word to describe Israel as a collectivity but rarely uses it to apply to the nation of Jews or Hebrews. Conversely, he never directly calls Israel a nation (ἔθνος) or a people (λαός), words which do not carry ambiguity as γένος does. When Philo speaks of the γένος Israel, then, he may mean the lineal race that has the ability to see, the class of people who can see, some sort of nebulous ideal, or perhaps a little bit of all these things.

A second characteristic of Philo's writings is that, with the exception of the treatise *Legat.*, the terms "Israel" and "Jew" never appear in the same work. *Legat.* is the only treatise in which one can find both words. In the Allegory and QGE, where Philo does mention "Israel," he never speaks of the Jews by name. By contrast, in the Exposition, Philo mentions the Jews by name, but he rarely mentions "Israel" and never mentions the two in the same treatise.

Philo's non-mention of "Israel" is particularly striking in the two treatises on Moses—part of the Exposition series—which are predominantly concerned with the Biblical nation Israel. In these treatises, Philo never calls the people "Israel," as they are called in the Bible, but instead uses the proper name "Hebrews" or else calls them simply "the nation" or "the people." Even when paraphrasing Scriptural quotations in which the word "Israel" appears, he changes this term to "Hebrews."

Finally, Philo frequently universalizes Biblical passages—whether through allegories of the soul or through presentation of specific figures like Abraham or Moses or even the nation Israel as generic wise or good people. This characteristic will be especially relevant when we examine Philo's exegesis of verses about the relationship between God and Biblical Israel. Since he can universalize these verses without taking a stand on their historical dimension, it is difficult to know whether or not these universalizing interpretations replace or simply augment the literal sense.

To evaluate the significance of the above observations, one may consult scholarly discussions about the types and uses of ambiguity in different kinds of literature. Writers have understood ambiguity to be purposeful or unconscious, a quality which can provide enhanced literary enjoyment, convey an unexpressed attitude about composition or interpretation, or even carry political significance. In some cases, ambiguity is seen as intentional deception or evasion.[53]

Regarding Philo specifically, David Winston, in his studies of philosophical themes in Philo's work, claims that he uses "a subtle and deliberate ambiguity" in order to sidestep clashes between Jewish and Greek ways of thinking. Winston suggests that Philo uses this technique to be intentionally esoteric. He writes, "Although [Philo] allows the Jewish side of his thought the dominant place in his presentation, he invariably

---

53 Two prominent book-length treatments of this subject are William Empson, *Seven Types of Ambiguity*, 3rd ed. (New York: New Directions, n.d.) and William B. Stanford, *Ambiguity in Greek Literature: Studies in Theory and Practice* (Oxford: Basil Blackwell, 1939; repr., New York: Johnson Reprint Corporation, 1972). Other useful discussions can be found in Daniel Boyarin, *Intertextuality and the Reading of Midrash* (Bloomington, Indiana: Indiana University Press, 1990), esp. 57–79; John A. Miles, Jr., "Radical Editing, *Redaktionsgeschichte* and the Aesthetic of Willed Confusion," *Traditions in Transformation: Turning Points in Biblical Faith*, ed. Baruch Halpern and Jon D. Levenson (Winona Lake, Indiana: Eisenbrauns, 1981), 9–31; Paul R. Rabbe, "Deliberate Ambiguity in the Psalter," *JBL* 110 (1991): 213–27; David Stern, "Midrash and Indeterminancy," *Critical Inquiry* 15 (1988): 132–61; Meir Sternberg, *The Poetics of Biblical Narrative: Ideological Literature and the Drama of Reading* (Bloomington, Indiana: Indiana University Press, 1985), esp. 186–263; Leo Strauss, *Persecution and the Art of Writing* (New York: Free Press, 1952; repr., Chicago: University of Chicago Press, 1988), esp. 22–37.

tones it down by introducing some philosophical twist and by allowing the perceptive reader a glimpse of his true position."[54]

Turning to the four features described just above, one cannot easily assess Philo's intentions. Do his ambiguity and silence on such issues as the precise meaning of "Israel," the relationship between being a Jew and being able to see God, the significance of the covenant between God and Biblical Israel, and the importance of being a Jew bespeak a wish to be esoteric about his position on these issues?

Let us take as an example Philo's use of the terms "Israel," "Jews," and "Hebrews." Is Philo deliberately hiding or avoiding something by using "Israel" and "Jew" in separate works or by speaking only of "Hebrews" rather than of "Israel" in his treatises on Moses?

Philo's separate uses of these terms are indeed puzzling to the modern reader, who may expect "Israel" and "Jews"—or, in the case of the Biblical nation in Moses's time, "Israel" and "Hebrews"—to be synonymous. For Philo, however, "Israel" may represent something else—namely, a loosely defined entity comprising those who can see God, which theoretically could include some Jews or all Jews and even some non-Jews. The very fluidity of the meaning of "Israel" is simply highlighted by his depiction of it as a γένος, another word with many meanings. The Jews, on the other hand, embody the clearly identifiable nation that worships God. Thus Philo may regard "Israel" and "Jews"—or "Hebrews"— as overlapping in meaning but not necessarily synonymous.

If "Israel" and "Jews" or "Hebrews" do indeed have different though perhaps overlapping meanings, then it is only logical that Philo would use these different terms in different places for different purposes. Moreover, the extent to which "Israel" does or does not overlap with "Jews" or "Hebrews" may not have been significant to Philo and his contemporary readers the way it is to us, his modern readers. Our puzzlement over Philo's ambiguity and silence on this and the other issues mentioned above may be more a reflection of our own expectations than the outcome of his deliberate design.

As to why Philo keeps "Israel" so separate from "Jews" and "Hebrews," one may speculate that instead of trying to be esoteric, he may simply be adapting his discussion to suit different audiences. Among his three exegetical series, for example, Philo speaks of "Israel" chiefly in the Allegory, occasionally in QGE, and only rarely in the Exposition. In contrast, he speaks of the Jews by name only in the Exposition. By recalling that these three series may be intended for readers with different spiritual

---

[54] David Winston, "Judaism and Hellenism: Hidden Tensions in Philo's Thought," *SPhA* 2 (1990): 18, cf. 3; see also idem, *Logos and Mystical Theology*, 14.

sensibilities and levels of familiarity with the Bible, we may perhaps account for the variation in Philo's use of terms.

Accordingly, if "Israel" represents a soul, person, or group that can see God, Philo may confine his discussion of "Israel" to the Allegory and, to a lesser extent, to QGE in order to address people like himself who understand this goal of seeing God and strive toward it. Moreover, since the term "Israel" would be more meaningful for Jews familiar with the Bible and Jewish tradition than it would be for people less knowledgeable about these sources, those more familiar with the term would associate it with their own heritage and take pride in the identification of "Israel" with the goal of seeing God.

At the same time, Philo may avoid speaking of "Israel" in the Exposition, where his readers may be Jews and non-Jews who have yet to acquire the spiritual sensibility to appreciate what "Israel" stands for. Let us not forget, however, that although Philo mentions "Israel" only twice in the Exposition, he does not completely omit speaking about it or about seeing God. This suggests that Philo is not deliberately trying to hide something from his readers but instead may be adjusting his discussion to fit their needs and interests.

As for why Philo discusses Jews only in the Exposition, we might reasonably expect him to discuss the Jews in a series aimed primarily at people not well acquainted with Jewish history, beliefs, and practices. He would have no need, however, to speak about the Jews and their ways to his more knowledgeable readers in the Allegory and QGE.

In analyzing the various literary uses of ambiguity, William Empson comments about the ambiguity of "ambiguity" itself. He writes,

> 'Ambiguity' itself can mean an indecision as to what you mean, an intention to mean several things, a probability that one or other or both of two things has been meant, and the fact that a statement has several meanings. It is useful to be able to separate these if you wish, but it is not obvious that in separating them at any particular point you will not be raising more problems than you solve.[55]

With this caveat in mind, we begin this investigation. The chapters that follow will present and elaborate upon the various features of Philo's writings described above, paying heed to the implications of these features for understanding how he negotiates between the poles of particularism and universalism. After reflecting upon the significance of what he does and does not say, we shall be in a better position to address the question of how and why it is important to Philo to be a Jew. Let us now consider the evidence.

---

[55] Empson, *Seven Types of Ambiguity*, 5.

CHAPTER ONE

"ISRAEL" AND THE JEWS:
A SURVEY OF APPROACHES AND SOME
PRELIMINARY OBSERVATIONS

Scholars have often noticed that it is difficult to pinpoint exactly what Philo means by "Israel." Although the Biblical designation "Israel" may refer—depending upon the context—to the patriarch Jacob, the nation of his descendants, or the Northern Kingdom, in Philo's works, the precise identity of "Israel" is not easily defined.

Two features of Philo's discussion contribute to this ambiguity. First, as he often explains, etymologically "Israel" means ὁρῶν θεόν, one that sees God.[1] By understanding "Israel" as an entity that sees God, Philo assigns the term a meaning that has nothing to do with birth and origin, but rather with spiritual capacity. Indeed, theoretically, those who see God may include non-Jews, while some Jews may not be able to see God. Moreover, since the participle ὁρῶν can be either masculine or neuter, it is sometimes unclear about whom or what Philo is speaking when he describes "Israel" using the etymology.[2]

Second, Philo frequently understands "Israel" in a figurative sense—for example, as a collectivity that cannot be identified with a particular social group, as an individual, a soul, or even part of a soul. Because these general or symbolic terms can apply both to Jews and non-Jews, the relationship between "Israel" and the Jews remains unclear.

Scholars have assessed the ambiguous relationship between "Israel" and the Jews in Philo's writings in different ways. As we shall see, their methods and assumptions can determine their conclusions. Below is a survey of various scholarly approaches, followed by my own examination of how Philo uses the words "Israel," "Jew," and other related terms.

---

[1] *Congr.* 51, *Somn.* 2.173, *Abr.* 57, *Praem.* 44, et al.

[2] When explaining the meaning of the word "Israel," Philo gives the etymology without an article (e.g., *Congr.* 51, *Fug.* 208, *Somn.* 2.173, *Abr.* 57, *Praem.* 44, *Legat.* 4). When describing the entity "Israel," however, Philo does use an article with the etymology. Usually, the article is masculine (e.g., *Leg.* 3.172, 212; *Post.* 92; *Somn.* 1.171), but in *Leg.* 3.186, it is neuter. One cannot determine the gender of the participle when it appears with the definite article in the genitive case (e.g., *Leg.* 3.38, *Sacr.* 134, *Conf.* 56).

A Survey of Approaches

Of special interest are works by Peder Borgen, Erwin R. Goodenough, Annie Jaubert, Gerhard Delling, Karl Georg Kuhn, Walter Gutbrod, Jacob Neusner, and Nils Dahl. To highlight the importance of methodological and conceptual issues, I shall consider these works according to these issues, instead of in their chronological order.

Peder Borgen. Peder Borgen's impressive variety of studies on Philo ranges from broad surveys to very specific investigations.[3] While he briefly discusses the relationship between "Israel" and the Jews in some of these works, Borgen addresses this question in most detail in his book *Bread From Heaven: An Exegetical Study of the Concept of Manna in the Gospel of John and the Writings of Philo.* Here he is interested in the relationship between "Israel" and the Jews because one of the Philonic passages he analyzes (*Mut.* 253–63) refers indirectly to "Israel" as "the one that can see" (ὁ [τὸ] ὁρατικός [όν]).

As it appears in the dative case (ὁρατικῷ), we cannot tell whether the word is masculine or neuter. Borgen himself implicitly acknowledges this ambiguity by first translating the term as "the seeing one." He goes on, however, to use F. H. Colson's LCL translation, "nation of vision,"[4] which gives the term a more concrete meaning than it has.

After explaining that Philo's etymology for "Israel" pertains to seeing God, Borgen asks, "Does Philo by this etymology refer to the Jewish race in the concrete sense or does he develop it allegorically as a spiritualized concept only?" Having thus posed the question in either-or terms, he surveys scholars that line up on one side or the other.[5]

---

[3] Peder Borgen, *Bread From Heaven: An Exegetical Study of the Concept of Manna in the Gospel of John and the Writings of Philo*, Supplements to Novum Testamentum, vol. 10 (Leiden: E. J. Brill, 1965); idem, "Philo of Alexandria: A Critical and Synthetical Survey of Research since World War II" (hereafter referred to as "Survey"), 98–154; idem, "Philo of Alexandria," *Jewish Writings of the Second Temple Period: Apocrypha, Pseudepigrapha, Qumran Sectarian Writings, Philo, Josephus*, ed. Michael E. Stone, CRINT, sec. 2, vol. 2 (Philadelphia: Fortress Press, 1984), 233–82. Several of Borgen's independent studies are collected in *Paul Preaches Circumcision and Pleases Men and Other Essays on Christian Origins*, Relieff, no. 8 (Trondheim: Tapir, 1983) and in *Philo, John and Paul: New Perspectives on Judaism and Early Christianity*, Brown Judaic Studies, ed. Jacob Neusner et al., no. 131 (Atlanta: Scholars Press, 1987). See also idem, "There Shall Come Forth a Man."

[4] Borgen, *Bread From Heaven*, 115.

[5] Ibid., 116–17. Among the scholars mentioned who consider "Israel" and the Jews as the same are Harry A. Wolfson, Edmund Stein, Walther Völker, and Norman Bentwich. Those cited who believe "Israel" designates only a group with the ability to see God are Joseph Pascher, Richard Reitzenstein, Hans Leisegang, and Hans Jonas. Borgen discusses Nils Dahl as an example of the attempt "to mediate between these

Borgen's own sympathies lie with those who believe that Philo intends "Israel" and the Jews to be the same. Although he bases the following comment specifically upon *Mut.* 253–63, Borgen elsewhere applies his conclusion to Philo's work in general.[6] He writes,

> The idea of the vision in *Mut.* 253–263 is ... determined both by Greek educational ideas and the actual study of the Jewish philosophy in the synagogues on the Sabbath. Thus the nation of vision is the people that is selftaught by nature, even the Jews, especially as they study the laws of Moses on the Sabbath.[7]

Consideration of *Mut.* 253–63 shows that the above observation brings together concepts which Philo himself does not. In *Mut.* 253–63, Philo strings together—as he often does—individual units of interpretation whose boundaries must be recognized.[8] Reference to τῷ ὁρατικῷ, or the one that can see, falls in *Mut.* 258, where Philo introduces the subject of manna. Strictly speaking, this discussion of manna, which interprets Exod. 16:4 and 22–30, is confined to *Mut.* 258–60. The term ὁρατικῷ falls only within this smaller unit and does not directly relate to what immediately precedes it in *Mut.* 253–57 or what follows it in *Mut.* 261–63.

Borgen, however, adopting the translation "nation of vision," explains ὁρατικῷ using notions which function independently either in other exegetical units within the same larger passage (*Mut.* 253–63) or else in completely different contexts (*Mos.* 2.215–16 and *Prob.* 81). In the comment quoted above, for example, he links vision (derived from ὁρατικῷ in *Mut.* 258) with Greek educational ideas (from *Mut.* 263), with Sabbath study (from *Mos.* 2.215–16 and *Prob.* 81), and with the Jews (from *Mos.* 2.215–16). In so doing, he disregards the integrity of the unit (*Mut.* 258–60) and makes connections between concepts which Philo himself keeps separate.

In *Bread From Heaven*, then, Borgen gives the ambiguous term ὁρατικῷ the concrete meaning "nation of vision." He then equates this "nation" with the Jews by harmonizing discrete notions from different exegetical contexts. Finally, he maintains that the "nation of vision" and the Jews are the same throughout Philo's works, based upon his analysis of this one passage (*Mut.* 258).

Erwin R. Goodenough. While Borgen attempts to harmonize separate Philonic passages, each with its own separate context, Erwin R. Good-

---

two conflicting views of 'the nation of vision.'" For discussion of Dahl's work, see further below.

[6] Borgen, "Survey," 114; idem, "Philo of Alexandria," 269.

[7] Borgen, *Bread From Heaven*, 118. For his analysis of the entire passage, see ibid., 99–121.

[8] See, e.g., Mack, "Exegetical Traditions in Alexandrian Judaism," 75–76.

enough examines two different passages, arriving at two different conclusions about the identity of "Israel." Based upon one Philonic passage (*Abr.* 56–59), Goodenough writes in *By Light, Light,*

> This race has got the name of Israel, that is 'Seeing God,' and is distinguished by the fact that it has the vision of God at the end of the mystic Road, the highest possible achievement, to which vision God draws the soul up the Road by the action of the divine Powers. This is not a reference to the race of Israel, but first to the Patriarchs, and then to those who got the vision, whether Jew or Gentile, and only to those. For the true successors of the Patriarchs, who have themselves been thus elevated, are not those descended from them in the flesh but their spiritual successors.[9]

Here Goodenough argues that for Philo "Israel" refers only to those who have the vision of God—be they Jews or non-Jews. Based upon a completely different Philonic passage (*Legat.* 1–7), however, this same scholar arrives at a different conclusion about "Israel." In *The Politics of Philo Judaeus,* he writes,

> The Jews are Israel, which means, [Philo] says, 'seeing God.' The mystic vision given to Jews, vision of that Deity which is beyond all categories, even the categories of virtue, is hidden from other men, since they have no higher gift than reason, and reason can rise not even to the Powers of God, the Creative and Ruling Powers.[10]

It is not Goodenough's purpose, of course, to investigate Philo's overall understanding of "Israel." Instead, he is analyzing two separate passages in two different contexts—one, in a study of Philo's religious beliefs and the other, in a study of his political attitudes. That he can arrive at two contradictory conclusions based upon different Philonic passages, however, suggests that Philo may indeed use the term "Israel" in a variety of ways. If Goodenough is correct, then "Israel" may require different interpretations, depending upon the context. Accordingly, to determine whether Philo considers "Israel" and the Jews to be identical, one must first examine how he uses the terms "Israel" and "Jews" throughout his works.

Annie Jaubert. One scholar who does survey a range of Philo's uses of "Israel" is Annie Jaubert. In her examination of the covenant idea in Judaism during the Hellenistic period,[11] she considers various Philonic passages in which "Israel" appears, taking note of the different levels on which Philo interprets this term—as a concrete people, a company of souls, an individual sage, and the purest part of the soul. Jaubert argues for

---

9 Goodenough, *By Light, Light,* 136.
10 Goodenough, *The Politics of Philo Judaeus,* 12.
11 Jaubert, *La notion d'Alliance.*

a continuity among these levels: "Because Israel is a spiritual people, it is the collection of pious souls; what applies to all counts also for each one."[12]

According to this scholar, then, Philo's statements about "Israel" applied to the individual or the soul do not negate that "Israel" as a real community has a special standing with God; they simply convey his preference for internalized religion. For Philo, spiritual unity is more important than blood kinship, and internal worship more essential than external.

Since Jaubert's purpose is to examine the status of the covenant and related themes in Philo's works, she does not pursue the possible ambiguities introduced by his interpretations of "Israel." In keeping with the scope of her study, she affirms the particularist aspects of Philo's thought—i.e., the special standing "Israel" has with God—without fully exploring his universalist dimensions, though she seems to be aware of them.[13]

The limits of Jaubert's study, however, may be instructive for us, if we reflect upon how her observations might be extended. We have noted at least two reasons why Philo's use of the term "Israel" is ambiguous and why this group may not be identical with the Jews. First, he redefines "Israel" in spiritual terms apart from ethnic origin, as the one that sees God. Second, he interprets "Israel" symbolically—as a company of souls, the individual sage, the soul, or even a part of the soul—without commenting upon the literal meaning of "Israel."

Jaubert acknowledges—though she does not pursue—the second point, namely, that Philo's symbolic interpretations may not apply strictly to the Jews. She does not, however, mention the first point, i.e., that the etymology of the term as "one that sees God" may also lead to a rather different understanding of who belongs to the community of "Israel." Instead she assumes that Philo uses the words "Israel" and "Jews" interchangeably.

In arguing, for example, that the unity and harmony of "Israel" derive from its laws and beliefs rather than from blood kinship, Jaubert quotes generously from texts in the Exposition.[14] These passages, however, lack any mention of the term "Israel" but instead speak about the Jews. Indeed, if Philo equates "Israel" and the Jews in these passages, he does not do so explicitly.

Jaubert may well be correct that Philo preserves the special relationship between "Israel" and God. We do not, however, know precisely who he thinks "Israel" is. Moreover, he may view the relationship between God and "Israel" as different from the relationship between God and the Jews.

---

[12] Ibid., 407.

[13] See, e.g., ibid., 402–3, 412–14.

[14] Ibid., 408–9.

We shall see, in fact, that for Philo, "Israel"'s relationship with God is linked to its ability to see Him, whereas the Jews' relationship with God is based upon their belief in Him and worship of Him through observance of the special laws.

Gerhard Delling. Gerhard Delling's study "The 'One Who Sees God' in Philo,"[15] provides an interesting contrast to Jaubert, because he approaches the relationship between "Israel" and the Jews solely from the perspective of the etymology of "Israel" and ignores Philo's symbolic interpretations of the term. Viewing consideration of these interpretations as a "new task," Delling simply asserts that they do not negate the application of statements about "Israel" to the "past and present people of God," namely, the Jews.[16]

Like Jaubert, Delling too assumes that "Israel" and the Jews are one and the same, and this assumption underlies his entire argument. Indeed, he believes that "Israel" is neither more nor less than all the Jews, with the exclusion of apostates. Delling writes, "Seeing God is, after all, not a particular gift to a selected circle within Judaism, but (as the name indicates) to all 'Israel.' Philo does not mark off from the rest of Jewry an elite of those who see God, but rather the apostates ..."[17]

If Delling does not allow that only some rather than all Jews might be able to see God, neither does he directly address the possibility that non-Jews might also have this ability. Instead, he writes, "The gift of seeing God is bound up with the particular relationship to God that God accords the Jews ..." In a note to this comment, he adds, "Through conversion to Judaism, one becomes a member fully entitled to [this gift]," citing *Spec.* 1.51f. as his reference.[18] A look at this passage, however, reveals that although Philo mentions proselytes, he does not talk about the gift of seeing God at all. Instead, he exhorts Jews to accept proselytes as their equals.

As its title suggests, Delling's study focuses upon the etymology of "Israel" as "one who sees God." He takes up such issues as the vocabulary of seeing as it pertains to "Israel," the theological significance of seeing for the Jewish people, and parallel occurrences of the etymology in other literature. Here we shall concentrate upon Philo's vocabulary, as this issue is the most relevant to our present discussion.

---

[15] Gerhard Delling, "The 'One Who Sees God' in Philo," *Nourished With Peace: Studies in Hellenistic Judaism in Memory of Samuel Sandmel,* ed. Frederick E. Greenspahn, Earle Hilgert, and Burton L. Mack, Scholars Press Homage Series (Chico, California: Scholars Press, 1984), 28–41.

[16] Ibid., 40.

[17] Ibid., 39; see also 28.

[18] Ibid., 35.

Indeed, Delling is particularly helpful when he surveys Philo's special vocabulary for "seeing" in connection with "Israel." He points out, for example, that the etymological interpretation of "Israel" is "so firmly bound up with the name that an abbreviation is sufficient to indicate it. 'The one who sees God' is simply 'the one who sees.'" Similarly, he notes that the expression for the "race able to see" (ὁρατικὸν γένος) is *always* a periphrasis for "Israel." In contrast, although the word which means "one who loves the vision" (φιλοθεάμων) occasionally refers to "Israel," it "does not belong to the special vocabulary of the meaning of the name 'Israel.'"[19]

Since Philo's understanding of "Israel" as the one that sees God may or may not encompass all Jews, it would seem essential to distinguish precisely how Philo refers to Jews, "Israel," and those who see God. Unfortunately, however, although Delling discusses the range of Philo's terminology, he never questions his own assumption that "Israel" and the Jews are identical. While Delling is careful to note, for example, where and how many times the term "Jews" occurs, how many times the term "Israel" occurs, and how often "Israel" appears in connection with the vocabulary for seeing, he fails to observe that Philo uses the words "Israel" and "Jews" in the same treatise only once.[20]

By calling attention to Philo's varied vocabulary connected to "Israel," Jews, and those who see God, Delling does incorporate an important methodological consideration. His equation of "Israel" and the Jews, however, prevents him from fully developing the implications of his many useful observations.[21]

Approaches to "Israel" and the Jews From a Broader Perspective

With the exception of Annie Jaubert—whose interest is in the covenant idea in Second Temple literature—the scholars discussed up to this point have focused exclusively upon Philo in trying to understand the meaning

---

[19] Ibid., 30–31 and 37. The translation for ὁρατικὸν γένος as "a race able to see" is Delling's. I shall argue in the second part of this chapter that γένος is ambiguous and may be understood as, among other things, a race defined by birth or a class defined by certain characteristics.

[20] Ibid., 27, n. 3; 37. (Philo mentions "Israel" and the Jews together in the same treatise only in *Legat.*)

[21] Like Delling and Jaubert, E. P. Sanders also assumes that "Israel" and the Jews are identical, in "The Covenant as a Soteriological Category and the Nature of Salvation in Palestinian and Hellenistic Judaism," *Jews, Greeks and Christians: Religious Culture in Late Antiquity. Essays in Honor of William David Davies*, ed. Robert Hamerton-Kelly and Robin Scroggs (Leiden: E. J. Brill, 1976), 11–44, esp. 25–38. Although Sanders discusses several issues relevant to our study, he frames these issues in a soteriological context. Since Philo uses the language of salvation only rarely, if ever, Sanders's framework does not ultimately clarify Philo's own ideas.

of "Israel." The scholars we are about to review—Karl Georg Kuhn, Walter Gutbrod, Jacob Neusner, and Nils Dahl—all provide, in one way or another, a larger context in which to consider Philo. Although this larger context is beyond the scope of this study, it offers a useful perspective from which to understand Philo's use of the terms "Israel" and "Jew."[22]

Karl Georg Kuhn and Walter Gutbrod. As part of an entry under "Ἰσραήλ [Israel]" in the *Theological Dictionary of the New Testament (TDNT)*, Karl Georg Kuhn and Walter Gutbrod survey how the terms "Israel," "Jew," and "Hebrew" are used in a variety of writings.[23] Kuhn reviews a broad range of post-Biblical Jewish works, excluding those of Philo and Josephus, while Gutbrod reports on these two Jewish authors in a section on Greek Hellenistic literature, which also includes pagan writers. Since Kuhn's essay provides a larger Jewish context for considering Philo, we shall briefly consider his remarks before turning to Gutbrod.

As a general observation about post-Biblical usage, Kuhn notes that both terms "Israel" and "Jews" refer to a people and "express both national and religious allegiance." He observes that the designation "Jews" can be a non-Jewish way of referring to the people, but that "Israel" is what the people calls itself: "Thus ישראל always emphasises [*sic*] the religious aspect, namely, that 'we are God's chosen people,' whereas Ἰουδαῖος may acquire on the lips of non-Jews a disrespectful and even contemptuous sound, though this is not usual, since Ἰουδαῖος is used quite freely without any disparagement."[24] According to Kuhn, then, in other Jewish literature as well as in Philo, the term "Israel" suggests the spiritual dimension of the people in a way that "Jew" may not.

In his review of Hellenistic literature, Gutbrod, like Kuhn, also distinguishes between Jewish and non-Jewish usage. Gutbrod notes that pagans do not use "Israel," since it is "a specifically Jewish term which is

---

[22] Other studies of these and related terms which may shed light upon Philo's usage can be found in Renée Bloch, "Israélite, juif, hébreu," *Cahiers Sioniens* 5 (1951): 11–31, 258–80; Dieter Georgi, *The Opponents of Paul in Second Corinthians* (Philadelphia: Fortress Press, 1986), 40–60; Peter J. Tomson, "The Names Israel and Jew in Ancient Judaism and in the New Testament," *Bijdragen* 47 (1986): 120–40, 266–89; Solomon Zeitlin, "The Names Hebrew, Jew and Israel: A Historical Study," *Jewish Quarterly Review* 43 (1952–53): 365–79. For reflections on the meaning of these terms from a writer who lived closer to Philo's time, see Eusebius, *Praeparatio Evangelica* 7:6 and 8.

[23] Karl Georg Kuhn, "Ἰσραήλ, Ἰουδαῖος, Ἑβραῖος in Jewish Literature after the OT," *Theological Dictionary of the New Testament (TDNT)*, ed. Gerhard Kittel, trans. and ed. Geoffrey W. Bromiley (Grand Rapids, Mich.: W. B. Eerdmans, 1965), 3:359–69. Walter Gutbrod, "Ἰουδαῖος, Ἰσραήλ, Ἑβραῖος in Greek Hellenistic Literature," *TDNT*, 3:369–75.

[24] Kuhn, "Ἰσραήλ, Ἰουδαῖος, Ἑβραῖος," 360.

not based primarily on nationality or external factors."[25] Moreover, Josephus—who may be writing for a non-Jewish audience—does not use Ἰσραήλ (Israel) to describe the whole people but only the patriarch Jacob. Instead Josephus uses Ἰσραηλίτης (Israelite) "for members of the people of God in past days," but not for those in the present. Gutbrod observes, "This use is in keeping with the Biblical text and is also suitable for the readers whom he has in view."[26]

As a dictionary entry, Gutbrod's consideration of Philo is necessarily brief, but he makes some useful observations, particularly about Philo's etymological understanding of "Israel." He writes,

> The vision of God expressed in the name is the essential thing for Philo (Abr. 57-59; Leg. Gaj., 4). But this means that Ἰσραήλ may easily come to transcend the limits of the Jewish people. All οἱ τοῦ ὁρατικοῦ γένους μετέχοντες [those who belong to the race/class that can see] are Ἰσραήλ (Deus Imm., 144; Sacr. AC, 134). This extension is not directly stated; nevertheless, the way is clearly prepared for it.[27]

In these few words, Gutbrod captures the essence of the problem in Philo's definition of "Israel." By explaining the term as "one that sees God," Philo opens the way to understanding "Israel" as different from the entire Jewish people. Philo himself, however, never addresses this possibility directly, leaving his readers to puzzle—as indeed many still do—over the ambiguous relationship between the Jews and "Israel, the one that sees God."

Jacob Neusner. One scholar who especially emphasizes the different connotations of "Israel" and "Jews" in various writings from antiquity is Jacob Neusner. Neusner presents his arguments in a book entitled *Judaism and Its Social Metaphors: Israel in the History of Jewish Thought.*[28]

Neusner contends that one must speak of "Judaisms" in the plural rather than "Judaism" in the singular. "A Judaism" describes a religious system, which consists of "a worldview, way of life expressive of that worldview, and the social entity to which the worldview is addressed and that embodies the way of life."[29] Within such a system, "Israel" is a metaphor for the social entity which may be, among other things, a group, a class, a caste, family, nation, or "population."[30] As a social metaphor,

25　Gutbrod, "Ἰουδαῖος, Ἰσραήλ, Ἑβραῖος," 371.
26　Ibid., 372.
27　Ibid.
28　Jacob Neusner, *Judaism and Its Social Metaphors: Israel in the History of Jewish Thought* (Cambridge: Cambridge University Press, 1989). Neusner also usefully summarizes the main points of this book in "Israel: Judaism and Its Social Metaphors," *Journal of the American Academy of Religion* 50 (1978): 331–61.
29　Neusner, *Judaism and Its Social Metaphors*, 205.
30　Ibid., 3 and idem, "Israel," 333.

"Israel" conveys a group's self-definition by expressing "the things with which [they] compare themselves in accounting for their society together."[31]

Neusner focuses upon what he calls "the Judaism of the dual Torah," i.e., the written and oral Torah, whose literature encompasses the Mishnah, two Talmuds, and a variety of other midrashic writings produced during the first five centuries C.E. He also briefly considers some other religious systems, namely, those of Paul, Philo, and the Essenes of Qumran. Among other things, Neusner maintains that the definition of "an Israel" reflects the larger interests of a particular Judaism and that the importance of "Israel" within a system depends upon "the generative problematic—urgent question—of the system-builders, and not on their social circumstance."[32]

"Israel," then, is a rather elastic term, which takes its shape according to the interests of the shapers: "What an 'Israel' is depends on who wants to know. Philosophers imagine a philosophical 'Israel,' and politicians conceive a political 'Israel.'"[33] Regarding Philo, Neusner writes,

> What makes an 'Israel' into 'Israel' for Philo is a set of essentially philosophical considerations, concerning adherence to or perception of God. In the philosophical system of Philo, 'Israel' constitutes a philosophical category, not a social entity in an everyday sense.[34]

While closer examination of Neusner's hypotheses and observations would take us beyond the scope of our study, their significance for our investigation must be acknowledged. Indeed, by arguing that "Israel" functions differently in different kinds of Judaisms, Neusner illuminates a larger canvas upon which we might draw a detailed sketch of Philo.

Nils Dahl. Nils Dahl is another scholar who approaches the problem of "Israel" and the Jews in Philo's works from a broader perspective.[35] Dahl begins his book, *Das Volk Gottes*, by noting that in Gal. 6:16 Paul uses the term "Israel" to describe the Christian Church.[36] Recognizing that "Israel" must be a flexible concept for Paul to be able to use it this way, he poses as the central task of his book to understand how Paul's use of the term "Israel" became possible. Toward this end, Dahl surveys a broad range of

---

[31] Neusner, *Judaism and Its Social Metaphors*, 1.
[32] Ibid., 212.
[33] Ibid., 220.
[34] Ibid., 221.
[35] Nils A. Dahl, *Das Volk Gottes. Eine Untersuchung zum Kirchenbewusstsein des Urchristentums* (Oslo: Jacob Dybwad, 1941), 107–14.
[36] Ibid., 1.

Biblical and post-Biblical literature to see how "Israel" and "the people of God" are understood. It is in this context, then, that he takes up Philo's works specifically.

Dahl begins his discussion of Philo with an open-ended approach by asking simply what perceptions Philo sets forth about "Israel" and the Jews. He distinguishes among the terms "Israel," "Jews," and "Hebrews," noting that Philo mentions "Jews" most often in his political treatises, *Flacc.* and *Legat.*, but never in the Allegory, and that "Israel" appears most frequently in the Allegory.[37]

Dahl then incorporates "Israel" and the Jews into the much larger framework of all religious seekers mentioned by Philo. Indeed, Philo uses a broad range of generic terms for these seekers, terms which have no reference to ethnic origin. He speaks, for example, of the sage (σοφός); man of worth (ἀστεῖος, σπουδαῖος); lover of wisdom (ἐραστὴς σοφίας); disciple (γνώριμος, ὁμιλητής, φοιτητής) of Moses, of wisdom, of the Logos and of God; citizen of the world (κοσμοπολίτης) and the perfect man (τέλειος).

Dahl suggests that Philo presents these seekers according to a scheme— influenced by what Dahl calls the "Alexandrian world-scheme"— which consists of different levels that correspond to Philo's different levels of religious identification. Dahl's presentation is rather intricate and requires careful analysis.

On the lowest rung of the scheme is Philo's contemporary Jewish community. Philo's political activity in behalf of the Jews, expressions of communal feeling, and messianic hope exemplify his strong identification with this community.[38]

Dahl perceives a distinction in Philo's writings between what he calls the "visible" and the "invisible church," arguing that the next rung corresponds to the "invisible church." While the Jews supposedly represent the "visible community," this "invisible community" is composed of groups characterized and united by their spiritual qualities. Such groups would include, for example, the patriarchs as models of virtue rather than as historical figures and other seekers described by generic terms such as those listed above.[39]

Following the "invisible church," Dahl describes the next stage, which differentiates between earthly and heavenly existence. On this level, all people are considered sojourners on earth because their true home is in heaven. Dahl argues that Philo combines various motifs here. On the one

---

[37] Ibid., 107–8.
[38] Ibid., 108.
[39] Ibid., 109–10.

hand, according to the Stoic ideal, the sojourner theme applies to the individual sage, whose real homeland is virtue. On the other hand, according to Platonic-Gnostic ideas, the sojourner motif applies to the soul, which is a mere visitor to the corporeal world.

As Philo moves to higher levels, he leaves behind the concrete Jewish people and uses what Dahl calls the language of mystery religions. Here, for example, Philo speaks about the practicer, lover of virtue, prophet, seer, or student of God.[40]

Concerning the unique role of the Jewish nation in this whole scheme, Dahl concludes that Philo neither emphasizes nor denies Jewish particularity. Philo rarely alludes to the special position of the Jews, for example, when he speaks about the so-called "visible community." Instead he emphasizes virtue rather than blood ties as the basis of common citizenship. In discussing the so-called "invisible community," Philo seems to mesh the attributes of the Jews with those of the sage: "For Philo, on the one hand, the Jewish people is the realization of the Stoic ideal of the sage; on the other hand, he transfers all the noble predicates of God's people to the (Stoic) sage."[41]

As to the other levels of the scheme, Dahl points out that Philo's tendency to see specific Jewish characteristics as symbols of the cosmos does not cancel Jewish particularity but instead gives it deeper meaning. Similarly, Philo's mystery is not a different kind of Judaism from the "normative," but rather an interpretation on the level of the soul.

Regarding the place of "Israel" in this scheme, Dahl explains that according to Philo's understanding, "Israel" operates on each of the different levels. Thus the term can refer to the empirical Jewish nation, which alone sees God; the "invisible community," or the race that can see; the sage or the individual God-seer; the soul or the part of the soul that sees God; the abstract vision of God; and finally the Logos.[42]

After arguing that Philo's use of "Israel" encompasses different levels in this "Alexandrian world-scheme," Dahl raises the question of "Israel"'s special role. Specifically, he asks "whether this structure of piety permits that in Philo too 'Israel according to the flesh' holds a special place as the people of God or whether the political and philosophic-mystic ideas in Philo part ways entirely."

"Without a doubt," he answers,

> Philo embraces both trains of thought with equal passion, although he considers politics to be an intrusion. We could say that for him 'Israel according to the flesh'

---

[40] Ibid., 110–12.
[41] Ibid., 111.
[42] Ibid., 113.

is an image and representation of 'Israel according to the spirit,' if these
expressions are allowed here. Just as the body is a house of the soul for him and
the letter of the law a house of the spiritual content, so too the Jewish synagogue
becomes for him the home of the invisible community.[43]

Dahl's analysis has several merits. He is careful to distinguish how
Philo uses vocabulary for "Jews," "Hebrews," and "Israel," noting patterns
in where these terms appear in the different series. He presents a strong
case for Philo's commitment to the Jewish community but also demon-
strates how his thought poses several challenges to the importance of
being a Jew by birth. Dahl points out, for example, that Philo emphasizes
virtue rather than blood as a bond of kinship, presents the Jew as a Stoic
sage, and elaborates upon the internal and individual aspects of religion
besides the external and group dimensions. Last and most significant,
Dahl shows that "Israel" can indeed have several referents. Unlike those
who ask whether or not "Israel" is equivalent to the Jews, Dahl allows for
several possible ways to understand "Israel."

At the same time, however, Dahl's schematic presentation is perhaps
too ambitious in its attempt to encompass and classify Philo's many
expressions for religious seekers. Indeed, to elucidate the relationship
among all the Philonic terms for these seekers would be a great contri-
bution to our understanding of this complicated exegete. In trying to do
this, however, Dahl imposes upon Philo's thought an external structure,
which he calls the "Alexandrian world-scheme," and introduces distinctions between a "visible" and an "invisible community" and between
"Israel according to the flesh" and "Israel according to the spirit"—
distinctions which Philo himself does not make.[44]

Because he uses categories and terminology not found in Philo's
writings, one might argue that Dahl complicates the issue further. Despite
this criticism, however, of all the Philonic scholars discussed above,
perhaps Dahl allows for the greatest flexibility in understanding the
various ways "Israel" may function in Philo's thought.

---

[43] Ibid., 114.

[44] The distinction between "Israel according to the flesh" and "Israel according to
the spirit" is suggested in several passages in the New Testament. 1 Cor. 10:18
explicitly mentions Ἰσραὴλ κατὰ σάρκα (Israel according to the flesh) but not Ἰσραὴλ
κατὰ πνεῦμα (Israel according to the spirit). Other passages suggest that Abraham's
descendants or Israel may be determined not by birth, but rather by faith (Matt. 3:7–
10; Rom. 4:16, 9:6–8, 11:17–24). Rom. 2:28–29 contrasts the visible (ἐν τῷ φανερῷ) Jew
with the private (ἐν τῷ κρυπτῷ) one and circumcision in the flesh (ἡ ἐν σαρκὶ περιτομή)
with circumcision of the heart (περιτομὴ καρδίας).

A Survey of Approaches: Summary

Our review of how various scholars have approached the relationship between "Israel" and the Jews in Philo's works offers some useful lessons. Consideration of Borgen and Goodenough highlights the importance of taking into account all Philo's extant writings, not just individual passages, and of approaching the relationship between "Israel" and the Jews in a way that allows for several possible interpretations. Analysis of the work of Jaubert and Delling shows that to understand the ambiguity posed by Philo's use of "Israel," one should keep in mind both that he interprets the term symbolically and that the etymology allows "Israel" to be defined by spiritual capability rather than common origin.

By observing that the words "Israel" and "Jews" have different connotations in various kinds of Jewish discourse, Kuhn, Gutbrod, Neusner, and Dahl remind us that these different connotations are a phenomenon that goes beyond Philo's works alone. Finally, the studies of Delling, Gutbrod, and Dahl yield important observations, which can be further explored, about Philo's vocabulary and patterns of usage throughout his various writings. With these lessons in mind, we are now ready to consider Philo's discussion of "Israel" and the Jews.

Philo's Discussion of "Israel" and the Jews

Several word studies reveal some distinct characteristics and patterns in the way Philo talks about "Israel" and the Jews throughout his works. When discussing the real people, however—either the Biblical nation or his Jewish contemporaries—he does not always name them with a proper noun or even a common noun but sometimes simply uses pronouns. Thus we must consider both how Philo uses specific words like "Israel" and "Jews" and also how he speaks generally about the nation—in the past or present.

A careful examination of Philo's works yields the following observations:

1. *To describe the real nation, Philo uses "Jews" or "Hebrews" but not "Israel." Instead "Israel" seems to describe an entity which cannot be easily identified with a particular social group.* In every case where Philo uses the word "Jews," the context makes clear that he is referring to the real nation, whether in the past or present. Similarly, "Hebrews" also indicates an identifiable people —either the Biblical nation or past or present speakers of the Hebrew language—except in a very few passages where the word has a symbolic connotation.[45] By contrast, when Philo uses "Israel"—with the exception

---

[45] See below, n. 50.

of *Legat.* 4, in which the term denotes the Jews—we cannot easily identify the group to which he is referring.

2. *To describe "Israel" and the Jews as collectivities, Philo uses different words with different connotations.* Thus he refers to "Israel" as a γένος (race or class), but to the Jews and Hebrews predominantly as a nation (ἔθνος) or a people (λαός), but only rarely as a γένος. Although γένος may overlap in meaning with ἔθνος or λαός, as Philo applies these words to "Israel" and "Jews" or "Hebrews," their differences in meaning are significant. Finally, Philo occasionally uses the word πολιτεία (polity) to describe the Jews in the past or present, but never to describe "Israel."

3. *With one exception (the political treatise* Legat.*), Philo speaks about "Israel" and the Jews by name in different treatises.* Generally, the terms "Israel" and "Jew" appear in different series, which are probably intended for different audiences. Among the exegetical works, the Exposition stands apart from the Allegory and QGE as the only series in which Philo clearly mentions the Jews by name. It is also striking that he refers to "Israel" only twice in the Exposition (*Abr.* 57 and *Praem.* 44), whereas in the Allegory he frequently speaks about "Israel" and occasionally mentions it in QGE. The nature and number of references to Jews in the political treatises, *Flacc.* and *Legat.*, set these writings apart from the exegetical commentaries, since Philo mentions the Jews quite frequently in these treatises. In the non-exegetical works, "Israel" appears only once (*Legat.* 4). Finally, "Hebrews" and "Israel" appear in the same works only when "Hebrews" designates speakers of the Hebrew language, but never when it refers to the Biblical nation.

4. *Among the three exegetical series, only in one—the Exposition—does Philo speak at length about the Biblical nation and his Jewish contemporaries as real historical or social entities.* In the Exposition, especially in the treatises from *Mos.* 1 through *Praem.*, Philo's main purpose is to present the history and practices of his people. In the Allegory and QGE, however, Philo's primary purpose is to explicate Biblical passages, not to narrate historical events. Therefore when Philo refers to the Biblical people in the Allegory and QGE, their real existence is beside the point he wishes to make. In the Allegory, Philo does refer at least twice to Jewish contemporaries,[46] but these references are to individuals in specific social situations, not to the entire people. In QGE, Jews are mentioned once in the translation (*QG* 3.48, discussed below), but since we do not have the Greek text, we do not know Philo's original designation for them.

---

[46] *Migr.* 89–93 and *Somn.* 2.123–24. Here, he seems to be addressing (*Migr.* 89–93) or referring to (*Somn.* 2.123–24) his fellow Jews in Alexandria. Throughout all three exegetical commentaries, he also alludes to other exegetes, who are presumably Jews.

To support these various observations, below are the results of several word studies.[47] We shall first consider the exegetical works—namely, the Allegory, Exposition, and QGE—and then the non-exegetical works.

The Exegetical Works

Proper Nouns

Ἰουδαῖος (Jew)

Perhaps the simplest observation is that the Exposition is the only exegetical series to use the word "Jew" (Ἰουδαῖος), which appears twenty times.[48] This word never occurs in the Allegory and, although the English translation of QGE has it once (QG 3.48), the translator notes that in the Armenian, the word is "Hebrews." Unfortunately we have no Greek text to tell us whether the original word is "Jews." The context makes clear, however, that Philo is speaking about a contemporary people. Since "Hebrews" has a different connotation—as either the Biblical nation or people who speak the Hebrew language—use of the word "Jews" in this passage makes sense.

In all the cases where Philo uses "Jews" in the Exposition, he is referring to the real nation—usually in the present, but sometimes in the past.[49] He never interprets the term symbolically. Philo's exact way of referring to the people varies. Usually he calls them Jews (Ἰουδαῖοι), the nation of Jews (τὸ Ἰουδαίων ἔθνος), or simply the nation (τὸ ἔθνος). In *Virt.* 108, he calls them the polity of Jews (ἡ Ἰουδαίων πολιτεία).

---

[47] For most of the Philonic writings, we have fairly reliable word indexes. See Mayer, *Index Philoneus* and the TLG database. (See also Runia, "How to Search Philo," 106–39.) QGE presents a particular challenge for conducting word studies, since most of this commentary is extant only in the ancient Armenian translation, and even this text may be incomplete. (We also have a portion of QG 4 in Latin translation, and when this agrees with the Armenian, we can be more confident of the text.) Greek sections of QGE preserved in the works of other writers are mere fragments. Observations about QGE—based upon the English translation in LCL and Greek fragments, when these are available—are necessarily of a very general nature. For the Greek fragments of QGE, see Françoise Petit, ed., *Quaestiones in Genesim et in Exodum: Fragmenta Graeca*, vol. 33 of *Les oeuvres de Philon d'Alexandrie*, ed. Roger Arnaldez, Claude Mondésert, and Jean Pouilloux (Paris: Éditions du Cerf, 1978). (Hereafter the French translation is referred to as *OPA.*) Earle Hilgert has summarized the current state of scholarship on QGE in "The *Quaestiones*: Texts and Translations," *Both Literal and Allegorical*, ed. David M. Hay, 1–15.

[48] *Mos.* 1.1, 7, 34; *Mos.* 2.17, 25, 41, 193, 216; *Decal.* 96; *Spec.* 1.97; *Spec.* 2.163, 166; *Spec.* 3.46; *Spec.* 4.179, 224; *Virt.* 65, 168, 206, 212, 226.

[49] In two instances, Philo uses Ἰουδαῖος (Jew) in the treatises on Moses to refer to the Biblical people (*Mos.* 1.34, *Mos.* 2.193).

Ἑβραῖος (Hebrew)

"Hebrews" is another word that designates a clearly identifiable people. Of the more than fifty occurrences in the Allegory and the Exposition, "Hebrews" is rarely interpreted symbolically.[50] Philo uses it in the Allegory and the Exposition chiefly in two ways, to refer to the historical nation mentioned in the Bible and to those people either before or contemporary to him who speak the Hebrew language. The first use, whereby "Hebrews" indicates the Biblical nation, occurs occasionally in the Allegory, in which the real existence of the nation is beside the point of the passage.[51] In the Exposition, however, and especially in the treatises on Moses, "Hebrews" regularly designates the Biblical nation, whose real existence is clearly presupposed.[52] The second use of "Hebrews," whereby the word denotes those who speak the Hebrew language, is found in both series, almost exclusively where Philo provides etymologies of Biblical terms.[53]

When speaking about the Biblical people as a real entity, Philo calls them Hebrews (Ἑβραῖοι), the people (ὁ λαός), or the nation (τὸ ἔθνος). He never calls them specifically the Hebrew nation or Hebrew people.[54]

As for QGE, Philo uses "Hebrews" somewhat differently in QG and QE.

---

[50] In the Allegory, in *Migr.* 20, Philo gives an etymology of "Hebrew" as meaning "migrant." He writes that, in contrast to the Egyptian preoccupation with the body, a characteristic of the Hebrew race is to move away from the sense-perceptible realm to the noetic. Similarly, *Migr.* 141 speaks of Hebrew souls in contrast to Egyptian women, associating the former with the intellectual world, the latter with the material. Preference for the non-material as a trait of the Hebrews is also suggested in *Abr.* 251, but the word is not given an allegorical meaning nor is it applied to the soul. These are the only three instances in which Philo gives "Hebrews" a symbolic association.

[51] "Hebrews" refers to the Biblical nation in the following seven out of nineteen references: *Migr.* 20 (2 references), 141 (see above, n. 50); *Her.* 128; *Fug.* 168; *Mut.* 117 (2). The remaining twelve references denote speakers of the Hebrew language.

[52] "Hebrews" denotes the Biblical people in thirty out of forty references in the Exposition. The remaining ten denote speakers of the Hebrew language. All but one (see n. 53) of twenty-four references to "Hebrews" in *Mos.* 1 and 2 denote the Biblical nation. In addition, all three occurrences of Ἑβραϊκός (Hebrew)—a word which appears only in *Mos.* 1.16, 240, and 285—describe the Biblical people.

[53] See, e.g., *Somn.* 1.58, *Somn.* 2.250, *Spec.* 2.145. One case in which "Hebrews" is used outside of an etymological explanation to refer to speakers of the Hebrew language is *Mos.* 2.32. This passage describes how the high priest chose and sent the most esteemed of the Hebrews (οἱ δοκιμώτατοι Ἑβραίων) to Egypt to translate the Bible from Hebrew into Greek. Tomson ("The Names Israel and Jew," 128 and 137) makes the imaginative—though unprovable—suggestion that Philo may use "Hebrews" not only for Hebrew speakers but also for Hebrew readers, i.e., those Jews who read the Bible in Hebrew rather than in Greek.

[54] *Mos.* 1.285 and 289 refer to the Hebrew host (ἡ Ἑβραϊκὴ στρατιά, στρατιὰ Ἑβραίων) in the episode with Balaam and Balak. This expression does not appear in the corresponding Scriptural passages. For *Mos.* 1.289, e.g., see below, n. 65.

In *QG*, the word appears predominantly in etymological explanations to denote Hebrew speakers.[55] *QE*, in which Philo interprets verses about the Biblical nation, has very few occurrences of the word "Hebrew" to denote the nation and no occurrence to denote speakers of the Hebrew language.[56] One passage, which has a parallel Greek fragment, mentions the Hebrew race (τὸ Ἑβραῖον γένος, *QE* 2.2, discussed later in the chapter). Instead of using the proper noun "Hebrew," QGE often speaks of the Biblical nation as "they," "the nation," or "the people."[57]

Excursus: Χαλδαῖος (Chaldean)

In the Exposition and QGE, Philo occasionally uses "Chaldean" (Χαλδαῖος) or forms of this word as a synonym for "Hebrew," generally to mean speakers of the Hebrew language[58] and once to denote Hebrew race or descent.[59] "Chaldean" is never used as a synonym for "Hebrew" in the Allegory, however, in either sense. A different association with the Chaldeans as astrologers whose land Abraham leaves appears throughout all the exegetical writings.[60]

Ἰσραήλ (Israel)

Especially interesting is Philo's use or non-use of the word "Israel," both with regard to where he uses (or does not use) the term and what it

---

[55] See, e.g., *QG* 1.13; *QG* 2.45, *QG* 4.97, 102, 122, 147, 163, 191, 245.

[56] The English translation, for example, has "Hebrew" in *QE* 1.7, 10; *QE* 2.2, 6. Only the latter two passages have Greek fragments. The word "Hebrew" appears in the Greek for *QE* 2.2, but not in *QE* 2.6. Petit (*Quaestiones*, OPA, 33:243) notes that the Armenian text of *QE* 2.6 is obscure and differs from the Greek.

[57] *QG* 3.18, 38, 49 (here Philo gives the name of the nation as "Israel"; see below, n. 67); *QG* 4.153, 200; *QE* 1.2, 4, 9, 10; *QE* 2.22, 30, 31, 35, 49. Of these passages, only *QG* 3.18 and *QG* 4.153 have parallel Greek fragments. For a discussion of *QG* 3.18, see the section below on QGE under "Common Nouns." *QG* 4.153 uses the word γένος for the people in speaking about Abraham (though not by name) as "the origin and forefather of the race" (ἀρχὴ καὶ προπάτωρ γένους).

[58] *Abr.* 8, 12; *Mos.* 2.40 (2); *Praem.* 14, 23, 31; *QG* 2.43; *QG* 3.38, 43, 49; *QG* 4.1, 17, 97, 147, 239; *QE* 2.68. See also the following passages in which Χαλδαϊστί, in the Chaldean language, is used to denote the Hebrew language: *Abr.* 99, 201; *Mos.* 2.224; *Praem.* 44. Χαλδαϊκός, Chaldean, refers to the Hebrew language in *Mos.* 2.26, 38, 40.

[59] *Mos.* 2.5. *Hypoth.* 6.1 also speaks about an ancestor of Chaldean descent, but this may refer to Abraham who in fact was of Chaldean descent. See below, n. 97.

[60] *Gig.* 62; *Migr.* 178, 187; *Her.* 96–97, 277; *Congr.* 50; *Somn.* 1.52, 53; *Abr.* 67, 69, 72, 188; *QG* 3.1; *QG* 4.88. See also the following passages in which χαλδαΐζω, to follow Chaldean beliefs, appears: *Migr.* 184; *Her.* 99; *Mut.* 16; *Somn.* 1.161; *Abr.* 70, 77 (2). In the following passages, Χαλδαϊκός, Chaldean, refers to Chaldean beliefs: *Ebr.* 94; *Migr.* 177, 184; *Her.* 97, 280, 289; *Congr.* 49; *Mut.* 16; *Abr.* 71, 82; *Mos.* 1.23, *Praem.* 58. For a somewhat different classification of Philo's usage, see C. K. Wong, "Philo's Use of *Chaldaioi*," *SPhA* 4 (1992): 1–14.

represents. In contrast to the Allegory, in which it appears over seventy times—both in Biblical quotations and in the commentary—in the Exposition, "Israel" appears only twice, in the commentary.[61] Similarly, QGE has very few direct references to "Israel."[62] Instead, here, Philo frequently substitutes for "Israel" the periphrastic designation "the race or class that can see" (τὸ ὁρατικὸν γένος), both in Biblical quotations and in the interpretations. Without the Greek text of QGE, however, it is difficult to assess the significance of either the presence or absence of the actual word in this series.

The restricted use of "Israel" in the Exposition is especially striking when one looks at the two treatises on Moses, for there, more than in any other work, Philo recounts on a literal level the Biblical narrative of the nation called "Israel." The Scriptural account uses "Hebrews" along with "sons of Israel" (or some slight variation of this expression) while the nation is still in Egypt, through Exodus 10. After Exodus 10, the Biblical narrative begins to refer to the people regularly as "sons of Israel." "Hebrew" appears only twice later in the Pentateuch.[63] In *Mos.* 1–2, however, even after narrating the exodus from Egypt, Philo consistently refers to the nation as the Hebrews, or simply as the nation (τὸ ἔθνος) or the people (ὁ λαός). The word "Israel" never appears in these two treatises. Philo's mention of "Hebrews" throughout this paraphrase, then, goes well beyond the Biblical usage.

Philo's non-use of "Israel" here to denote the actual Biblical people seems to be a purposeful avoidance. One cannot argue that he simply uses "Hebrews" instead of "Israel" to be consistent, since he occasionally uses other names as synonyms for the Biblical people, such as "Chaldean" and "Jew."[64] Also, we have seen that Philo can use one word, like "Hebrew" or "Chaldean," in more than one way.

The *Mos.* 1 renditions of Balaam's prophecies in Num. 23:7, 23:21, and 24:5 provide striking examples of Philo's choice of terms. In Num. 23:7, Balaam tells how Balak brought him to curse the people:

---

[61] Philo's numerous references to "Israel" in the Allegory are discussed extensively in the next chapter. The two Exposition references are *Abr.* 57 and *Praem.* 44.

[62] *QG* 3.49; *QG* 4.233; *QE* 2.30, 37. In *QG* 3.49 and *QG* 4.233, Philo mentions the word in an interpretation. In *QE* 2.30, he mentions "Israel" in a paraphrase of Exod. 24:4; in *QE* 2.37, he mentions it in a quotation of Exod. 24:10.

[63] Exod. 21:2 and Deut. 15:12. The Bible frequently uses "Hebrews" when speaking about Israel in relation to other peoples. See Anson F. Rainey, "Hebrews," *Harper's Bible Dictionary*, ed. Paul J. Achtemeier (San Francisco: Harper & Row, 1985), 379. Cf. Tomson, "The Names Israel and Jew," 128.

[64] *Chaldean*: *Mos.* 1.5; *Jew*: *Mos.* 1.34, *Mos.* 2.193.

From Mesopotamia Balak summoned me,
  the king of Moab out of the mountains of the east,
'Come, curse Jacob for me,
  and come, call down curses for me upon Israel.' (my translation)

In *Conf.* 72, a passage in the Allegory, Philo quotes the second part of this verse exactly as the Greek Bible has it, including the names "Jacob" and "Israel." In *Mos.* 1.278, however, he transforms Balaam's words as follows: "From Mesopotamia hath Balak called me, a far journey from the East, that he may avenge him on the Hebrews through my cursing." Num. 23:21 and 24:5 also mention Jacob and Israel. When Philo recasts these verses in *Mos.* 1.284 and 289, however, he again substitutes "Hebrews" for the two names.[65] Because Balaam's oracles appear as direct quotations both in the Bible and in Philo's rendition, the consistent change from the original "Jacob" and "Israel" to "Hebrews" is especially salient.

If Philo's non-use of "Israel" is striking, so too is his use of the term. We have just noted that "Israel" is entirely absent from Philo's literal retelling of the Biblical narrative about the nation in *Mos.* 1 and 2. This observation and the following ones suggest that Philo understands "Israel" in a special, nonliteral way.

In all three series, Philo frequently interprets "Israel" using the etymology. In the Allegory, which has "Israel" over seventy times, the word appears either as part of a Scriptural quotation, which is not expounded, or in a symbolic interpretation that frequently refers to the etymology either directly or indirectly. In the two passages in which Philo uses "Israel" in the Exposition (*Abr.* 57 and *Praem.* 44), he also provides interpretations based upon the etymology. QGE includes "Israel" twice in the questions and twice in the commentary.[66] Both latter instances give the etymology. Although Philo never rejects a literal understanding of the term as the real nation in any of his exegetical works, neither does he explicitly affirm this literal sense.

Finally, when "Israel" connotes a group, Philo most frequently calls it a race or class (γένος). He never calls it a people (λαός). Although Philo does use "Israel" in connection with ἔθνος (nation) five times, whether or not "Israel" is a nation is beside the point of the passages.[67] Thus Philo's

---

[65] Num. 23:21: "There shall not be trouble in Jacob, nor will hardship be seen in Israel" (my translation). Cf. *Mos.* 1.284: "There shall be no trouble or labour among the Hebrews."

Num. 24:5: "How fair are your tents, O Jacob, Your encampments, O Israel!" Cf. *Mos.* 1.289: "How goodly are thy dwellings, thou host of the Hebrews!"

[66] See above, n. 62.

[67] In *Her.* 279, *Abr.* 57, and *QG* 3.49, Philo writes that "Israel" is the *name* of the

use of γένος to describe "Israel" as a collectivity also distinguishes this entity from Hebrews and Jews, who are usually either an ἔθνος (nation) or a λαός (people).[68]

Common Nouns

Studies of how Philo uses λαός (people), ἔθνος (nation), πολιτεία (polity), and γένος (race or class) support the above observations. The Greek Pentateuch—i.e., the part of the Bible upon which Philo concentrates—commonly uses λαός, a translation of the Hebrew word עם, to refer to the people of Israel. ἔθνος, usually a translation of the Hebrew word גוי, rarely designates this people, and γένος is almost never used for them.[69] The term πολιτεία does not occur in the Greek Pentateuch.

Below I shall discuss these common nouns separately as they appear in the Allegory and Exposition, and then all together as they occur in QGE. Since Philo uses λαός (people) and ἔθνος (nation) almost interchangeably, I shall consider these two words in the same section.

λαός (People) and ἔθνος (Nation)

In Philo's Allegory, when λαός (people) and ἔθνος (nation) refer to the Biblical people Israel, they often appear first in a Scriptural quotation and are then interpreted symbolically.[70] When Philo does not interpret these words,[71] he neither affirms nor denies their literal sense.

---

nation, but he does not define "Israel" itself as a nation. Instead he focuses upon the significance of the name. *Deus* 148 and *QE* 2.30 have a word for "nation" in interpretations of verses in which "Israel" appears. The word ἔθνος occurs explicitly in *Her.* 279, *Abr.* 57, and *Deus* 148. As we have no Greek fragments for *QG* 3.49 or *QE* 2.30, we cannot know Philo's original term for "nation" in these passages. In fact, the Armenian word for nation used here (*azg*) is ambiguous, and it is possible that the original Greek was γένος. (I am indebted to Prof. Sze–kar Wan for this information.) See also further below concerning *QG* 3.18.

68 Philo's use of γένος to describe "Israel" is amply discussed in Chapter Three. Other words to describe "Israel" as a collectivity can be found in *Plant.* 58, in which he calls "Israel" a band of wise souls (ψυχῶν σοφῶν ὁ θίασος), and in *Her.* 203, in which he refers to the Egyptian and Israelite host (ἡ Ἀιγυπτιακὴ καὶ ἡ Ἰσραηλιτικὴ στρατιά). The latter passage has the only occurrence of the word Ἰσραηλιτικός in Philo.

69 An exception is Exod. 1:9, which speaks of the race of the sons of Israel (τὸ γένος τῶν υἱῶν Ἰσραήλ). In *Migr.* 54, Philo interprets this as the race that can see the Existent (τὸ ὁρατικὸν τοῦ ὄντος γένος). This is consistent with many of his other interpretations of "Israel."

70 For λαός, see, e.g., *Leg.* 2.77; *Leg.* 3.162–63; *Agr.* 44, 84, 88; *Ebr.* 37, 96; *Migr.* 14, 47; *Congr.* 83; *Somn.* 1.71, 89. For ἔθνος, see *Deus* 148. The two words appear together in *Post.* 89–91; *Plant.* 59; *Migr.* 56–60, 68.

71 For λαός, see *Leg.* 2.94; *Cher.* 87; *Ebr.* 67; *Sobr.* 10; *Conf.* 58, 94; *Migr.* 81; *Her.* 251 (2); *Congr.* 163; *Mut.* 125. For ἔθνος, see *Her.* 174, 278; *Fug.* 185; *Mut.* 191; *Somn.* 1.167.

In contrast, in the Exposition, Philo regularly uses λαός (people) and ἔθνος (nation) to indicate the real nation. These words appear to describe the nation as a social or political entity; neither word specifically delimits it as a group with common origins. As a rule, λαός denotes the ancient Hebrews rather than Philo's Jewish contemporaries.[72] Of the dozen or so appearances of λαός in the Exposition, only two are explained symbolically.[73]

Philo uses ἔθνος more frequently than λαός, whether he is speaking of the Biblical people or his Jewish contemporaries. Although the Pentateuch prefers λαός to ἔθνος for the ancient Hebrews, Philo uses both words interchangeably to refer to them. For the contemporary nation, however —with the exception of *Spec.* 2.145—he generally uses ἔθνος instead of λαός. In fact, Philo's usual way of speaking about either the Hebrews or the Jews—that is, the historical or the contemporary people—is simply to call them "the nation" (τὸ ἔθνος). The term ἔθνος is never allegorized in the Exposition.

πολιτεία (Polity)

In both the Allegory and the Exposition, the word πολιτεία has a range of meanings. It can denote a constitution of laws, a form of government, political life in general, the political life of a specific community, citizenship, or the people who live under a common form of government. To be sure, occasionally more than one meaning may obtain.[74]

Of the two dozen occurrences of πολιτεία in the Allegory, three passages specifically mention the πολιτεία of Moses, noting that he has banished from his πολιτεία painters, sculptors, and their idolatrous crafts. In these passages, πολιτεία twice refers to Moses's legislation (*Gig.* 59, *Her.* 169) and once (*Ebr.* 109) to the community of people who live according to this legislation. This last reference, however, is vague and does not necessarily indicate a particular social group.

---

[72] *Spec.* 2.145 is an exception where λαός refers to the contemporary nation.
[73] *Virt.* 184 and *Praem.* 123. For discussion of these passages, see Chapter Four.
[74] See, e.g., Aryeh Kasher, "The Term *Politeia* in Philo and Josephus," *The Jews in Hellenistic and Roman Egypt: The Struggle for Equal Rights*, Texte und Studien zum Antiken Judentum, ed. Martin Hengel and Peter Schäfer (Tübingen: J. C. B. Mohr [Paul Siebeck], 1985), 358–64. For varied uses of πολιτεία and other related words, see also Hermann Strathmann, "πόλις, κτλ," *TDNT*, 6:516–35; Harold W. Attridge, *The Interpretation of Biblical History in the* Antiquitates Judaicae *of Flavius Josephus*, Harvard Theological Review; Harvard Dissertations in Religion, no. 7, ed. Caroline Bynum and George Rupp (Missoula, Montana: Scholars Press, 1976), 62–63; Smallwood, *Philonis Alexandrini*, 3–4. Philo uses πολιτεία figuratively in the Allegory passages *Gig.* 61, *Conf.* 108, and *Somn.* 1.78.

52 CHAPTER ONE

In the Exposition, Philo speaks more frequently about the πολιτεία of Moses, both as a form of government and as a specific community of people who live according to this form of government.[75] In contrast to the Allegory, in which this community is only a vague reference, we can tell from the context in the Exposition that Philo has in mind the Jews. Indeed, in *Virt.* 108, he specifically calls them the polity of the Jews (ἡ Ἰουδαίων πολιτεία).

γένος (Race or Class)

Finally, a study of γένος in the Allegory and the Exposition shows that in both series Philo uses this word in a variety of ways. Thus γένος may denote a class or order of people or things; common origin, birth, or descent; an abstract kind or nature; a genus composed of several species; and, in the philosophical sense, an ideal. Though we are now interested only in Philo's use of γένος to refer to people, I shall presently consider the philosophical nuances of the word.

With regard to people, γένος most frequently denotes a class or order. (While the English word "race" may also be used in this sense, to avoid confusion, I shall use the word "race" only to apply to a group that shares common birth or origins.) When γένος denotes a class or order, Philo describes the γένος either with a noun in the genitive case or with an adjective. Thus he frequently speaks about the class or order of humans (γένος ἀνθρώπων)[76] or the mortal class (θνητὸν γένος). Philo also uses other adjectives with γένος to describe a more specific class of people distinguished by a certain quality or pursuit. Examples include the poetic class (ποιητικὸν γένος), the class of sophists (σοφιστικὸν γένος), or the prophetic class (προφητικὸν γένος).[77]

Besides class or order, γένος may also indicate common origin, birth, or descent. It can, for example, refer to a race of people with common ancestry, such as the Greeks or Egyptians, who also constitute a political nationality.[78] In the Allegory and the Exposition, Philo does not mention γένος specifically with Hebrews or Jews, although he does use γένος

---

[75] *Mos.* 2.211; *Decal.* 98; *Spec.* 1.60, 63, 314, 319; *Spec.* 2.123; *Spec.* 3.24, 51; *Spec.* 4.55, 100, 105; *Virt.* 87, 127, 175.

[76] Cf. class or kind (γένος) of Magi, *Spec.* 3.100; of fish, *Opif.* 63, 65; *Mos.* 1.100; of birds, *Opif.* 63; of living creatures, *Opif.* 64; of grasshoppers, *Opif.* 163; of trees, *Praem.* 141; et al.

[77] Poets: *Opif.* 133, 157; *Sacr.* 78; *Agr.* 41; *Ios.* 2; *Spec.* 2.164. Sophists: *Opif.* 157. Prophets: *Her.* 249, 265; *Migr.* 84; *Fug.* 147; *Mut.* 110, 120. In some of these passages, γένος may also mean nature or kind, in an abstract sense, rather than class of people.

[78] *Conf.* 70: the body-loving race of the Egyptians (τὸ φιλοσώματον γένος τῶν Ἀιγυπτίων); *Ios.* 56: the Greek and barbarian race (τό τε Ἑλληνικὸν καὶ βαρβαρικὸν γένος).

alone—albeit infrequently—in a way that might refer to the race united by Hebrew or Jewish descent.[79]

In addition to race by birth, γένος can also denote a smaller group, such as a family or clan, a line of descent, a single offspring, kinship or blood relationship, and birth or common origin in general.[80] Because these senses often overlap, assignment of one meaning over another can sometimes be difficult.

With respect to people, then, Philo uses the word γένος to indicate either class or descent. The second meaning occurs mostly in the Exposition, in which Philo often discusses kinship and origin. This meaning rarely occurs in the Allegory.[81]

In light of these observations, we can now recognize that when Philo refers to Israel as the ὁρατικὸν γένος, or the γένος that can see, "Israel" may be the proper name of the class of people who are able to "see" or of a group with this ability that shares a common ancestry. Perhaps too Philo may intend both senses at once. In these cases, then, when translating γένος, I shall use the designation "race/class" to indicate the ambiguity.

Without a doubt, the correct meaning of γένος in connection with "Israel" goes beyond linguistic concerns and touches upon the very issue of this whole investigation. Is the ability to "see"—which "Israel" possesses—inherited or acquired? If it is only inherited, then the racial group Israel and the Jews are the same. If it is only acquired, then "Israel" becomes a different sort of entity. If this vision is inherited but can also be acquired, then the identity of the group changes again. In Chapter Three, we shall explore further the various possibilities for understanding the identity of "Israel."

Besides ὁρατικόν, Philo uses other adjectives with γένος to describe the race/class "Israel." He calls this γένος the chosen (ἐπίλεκτον, Post. 92; cf.

---

[79] Her. 278, Fug. 73, Mut. 88, Somn. 1.159, Ios. 42, Mos. 1.324, Spec. 2.217, Virt. 206; see also n. 84 below. In Migr. 20, Philo speaks of Moses as a single offspring of the Hebrews (γένος Ἑβραίων).

[80] Family or clan: Det. 25; Post. 109; Fug. 107, 114; Mut. 117; Abr. 50; Ios. 233; Mos. 1.302, 304; Mos. 2.8, 142, 245; Decal. 130; Spec. 1.118; Spec. 2.111, 129; Spec. 3.157; Virt. 191, 193, 197.

Line of descent: Her. 61, 82; Somn. 2.16; Mos. 1.147; Mos. 2.289; Spec. 1.110; Spec. 3.21; Spec. 4.192, 206; Virt. 60.

Single offspring: Migr. 20, Congr. 132, Virt. 212.

Kinship: Det. 99; Somn. 1.166; Spec. 2.237, 239; Spec. 3.11, 162; Virt. 225.

Birth or common origin: Congr. 41; Abr. 211; Mos. 1.5; Mos. 2.8; Decal. 71; Spec. 1.160; Spec. 2.95, 114; Spec. 3.27, 113 (second appearance of γένος), 165, 192; Spec. 4.18; Virt. 123, 132, 199.

[81] In n. 80, of the fifty-six passages in which γένος denotes descent, only thirteen are from the Allegory. The rest are from the Exposition.

Conf. 56),[82] the best (ἄριστον, *Congr.* 51), the self-controlled and God-beloved (ἐγκρατὲς καὶ θεοφιλές, *Her.* 203; cf. *Migr.* 114, 158), and the race/class of wisdom (τὸ σοφίας γένος, *Migr.* 125, *Somn.* 1.175[83]). In some of these interpretations, γένος may no longer denote a class of people but instead an abstract nature or kind. Almost all of these examples occur in the Allegory, in which Philo usually uses γένος to mean class and rarely origin.[84] Moreover, when he clearly speaks of groups with common descent, he generally uses γένος without an adjective.[85] Nevertheless for now, we cannot rule out the sense of the γένος "Israel" as a race united by common descent.

QGE

Because so little of this series has survived in Greek, it is impossible to say very much about Philo's use here of the common nouns λαός, ἔθνος, πολιτεία, or γένος. Most of the passages which mention the Biblical nation are not extant in Greek. Ironically, in one of these passages, which does have Greek fragments (*QG* 3.18), one source has ἔθνος; another has γένος. To complicate matters, the Armenian word *azg* does not distinguish in meaning between ἔθνος and γένος.[86] In another passage which has Greek fragments (*QE* 2.2), Philo refers explicitly to the Hebrew race (τὸ Ἑβραῖον γένος). This is the only passage in all his works in which he uses γένος explicitly with Ἑβραῖον to denote the race.

Despite the difficulty in conducting a word study for QGE, we can still make some significant observations. With the exception of *QG* 3.48

---

[82] QGE also has several references to the Biblical people as chosen or as the "chosen race": *QG* 2.65; *QG* 3.49; *QE* 2.38, 42, 43, 46. Of these passages, "Israel" is mentioned by name only in *QG* 3.49. In some cases, it is difficult to ascertain whether or not Philo is talking about the real Biblical nation. For further discussion of these passages, see Chapters Three and Four.

[83] This reference does not mention "Israel" explicitly by name but refers to Jacob's descendants.

[84] Two passages in the Exposition which use γένος with adjectives are *Mos.* 2.189, which speaks of "the race/class that worships Him" (τὸ θεραπευτικὸν αὐτοῦ γένος) and *Mos.* 2.196, which mentions "the seeing and knowing race/class" (τὸ ὁρατικὸν καὶ ἐπιστημονικὸν γένος). These expressions clearly refer to the actual Biblical nation, but "Israel" is never mentioned by name in this treatise. Strictly speaking, then, we cannot say that these expressions describe "Israel."

[85] Exceptions include *Conf.* 70, in which he mentions the body-loving race of the Egyptians (see above, n. 78); *Her.* 82: γένος τὸ ἱερωμένον, the consecrated line; *Virt.* 197: λαμπρὰ γένη, illustrious lineages; and *Virt.* 199: γένος ἐξαίρετον, extraordinary origin. When Philo speaks about the priestly (ἱερατικὸν) γένος in *Spec.* 1.243, the word γένος may mean either class or family, though family is more likely. Cf. *Spec.* 1.111, in which γενεὰ ἱερατική is clearly "priestly family."

[86] Petit, *Quaestiones*, OPA, 33:131.

(discussed earlier), this series does not mention contemporary Jews. Some Questions and Answers in the English translation refer to the Biblical people as "they," "the nation," or "the people."[87] While some of these passages specifically describe as "literal" (τὸ ῥητόν) the interpretations in which these words appear, others do not describe the interpretation at all.[88] Nonetheless, since Philo's purpose here is to explicate the text rather than to narrate Biblical history, the real existence of the people is beside the point of the passages.

In addition, both within Biblical quotations and in the interpretations, Philo commonly substitutes for the proper name "Israel" such etymologically derived designations as "the race/class that can see" (τὸ ὁρατικὸν γένος) or "the seeing one" (ὁ [or τὸ] ὁρῶν).[89] These phrases are always interchangeable only with "Israel"; they never replace any other proper name and never indicate any other group apart from "Israel." Two of the six interpretations which have such periphrases for "Israel" describe the interpretation as "literal" (QE 1.12, 21). Here, "the one that can see" or "the race/class that can see" may possibly be understood as the Biblical nation Israel in addition to an entity defined by its spiritual ability. We shall explore the possible interpretations of these periphrases in Chapter Three.

Philo's Discussion of "Israel" and the Jews in the Exegetical Works: Summary and Conclusions

In his exegetical works, Philo uses different vocabulary to describe the real historical and contemporary nation, on the one hand, and "Israel," on the other. For the most part, he speaks about the real nation—either past or present—and "Israel" in separate works.

One may perhaps attribute this second observation to Philo's different audiences for his exegetical series, as discussed in the Introduction. That is, Philo does not speak of his Jewish contemporaries in the Allegory or

---

[87] See above, n. 57.

[88] Passages in which reference to the nation is included in a "literal" interpretation: *QG* 3.18; *QG* 4.153, 200; *QE* 1.2, 4; *QE* 2.31. Passages that do not describe the interpretation in which reference to the nation is made: *QG* 3.38, 49; *QE* 1.9, 10; *QE* 2.22, 35, 49.

[89] A periphrasis—most likely ὁρατικὸν γένος (race/class that can see)—occurs in Philo's commentary, not the Biblical citation, in *QE* 1.21; *QE* 2.42, 43, 46, 76. Only *QE* 2.46 exists (in part) in the Greek, but this fragment attests to Philo's use of the phrase ὁρατικὸν γένος. *QE* 1.12 may have the adjective, ὁρατικός (able to see), alone—that is, without γένος—as a substantive. *QE* 2.38 substitutes "the chosen seeing ones" for "Israel" in the Biblical quotation of Exod. 24:11, and *QE* 2.47 substitutes "the seeing one" for "Israel" in the Biblical quotation of Exod. 24:17.

QGE, possibly because his readers are already quite familiar with the Jews and their ways. Likewise, these readers are probably more likely than those in the Exposition to understand and appreciate the special significance of "Israel." In contrast, Philo discusses Jews at length in the Exposition, in which his audience may be less familiar with their history and practices. Finally, QGE may have more expressly "literal" interpretations about the nation than the Allegory does, perhaps because QGE is intended for a wider range of Jewish readers, including those who value the literal approach to Scripture.

Philonic Reflections Upon the Meaning of λαός and γένος

I have suggested that Philo's way of referring to "Israel" is significant because he describes it as a γένος (race/class) but not a λαός (people) or an ἔθνος (nation). Moreover, in describing "Israel" specifically as the ὁρατικὸν γένος, or the race/class that can see, he may understand this γένος as a class of people that can see in addition to or instead of as a race united by birth that inherits this ability. Before we examine Philo's vocabulary in the non-exegetical works, therefore, it may be instructive to consider one instance in which he himself comments directly about two of the relevant terms, λαός (people) and γένος (race/class).[90]

The passage is *Sacr.* 6–7, which interprets Gen. 35:29. Philo notices that this verse mentioning Isaac's death differs in one word from the verses mentioning the deaths of Abraham (Gen. 25:8) and Jacob (Gen. 49:33). In the Masoretic text, all three expressions are the same: ויאסף אל עמיו, "And he was gathered to his people." The Greek Bible, however, translates עמיו as λαός in both verses about Abraham and Jacob (καὶ προσετέθη τὸν λαὸν αὐτοῦ) but renders the noun as γένος in the verse about Isaac.

To explain this discrepancy, Philo uses a paradigm in which the three patriarchs represent differently acquired virtues. According to this paradigm, which is commonplace in his interpretations, Abraham symbolizes virtue acquired by learning; Isaac, virtue acquired by nature; and Jacob, virtue gained by practice.[91] In *Sacr.* 6–7, Philo explains that Isaac is distinguished from the other two patriarchs because natural or inherent virtue is superior to that acquired by learning or practice:

> Once more there is Isaac to whom was granted the higher gift of self-learnt knowledge. He too abandon[s] all such bodily elements as had been interwoven

---

[90] Philo may also comment on the distinction between people (λαός) and nation (ἔθνος) in *QG* 4.157, which interprets Gen. 25:23, the prophecy to Rebecca: "Two nations (ἔθνη) are in thy womb, and two peoples (λαοί) will be separated from thy womb." Unfortunately, the meaning of the interpretation is obscure.

[91] See, e.g., *Congr.* 34–38, *Mut.* 88, *Abr.* 52–55, *Praem.* 24–27, et al.

with the soul, and is added and allotted to another company; but not this time, with the others, to a people (λαός), but to a 'race' or 'genus' (γένος), as Moses says. For genus is one, that which is above all, but people is a name for many. Those who have advanced to perfection as pupils under a teacher have their place among many others; for those who learn by hearing and instruction are no small number, and these he calls a people. But those who have dispensed with the instruction of men and have become apt pupils of God receive the free unlaboured knowledge and are translated into the genus of the imperishable and fully perfect. Theirs is a happier lot than the lot of the people, and in this sacred band Isaac stands confessed as a chorister. (*Sacr.* 6–7)

In this interpretation, Philo's reasoning seems to be as follows: Unlike Abraham and Jacob, who learn from a teacher, Isaac acquires his self-taught knowledge from God. Since many people learn from teachers, Abraham and Jacob belong with "people," a word that indicates several individuals. Isaac, however, is one of the few students of God. He therefore goes to a race or γένος, which is one.

Undoubtedly the literal meaning of γένος in Gen. 35:29 amounts to the same thing as λαός, a people, and there is no obvious reason why the Greek translator uses γένος instead of λαός in this verse. Philo, however, understands γένος here in a philosophical sense, describing it as one (ἕν), the highest (ἀνωτάτω), imperishable (ἄφθαρτον), and most perfect (τελειώτατον). These remarks about γένος echo statements he makes elsewhere about the relationship between genus and species.[92]

From one perspective, this relationship describes one whole and many parts. While there are many species, they belong to one genus.[93] Although an exact correspondence between people and species would require Philo to refer to many peoples, the thought here is simply that "people" is a collectivity of many, to which the one genus stands in contrast. Thus, γένος is logically the "highest" or stands above all in the sense that the whole comes before the parts and can be divided into parts.

The notion that a γένος is imperishable and perfect is connected to the idea that God first creates the genus as an original or archetype of the particular or the species. All that is generic is imperishable, while all that is specific is perishable.[94] Thus, γένος is closer to God and is "the highest" in a temporal or metaphysical sense as well as a logical one, because God creates the genus before the species. As a direct pupil of God rather than of humans, Isaac ranks among the imperishable generic rather than the perishable specific.

---

[92] Thomas H. Tobin discusses the philosophical nuances in Philo's use of the word γένος in *The Creation of Man*, 113–19.

[93] Cf. *Conf.* 192.

[94] Cf. *Leg.* 1.22–23, *Leg.* 2.13, *Cher.* 5–7, *Mut.* 78–80, *Her.* 118, *QG* 3.53.

In *Sacr.* 6–7, Philo takes advantage of the Scriptural irregularity where λαός is used in verses about Abraham and Jacob and γένος is used in the verse about Isaac, to expand upon the differences between Abraham and Jacob, on the one hand, and Isaac, on the other, in the way they acquire virtue. By juxtaposing the philosophical sense of γένος with the literal sense of λαός, or people, he underscores Isaac's superiority to the other patriarchs, as well as the superiority of γένος to λαός.

Clearly, Philo has a broad range of associations with γένος, and he can apply these different associations simultaneously on different levels. *Sacr.* 6–7 is the only passage in which he explicitly attaches philosophical import to this word when he recognizes that it also functions literally to mean a race or a people in Scripture. Nonetheless, this example is enough to show that γένος—the term Philo uses most frequently to describe "Israel" as a collectivity—carries for him significant nuances.

The Non-Exegetical Works

Unlike the exegetical treatises, which can be organized by series, the non-exegetical works represent a miscellaneous collection of writings. For our purposes, the most relevant are Philo's two political treatises, *Flacc.* and *Legat.*, in which he speaks about the contemporary Jewish nation, and the fragmentary *Apology for the Jews* (*Hypoth.*), in which he mentions both the Biblical and the contemporary nations. In *Contempl.*, Philo also refers to the Biblical nation briefly. Finally, in the philosophical treatises *Prob.* and *Aet.*, Philo mentions the Jews in passing, most frequently when citing Moses as their lawgiver.[95] These references in *Prob.* and *Aet.*, however, are not significant to our study.

The following discussion is organized according to references— whether by proper or common nouns—to Philo's Jewish contemporaries, the Biblical people, and finally to Israel.

Philo's Jewish Contemporaries

Throughout the political treatises, *Flacc.* and *Legat.*, Philo talks extensively about his Jewish contemporaries, referring to them as the Jews ('Ιουδαῖοι), the nation of Jews (τὸ 'Ιουδαίων ἔθνος), or the nation (τὸ ἔθνος). The word λαός (people) does not appear at all. In all these instances, the Jews are understood to be the contemporary nation and usually, more specifically,

---

[95] Occasionally Philo mentions the legislation or the lawgiver of the Jews when he wishes to bring in a Biblical interpretation to buttress a philosophical point (*Prob.* 29, 43, 57, 68; *Aet.* 19). He also speaks of the Essenes as belonging to the populous Jewish nation (*Prob.* 75).

the Jewish community in Alexandria.[96] In a few cases in *Legat.*, Philo also refers to the Jewish race (τὸ Ἰουδαίων γένος, 178, 346; τὸ Ἰουδαϊκὸν γένος, 201). This designation seems to encompass all Jews everywhere—whether by birth or choice—rather than just the Alexandrian community. The combination of γένος specifically with the words "Jews" or "Jewish" appears only here among Philo's works. In general, the non-exegetical works do not reveal any new applications of the word γένος. As in the Biblical commentaries, here too γένος refers to race, family, kinship, or class. The non-exegetical treatises do not use γένος in the philosophical sense at all.

Finally, in *Flacc.* and *Legat.*, Philo also uses the word πολιτεία (polity) in connection with the Jews, referring explicitly to the polity of the Jews (ἡ πολιτεία ἡ Ἰουδαίων) in *Legat.* 194. In these treatises, he appears to apply the term more broadly with reference to the Jews than he does in the Exposition. In the Exposition, when Philo describes the Jewish community as having or being a πολιτεία, he seems to associate the word either with Moses's legislation or with the people living under this legislation. In *Flacc.* and *Legat.*, however, when Philo uses πολιτεία to refer to the Jews and their form of government, he seems to understand their form of government as including both their ancestral customs—presumably embodied in Moses's legislation and in the interpretation of this legislation— and their contemporary political organization (see, e.g., *Flacc.* 53).

Philo also speaks about the contemporary nation in *Hypoth.* 7.1–20, in which he describes its laws and customs. In this treatise, he seems to have in mind the whole people, not just the Alexandrian community. Although he refers to them once as the nation, (τὸ ἔθνος, *Hypoth.* 6.1), in general, he talks about the Jews of his day with a third person pronoun (αὐτοί, ἐκεῖνοι), without any proper or common nouns.

The Biblical Nation

The Biblical nation is mentioned in *Hypoth.* and in *Contempl. Hypoth.* 6.1–9 discusses the Biblical people in a description of their exodus from Egypt and conquest of the promised land, and *Contempl.* 85–87 briefly mentions the crossing of the Red Sea. In both of these treatises, Philo uses the common noun λαός, people, for the Biblical nation, as he does in the Exposition.

Neither of these two works uses a proper noun for the Biblical people. In fact, "Hebrews" is missing completely from the non-exegetical writings.

---

[96] In contrast, when Philo speaks of the Jews in the Exposition, he seems to mean the entire people rather than just the Alexandrian community.

When he gives an etymology in *Legat.* 4, Philo uses a form of the word for Chaldean (Χαλδαϊστί) as a synonym for the Hebrew language. Also, in *Hypoth.* 6.1, he calls the ancient ancestor (ὁ παλαιὸς πρόγονος) of the people a Chaldean (ἀπὸ Χαλδαίων). This may be a reference to Abraham, however, who actually was from the land of Chaldea.[97]

Israel

Among all the extant non-exegetical works, "Israel" is mentioned only once, in *Legat.* 4, in the introduction to Philo's treatise about the political woes of his Jewish contemporaries. There, Philo identifies "Israel" as the name of the suppliants' race (τὸ ἱκετικὸν γένος) and explains that the word means "one who sees God" (ὁρῶν θεόν). By describing "Israel" as a γένος (race/class) rather than an ἔθνος (nation) or λαός (people) and by incorporating the etymology, Philo uses the term "Israel" consistently with his references in the exegetical treatises. This is the only treatise, however, in which he mentions "Israel" and the Jews by name in the same context. To assess the significance of this important passage, we shall have to examine it together with Philo's other references to "Israel" and "the Jews." To that task we now turn.

---

[97] In a note to the passage in LCL, F. H. Colson identifies this ancestor as Jacob and defends Philo's use of "Chaldean" by mentioning *Mos.* 1.5, in which he calls Moses a Chaldean. The description in *Hypoth.*, however, can also suit Abraham and may make more sense if taken this way since Abraham *was* from Chaldea, and Philo usually mentions him as the prominent ancestor (*Her.* 278, *Virt.* 212) but does not single out Jacob in this way. Like Jacob, Abraham also went down to Egypt and prospered greatly (Genesis 12–13). On the other hand, the chief problem in associating this ancestor with Abraham instead of with Jacob is that Philo implies that the nation had a continuous presence in Egypt from his time until the Exodus, a description that does not apply in Abraham's case.

CHAPTER TWO

"ISRAEL" AND THE VISION OF GOD

In the previous chapter we saw that Philo uses "Israel" differently from "Jews" and "Hebrews" and that he speaks of "Israel" and the Jews in different works, mentioning them in the same treatise only once. We shall now look more closely at how Philo talks about "Israel" and consider such related issues as the source of the etymology ὁρῶν θεόν, or one that sees God; Philo's ideas about seeing God and possible influences upon his ideas; and finally, his understanding of the experience itself.

Philo's Discussion of "Israel"

By far, most of Philo's explicit references to "Israel" include the etymology either directly or indirectly. In addition, instead of using the term "Israel" itself, he frequently substitutes for it a variety of expressions, which in one way or another pertain to seeing or seeing God. Philo's predominant association with "Israel," then, whether the word occurs explicitly or not, depends upon his understanding of its etymology as ὁρῶν θεόν, one that sees God.

Below we shall focus upon the explicit occurrences of "Israel" in Philo's works and then briefly upon periphrastic expressions that substitute for "Israel" where the word itself does not appear. These periphrastic expressions will be discussed more extensively in the next chapter.

Explicit Occurrences of the Word "Israel"

In all, the word "Israel" appears seventy-eight times in Philo's extant Greek works. To these we might add four occurrences in the English translation of QGE, though we have no parallel Greek fragments to verify Philo's use of the word here.[1] In addition, the adjective Ἰσραηλιτικός (Israelite) appears once (*Her.* 203).

These eighty-three explicit citations of Ἰσραήλ and Ἰσραηλιτικός can be divided roughly into the four categories listed below. For reasons to be explained presently, the numbers in parentheses provide only a general

---

[1] For the extant Greek works (fragments are not included), see under "Ἰσραήλ" in Mayer, *Index Philoneus*, 150. "Israel" appears in the English translation of QGE in *QG* 3.49, *QG* 4.233, and *QE* 2.30 and 37.

rather than an exact picture of how these references can be classed. The categories are as follows:

A)   References, usually in Biblical quotations, that are not interpreted (15 references);
B)   References that are interpreted in a way not related to the etymology (17);
C)   References that are interpreted in a way related to the etymology (49); and
D)   References in which the exact interpretation of "Israel" is unclear, but the metaphor of seeing is used (2).

Methodological Considerations

The attempt to categorize Philo's usage of "Israel" is beset by methodological difficulties, which are not unique to the term "Israel" but instead inhere in the nature of Biblical interpretation and Philo's style of writing in general. It is difficult, for example, to be numerically precise in classifying Philo's eighty-three references. On the one hand, a passage may mention "Israel" explicitly several times—either in the Biblical verse or in the interpretation—but Philo may interpret these references only once.[2] On the other hand, a Biblical verse may cite "Israel" only once, but the ensuing discussion may offer several associations with or interpretations of the term, some of which may repeat the word "Israel" and some of which may not. Moreover, some associations or interpretations may include or be related to the etymology, while others may not. Finally, it is sometimes unclear whether or not "Israel" per se is being interpreted at all.

To provide a general impression of how Philo uses the term "Israel" relative to the number of times the term occurs, I have assigned each reference to "Israel" to only one category. (All references in the discussion of categories are only to the passage in which "Israel" appears, even though interpretations of the term may be found in one or more nearby

---

[2] Two examples are *Sacr.* 118 and *Somn.* 1.171–72. *Sacr.* 118 quotes Num. 3:12–13, which mentions "Israel" three times. In his interpretation (in the first part of *Sacr.* 119), however, Philo understands all three references to "Israel" in the same way, namely, as the soul. *Sacr.* 118, then, contributes three citations to Category B— references that are interpreted without mention of seeing—but the numbers are misleading, since all three terms are collectively given only one interpretation. (On this passage, see also below, n. 4.) Similarly, in *Somn.* 1.171–72, "Israel" is mentioned three times—once in the Biblical verse (Gen. 46:1) and twice in Philo's commentary—but the term is given only one interpretation. Because this exegesis depends upon the etymology, these three references are assigned to Category C.

passages.) When one Biblical reference to "Israel" spawns several interpretations or associations, at least one of which includes or is based upon the etymology, that reference is assigned to Category C, "the seers," even though the passage may include other interpretations that do not mention either the etymology or seeing in general. These other associations are cited in the notes.[3] Whenever "Israel" is mentioned explicitly in a separate interpretation within a chain, this citation is classified separately.[4]

Finally, where it is difficult to determine whether or not Philo is interpreting "Israel" intentionally, I have used my own judgment about how to classify the reference.[5] In two cases (*Somn.* 1.117 and *Somn.* 2.271), the metaphor of seeing is part of the interpretation, but it is unclear whether or not "Israel" itself is meant to be interpreted. Because these interpretations may be related to the etymology—and therefore because the understanding of "Israel" as the one that sees God may be significant—these passages are included separately in Category D, the unclear references.

---

[3] Examples of passages in Category C that have multiple interpretations, not all of which are based upon the etymology, are *Post.* 92, *Plant.* 59, *Ebr.* 82, *Migr.* 113, *Fug.* 208, *Somn.* 1.114, and *Somn.* 2.280. In *Post.* 92, "Israel" is the chosen race/class (τὸ ἐπίλεκτον γένος) and the one that sees God (ὁ ὁρῶν τὸν θεόν). In *Plant.* 59, "Israel" is the company of wise souls that sees most sharply (ψυχῶν σοφῶν ὁ θίασος, ὁ ὀξυωπέστατα ὁρῶν), the character that can see Him and is a genuine worshipper (ὁ ὁρατικὸς αὐτοῦ καὶ γνήσιος θεραπευτὴς τρόπος), and virtue (ἀρετή). *Ebr.* 82 associates "Israel" with eyes in contrast to ears, deeds in contrast to words, and perfection in contrast to progress. In *Migr.* 113, "Israel" is the seer (ὁ ὁρῶν) and the God-beloved race/class (γένος τὸ θεοφιλές). *Fug.* 208 describes "Israel" as the genuine and firstborn son (ὁ γνήσιος υἱὸς καὶ πρωτόγονος), associates "Israel" with sight (ὅρασις), and provides the etymology, ὁρῶν θεόν. *Somn.* 1.114 associates "Israel," the seeing one (ὁ βλέπων), with reason (ὁ λόγος). In *Somn.* 2.280, "Israel" is the ὁρατικὸν γένος, the race/class that can see, and also virtue (ἀρετή).

[4] "Israel" appears in separate interpretations in *Sacr.* 118–20, *Deus* 144–45, and *Conf.* 92–93. I have assigned sections of these compound passages to separate categories on the basis of whether the interpretation of "Israel" pertains to seeing or not.

[5] Examples which I have assigned to Category A, the uninterpreted references, include *Leg.* 3.214, *Plant.* 63, *Migr.* 168–69, and *Congr.* 86. In *Leg.* 3.214, the cry of "Israel" is interpreted as the suppliant word (ὁ ἱκέτης λόγος). Here the emphasis is upon the cry, and it seems incidental that the cry belongs to "Israel" per se. *Plant.* 63 implies a literal interpretation of "Israel" as the twelve tribes, but this is beside the main point. In *Migr.* 168–69, Exod. 24:1, which mentions the seventy elders of Israel, is interpreted as an allegory of the soul. Here again, mention of "Israel" seems incidental to the interpretation. In *Congr.* 86, "Israel" may be linked to "our mortal race" (mentioned in *Congr.* 85), but the correspondence is not certain.

Examples which I have assigned to Category B, references with interpretations unrelated to the etymology, include *Post.* 158, *Her.* 124, and *Somn.* 1.89. In *Post.* 158, "Israel" may be connected with the industrious soul (ψυχὴ ἀσκητική); in *Her.* 124, "Israel" corresponds to mind (διάνοια) or perhaps to soul (ψυχή, in 123); and in *Somn.* 1.89, "Israel" corresponds to mind (διάνοια, 91).

Categories Describing Philo's Uses of "Israel"

Of all four categories, the most relevant to this study are Categories C and D, which include interpretations that pertain to seeing or seeing God and are therefore connected—or, in the case of Category D, may be connected —to the etymology. These fifty-one interpretations constitute the majority of the eighty-three citations to "Israel." Since the citations in Categories A and B are generally too diffuse to permit any further classification that might be helpful, these categories are ultimately not relevant to this investigation. Below is a brief description of all four categories.

Category A: Uninterpreted References (15)

Simplest to describe, perhaps, are the references in which "Israel" remains uninterpreted.[6] Typically in these instances, the term appears in a Biblical quotation and is either ignored in or remains insignificant to the interpretation, which focuses upon another issue in the Scriptural verse. In three cases, Philo alludes to "Israel" outside of a direct Scriptural quotation, once in a paraphrase of a verse (*Leg.* 3.11, paraphrasing Deut. 16:16—it is curious that in the Biblical verse "Israel" is not mentioned) and twice in references to Jacob's change of name to "Israel" (*Leg.* 3.15, *Mut.* 83). As with the other citations in this category, here too Philo does not interpret the term but concentrates instead upon another point.

Category B: Interpretations Unrelated to the Etymology (17)

These passages,[7] which occasionally interpret "Israel" more than once, offer a range of associations for the term. "Israel" is presented as the soul;[8] the mind;[9] education and creation (παιδεία, γένεσις, *Ebr.* 77); higher (male) parentage (*Deus* 121); the sage (ὁ σοφός, *Conf.* 36); the God-beloved (ὁ, ἡ [or τὸ] θεοφιλής [ες], *Sobr.* 19); the self-controlled and God-beloved race/class (τὸ ἐγκρατὲς καὶ θεσφιλὲς γένος, *Her.* 203);[10] suppliants (ἱκέται, *Det.* 94); men of worth (σπουδαῖοι, *Conf.* 36); the wisely-minded (οἱ εὖ φρονοῦντες, *Conf.* 93); the virtue-loving host (ἡ φιλάρετος πληθύς, *Post.* 54);

---

[6] *Leg.* 2.94; *Leg.* 3.11, 15, 133, 214; *Det.* 67; *Plant.* 63; *Migr.* 168; *Her.* 113, 117; *Congr.* 86; *Mut.* 83; *Somn.* 1.62; *Somn.* 2.222; *QE* 2.37.

[7] *Leg.* 2.77; *Sacr.* 118 (3); *Det.* 94; *Post.* 54, 158; *Deus* 121, 145; *Ebr.* 77; *Sobr.* 19; *Conf.* 36, 93; *Her.* 124, 203 (here the word is Ἰσραηλιτικός, see below, n. 10); *Somn.* 1.89; *QE* 2.30.

[8] ψυχή: *Leg.* 2.77; *Sacr.* 118; *Det.* 94 (suppliant souls, ψυχαὶ ἱκέτιδαι); *Post.* 158 (industrious soul, ψυχὴ ἀσκητική); *Deus* 145 (the soul of each of his [Moses's] disciples, ἡ ἑκάστου ψυχὴ τῶν γνωρίμων αὐτοῦ).

[9] διάνοια: *Somn.* 1.89; *Her.* 124 ("Israel" may also correspond to soul [ψυχή] in *Her.* 123); *Her.* 203 (thriving minds, διάνοιαι ἀρετῶσαι).

[10] Here reference is not to "Israel" but to the Israelite host (Ἰσραηλιτικὴ στρατιά).

an entire, very populous nation (ὅλον ἔθνος πολυανθρωπότατον, *Deus* 145), and the Biblical nation (*QE* 2.30).

None of these interpretations appears with sufficient frequency to establish a significant pattern among Philo's "non-seeing" interpretations of "Israel." Even when Philo's "non-seeing" associations from Category C are considered, we still do not have a significant pattern among interpretations of "Israel" that are unrelated to the etymology.[11]

Since we are interested in determining whom Philo has in mind when he uses the term "Israel" to refer to a group of people, the most pertinent passages are those in which he seems to discuss "Israel" as a collective entity. None of these passages, however, contributes significantly to this study. Some interpretations describe "Israel" as a fairly general group—e.g., men of worth, suppliants, the virtue-loving host, the God-beloved, or the self-controlled and God-beloved race/class—and these descriptions may refer to all people who fit the description, not necessarily the Biblical nation alone. Even where these descriptions may be intended for the Biblical nation (e.g., the virtue-loving host, *Post.* 54; the God-beloved, *Sobr.* 19; or the self-controlled and God-beloved race/class, *Her.* 203), the real existence of the nation is not the focus of the interpretation. Similarly, passages in which "Israel" is actually called a nation (*Deus* 145 and *QE* 2.30) add little to this investigation, again since the real existence of the nation is beside the point of the interpretation.

In one case (*Det.* 94), Philo rejects the literal meaning of a Scriptural verse (Exod. 2:23) and allegorizes on the level of the soul. Here again, however, his focus is upon explaining a particular difficulty in a Biblical passage (Exod. 2:23), not upon affirming or denying the historical existence of the Biblical people.

Category C: Interpretations Related to the Etymology (49)

Philo discusses "Israel" most frequently in connection with his etymology of the term as ὁρῶν θεόν, one that sees God.[12] It is worth noting that he never includes in the etymology a word for man (ἀνήρ) or person

---

[11] See n. 3.

[12] The forty-nine passages included in Category C are listed below. Again, references indicate the passage in which "Israel" appears, although the expression that pertains to seeing may occur in a nearby passage. Numbers in parentheses indicate the number of times "Israel" occurs in the passage. Also, some references are interpreted with more than one expression that pertains to seeing. The passages are as follows: *Leg.* 2.34; *Leg.* 3.186 (2), 212; *Sacr.* 119, 120, 134 (2); *Post.* 63, 89, 92; *Deus* 144; *Plant.* 59; *Ebr.* 82 (2); *Conf.* 56, 72 (2), 92, 146, 148; *Migr.* 15, 39, 54, 113, 125, 201, 224; *Her.* 78, 279; *Congr.* 51; *Fug.* 208; *Mut.* 81 (2), 207; *Somn.* 1.114, 129, 171, 172 (2); *Somn.* 2.44, 172, 173, 280; *Abr.* 57; *Praem.* 44; *Legat.* 4; *QG* 3.49; *QG* 4.233.

(ἄνθρωπος). Although he most often mentions the etymology explicitly,[13] he sometimes alludes to it indirectly using other expressions that pertain to seeing, other or additional expressions for God, or other or additional descriptions of the object that is seen.[14] Occasionally, Philo omits an object altogether, referring to "Israel," for example, simply as the seer (ὁρῶν or βλέπων) or the one that can see (ὁρατικός).[15] Usually ὁρατικός appears together with another word like γένος (race/class), τρόπος (character), διάνοια (mind), or νοῦς (mind). In some passages about "Israel," Philo does not speak of a subject that sees but instead mentions sight (ὅρασις, *Conf.* 72); the vision of God (ὅρασις θεοῦ, *Ebr.* 82); or contemplation of the only wise one (θεωρία ἡ τοῦ μονοῦ σοφοῦ, *Sacr.* 119–20).

Category D: The Unclear References (2)

Two passages—*Somn.* 1.117 and *Somn.* 2.271—use the metaphor of seeing, but it is unclear how the metaphor is related to "Israel." In *Somn.* 1.117, "Israel" serves as an implied contrast to "those who are blind in the eyes of the soul rather than of the body and do not know the rays of virtue"

---

[13] The etymology occurs in relation to twenty-two appearances of the term "Israel" in the passages noted below. Numbers in parentheses indicate the number of times "Israel" appears in the passage. The passages are as follows: *Leg.* 3.186 (2), 212; *Sacr.* 134 (2); *Post.* 63, 89, 92; *Congr.* 51; *Conf.* 56; *Her.* 78; *Fug.* 208; *Mut.* 81; *Somn.* 1.171, 172 (2); *Somn.* 2.172, 173; *Abr.* 57; *Praem.* 44; *Legat.* 4; *QG* 3.49 (no parallel Greek fragment exists).

[14] The most frequent alternative expressions that pertain to seeing are mentioned immediately in the text and listed below in n. 15. Often an interpretation of "Israel" includes many words related to seeing. In *Conf.* 92, for example, Philo describes "Israel" as "the eye of the soul, most translucent, most pure, most sharp-sighted of all, to which alone it is permitted to behold God" (my translation). Here the words connected to seeing include ὀφθαλμός (eye), ὀξυωπέστατος (most sharp-sighted), and καθορᾶν (to behold). Sometimes, Philo gives "Israel" more than one interpretation related to seeing; see, e.g., *Plant.* 59, described above in n. 3.

Examples of other or additional expressions for God or for the "object" seen include the following: ὁ [τὸ] μόνος[ον] σοφός [όν] (the only wise one, *Sacr.* 120); ἀρχεγονώτατον ὄν (the most original being, *Post.* 63); φῶς τὸ θεῖον (the divine light, *Migr.* 39); ὁ [τὸ] ὤν [όν] (the Existent, *Migr.* 54; cf. *Mut.* 81, which clearly has the masculine form); τὰ τῆς φύσεως πράγματα (the things of nature, *Her.* 279); τὸ ἄριστον, τὸ ὄντως ὄν (the best, the truly Existent, *Congr.* 51); θεὸς τε καὶ κόσμος (God and the universe, *Somn.* 2.172–73); ὁ πατὴρ καὶ ποιητὴς τῶν συμπάντων (the Father and Creator of all, *Abr.* 57). (Translations are mine. When the gender of words cannot be determined because they appear in cases in which masculine and neuter have the same endings, I have put neuter articles, forms, or endings in brackets.)

[15] ὁρῶν: *Leg.* 2.34; *Plant.* 59; *Conf.* 146, 148; *Migr.* 39, 113, 125; *Somn.* 1.129; *Somn.* 2.44; *QG* 4.233 (no parallel Greek fragment exists; the Latin translation and the French, which is based on the Latin, have "nature" as the object seen). βλέπων: *Migr.* 224, *Somn.* 1.114. ὁρατικὸν γένος: *Deus* 144, *Migr.* 54 (has ὁ [τὸ] ὤν [όν], the Existent, as the "object" seen), *Somn.* 2.280. ὁρατικὸς τρόπος: *Plant.* 59. ὁρατικὴ διάνοια: *Migr.* 15. ὁρατικὸς νοῦς: *Mut.* 207.

(my translation). Philo does not, however, say explicitly what "Israel" itself represents. In *Somn.* 2.271, Philo speaks about knowledge which waters "the reasoning grounds in the souls of those who are fond of seeing (φιλοθεάμονες)" (my translation). It is unclear, however, whether or not "Israel" corresponds to "those who are fond of seeing." Since Philo's interpretations of "Israel" remain ambiguous here, I shall simply note that they may be connected—albeit indirectly—to the etymology.

Periphrastic Expressions for "Israel"

Philo frequently uses expressions pertaining to seeing to represent "Israel" in passages where the word "Israel" does not appear explicitly. The expressions he uses most often are ὁ [or τὸ] ὁρῶν [τὸν] θεόν (the one that sees God), ὁ [or τὸ] ὁρῶν (the one that sees), and τὸ ὁρατικὸν γένος (the race/class that can see). These expressions may replace "Israel" within a Biblical quotation or else in an interpretation in which "Israel" is clearly understood to be the referent. In the next chapter, we shall examine these periphrastic expressions in more detail.

For our present purposes, these periphrases are significant because they further support the observation that Philo most frequently interprets "Israel" with direct or indirect reference to the etymology ὁρῶν θεόν. Before devoting attention, then, to these specific expressions and to the question of how Philo identifies these "seers" with real people, we shall first consider the sources for his etymology, Philo's notions about seeing God and the possible influences upon these notions, and Philo's understanding of the experience itself.

Philo's Etymology for "Israel"

In discussing Philo's etymology for "Israel"— ὁρῶν θεόν, or one that sees God—scholars have investigated the source of this etymology and of Philo's etymologies in general; the Hebrew basis for ὁρῶν θεόν; and parallel occurrences of this etymology in other literature. Various approaches to these three issues are surveyed below.

The Source of Philo's Etymologies

Consideration of Philo's etymology for "Israel" touches upon the larger issue of how he derives all the etymologies found in his works. Scholars have debated whether these word explanations are Philo's own creations, and this question in turn has led to the problem of whether or not he knew Hebrew. Although the two questions are not necessarily related, scholars have often addressed them together.

Philo's etymologies have in fact been used to buttress both sides of the question of whether or not he knew Hebrew.[16] It is generally agreed that some of his etymologies fit an original Hebrew quite closely, while others do not.[17] Some are based upon readings in the Septuagint that differ from the Hebrew Bible, and some are Greek etymologies for Biblical terms. Occasionally, those etymologies which defy a close fit to the Hebrew have given rise to some imaginative speculations about possible derivations.[18]

Scholars also agree that Philo may have drawn at least some of his etymologies from outside sources. We know of various onomastica from antiquity, and he could have had one or more such lists available to him.[19]

---

[16] For a good overview of whether or not Philo knew Hebrew, see Nikiprowetzky, *Le commentaire de l'Écriture*, 50–96. Nikiprowetzky concludes that Philo did not know Hebrew. Other scholars who agree are Edmund Stein, *Die allegorische Exegese des Philos aus Alexandreia*, Beihefte zur Zeitschrift für die Alttestamentliche Wissenschaft, no. 51 (Giessen: Alfred Töpelmann, 1929), 20–26; Isaak Heinemann, *Philons griechische und jüdische Bildung: Kulturvergleichende Untersuchungen zu Philons Darstellung der jüdischen Gesetze* (Breslau: Marcus, 1932; repr., Hildesheim: Olms, 1962), 524; Goodenough, *Introduction to Philo Judaeus*, 9; Sandmel, *Philo's Place in Judaism*, 11–13, and idem, "Philo's Knowledge of Hebrew," *SP* 5 (1978): 107–11. Among those who think Philo did know Hebrew are Carl Siegfried, *Philo von Alexandria als Ausleger des alten Testaments: an sich selbst und nach seinem geschichtlichen Einfluss betrachtet* (Jena: Hermann Dufft, 1875), 142–45; Samuel Belkin, *Philo and the Oral Law*, Harvard Semitic Series, vol. 11 (Cambridge: Harvard University Press, 1940), 29–48; idem, "Interpretation of Names in Philo," *Horeb* 12 (1956): 3–61 (Hebrew); Suzanne Daniel, "La Halacha de Philon selon le premier livre des 'Lois Speciales,'" *Philon d'Alexandrie*, Colloques Nationaux du Centre National de la Recherche Scientifique (Paris: Centre National de la Recherche Scientifique, 1967), 221–40; and Wolfson, *Philo*, 1:88–90.

On this question, see also Yehoshua Amir, "Explanation of Hebrew Names in Philo," *Tarbitz* 31 (1962): 297 (Hebrew); Hugo D. Mantel, "Did Philo Know Hebrew?" *Tarbitz* 32 (1962): 98–99 (Hebrew); and Jean-George Kahn, "Did Philo Know Hebrew?" *Tarbitz* 34 (1965): 337–45 (Hebrew).

[17] For a full-length work on Philo's etymologies, see Lester L. Grabbe, *Etymology in Early Jewish Interpretation: The Hebrew Names in Philo*, Brown Judaic Studies, ed. Jacob Neusner et al., no. 115 (Atlanta: Scholars Press, 1988). See also Goulet, *La philosophie de Moïse*, 46–52, 58–62. For different classifications of Philo's etymologies, see further: Stein, *Die allegorische Exegese*, 50–61; Siegfried, *Philo von Alexandria*, 190–96; Jean-George Kahn, ed., *De Confusione Linguarum*, OPA, 13:19–21; and Anthony T. Hanson, "Philo's Etymologies," *JTS* 18 (1967): 128–39.

[18] See especially Hanson, "Philo's Etymologies," and Nikiprowetzky's discussion of this topic in *Le commentaire de l'Écriture*, 75–81.

[19] Grabbe, *Etymology in Early Jewish Interpretation*, 102–11; David Rokeah, "A New Onomasticon Fragment from Oxyrhynchus and Philo's Etymologies," *JTS* 19 (1968): 70–82. Rokeah lists various editions of Greek onomastica, 71, n. 6. See also Adolf Deissmann, *Veröffentlichungen aus der Heidelberger Papyrus-Sammlung* (Heidelberg: Carl Winter, 1905), Papyrology on Microfiche, ser. 2, vol. 31 (Missoula, Montana: Scholars Press, n.d.), 1:86–93. Deissmann believes Philo himself may have authored such a list. In contrast, Sandmel writes, "Philo says plainly on many occasions that the etymologies are not his own, but that he has heard them" (*Philo's Place in Judaism*, 12).

Unfortunately, since the evidence dates from after Philo's time, his reliance on such lists can only be hypothesized.

While most scholars generally concur that Philo used outside sources, they do not agree upon which etymologies he derived from these sources and which he invented himself. Since the etymological lists which may have been available to Philo are no longer available to us, however, it becomes impossible to determine, without prejudging the issue, which of his etymologies are original and which are derived. Moreover, since even the onomastica include etymologies which range in their fit to an original Hebrew, the etymologies alone—be they original or borrowed— do not provide sufficient evidence to determine whether or not Philo knew Hebrew.[20]

Aside from the problem of which etymologies are Philonic and which are pre-Philonic, the evaluation of etymologies according to their precise fit to an original Hebrew deserves some attention. The etymologies in the Bible itself do not always precisely fit the words they are meant to explain, yet no one questions the Hebrew language skills of their source.[21] The purpose of Biblical etymologies seems to be etiological, explaining after-the-fact how people and places acquired their names. These explanations do not answer questions about philology but rather questions about why people or places are called what they are.

Later interpreters of the Bible frequently invent their own new etymologies for Biblical terms. In so doing, these interpreters are trying to understand the text from the perspective of their own time and place. The Rabbis, for example, do not hesitate to use their imaginations to create new etymologies, and their creations reflect a playfulness with the Hebrew language rather than a precise fit.[22] By developing new etymologies for Biblical terms, the Rabbis are making the Bible meaningful for their own contemporary contexts.

Philo too uses some non-Biblical etymologies to support his understanding of the text. It is especially noteworthy that he usually does not

---

(Unfortunately, Sandmel does not cite specific references for such statements, and I have not scanned Philo's works with this question in mind.)

[20] Another important issue for evaluating this question is whether or not Philo used the Hebrew Bible. For various positions, see the authors cited above in n. 16.

[21] See especially Immanuel M. Casanowicz, *Paronomasia in the Old Testament* (Jerusalem: Makor, 1970; repr. of 1892 dissertation), 36–40; Hermann Gunkel, *The Legends of Genesis: The Biblical Saga and History*, trans. W. H. Carruth (n.p., 1901; repr., New York: Schocken Books, 1964), 27–30.

[22] Isaak Heinemann, *Ways of the Aggadah* (Jerusalem: Magnes Press, 1954), 110–12 (Hebrew); James Kugel, "Two Introductions to Midrash," *Prooftexts* 3 (1983): 131–55. For examples of rabbinic etymologies, see Heinemann, *Ways of the Aggadah*, and Belkin, "Interpretation of Names in Philo," 3–6.

build up to the etymology—that is, he does not explain how a certain name came to be, as the Bible does, or as rabbinic interpretations do.[23] More frequently, he simply gives the meaning of the name and then builds upon the etymology that he already takes for granted. An etymology, then, is not usually the end-point of his exegesis but rather the starting point. This characteristic lends additional support to the thesis that he probably derived his etymologies from another source.

Philo's tendency to take for granted familiarity with an etymology is particularly apparent in his discussion of "Israel" as the ὁρῶν θεόν, or God-seer.[24] Indeed, he frequently calls "Israel" the God-seer or the seer (ὁρῶν), without mentioning specifically that this is the etymology or part of the etymology. Similarly, his other periphrastic expressions, such as τὸ ὁρατικὸν γένος, the race/class that can see, seem to be based upon or to presuppose the etymology.[25] Given the possibility that Philo drew his etymologies from other sources and that he seems to take for granted familiarity with the specific etymology for "Israel," it would appear that he himself did not originate the explanation that "Israel" means ὁρῶν θεόν. As we shall see later, this conclusion gains additional support from parallel occurrences of the etymology in other literature.

The Hebrew Derivation of the Etymology

In trying to understand Philo's etymology of "Israel" as ὁρῶν θεόν, scholars have suggested the following possible derivations from the Hebrew:

1) איש ראה אל, a man [who] saw/sees God (depending upon the pointing);
2) ראה אל, one [who] saw/sees God; and
3) ישר אל, he will see God.[26]

---

[23] In the cases of Abraham and Sarah, Philo does explain how their names are derived, but these explanations are based upon the Greek letters rather than the Hebrew. The explanations, therefore, have nothing to do with the meanings he then provides that are based upon the Hebrew. See *Mut.* 60–80, esp. 77; *QG* 3.43, 53; cf. Rokeah, "A New Onomasticon Fragment," 78.

[24] See, e.g., *Leg.* 3.212, *Post.* 63, *Conf.* 56. Jonathan Z. Smith comes to a similar conclusion about Philo's etymology for "Israel." He writes, "As the derivation rests on a Hebrew *jeu de mots* and as it is never argued but rather assumed by Philo, there is good reason to suggest that he is drawing upon an earlier tradition" ("The Prayer of Joseph," *Religions in Antiquity: Essays in Memory of Erwin Ramsdell Goodenough*, ed. Jacob Neusner, Studies in the History of Religions (Supplements to *Numen*), no. 14 (Leiden: E. J. Brill, 1968), 266. (Hereafter this article will be cited as "Smith, 'The Prayer of Joseph,' *Religions.*")

[25] The relationship between the etymology and the expression ὁρατικὸν γένος is explored in the next chapter.

[26] Wilhelm Michaelis, "ὁράω," *TDNT* 5:337, n. 113; Smallwood, *Philonis Alexandrini*,

Unlike the first two suggestions which come from the root ראה, to see, the last comes from the less common root, שור, to see (cf. Num. 23:9, 24:17; Hos. 14:9; Job 34:29).

Of these three proposals, the most attractive is the first, that "Israel" is based upon איש ראה אל. This proposal gains support from:

a) Jacob/Israel's words in Gen. 32:31;
b) the fit between the letters of ישראל and איש ראה אל; and
c) parallels in other Hellenistic Jewish writings and patristic literature.

Here I shall comment upon the first two factors and consider the third in a separate section.

A particularly strong argument for both proposals that are based upon ראה comes from the Bible itself. The passage in which Jacob's name is changed to "Israel" includes two etymologies, one for "Israel" (Gen. 32:29) and one for "Peniel" (Gen. 32:31). As to the first, when Jacob's adversary dubs him "Israel," he says, "Your name will no longer be called Jacob but Israel because you strove with God and with people and you prevailed" (לא יעקב יאמר עוד שמך כי אם ישראל כי שרית עם אלהים ועם אנשים ותוכל; Gen. 32:29 [my translation]).

Two verses later, Jacob gives the name "Peniel" to the spot where the struggle occurs, explaining, "because I saw God face to face and my soul was preserved" (כי ראיתי אלהים פנים אל פנים ותנצל נפשי; Gen. 32:31 [my translation]).

The Biblical etymology for "Israel" then is based upon שרית and אלהים, while Peniel derives from פנים and אלהים. Jacob's very first words after his name becomes "Israel," however, are "I have seen God" (כי ראיתי אלהים, Gen. 32:31). Noticing this, a Biblical exegete might easily come to associate "Israel" with seeing God.[27]

Another argument for the first Hebrew derivation proposed above is that ישראל is a contraction of איש ראה אל, and thus the letters of ישראל are all accounted for. Although this suggestion is plausible, one ought to recall

153–54; G. A. Danell, *Studies in the Name Israel in the Old Testament* (Uppsala: Appelbergs boktrychkeri-A.-B., 1946), 15–28; E. Sacchse, "Die Etymologie und älteste Aussprache des Namens ישראל," *Zeitschrift für die alttestamentliche Wissenschaft* 34 (1914): 1–15; Kahn, "Did Philo Know Hebrew?" 342–43.

27 Clement connects the name of Israel with Gen. 32:31: "Then also he was named Israel because he saw God the Lord" (τότε καὶ Ἰσραὴλ ἐπωνόμασται, ὅτε εἶδε τὸν θεὸν τὸν κύριον; *Paedagogus* 1:7). Clement does not give the etymology and seems to assume that his readers are familiar with it.

Nikiprowetzky notes other examples in which Philo's etymologies can be linked with the Biblical context rather than with the linguistic construction of the word; see *Le commentaire de l'Écriture*, 53–54 (examples of Sodom and Noah), 57 (Rebecca).

that the letters of etymologies do not always precisely match the letters of the words they explain.

Those who object to this proposal for the Hebrew emphasize that Philo never uses the full formulation ἀνήρ or ἄνθρωπος ὁρῶν θεόν and thus never includes a Greek equivalent for איש.[28] I shall discuss this objection in the section on parallels to Philo's etymology.

The proposal that the etymology comes from ראה אל, that is, without איש, does not get much attention. In its favor, this formulation is more in accord with Philo's etymology, which has ὁρῶν as a substantive without a noun for "man." Moreover, unlike איש ראה אל, ראה אל adds no new words to the Biblical expression in Gen. 32:31, כי ראיתי אלהים.

As Wilhelm Michaelis points out, however, ראה אל leaves the first two letters of ישראל, namely, יש, unaccounted for.[29] Again, since this kind of precision is a poor criterion for judging etymologies, Michaelis's objection on its own need not eliminate this possibility. Parallels in other literature, however, provide stronger support for the full formulation איש ראה אל.

The last suggestion, ישר אל, offers the best fit—in terms of matching letters—to an original Hebrew. E. Mary Smallwood observes that this alternative "would involve different pointing but no elimination of letters" from ישראל.[30] Unlike the two proposals based upon the verb ראה, however, this one is not supported by the Biblical passage that reports Jacob's words after his name is changed. Nor do we have parallels that attest to this formulation in any other literature. Although the letters may fit the Hebrew more precisely, then, this criterion alone does not provide a strong enough argument, and ישר אל appears least convincing of the possible Hebrew expressions behind the etymology.

Parallel Occurrences of the Etymology in Other Literature

Parallels to and variants of the etymology found in Philo are abundant in patristic literature and less abundant in Hellenistic Jewish literature (a literature which is itself less abundant!). A Gnostic text from the third or fourth century includes a Coptic parallel to "a man who sees God."[31] A Hebrew instance of איש ראה אל is found in *Seder Eliahu Rabbah*, probably a tenth century work.[32] Finally, the etymology איש ראה אל is also referred to

---

28 Michaelis, "ὁράω ," 337, n. 113.
29 Ibid.
30 Smallwood, *Philonis Alexandrini*, 154.
31 "On the Origin of the World," trans. Hans-Gebhard Bethge and Bentley Layton, *The Nag Hammadi Library*, 3rd ed., ed. James M. Robinson (San Francisco: Harper & Row, 1988), 176; see also Smith, "The Prayer of Joseph," *Religions*, 264.
32 *Seder Eliahu Rabbah* 25 (27), ed. Meir Friedmann (Vienna: n.p., 1902), 138–39.

in a Syriac thesaurus.[33] With one possible exception—the *Prayer of Joseph* (*PJ*), to be examined below—all these sources are later than Philo, and most of the patristic parallels are probably dependent upon him.

The one Hebrew instance, found in *Seder Eliahu Rabbah*, appears centuries after Philo. Nevertheless this occurrence provides important evidence of a Hebrew formulation for the etymology איש ראה אל, which may indeed reflect an earlier tradition.[34]

As to Greek and Latin parallels, patristic writings include the etymology in various forms. Thus we find ὁρῶν θεόν, one who sees God; νοῦς ὁρῶν θεόν, a mind that sees God; and ἄνθρωπος ὁρῶν θεόν, a person who sees God—as well as their Latin equivalents.[35] A reference in Clement (*Paedagogus* 1:7), moreover, explicitly connects the name "Israel" with Gen. 32:31, in which Jacob, newly named Israel, exclaims, "I have seen God."[36] It is especially striking that these writings include the full form ἄνθρωπος ὁρῶν θεόν . These instances of the fuller etymology lend support to the proposition that it comes originally from the Hebrew, איש ראה אל.

In the scanty Hellenistic Jewish literature, we can find parallels to Philo's etymology for "Israel" in the *Prayer of Joseph*. We can also find them in a Christian work, the *Constitutiones Apostolorum*, a guide for

---

[33] *Thesaurus Syriacus*, ed. R. Payne Smith (1879), 1:163, cited by Smallwood, *Philonis Alexandrini*, 153–54.

[34] The text reads,

ד'א בשעה שמצאתי שנים עשר שבטים שעשו רצון יעקב אביהם. שנאמר כענבים במדבר מצאתי ישראל (הושע ט' י'). אל תיקרי ישראל. אלא איש ראה אל. שכל מעשיו מכוונין לפניו. לכך נאמר הנה עתך עת דודים.

Another point: At the time when I found the twelve tribes who were doing the will of Jacob their father. As it is said, 'Like grapes in the desert I found Israel' (Hosea 9:10). Do not read 'Israel' but איש ראה אל [a man (who) saw, or sees, God]. Because all his deeds are upright before Him. Therefore it is said, 'Behold your time is the time of love.' (my translation)

This section forms part of a chain of examples illustrating what is meant by the time of love (עת דודים), cited in Ezek. 16:8. The passage interprets Hos. 9:10 as a proof-text to show that God found Israel acting in proper fashion and this is an example of the time of love. (The Friedmann edition cites the verse from Hosea erroneously as 9:6 instead of 9:10. I have corrected this citation in the Hebrew quoted above and in my translation.) Cf. Kahn, "Did Philo Know Hebrew?" 342–43. Kahn quotes the etymology as מי שראה אל rather than איש ראה אל, as it appears in the Friedmann edition.

[35] For specific references, see Geoffrey William Hugo Lampe, *A Patristic Greek Lexicon* (Oxford: Clarendon Press, 1961), 678; Smallwood, *Philonis Alexandrini*, 153–54; Smith, "The Prayer of Joseph," *Religions*, 266, n. 3; and Louis Ginzberg, *The Legends of the Jews* (Philadelphia: Jewish Publication Society, 1925), 5:307, n. 253. A related citation to "Israel" as ὁ τῷ ὄντι διορατικός, the one that discerns the Existent, is found in Clement, *Stromata* 1:5, and other sources; see Lampe, *Patristic Greek Lexicon*, 373, under "διορατικός."

[36] See above, n. 27.

Christian living compiled in the late fourth century, which contains prayers considered likely to be of Jewish origin. Although "Israel" is identified in these prayers with the Gentiles and with Christians, the language describing "Israel" directly does not vary from Philo's usage in that neither reference mentions a word for "man." These references therefore are not immediately helpful.[37]

Of all the literature, the most interesting evidence comes from *PJ*, fragments of which have been preserved by patristic writers.[38] The relevant excerpt is spoken by Jacob/Israel and seems to reflect Jacob's encounter with his adversary in Gen. 32:25–33. *PJ* has illuminating parallels to Philo as well as important differences. Since the *Prayer* may be contemporary to Philo,[39] it provides information which may shed light upon how he derived his etymology and adapted his sources.

Comparing *PJ* and a passage from Philo, *Conf.* 146, Edmund Stein juxtaposes the names used by the speaker in *PJ* with similar epithets used by Philo for the λόγος.[40] The pertinent part of *PJ* is as follows:

> I, Jacob, who is speaking to you, am also Israel, an angel of God and a ruling spirit. Abraham and Isaac were created before any work. But I, Jacob, who[m] men call Jacob but whose name is Israel, am he who[m] God called Israel which means, a man seeing God, because I am the firstborn of every living thing to whom God gives life... Are you not Uriel, the eighth after me? and I, Israel, the archangel of the power of the Lord and the chief captain among the sons of God? Am I not Israel, the first minister before the face of God?...

[37] David A. Fiensy, *Prayers Alleged To Be Jewish: An Examination of the* Constitutiones Apostolorum, Brown Judaic Studies, ed. Jacob Neusner, no. 65 (Chico, California: Scholars Press, 1985); and D. R. Darnell and D. A. Fiensy, "Hellenistic Synagogal Prayers," *Old Testament Pseudepigrapha* (*OTP*) ed. James H. Charlesworth (Garden City, New York: Doubleday, 1985), 2:671–97. See also Goodenough, *By Light, Light*, 306–58. The following text and translation are found in Fiensy, *Prayers Alleged To Be Jewish*:
  Const. Ap. 7.36.2 (Fiensy, 76–77): ὁ ἀληθινὸς Ἰσραήλ, ὁ θεοφιλής, ὁ ὁρῶν θεόν, "the true Israel, the beloved of God, the one who sees God." Here Israel is identified with the Gentiles (τὰ ἔθνη).
  Const. Ap. 8.15.77 (Fiensy, 110–11): ὁ θεός Ἰσραήλ τοῦ ἀληθινῶς ὁρῶντος, "the God of Israel which truly sees." Here Israel is identified with believers in Christ (ὁ εἰς Χριστὸν πιστεύσας λαὸς σός).
[38] Smith, "The Prayer of Joseph," *Religions*, 253–4, and idem, "Prayer of Joseph," *OTP*, 2:699–714. Citations in the text of the chapter are taken from the translation provided in *OTP*.
[39] "The various parallels to both hellenistic and Aramaic materials would suggest a first century date" (Smith, "Prayer of Joseph," *OTP*, 2:700). See also the discussion of Edmund Stein in the text of the chapter.
[40] Edmund Stein, "Zur apokryphen Schrift 'Gebet Josephs,'" *Monatsschrift für Geschichte und Wissenschaft des Judentums* 81 (1937): 280–86, esp. 282–83.

Conf. 146 reads,

> But if it happens that someone is not yet worthy to be called son of God, let him
> hasten to be placed with the Logos, His firstborn, the eldest of angels, a kind of
> archangel, being many-named; for he is called 'beginning' and 'name of God'
> and 'Logos' and 'the man according to the image' and 'the seer, Israel.' (my
> translation)

A comparison between the epithets in *PJ* and those in *Conf.* 146 reveals the
parallels shown below and suggests that the two passages might be
connected. We can see that *PJ* provides the etymology for Israel as ἀνὴρ
ὁρῶν θεόν, while *Conf.* 146 has simply ὁ ὁρῶν. It is interesting that
although the etymology in *PJ* means "a man who sees God," the passage
also describes "Israel" as an angel.

A *Comparison of Epithets in* PJ *and* Conf. 146

PJ	Conf. 146
ἄγγελος θεοῦ angel of God	ὁ ἀγγέλων πρεσβύτατος the eldest of angels
πνεῦμα ἀρχικόν ruling spirit	[ἀρχάγγελος]* [archangel]*
Ἰσραήλ Israel	Ἰσραήλ Israel
ἀνὴρ ὁρῶν θεόν a man who sees God	ὁ ὁρῶν the seer
πρωτόγονος παντὸς ζώου ζωουμένου ὑπὸ θεοῦ firstborn of every living thing to whom God gives life	ὁ πρωτόγονος αὐτοῦ His [God's] firstborn
ἀρχάγγελος δυνάμεως Κυρίου archangel of the power of the Lord	ἀρχάγγελος archangel
ἀρχιχιλίαρχος ἐν υἱοῖς Θεοῦ chief captain among the sons of God	[ἀρχάγγελος]* [archangel]*

*These brackets indicate similar terms but not real parallels.

For reasons he does not explain, Stein assumes that *PJ* is dependent
upon Philo. Since *PJ* is not clearly later than Philo, such a dependency is
not necessarily indicated.[41] Stein, however, believing that Philo did not

---

41 See, e.g., Delling, "The 'One Who Sees God' in Philo," 38, n. 70.

know Hebrew, contends that the etymology for "Israel"—found in both sources—is pre-Philonic.

Like the similar occurrences in patristic literature, the full form ἀνὴρ ὁρῶν θεόν in *PJ* suggests that this etymology may be based upon an original Hebrew, איש ראה אל. Because *PJ* may be contemporary to Philo, the presence of the etymology in this source indicates that Philo may not have been the original inventor of the etymology. Indeed, he may have borrowed it from *PJ*, both may have drawn upon a common tradition, or *PJ* may have taken the etymology from Philo. We have no way to determine who borrowed from whom or what source may have served both writers.

Besides providing a parallel to the etymology, the *PJ* passage is illuminating for yet another reason. While the epithets in *PJ* describe the angel named "Israel," Philo uses these same epithets for the λόγος in *Conf.* 146 and elsewhere.[42] In discussing *PJ*, Jonathan Z. Smith observes that different groups use the same cluster of titles for different figures. Thus, these epithets are applied by *PJ* to "Israel," "by Philo to the *Logos*, by rabbinic literature to Michael, by Jewish mystical literature to Metatron and by Jewish Christianity to Jesus."[43] Citing parallels in other works that describe "Israel" with some of the same titles found in *PJ*, Smith suggests that behind these various parallels may lie a common, evolving tradition: "In the *PJ* we are given a precious fragment of a mythology concerning the Mystery of Israel, a mythology which continues in the later Merkabah and Metatron speculation and which is present in a 'de-mythologized' form in the writings of Philo."[44]

The "de-mythologizing" character of the passage in Philo highlights an interesting issue related to his etymology for "Israel." If indeed the original Greek etymology was ἀνὴρ or ἄνθρωπος ὁρῶν θεόν, that is, if the etymology originally included a word for "man," one might well ask why this fuller form never appears in Philo's works. The contrast with *PJ* is especially interesting, since *PJ* retains a word for "man" even though the author also calls "Israel" an angel.

The consistent absence of a word for "man" in Philo's etymology for "Israel" raises the possibility that he—or perhaps one of his predecessors—may deliberately omit a word for "man" because the ambiguous participle ὁρῶν better suits his exegetical purposes—or those of the tradition upon which he draws. For example, in *Conf.* 146, discussed above, ὁρῶν refers to the λόγος—not a man, but an abstraction. Elsewhere, as we have seen,

---

[42] Smith lists these parallel epithets in "Prayer of Joseph," *OTP*, 2:701, n. 11.

[43] Smith, "The Prayer of Joseph," *Religions*, 259.

[44] Ibid., 260. See also Smith, "Prayer of Joseph," *OTP*, 2:704.

Philo also speaks of "Israel" as an abstraction—for example, as the mind or the soul. In addition, even where "Israel" may represent an individual or a collectivity instead of an abstract concept, its identity remains vague. Finally, as we shall soon discuss, Philo is equivocal about whether or not it is possible for a person to "see" God. Thus Philo—or a tradition upon which he relies—may deliberately drop a word for "man" from the etymology to dehistoricize the patriarch Jacob and his descendants, to allow for flexibility in representing "Israel" as an abstraction, or to avoid giving the impression that it is possible for a man to see God.[45]

Whether or not Philo deliberately omits a word for "man" from an earlier etymology, he most certainly uses the etymology to link "Israel" with a well-developed set of notions about seeing and seeing God. According to him, seeing God represents the greatest human happiness and the best of all possessions.[46] Indeed, the very ability to see Him is what confers upon "Israel" its distinct standing.[47]

Thus, while Philo may derive from tradition the etymology for "Israel" as "one that sees God," this etymology serves to place "Israel" in a position of prime importance in his thought because of the very significance he ascribes to this ability to see Him. Besides concentrating upon the derivation of and parallels to Philo's etymology for "Israel," then, we must also examine how and why the phenomenon of seeing and seeing God carries so much significance in his thought.

Philo's Ideas About Seeing God and Possible Influences Upon These Ideas

However Philo may arrive at the etymology for "Israel" as "one that sees God," it is clear that the motif of seeing God runs throughout his works and extends well beyond his interpretations of "Israel." Sometimes Philo discusses this motif in relation to Biblical verses about seeing God, which we shall consider below, and sometimes he introduces this theme when it is not immediately indicated either by a Biblical verse or by mention of "Israel."[48] Also noteworthy is that Philo refers to seeing God throughout all three exegetical series, and occasionally in his non-exegetical works as well.[49] Finally, besides expounding upon seeing God per se, Philo also frequently extols the sense of sight in general.[50]

---

45 This last possibility was suggested to me by Prof. John Strugnell in private conversation.

46 *Ebr.* 83, *Abr.* 57, *Legat.* 4; cf. *Praem.* 43–46.

47 *Post.* 63, 92; *Congr.* 51; *Plant.* 58–60; cf. *Praem.* 43–46.

48 E.g., *Opif.* 69–71, *Somn.* 1.64–67, *Somn.* 2.226–27, *QG* 4.196.

49 Examples of references in his exegetical series are listed above, in n. 48, and below, in n. 51. References in his non-exegetical writings include *Contempl.* 11 and *Legat.* 4–6.

50 *Abr.* 57; *Ebr.* 82; *Conf.* 72, 148; *Migr.* 39; *Fug.* 208. See also the discussion and

Seeing God in the Bible

Biblical verses vary in the way they present the experience of seeing God. Although this theme appears throughout Scripture, Philo develops it especially in connection with the following passages from Genesis and Exodus: Gen. 12:7, 17:1, 32:25–33, and Exod. 24:9–11 and 33:12–23.[51] (The following discussion is based upon the Greek Bible, which differs in places from the Hebrew.)

Occasionally Scripture depicts the experience of seeing God in the passive. In Gen. 12:7 and 17:1, for example, it says, "And the Lord appeared to (was seen by) Abram and He said..."[52] Neither verse elaborates upon God's appearance, which simply precedes and introduces His message.

At other times, Scripture presents the experience of seeing God in more active, physical terms. In Gen. 32:25–33—the all-important passage for Philo's thought that narrates Jacob's change of name to "Israel"—the patriarch wrestles with a man (ἄνθρωπος). Afterwards, however, in naming Peniel, he says, "I have seen God face to face."

Another passage, Exod. 24:9–11, also describes physical sight, though God Himself is not directly seen. It says,

> And Moses went up, and Aaron and Nadab and Abihu and seventy of the elders of Israel, and they saw the place where the God of Israel was standing; and there was under His feet as it were a work of sapphire stone, just like the appearance of the firmament of heaven in purity. And not one of the chosen ones of Israel perished; and they appeared in the place of God and ate and drank. (my translation)[53]

Finally, the Bible also carries the idea that humans are not permitted to see God and live. This is implicit above in Exod. 24:11, where it says that "not one of the chosen ones of Israel perished." In Exod. 33:12–23,

---

passages cited by Runia, *Philo of Alexandria and the* Timaeus *of Plato*, 270–76.

[51] Passages in which Philo discusses the vision of God in connection with these verses include the following: Gen. 12:7: *Abr.* 77–80, *Det.* 159. Gen. 17:1: *Mut.* 3–6, 15–17; *QG* 3.39. Gen. 32:25–33: *Ebr.* 82–83; *Migr.* 199, 201; *Mut.* 81–82; *Somn.* 1.129; *Praem.* 36–46. Exod. 24:9–11: *Conf.* 96–97, *QE* 2.37–39. Exod. 33:12–23: *Post.* 13–16, *Mut.* 8–10, *Spec.* 1.41–50.

[52] Both Gen. 12:7 and 17:1 have the Hebrew: וירא יי אל אברם. For both verses, the LXX has καὶ ὤφθη κύριος τῷ Ἀβράμ. In *Abr.* 77 and *Det.* 159, Philo's citation of Gen. 12:7 has θεός instead of κύριος. On Gen. 17:1, see *QG* 3.39; *Mut.* 1, 15–17. Here he uses κύριος as does the LXX.

[53] In Hebrew, the relevant parts of Exod. 24:10 and 11 are as follows: ויראו את אלהי ישראל...ויחזו את האלהים...; "And they saw the God of Israel... And they beheld God..." The LXX, which Philo uses, has a slightly different reading for these phrases: καὶ εἶδον τὸν τόπον, οὗ εἱστήκει ἐκεῖ ὁ θεὸς τοῦ Ἰσραήλ ... καὶ ὤφθησαν ἐν τῷ τόπῳ τοῦ θεοῦ ... "And they saw the place where the God of Israel was standing... And they appeared in the place of God..." See Michaelis, "ὁράω," 331–32.

however, in which Moses petitions God to reveal Himself, the notion is made explicit. God tells Moses, "You cannot see my face; for man shall not see me and live" (Exod. 33:20; cf. Exod. 3:6 and 19:21). Therefore God shows him His back but not His face (Exod. 33:23).

Even in these few sample passages, then, the Bible is inconsistent about seeing God. Gen. 12:7 and 17:1 do not describe the experience but instead take it for granted. Exod. 24:9–11 depicts an ascent with direct physical vision of the place where God was standing. In Gen. 32:25–33, Jacob wrestles with a man, yet later he declares that he has seen God "face to face." In contrast, Exod. 33:12–23 stresses that such direct vision is life-threatening to humans. None of these passages claims, however, that seeing God is impossible; rather it is dangerous and indeed can be fatal.[54]

General Features of Philo's Discussion

Philo's notions about seeing God differ from and go well beyond the Biblical verses he interprets. As with so much else in Philo's writings, his disquisitions about seeing God are sometimes inconsistent and even contradictory. Nonetheless, certain features do recur.[55]

A fairly constant theme is that God is seen not with the eyes of the body but with the eyes of the soul or mind (*Mut.* 3–6, *Abr.* 57–58). Indeed a turning away or withdrawal from the body seems to be a prerequisite for the mind or soul to see God (*Det.* 158–60, *Ebr.* 99–103). While Philo occasionally discusses seeing God as a function of the mind, however, he also declares that one can reach God only after recognizing the mind's limits (*Leg.* 3.39–48, *Her.* 68–74). Some passages about the limits of the mind also suggest that seeing God involves the experience of ecstasy (*Opif.* 70–71; *Her.* 69–70, 263–65). Occasionally too, Philo uses the language of the mysteries to describe seeing God as a process of initiation (*Leg.* 3.100, *Abr.* 122).

Although one may not always succeed in the quest, seeing God is a goal that can be achieved during one's lifetime (*Leg.* 3.47, *Post.* 13–21, *Spec.* 1.32); it is implicit that the goal is not reserved for after death. People may arrive at a vision of God via different paths. Some may be led to it by contemplating creation (*Abr.* 69–71, *Praem.* 41–43); others by practicing virtue (*Ebr.* 82–83, *Mut.* 81–82); still others—though very few—see God

---

[54] For Philo, seeing God is impossible rather than dangerous. See, e.g., *Fug.* 141 on Exod. 3:6. See also Michaelis, "ὁράω," 337, n. 110.

[55] References provided in the ensuing discussion are representative, not comprehensive. For good overviews of how Philo discusses seeing God, see Michaelis, "ὁράω," 334–38; Donald A. Hagner, "The Vision of God in Philo and John: A Comparative Study," *Journal of the Evangelical Theological Society* 14 (1971): 81–93; Kenneth E. Kirk, *The Vision of God: The Christian Doctrine of the Summum Bonum* (New York: Harper & Row, 1931), 38–46; Winston, *Logos and Mystical Theology*, 54–55.

through God Himself (*Leg.* 3.100–3, *Praem.* 43–46). In contrast, Philo sometimes declares that a person cannot by his or her own abilities see God at
all, but only God can reveal Himself to the seeker (*Post.* 16, *Abr.* 80).

Although Philo occasionally seems to speak without qualification about
the possibility of seeing God, at other times he claims that God can be seen
only through apprehension of His various intermediaries (*Conf.* 95–97,
Somn. 1.64–67, *QG* 4.2). He is also careful to warn that God cannot be seen
as He is; instead, one sees only "that He is, not what He is" (*Fug.* 141,
Praem. 39–40).

Finally, as the one that sees God, "Israel" holds a special place in
Philo's thought. The passage below expresses this and other ideas characteristic of Philo. He writes of "Israel":

> Its high position is shewn by the name; for the nation is called in the Hebrew
> tongue Israel, which, being interpreted, is "He who sees God." Now the sight of
> the eyes is the most excellent of all the senses, since by it alone we apprehend the
> most excellent of existing things, the sun and the moon and the whole heaven
> and world; but the sight of the mind, the dominant element in the soul, surpasses
> all the other faculties of the mind, and this is wisdom which is the sight of the
> understanding. But he to whom it is given not only to apprehend by means of
> knowledge all else that nature has to shew, but also to see the Father and Maker of
> all, may rest assured that he is advanced to the crowning point of happiness; for
> nothing is higher than God, and whoso has stretched the eyesight of the soul to
> reach Him should pray that he may there abide and stand firm... (*Abr.* 57–58)

Clearly, Philo's notions about seeing God are quite complex, and it is
beyond the scope of this study to address these complexities in depth.
Instead, our chief concern is to understand how and why "Israel"—as the
one that sees God—holds such an important place in Philo's thought. I
shall therefore concentrate upon Philo's high estimation of the faculty of
seeing in general and seeing God in particular and upon his notion of
God as the "object" seen. To understand these ideas, we must consider
their philosophical background.[56]

The Philosophical Background Behind Philo's Ideas About Seeing God

Plato. Many of the individual strands found woven together in Philo's
comments about seeing God can be traced back to Plato. Plato himself,

---

[56] For a broader perspective on the Hellenistic background of Philo's ideas, see
Charles Harold Dodd, "Hellenism and Christianity," *Harvard Divinity School Bulletin*
(1937), esp. 26–31; Alan F. Segal, "Heavenly Ascent in Hellenistic Judaism, Early
Christianity, and their Environment," *ANRW*, 2.23.2: *Religion (Vorkonstantinisches
Christentum: Verhältnis zu römischem Staat und heidnischer Religion [Forts.])*, ed. Wolfgang
Haase (Berlin: de Gruyter, 1980), 1333–94; idem, *Paul the Convert: The Apostolate and
Apostasy of Saul the Pharisee* (New Haven: Yale University Press, 1990), 38–56.

however, often does not combine these strands, nor does he address how certain notions in his writings are meant to be connected.

Regarding the sense of sight and its relation to the intellect, Plato declares that sight is to be highly regarded because it leads to contemplation of the universe and thereby to philosophy (*Timaeus* 47a–c).[57] The true value in contemplating what is visible is that it leads to contemplation of what really is and is invisible (*Republic* 529–31). In the visible world, the sun is the source of light and therefore enables sight to see; in the same way the idea of the Good in the intelligible world is the source of truth and enables the knower to know (*Republic* 507–8). The objects of thinking are invisible (*Phaedo* 79a, *Timaeus* 52a); and the supreme idea of the Good is beyond Being (*Republic* 508–9).[58]

As for what one should strive for in life, Plato observes that it is a task to discover the Creator and Father of the universe, and once one discovers Him, it is impossible to report it to everyone (*Timaeus* 28c). It behooves humankind to become like God (*Theaetetus* 176b, *Republic* 613b); and the goal of life is to assimilate that which thinks to that which is thought (*Timaeus* 90d).

Finally, regarding the process of seeing what is ultimate, the body interferes with the ability of the soul to behold the truth, and only freedom from the body after death will permit attainment of the desired wisdom (*Phaedo* 66–67).[59] One passage (*Symposium* 210d–212a) describes ascent to a vision of the beautiful (τὸ καλόν) or divine beauty (τὸ θεῖον καλόν). Here the subject of the ascent is left vague, though the mind or soul is understood. Another passage (*Phaedrus* 246e–247e, 249c) speaks specifically of the ascent of the soul to a vision of the Existent (τὸ ὄν), which is visible only to the mind, the pilot of the soul. Both passages use the language of the mysteries to describe initiation into the lore of these visions (*Symposium* 210a, *Phaedrus* 249c).

Thinkers After Plato. Since Plato himself discusses certain concepts without relating them to each other, his followers are left to ponder how such entities as God, the Creator and Father of the universe, the world of Ideas in general, and especially the idea of the Good are all connected.[60] Plato's immediate successor, Speusippus, already mentions a first principle, the

---

[57] References provided here are to representative or especially important passages.

[58] Philo does not go so far as to claim that God is beyond Being; see Runia, *Philo of Alexandria and the* Timaeus *of Plato*, 135, 435.

[59] Although Philo similarly believes that the body impedes the soul, he does not assert that vision of God is possible only after death. Cf., however, *Leg.* 3.45.

[60] Wolfson, *Philo*, 1:200–2; Drummond, *Philo Judaeus*, 1:59–60; Runia, *Philo of Alexandria and the* Timaeus *of Plato*, 442.

One, which is prior to and separate from all being. We find a similar notion in Neopythagorean writings, namely, that God, the craftsman, is superior to mind and stands above the two principles of Form and Matter, which correspond to the Monad and Dyad.[61]

Acknowledging the supreme One of the Pythagoreans, the Alexandrian Platonist Eudorus (latter part of the first century B.C.E.) associates this first principle with the cause of matter and created things and calls this entity the supreme God (ὁ ὑπεράνω θεός). Eudorus appears to be a significant witness to the presence in Alexandria of a philosophical approach that has come to be known as Middle Platonism. Characteristic of this approach is belief in the transcendence and immateriality of God— a belief which leads to speculation about the intermediary world between this transcendent Being and creation—and, in general, a more religious or theocentric outlook.[62]

In his impressive study of how Philo understands and uses the *Timaeus* of Plato, David T. Runia portrays the development of this outlook as follows:

> The difference between Plato and his later followers obviously does not lie in their theological concern as such. Plato is passionately concerned with the subject of Divinity and proposes distastefully heavy punishments for atheists and those who deny the workings of divine Providence. He does retain, however, an (admittedly tenuous) separation of abstract philosophical principles (the Ideas, the Good, the One) and theological entities (the demiurge, the cosmic soul, the gods of myth). The Middle Platonists disregard this separation. Abstract principles and theological conceptions are brought into relation with each other and fused in θεολογία, the highest form of knowledge.[63]

Pervading the intellectual contemplation of Middle Platonism, then, is a deep concern for the divine and its relation to the world.

Philo in Relation to His Philosophical Background. Against this background, we can discern that Philo's ideas about seeing and seeing God are quite compatible with the spirit of his time. By his day, it was commonplace to esteem sight highly as the sense that leads to philosophy and to regard the contemplative life described by Aristotle as the best of human pursuits.[64]

---

[61] John Dillon, *The Transcendence of God in Philo: Some Possible Sources*, Protocol of the Colloquy of the Center for Hermeneutical Studies in Hellenistic and Modern Culture, ed. Wilhelm Wuellner, no. 16 (Berkeley: Center for Hermeneutical Studies, 1975), 1–3. Dillon emphasizes that the dating of pseudo-Pythagorean texts is far from certain. See also Winston, "Introduction," *Philo of Alexandria*, 22.

[62] Dillon, *The Transcendence of God*, 4; idem, *The Middle Platonists*, 119–21, 126–28; Tobin, *The Creation of Man*, 13–15. On Eudorus and Middle Platonism in general, see Dillon, *The Middle Platonists*, 114–39, and Tobin, *The Creation of Man*, 11–19.

[63] Runia, *Philo of Alexandria and the* Timaeus *of Plato*, 492–93.

[64] On the estimation of sight, see ibid., 271. Regarding Aristotle, see Michaelis,

Moreover, by emphasizing that God is the highest or best object of vision or contemplation, Philo is very much in accord with his philosophical environment.

To leave the impression that Philo is no more than a reflection of this environment, however, would be misleading. His discussion is distinguished by the way in which he describes God from both a philosophical perspective and a personal, Biblical, or, one might say, Jewish perspective.

One can hardly fail to notice the variety of formulations Philo applies to God and what is seen.[65] This range of descriptions may signify nothing more than that Philo is drawing upon vocabulary from different intellectual traditions without special regard for the philosophical implications. His occasional description of the object of contemplation as nature, for example, reflects the influence of Stoic philosophy.

Although Philo may indeed simply adopt the vocabulary of his environment without concern for any broader implications, however, some of his formulations may be construed as an intentional polemic against the philosophical equation of certain concepts.[66] Two passages about seeing God offer particularly striking examples. In one, Philo writes about God, "For that which is better than the Good, more important than the Monad, and purer than the One is impossible to be seen by anyone else, because it is permitted to Him alone to be comprehended by Himself" (*Praem.* 40, my translation).

In another noteworthy passage, Philo writes of

> souls whose vision has soared above all created things and schooled itself to behold the uncreated and divine, the primal good, the excellent, the happy, the blessed, which may truly be called better than the good, more excellent than the excellent, more blessed than blessedness, more happy than happiness itself, and any perfection there may be greater than these. (*Legat.* 5)

In these passages, Philo goes out of his way to present God as higher, better, and more important than such philosophical constructs as the Monad, the One, the Good, etc. From this perspective, then, he may be seen as criticizing certain philosophical trends in his environment.

"ὁράω," 322; Kirk, *The Vision of God*, 33, 475–79; and A. Hilary Armstrong, "Gotteschau (Visio beatifica)," *Reallexicon für Antike und Christentum: Sachwörterbuch zur Auseinandersetzung des Christentums mit der antiken Welt*, ed. Theodor Klauser (Stuttgart: Hiersemann, 1983), 12:8. Aristotle himself defines as the purpose (οὗ ἕνεκα) of human life to worship and contemplate God (τὸν θεὸν θεραπεύειν καὶ θεωρεῖν) (*Eudemian Ethics* 8:3:15–16 [1249b]; *Nichomachean Ethics* 10:7–8 [1177a–1178b]).

[65] Drummond provides an impressive list of Philonic appellations for God, *Philo Judaeus*, 2:63. See also Wolfson, *Philo*, 1:210–11, and n. 14 above.

[66] Dillon, *The Transcendence of God*, 9–12; the suggestion is put forth by Gerard E. Caspary, a respondent to Dillon's presentation. Note the list of passages Caspary adduces on p. 9. See also Wolfson, *Philo*, 1:201–2.

Some of Philo's descriptions of God, however, have nothing to do with the philosophical formulations he occasionally criticizes but instead accord more closely with the personal God of the Bible. In contrast, for example, to the abstract, philosophical formulation τὸ ὄν (the Existent), Philo sometimes calls God ὁ ὤν (He that exists), based upon the name God expresses to Moses in Exod. 3:14. As opposed to the remote and transcendent God of philosophy, the Biblical God—the God of Abraham, Isaac, and Jacob—relates to people. The juxtaposition of the two different portrayals of God can be somewhat perplexing.[67]

Perhaps few passages so capture the paradox of Philo's transcendent yet personal God as *Spec.* 1.41–50, an interpretation of Moses's request to see God (Exod. 33:12–23). In his interpretation, Philo presents a dialogue between Moses and God in which Moses pleads with God, using the second person singular, to reveal Himself to him. Philo writes,

> In these words we may almost hear plainly the inspired cry 'This universe has been my teacher, to bring me to the knowledge that Thou art and dost subsist. As thy son, it has told me of its Father, as Thy work of its contriver. But what Thou art in Thy essence I desire to understand, yet find in no part of the All any to guide me to this knowledge. Therefore I pray and beseech Thee to accept the supplication of a suppliant, a lover of God, one whose mind is set to serve Thee alone; for as knowledge of the light does not come by any other source but what itself supplies, so too Thou alone canst tell me of Thyself.' (*Spec.* 1.41–42)

To this request, Philo has God reply,

> Thy zeal I approve as praiseworthy, but the request cannot fitly be granted to any that are brought into being by creation. I freely bestow what is in accordance with the recipient, for not all that I can give with ease is within man's power to take and therefore to him that is worthy of my grace I extend all the boons which he is capable of receiving. But the apprehension of me is something more than human nature, yea even the whole heaven and universe will be able to contain. (*Spec.* 1.43–44)

In this and the ensuing dialogue, Philo presents what is essentially a personal conversation in which God explains His transcendence and unknowability to Moses![68] Here and elsewhere, the qualities of a remote and transcendent Being are counterpoised by the qualities of the Father and Creator who cares for His creation.

---

[67] As to how Philo reconciles the two approaches to God, Runia writes, "On this question we can do no better than highly to recommend the discussion [of Goodenough, Nikiprowetzky, and Sandmel], each of which is the fruit of a lifetime's study of Philo" (*Philo of Alexandria and the* Timaeus *of Plato*, 436, n. 152). His references are to Goodenough, *Introduction to Philo Judaeus*, 86–87; Nikiprowetzky, *Le commentaire de l'Écriture*, 128–30; and Sandmel, *Philo of Alexandria*, 89–94.

[68] This passage goes on to discuss apprehension of God's powers (*Spec.* 1.46–49). For other interpretations of Exod. 33:12–23, see, e.g., *Post.* 13–16, 169; *Fug.* 164–5; and *Mut.* 8–10.

The Biblical passage (Exod. 33:20) upon which the above interpretation is based declares merely that seeing God is not permitted. According to Philo, however, seeing God is beyond the abilities of anything created. In postulating an invisible and unknowable God, Philo follows in the tradition of Greek philosophy.[69] At the same time, however, the God that is "seen" is not only τὸ ὄντως ὄν, the truly Existent, but also the Creator and Father of the world whose activity vis-à-vis His creation is narrated in the Bible. If Philo can quite capably talk about God in the lofty terms of a philosopher, so too is he able to present a solicitous God talking to His creatures about Himself.

Philo's Understanding of the Experience of Seeing God

Before we turn away from Philo's understanding of seeing God, it may be worthwhile to reflect briefly upon how he conceives of the experience itself. Scholars have debated whether Philo considers the human experience of seeing God to be rational or ecstatic—and whether Philo in particular ever experienced ecstatic vision—and also whether Philo believes that God Himself—or only His intermediaries, such as the powers or the Logos—can be seen.

Opinions on these questions vary widely. Some scholars distinguish between a rational and ecstatic kind of experience, while others do not see a necessary dichotomy between the two.[70] One claims that Philo uses the

---

[69] Dillon raises the question of whether or not Philo was the first to introduce the idea of an unknowable God into Greek thought (*The Middle Platonists*, 155), and Caspary wonders whether or not he may have been "the inventor (or at least the philosophical formulator) of the notion of Transcendent Being" (Dillon, *The Transcendence of God*, 12). Both acknowledge that the elements that contribute to Philo's formulations were readily present in his philosophical environment.

[70] In relation to these issues, many authors mentioned below also discuss prophecy. See Bréhier, *Philon d'Alexandrie*, 2:180–205; Hans Jonas, *Gnosis und Spätantiker Geist*, pt. 2/1: *Von der Mythologie zur mystischen Philosophie*, Forschungen zur Religion und Literatur des Alten und Neuen Testaments, no. 63 (n.s. 45) (Göttingen: Vandenhoeck & Ruprecht, 1954), 70–121; Jean-George Kahn, "Israel–Videns Deum," *Tarbitz* 43 (1971): 285–92 (Hebrew); Hans Leisegang, *Der heilige Geist: Das wesen und werden der mystisch-intuitiven Erkenntnis in der Philosophie und Religion der Griechen* (Leipzig: B. G. Teubner, 1919) 1:145–231; Hans Lewy, *Sobria Ebrietas: Untersuchungen zur Geschichte der antiken Mystik*, Beihefte zur Zeitschrift für die neutestamentliche Wissenschaft und die Kunde der älteren Kirche, no. 9 (Giessen: Alfred Töpelmann, 1929), 3–41; Andrew Louth, *The Origins of the Christian Mystical Tradition From Plato to Denys* (Oxford: Clarendon Press, 1981), 18–35; Joseph Pascher, ἡ βασιλικὴ ὁδός: *Der Königsweg zu Wiedergeburt und Vergottung bei Philon von Alexandria*, Studien zur Geschichte und Kultur des Alterums, vol. 17, nos. 3–4 (Paderborn: Schoningh, 1931; repr., n.d. [1968]), esp. 160–91; E. Vanderlinden, "Les divers modes de connaissance de Dieu selon Philon d'Alexandrie," *Mélanges de Science Religieuse* 4 (1947): 285–304; Völker, *Fortschritt und Vollendung*, esp. 279–317; David Winston, "Was Philo a Mystic?" *Studies in Jewish Mysticism*, ed. Joseph

language of ecstasy merely as a literary convention to appeal to his audience without actually knowing the experience firsthand.[71] Another thinks Philo can be understood only if one takes his discussions of these experiences seriously.[72] Still another writer holds that according to Philo, people can experience God only through His Logos, an experience which, though rational, may culminate in ecstasy.[73]

To enter into these sundry debates would take us beyond the scope of this study. It is difficult, if not impossible, to arrive at a definitive portrayal of what Philo may mean by seeing God because his presentation is filled with contradictions and inconsistencies. Rather than trying to resolve these various problems, I shall instead suggest additional perspectives from which to consider the issue.

In sorting out the several inconsistencies in what Philo writes about seeing God, scholars have often focused exclusively upon his ideas without taking note of such other factors as the relationship between these ideas and the Biblical text he is interpreting, the possible influence of earlier exegetical traditions, the literary genre of the work, Philo's audience(s), and finally, the very nature of seeing God. After presenting two examples below of Philonic passages about seeing God—one passage from QGE and one from the Allegory—I shall discuss how and why these various factors may be important.

Two Philonic Examples

QG 4.2 and 4. These two passages, which pertain to whether or not it is possible to see God without His intermediaries, illustrate the importance of considering the Biblical verse(s) under discussion and the literary genre of Philo's writings. A contradiction occurs between *QG* 4.2 and 4. In *QG* 4.2, Philo claims that one cannot see God alone without His powers. In *QG* 4.4, however, he declares that Abraham does in fact see God in His oneness.

Upon closer scrutiny, one can trace this contradiction to the two Biblical verses each passage is interpreting, Gen. 18:2 and 3. *QG* 4.2 addresses a difficulty posed by Gen. 18:1 and 2. In these verses, it says, "And God appeared to him by the oak of Mamre, as he sat at the door of his tent at midday. Lifting up his eyes, he saw, and behold, three men stood before him."[74]

Dan and Frank Talmage (Cambridge: Association for Jewish Studies, 1982), 15–39. For some other related treatments, see n. 55.

[71] Völker, *Fortschritt und Vollendung*, esp. 279–317.

[72] Goodenough, *Introduction to Philo Judaeus*, esp. 13–14, 134–60; this point of view is presupposed in idem, *By Light, Light*.

[73] Winston, "Was Philo a Mystic?" 15, 26.

[74] My translation, based upon the LXX. The Hebrew has YHWH, the Greek has θεός.

In *QG* 4.2, Philo responds to the contradiction posed between verse 1, which says that "God appeared," and verse 2, which says that "three men" were standing before Abraham. He solves this problem by arguing that God cannot be seen alone as a unity but only together with His two powers, thereby giving the appearance of three.

In Gen. 18:3, however, Abraham addresses the three men of verse 2 with a singular noun, Κύριε, Lord. Philo notices that Abraham addresses the three as one and claims that now Abraham's mind "forms an impression with more open eyes and more lucid vision," and therefore he is able to perceive God as one. In direct contradiction, then, to what he says in *QG* 4.2, namely, that "God cannot be seen in His oneness without something (else) ...," Philo states in *QG* 4.4 that God now shows Himself in His unity.[75]

The proximity of these contradictory statements is rather striking. Yet because the QGE commentary is written in a format of discrete questions and answers, the contradictions can stand side by side. Although this format is unique to QGE, it does highlight an important feature of Philo's writing that must be taken into account elsewhere when one deals with his many contradictions: as a careful exegete, Philo can be so verse-focused that he may contradict himself from one moment to the next.[76]

Her. 68–85. This passage concerning ecstasy illustrates the importance of taking into account the Biblical verse Philo is interpreting, because the passage shows how a particular phrase in a verse may "trigger" a certain kind of interpretation. In *Her.* 69–70, Philo discusses Gen. 15:4, in which God tells Abraham, "He who shall come out of thee shall be thy heir." Focusing upon the words, "He who shall *come out of* thee" (my emphasis), Philo interprets this verse allegorically to mean that the true "heir of divine and incorporeal things" (*Her.* 63) is the soul or mind that leaves behind or "comes out of" the body, sense perception, speech, and finally, itself. He thus exhorts the soul to

> escape from yourself and stand outside yourself, being inspired like possessed people and corybants and being God-possessed as if in a sort of prophetic trance. For when the mind is divinely possessed and no longer in itself but is wildly excited and driven mad by a yearning for heaven and is led by the One who really is and

---

75 *QG* 4.2 also says, "For when the mind begins to have an apprehension of the Existent One, He is known to have arrived there, making (Himself) unique, and appearing as chief and sovereign." While the meaning of this remark is somewhat unclear, it may be suggesting that the mind *is* capable of perceiving God as one. In *Abr.* 119–23, in which Philo interprets the same Biblical passage, he makes explicit that there are two stages of apprehension, thus resolving the ambiguity. In one stage, the mind can perceive God as one; in another, lower stage, it perceives Him as three.

76 See Kugel, "Two Introductions to Midrash," 145–47.

is drawn up to Him, with truth going ahead and removing [obstacles] before the feet so that it may walk upon a smooth road—this is the heir. (*Her.* 69–70, my translation)[77]

The Biblical words, "come out of," then, lead Philo to talk about the mind leaving itself behind. One can easily see how he might be moved to talk here about ecstasy which means, literally, a standing outside.[78]

Factors That May Influence Philo's Discussion of Seeing God

The examples just discussed illustrate how certain factors may influence what Philo says about seeing God. These and other factors are summarized below.

1. *Exegetical Context.* Both passages above highlight how important the exegetical function may be in Philo's remarks about seeing God. His interpretation in *QG* 4.2 and 4 about God's powers and the capacity of the human mind to see is completely different from the one in *Her.* 68–85, which focuses upon ecstasy and divine possession. In large part, this is because the Scriptural verses behind each passage present different problems. *QG* 4.2 and 4 mention God's powers as a way of addressing the Scriptural fluctuation in Gen. 18:1–3 in portraying the number of Abraham's visitors as one or as three. In contrast, *Her.* talks about ecstasy—to some extent at least—because of the textual trigger of the words in Gen. 15:4 about coming "out."

One can also point to other passages, however, in which·Philo similarly interprets going "outside" as the mind attributing the source of its powers to God but in which he does not speak about ecstasy.[79] Thus, while attention to the relationship between Philo's ideas and the verses he is interpreting is important, clearly this factor alone is not enough to account for his various inconsistencies in describing the experience of seeing God.

---

[77] In *Her.* 70, it is unclear whether Philo is speaking about God, the One that really is, as ὁ ὄντως ὤν (m.) or τὸ ὄντως ὄν (n.), since the expression appears in the genitive. Later in the passage, the pronoun αὐτό appears, though different manuscripts have different readings: αυτω, αὐτόν, αὐτήν (see Leopold Cohn and Paul Wendland, eds., *Philonis Alexandrini: Opera Quae Supersunt* [Berlin: Reimer, 1898; repr., Berlin: de Gruyter, 1962], 3:16). I have followed the reading "αὐτόν," understanding the first expression to be ὁ ὄντως ὤν.

[78] Philo goes on to explain that the mind leaving itself behind signifies that the mind recognizes the limits of its own abilities and acknowledges God as the true source of these abilities (*Her.* 73–74). In this way, the mind becomes the heir of divine things. In *Her.* 78, Philo links the one who goes "outside" with the one who sees God, "Israel," thereby implicitly connecting ecstasy with seeing God.

[79] See, e.g., *Her.* 75–78 on Gen. 15:5 and the series of interpretations of this verse and others in *Leg.* 3.39–48.

2. *Different Traditions.* Another possible explanation for these inconsistencies is that Philo may be drawing from different exegetical traditions which emphasize different elements.[80] Although the two examples given above are both about the experience of the soul, their different concerns may well reflect the existence of different pre-Philonic traditions. One tradition, for example, may focus upon God and His powers or intermediaries (*QG* 4.2 and 4), while another may concentrate upon the journey of the soul itself (*Her.* 68–85).

3. *Literary Genre.* The literary form of Philo's different commentaries may also influence his presentation. *QG* 4.2 and 4, for example, are from QGE—a series of separate questions and answers about individual verses or problems—whose form does not necessarily require resolution of contradictions from one unit to the next. Although the Allegory and the Exposition are also composed largely of discrete interpretations of different Scriptural problems, the treatise format in these series calls for linking together—however loosely—the units of interpretation and perhaps for smoothing over or at least addressing glaring contradictions.[81]

4. *Philo's Audience(s).* Since Philo may be addressing different audiences in his different commentaries, he may very well adapt his discussions to suit his readers.[82] It is particularly striking, for example, that on the whole he refers to seeing God much less frequently in the Exposition than in the other two exegetical series. Moreover, unlike the Allegory and QGE, in which he sometimes mentions seeing God in passing, when Philo does speak about seeing God in the Exposition, he generally provides some elaboration.[83] Finally—again, in contrast to the other two series—Philo's remarks in the Exposition rarely mention intermediaries.[84]

---

[80] The possible existence of earlier traditions in Philo's work has been explored in different ways by a number of scholars. See n. 49 in the Introduction.

[81] Similar requirements of literary genre, for example, may lead Philo to tie together in *Abr.* 119–23 the disparate explanations found in *QG* 4.2 and 4. See above, n. 75.

[82] For a consideration of Philo's audience(s), see the Introduction.

[83] Examples in which Philo discusses seeing God at length in the Exposition are *Opif.* 69–71; *Abr.* 57–59, 77–80, 119–123; *Spec.* 1.36–50; *Virt.* 215–17; and *Praem.* 36–46. He mentions seeing God considerably less, if at all, in *Ios.*, *Mos.* 1–2, *Decal.*, and *Spec.* 2–4. Cf., however, *Mos.* 1.66, 158, 272, 289, and *Mos.* 2.69, which report but do not expand upon vision experiences described in the Bible. This question of how Philo may approach this topic differently in his various writings requires further investigation.

[84] *Abr.* 119–23 (see nn. 75 and 81) and *Spec.* 1.45–50 are exceptions to this observation. As an example of the contrast between the Allegory and the Exposition, compare *Somn.* 1.129 of the Allegory with *Praem.* 43–46 in the Exposition. In *Somn.* 1.129, the λόγος (Logos) changes Jacob's name to "Israel, the one who sees," while in *Praem.* 43–46, "Israel" is granted the vision of God through God Himself. Philo's discussion of intermediaries in the three series requires further investigation.

A possible explanation for these observations is that in the Exposition, Philo may be addressing a less sophisticated readership than in the Allegory and QGE. This might account for why he refers to seeing God less frequently, why he goes out of his way to explain himself when he does talk about seeing God, and why he generally avoids the more complex issue of intermediaries, an issue he may reserve for "advanced seers."

5. *The Nature of Seeing God.* Finally, the factors listed above—though certainly important—may not be sufficient to explain Philo's many inconsistencies about seeing God, because the very experience itself may defy any single description. Thus, seeing God may vary from one individual to another and may also vary from one time to the next for the same person. Philo himself may experience or even just conceive of this vision in different ways, sometimes as a rational perception, and sometimes as an ecstatic rapture. Perhaps only when we consider all the perspectives mentioned here—including the possibility that the experience itself may vary—will we be closer to understanding Philo's many contradictory statements.

One may choose then from a number of solutions to how Philo perceives the experience of seeing God, what sources may influence his notions about this experience, and where he derives his etymology for "Israel." What remains important for this investigation, however, is the way he brings "Israel" together with seeing God and the way this combination functions in his works. Although the etymology ὁρῶν θεόν may have originally been linked with Jacob's vision narrated in Genesis 32, Philo understands seeing God in a radically different manner from the Bible. Because he places a supreme value upon seeing God, Philo accords "Israel," the ὁρῶν θεόν, a special place in his thought. It is now time for us to determine who belongs to this special Philonic entity.

CHAPTER THREE

"ISRAEL" AND THE ONES WHO CAN SEE

By examining passages which explicitly mention "Israel," we discovered that Philo uses "Israel" most frequently with reference to seeing or seeing God, an association that derives from his etymology for the term as ὁρῶν θεόν, or one that sees God. We shall now seek to understand how Philo identifies "Israel" as a group that can see and to determine what relationship, if any, this group may have to the historical Biblical people or to Philo's Jewish contemporaries.

To accomplish these aims, it is first necessary to collect all references to "Israel" as an entity that can see, whether Philo mentions "Israel" explicitly or uses substitute expressions such as ὁ [or τὸ] ὁρῶν [τὸν] θεόν, the one that sees God; ὁ ὁρῶν, the one that sees; or τὸ ὁρατικὸν γένος, the race/class that can see. Before we consider these references in detail, a few preliminary observations are in order about the selection of passages and Philo's vocabulary.

Selection of Passages

When Philo talks about "Israel" as an entity that sees God, he may interpret "Israel" as a soul, mind, individual, or race/class. Sometimes too he describes "Israel" as vision or contemplation. Since we are interested in learning about the possible social identity of "Israel," I shall concentrate only upon those etymologically-related interpretations of "Israel" which may refer to people—whether individuals or collectivities—and leave behind the abstract interpretations, like the soul or the mind, which are impossible to identify with real persons.[1]

---

[1] Below are Philo's etymologically-related interpretations that refer to abstractions. I have omitted some additional adjectives. Translations are mine. The interpretations are as follows: ἡ ὁρατικὴ διάνοια, the mind that can see (*Migr.* 14, *Congr.* 56 [here the phrase has αὐτός, Him, as an object, referring to God, θεός]); ὁ ὁρατικὸς καὶ φιλοθεάμων νοῦς, the mind that can see and loves to contemplate (*Mut.* 209); ἡ ὁρατικὴ ψυχή, the soul that can see (*Ebr.* 111, *Fug.* 139); ὁ ὁρατικὸς τρόπος, the character that can see (*Plant.* 60); ἡ φιλοθεάμων ψυχή, the soul that loves to contemplate (*Her.* 79, *Mut.* 88); αἱ φιλοθεάμονες διάνοιαι, minds that love to contemplate (*Fug.* 138); ὅρασις θεοῦ, vision of God (*Ebr.* 82); ὅρασις ψυχῆς, sight of the soul (*Conf.* 72); θεωρία ἡ τοῦ μονοῦ σοφοῦ, contemplation of the only wise being (*Sacr.* 120); ὁ νοῦς θεωρητικὸς θεοῦ τε καὶ κόσμου, the mind that is able to contemplate God and the cosmos (*Somn.* 2.173); τὸ θεωρητικὸν τῶν τῆς φύσεως πραγμάτων ἔρνος, the plant able to survey the things of nature (*Her.* 279);

Although in the Pentateuch—the focus of most of Philo's exegetical activity—"Israel" may refer to either the patriarch Jacob/Israel or the nation of his descendants, in Philo's exegesis, both the patriarch Israel and the nation Israel may be called ὁ [or τὸ] ὁρῶν [τὸν] θεόν. To understand, therefore, what Philo means by "Israel, the one that sees God," we shall consider all references to "Israel" as the one that sees, regardless of whether these references correspond in the Bible to the patriarch or the nation.

Finally, Philo often uses periphrastic expressions for "Israel" where the term itself does not appear, both within Biblical quotations and in interpretations where the periphrasis clearly signifies "Israel." To collect all references to seers whom Philo equates with "Israel," then, I have gathered evidence not only from passages in which "Israel" appears explicitly, but also from several studies of how Philo uses words related to seeing.[2]

"Israel Seers" and Others

What emerges from these several studies is that Philo mentions those who see in a variety of contexts, and it is sometimes difficult to determine whether or not he equates these seers with "Israel." Obviously, references to those who see in a purely physical sense are not relevant to this study since "Israel"'s distinction is its ability to see in a philosophical sense. The relevance of some other references, however, is less clear.

In a surprising number of cases, for example, Philo may be using the language of seeing metaphorically to describe people with keen intelligence, whom he does not necessarily identify with "Israel." He speaks, for instance, about Scriptural interpreters or simply people who have special insight as οἱ ὁρατικοί and οἱ ὁρᾶν δυνάμενοι (both of which mean

---

τὸ ψυχῆς ὄμμα ὃ δὴ μόνον τὸν θεὸν ὁρᾶν πεπαίδευται, the soul's best eye which alone has been trained to see God (*Mut.* 203); ὁ ψυχῆς ὀφθαλμὸς ὁ διαυγέστατος καὶ καθαρώτατος καὶ πάντων ὀξυωπέστατος ᾧ μόνῳ τὸν θεὸν ἔξεστι καθορᾶν, the eye of the soul, most translucent, most pure, and most sharp-sighted of all, the eye to which alone it is permitted to behold God (*Conf.* 92).

[2] The passages selected are based upon studies of the following words: ἀναβλέπω, look up; βλέπω, see; εἴδω, οἶδα, see, know; θέα, sight; θεάομαι, behold; θεωρέω, behold, contemplate; θεωρητικός, contemplative; θεωρία, contemplation; καθοράω, see distinctly; ὄμμα, eye; ὀξυδερκέω, see sharply; ὀξυδερκής, sharp-sighted; ὀξυωπής, sharp-sighted; ὅρασις, sight; ὁρατικός, able to see; ὁράω, see; ὀφθαλμός, eye; ὄψις, sight, eye; φιλοθεάμων, fond of contemplating. All of these words are suggested by the various expressions for seeing that occur in passages in which "Israel" appears explicitly, as discussed in Chapter Two. The list does not exhaust all Philonic words connected to sight and therefore some references to seers may be missing. Because the list does capture Philo's basic vocabulary in this area, however, the results are certainly representative of his references to those who see. I have also identified two additional passages about "seers" (*Prob.* 74 and *Spec.* 2.44–48) through a careful reading of Philo's works.

"those who can see") or οἱ ὀξὺ καθορᾶν δυνάμενοι (those who can see sharply). He also talks of οἱ φιλοθεάμονες, those who are fond of contemplating. Since these expressions may apply generally to any people who fit the description, and since Philo does not specifically call them "Israel," we cannot know for sure whether they are "Israel" or not.[3]

Besides these somewhat general characterizations of people whose identity remains vague, Philo sometimes describes specific persons like Abraham, Jacob, Moses, or an individual Israelite as seers.[4] He also points out—presumably on the basis of 1 Sam. 9:9—that prophets were formerly called seers (ὁρῶντες or βλέποντες).[5] All these people may be part of "Israel," though they are certainly not equivalent to it.

Finally, in a small number of cases, Philo refers unambiguously to particular contemporary social entities as people who can see. Especially significant is that some of these "seers" are not Jews. Examples include the Persian Magi, who "silently make research into the facts of nature to gain knowledge of the truth and through visions (ἐμφάσεις) clearer than

---

[3] Expressions for seers whom we cannot identify with "Israel" are listed below. Translations are my own. The expressions are as follows: οἱ ὁρατικοί, those who can see (Somn. 1.39, Decal. 26); οἱ ὁρατικοὶ ἄνδρες, men who can see (Plant. 36); οἱ ὀξυδερκέστερον ὁρῶντες, those who see fairly sharply (Decal. 7); οἱ ὀξὺ καθορᾶν δυνάμενοι, those who can see sharply (Opif. 76, Somn. 2.3); οἱ φιλοθεάμονες, those who are fond of contemplating (Opif. 158, Ebr. 124, Migr. 191, Somn. 1.39); οἱ ὀξυδερκοῦντες, those who see sharply (Ebr. 88); οἱ διάνοιαν ὀξυδερκοῦντες, those who see sharply with the mind (Somn. 1.11, Somn. 2.171, Decal. 82); οἷς τὸ τῆς διανοίας ὄμμα ὀξυδερκεῖ, those in whom the eye of the mind sees sharply (Ios. 106); οἱ ὀξὺ τῇ διανοίᾳ βλέπειν δυνάμενοι, those who can see sharply with the mind (Mos. 1.188); τὸ ὀξυωπέστατον γένος, the most sharp-sighted race/class (Migr. 46); ἀσώματα ὅσοι καὶ γυμνὰ θεωρεῖν τὰ πράγματα δύνανται, as many as can contemplate incorporeal and naked facts (Abr. 236).

In QGE, the following expressions are in the LCL English translation, but there are no parallel Greek fragments to verify Philo's original language: "those who are able to see from afar what is distant with the sharp-sighted eyes of the mind" (QG 2.65); "those who are able to see" (QG 4.2).

For more elaborate descriptions of seers who cannot be clearly identified with "Israel," see Spec. 1.37; Spec. 2.44–48 (see also below, n. 39); Spec. 4.115; Praem. 26; Prob. 63, 74. In one passage (Spec. 3.161), Philo speaks about people as "seers" who cannot clearly be equated with "Israel," at a specific historical moment. Here, he narrates an incident in which a regional tax collector wreaked vengeance upon the relatives of debtors who had fled. To escape torture, some of these relatives took their own lives. Philo describes them as people "who perceived more clearly through their souls than through their eyes."

[4] Expressions that describe specific individuals are as follows: ὁ βλέπων, the seeing one: Leg. 2.93 (Moses); ὁ ὁρῶν, the seeing one: Leg. 3.24 (Abraham), 38 (an individual Israelite); Cher. 67 (Jacob, but not "Israel"; here ὁρῶν has as an object ἡ ἄποιος φύσις, the nature without quality); Somn. 1.33 (Reuben—this reference, however, may imply physical seeing); ὁ τοῦ ὄντος ὁρατικός, the one that can see the Existent: Ebr. 107 (Abraham).

[5] Deus 139, Migr. 38, Her. 78, QG 4.138 (here the Greek is uncertain).

speech give and receive the revelations of divine excellency" (*Prob.* 74);
the Athenians, who are "the most sharp-sighted (ὀξυδερκέστατοι) in mind
—for as the pupil is in the eye or reason in the soul, so is Athens in
Greece" (*Prob.* 140, my translation); philosophers of Greek and foreign
lands, who are "the best observers (θεωροί) of nature and all things in it"
(*Spec.* 2.45, my translation); and the Therapeutae, who strive to see God
(*Contempl.* 11; cf. *Contempl.* 64, 66, 90). Even though the treatise about the
Therapeutae depicts them as people who strive to see God and portrays
them implicitly as Jews (Philo never calls them "Jews"), we still cannot
determine their relationship to "Israel." "Seers," "Israel," and "Jews,"
then, are not always synonymous.

To distinguish between those seers who are clearly identical to "Israel"
and those who are not, I shall call the two groups "Israel seers" and "other
seers," respectively. At present we are interested only in the "Israel seers,"
to learn whether or not they correspond to an identifiable social group. It is
interesting, however, that although Philo never calls the "other seers"
"Israel" per se, he does occasionally describe them with expressions quite
similar to ones he also uses for "Israel." Indeed, though he never says so
directly, Philo may even consider these people to be part of "Israel." I shall
address this possibility below, in the section entitled "The Members of
'Israel.'"

Philo's Vocabulary

Because Philo refers to "Israel seers" and "other seers" in a similar way,
we must pay careful attention to his vocabulary. Does he in fact have a
"technical" language for "Israel" apart from his expressions for "other
seers"? That is, does he use any expressions that always refer only to
"Israel"? Conversely, does he have a distinctive vocabulary for groups that
may or may not be "Israel"? Finally, what expressions, if any, does Philo
use both for "Israel" and for "other seers"?

The results of my examination show that Philo does indeed have a
"technical" vocabulary for "Israel"—the etymology ὁρῶν θεόν and the
phrase τὸ ὁρατικὸν γένος, the race or class that can see. Whenever these
expressions occur, they always signify "Israel," whether the word appears
explicitly or not.[6] In addition, Philo frequently uses a shortened form of

---

[6] The etymology ὁρῶν θεόν appears with or without the definite article eighteen
times in the extant Greek works and once in *QG* 3.49, where the Greek is uncertain.
The passages from the extant Greek works are as follows: *Leg.* 3.38, 172, 186, 212; *Sacr.*
134; *Post.* 63, 92; *Conf.* 56; *Her.* 78; *Congr.* 51; *Fug.* 208; *Mut.* 81 (2); *Somn.* 1.171; *Somn.*
2.173; *Abr.* 57; *Praem.* 44; *Legat.* 4. Two of these references are equated with abstractions
and are therefore not included in my examination of passages: *Leg.* 3.186, in which
the expression is τὸ ὁρῶν τὸν θεόν (n.) and refers to the part of the mind (νοῦς) that

the etymology (ὁρῶν or sometimes βλέπων) to mean "Israel," but these words can also describe any person that sees, whether the seeing is physical or philosophical.[7]

Philo's technical vocabulary for "Israel" may function in different ways. The etymology or one of its shortened forms, for example, may serve as an explanatory comment, an appositive, a substitute, or an alternative expression for "Israel." Similarly, the phrase ὁρατικὸν γένος may function as either a substitute or alternative phrase for "Israel." (Unlike the etymology, this phrase never serves as an explanation or an appositive.)

Thus, when Philo writes explicitly that "Israel" means "one that sees God" or when he uses similar words to indicate that the etymology provides the meaning of "Israel," then the etymology functions as an *explanation*.[8] When he writes, "Israel, the one that sees God," the etymology serves as an *appositive*. Sometimes, too, "Israel" serves as an appositive for the etymology.[9] Finally, ὁρῶν θεόν and ὁρατικὸν γένος function as *substitutes* for "Israel" when the word "Israel" does not appear in the immediate passage; when the word "Israel" does appear in the passage, then these phrases serve as *alternative expressions*.[10]

---

sees God, and *Somn.* 2.173, in which the etymology explains what "Israel" means, but "Israel" symbolizes "the mind that is able to contemplate God and the cosmos" (see n. 1).

The expression τὸ ὁρατικὸν γένος appears eleven times in the extant Greek works and possibly four other times in QGE where the Greek is uncertain. The extant Greek passages are as follows: *Deus* 144; *Conf.* 91; *Migr.* 18, 54 (here the phrase is τὸ ὁρατικὸν τοῦ ὄντος γένος, the race/class that can see the Existent); *Fug.* 140; *Mut.* 109, 189; *Somn.* 2.276, 279; *Mos.* 2.196 (here the phrase is amplified as follows: τὸ ὁρατικὸν καὶ ἐπιστημονικὸν γένος, the race/class that can see and know); *QE* 2.46 (this passage has a Greek fragment in which the phrase appears). The *QE* passages where the Greek is uncertain are *QE* 1.21; *QE* 2.42, 43, 76.

[7] ὁρῶν stands for "Israel" thirteen times in the extant Greek works and in QGE possibly four times, but the Greek is uncertain. Passages in which ὁρῶν stands for "Israel" in the extant Greek works are *Leg.* 2.34; *Leg.* 3.15; *Sobr.* 13; *Conf.* 146, 148, 159; *Migr.* 21, 39, 113, 125; *Somn.* 1.129; *Somn.* 2.23, 44. In *Somn.* 2.23, the plural ὁρῶντες is used. *Conf.* 146 is not included in the examination of passages because "Israel," the ὁρῶν, is equated with an abstraction, the λόγος (Logos). (This passage is discussed in the previous chapter in connection with the *Prayer of Joseph*.) Passages in QGE in which the Greek is uncertain are *QG* 4.233; *QE* 2.38, 47 (2). For passages in which βλέπων stands for "Israel," see below, n. 20.

[8] E.g., *Congr.* 51, *Fug.* 208, *Abr.* 57, *Praem.* 44, *QG* 3.49, *QG* 4.233, *Legat.* 4.

[9] E.g., *Leg.* 2.34; *Conf.* 56; *Migr.* 113, 125, 224; *Somn.* 1.129, 171; *Somn.* 2.44. In some of these examples, the shorter form of the etymology, i.e., ὁρῶν or βλέπων is used.

[10] For the etymology or a shorter form as a substitute, see, e.g., *Leg.* 3.15, 81, 172; *Sobr.* 13; *Conf.* 159; *QE* 2.47. For the etymology as an alternative expression, see, e.g., *Leg.* 3.212; *Sacr.* 134; *Post.* 63, 92. Passages in which the phrase ὁρατικὸν γένος serves as a substitute include *Migr.* 18; *Fug.* 140; *Mut.* 109, 189; *Somn.* 2.276; *Mos.* 1.196; *QE* 1.21; *QE* 2.42, 43, 46, 76. Passages in which ὁρατικὸν γένος serves as an alternative expression include *Deus* 144, *Conf.* 91, *Migr.* 54, *Somn.* 2.279.

In contrast to ὁρῶν θεόν and ὁρατικὸν γένος, Philo's other formulations cannot be categorized as technical expressions in the same way, either because they are used for both the "Israel seers" and the "other seers" or because no one expression occurs with significant frequency.

The only terms used for both sets of "seers" are οἱ ὁρατικοί, those who can see, and οἱ ὁρῶντες, those who see.[11] An expression for "Israel seers" which is used twice (*Agr.* 81, *Fug.* 19) and does not have an exact parallel among the "other seers" is οἱ ὀξὺ καθορῶντες, those who see sharply. On the other hand, examples of expressions for "other seers" which have no exact parallels among the terms for "Israel seers" are οἱ φιλοθεάμονες, those who are fond of contemplating; οἱ ὁρᾶν δυνάμενοι, those who can see; οἱ ὀξὺ καθορᾶν δυνάμενοι, those who can see sharply; and οἱ διάνοιαν ὀξυδερκοῦντες, those who see sharply with their minds.[12] These terms, however, do not differ significantly in meaning from those which clearly do describe "Israel." Indeed all these expressions carry much the same meaning and denote groups that can see.

The Relationship Between the Etymology ὁρῶν θεόν and the Phrase ὁρατικὸν γένος

Since ὁρῶν θεόν (one that sees God) and τὸ ὁρατικὸν γένος (the race/class that can see) are two expressions which always refer only to "Israel," it may be worth reflecting briefly upon how they may be related. While Philo uses ὁρῶν θεόν—which is singular—for both the patriarch Israel and the nation of his descendants, the expression ὁρατικὸν γένος by definition describes a collectivity.

As a term for collective Israel, ὁρατικὸν γένος represents an interpretation, or at least a further application, of the etymology ὁρῶν θεόν. First, the expression extends the ability to see from "one who sees"—as conveyed in the singular participle ὁρῶν—to an entire race or class (γένος). Second, "God" as the "object" seen drops out, so that while the ability to see is explicitly ascribed to collective "Israel," the ability to see God per se remains implicit.

As we observed in the previous chapter, Philo probably derived from another source his etymology for "Israel," which originally may have been linked to Jacob's struggle and his naming of Peniel (Gen. 32:25–33). In Philo's thought, this etymology holds great significance because of the supreme importance he places upon seeing God. Philo's understanding of

---

[11] οἱ ὁρατικοί, those who can see: *Plant.* 46 (here the referent is "Israel"); *Somn.* 1.39 and *Decal.* 24 (here the referent is unclear). οἱ ὁρῶντες, those who see: *Somn.* 2.23 (here the referent is "Israel"); *Deus* 139 and *Her.* 78 (here the word describes prophets).

[12] For other examples, see n. 3.

seeing God, however, is quite different from the kind of seeing implied in the Genesis narrative.

Like the etymology, the expression ὁρατικὸν γένος may have had a similar pre-Philonic history. Appearing throughout Philo's exegetical writings and within both literal and symbolic interpretations, this expression may also be an inherited commonplace, which originally served simply as a title for the nation Israel. Accordingly, ὁρατικὸν γένος may have been an exegetical "family name" adapted from the "eponymous ancestor" ὁρῶν θεόν, [the] one that sees God.[13] As such, the phrase ὁρατικὸν γένος may not originally have denoted the kind of seeing Philo associates with it. Instead, this expression too may have been linked to the experience narrated in Genesis 32 of its eponymous ancestor "Israel," [the] one that sees God, or perhaps to a separate experience in the nation's history, such as the revelation at Mount Sinai (see, e.g., Exod. 20:22).

Both ὁρῶν θεόν and ὁρατικὸν γένος, then, may have changed in meaning over time. We have just observed that the kind of seeing originally denoted by each term is quite different from Philo's philosophical conceptions of seeing God. A second important observation is that occasionally when Philo uses these expressions, the ability to see or to see God does not add any meaning to the discussion. (Here, of course, I am speaking of seeing in the philosophical sense.) Instead, the terms are simply equivalent names or automatic substitutes for "Israel."

When the ability to see or to see God is relevant to the passage, the titles carry their "semantic weight," that is, they seem to emphasize the sense of people who can really see or see God. When the ability to see is not relevant, then this ability appears to exist in name only. Thus, in the same way that someone today with the surname "Baker" is not necessarily a baker or someone with the surname "Little" is not necessarily of small stature, so too, the entity called ὁρῶν θεόν or ὁρατικὸν γένος may not necessarily be spiritually sighted.

In brief, then, the kind of seeing originally signified by ὁρῶν θεόν and ὁρατικὸν γένος may have been quite different from the kind of seeing which Philo so highly values; and, in some Philonic contexts, the ability to see or see God is not relevant, so that these expressions appear merely as automatic equivalents for "Israel." These two observations highlight the possibility that ὁρῶν θεόν and ὁρατικὸν γένος may have gradually

---

[13] In the Bible, the nation Israel derives its name from the patriarch Jacob/Israel. Thus Israel the patriarch is the eponymous ancestor, i.e., the original founder whose name becomes attached to the descendant nation. In the case of the etymology, my argument is that ὁρῶν θεόν serves somewhat inexactly as an "eponymous ancestor" of the "descendant" ὁρατικὸν γένος. While the γένος does not have precisely the same name, i.e., ὁρῶν θεόν, the adjective ὁρατικόν is adapted from the original etymology.

acquired different nuances from their original ones. In Chapter One, we also saw that the term "Israel" itself has a history in which it has been understood in different ways. Let us examine more closely, then, how all three terms—ὁρῶν θεόν (one that sees God), ὁρατικὸν γένος (race/class that can see), and "Israel"—evolved or may have evolved in meaning over time.

Evolution in Use of Terms: A Hypothesis

The Etymology

As we saw in the last chapter, external evidence suggests the etymology ὁρῶν θεόν was part of a common exegetical vocabulary which Philo inherited. Scholars have speculated that it may be based upon an original Hebrew etymology, איש ראה אל, a man [who] saw/sees God, and may be derived from Jacob's encounter described in Genesis 32. Although Philo himself never uses an equivalent for איש, man, some other Greek and Latin sources have ἀνὴρ or ἄνθρωπος ὁρῶν θεόν.[14] Most of these sources are later than Philo, but one—the *Prayer of Joseph*—may be contemporary to him. This work gives the etymology as ἀνὴρ ὁρῶν θεόν, a man who sees God.

In the last chapter, I also suggested that Philo himself—or perhaps an earlier tradition—may purposely drop a word for איש, man, from the etymology in order to separate it from identification with the historical patriarch and his descendants; to allow for more flexibility to interpret the etymology as an abstraction, like the mind, soul, or λόγος (Logos); or to downplay the impression that a man could possibly see God. Elimination of a word for "man," then, may enable Philo to distance the etymology from its original association with the patriarch's encounter in Genesis 32 and to emphasize instead the contemporary philosophical importance of seeing God.

As we have noted, Philo discusses the philosophical importance of seeing God not only in relation to "Israel," but also in other contexts.[15] Accordingly, seeing God may have had an independent philosophical significance, which eventually became connected with the etymology. At some point—perhaps even before Philo—the philosophical importance of the ability to see God may have added to or even replaced the original historical significance implied by the etymology. This specific case,

---

[14] For specific references, see Lampe, *Patristic Greek Lexicon*, 678, under "Ἰσραήλ"; and Smith, "The Prayer of Joseph," *Religions*, 266, n. 3.
[15] E.g., *Opif.* 69–71; *Somn.* 1.64–67; *Somn.* 2.226–27; *Abr.* 119–30; *Contempl.* 11; *QG* 4.138, 196; *QE* 2.51.

whereby "Israel, the one that sees God," acquires a contemporary meaning is simply representative of a broader approach to the Bible, whereby all of Scripture is read as the embodiment of contemporary truths.

The Phrase ὁρατικὸν γένος

The case for an evolution in meaning of ὁρατικὸν γένος is built upon similar assumptions to those just described. Unfortunately, we do not have external evidence, as we do with the etymology, to claim that ὁρατικὸν γένος belongs to a common vocabulary. Philo is the only writer who uses this precise phrase, and variations occur only twice in later patristic sources.[16] The argument offered below, then, is based upon observations only about Philo's works themselves.

Despite the lack of outside evidence, however, one *can* point to some distinct differences within the Philonic works. In *QE*, for example, as we shall see, the phrase ὁρατικὸν γένος appears to serve only as an automatic replacement for "Israel," because the ability to see is not relevant. Since the contexts of the *QE* interpretations do not provide positive information, we cannot decisively identify the ὁρατικὸν γένος with any particular group, although two passages favor understanding this entity as Biblical Israel.

In the Exposition, specifically in *Mos.* 2.196, the phrase ὁρατικὸν γένος occurs once as a description of the Biblical nation, although Philo does not use the word "Israel" in this treatise. Here, the ability to see does contribute to the meaning of the interpretation. In this passage, then, it is clear that Philo uses ὁρατικὸν γένος to designate the Biblical nation and that he also intends the phrase to highlight the nation's ability to "see."

Finally, in the Allegory, the phrase ὁρατικὸν γένος functions in a variety of ways. It may, for example, serve as an automatic substitute for "Israel" when the word itself does not appear or as an alternative expression when it does appear. In some contexts, the ability to see is relevant to the meaning of the passage, while in other contexts, it is not. Most important, none of the passages ever provides enough information to allow conclusive identification of the ὁρατικὸν γένος, so that whether the phrase is a mere title or a meaningful description, we cannot link it with any particular social group.

The different characteristics, just described, among Philo's various writings may be related to his different aims and audiences for each series, as I shall suggest at the end of this chapter. These differences may

---

16 The phrase διορατικὸν γένος occurs once in Origen, *Fragmenta in Evangelium Joannis* 26:1, and once in Eusebius, *Demonstratio Evangelica* 4:7:2.

also, however, reflect different stages in the way the phrase ὁρατικὸν γένος was understood.

Originally, this phrase may have served simply as a title for the Biblical or post-Biblical nation Israel, descendants of an ancestor who saw God, or themselves a nation that saw God (e.g., during the revelation at Sinai). At this stage, the phrase ὁρατικὸν γένος may or may not have signified literally their ability to see God. If, in fact, the phrase originally did signify this ability, the kind of seeing it denoted is rather different from Philo's understanding. Indeed, for Philo, the phrase carries added significance because of the contemporary philosophical importance he attaches to seeing and seeing God.

Besides the enhanced meaning conveyed by ὁρατικόν (able to see), we have noted that the word γένος too carries a range of associations in Philo's thought. It can mean a race of people with common ancestry, a class defined by acquired characteristics, an abstract nature or kind, or an original ideal.

In its beginnings, then, ὁρατικὸν γένος may well have been adapted from the etymology ὁρῶν θεόν as a name for the nation or race of Israel. By Philo's time, however, both ὁρατικόν and γένος have acquired additional nuances, allowing the combination of the two words to be understood in several senses at once.

"Israel"

This term began to evolve in meaning well before Philo. In the Five Books of Moses, "Israel" refers specifically to the patriarch Jacob/Israel or his descendant nation. In some prophetic books of the Bible, the name also indicates the Northern Kingdom as distinct from the Southern Kingdom of Judah. With time, "Israel" seems to have acquired a self-referential function. Depending upon who is using the word, "Israel" may designate any of a variety of groups—all Jews, a subset of the Jews, or a redefined group which may or may not include Jews.[17]

Philo most frequently interprets "Israel" in relation to seeing or seeing God. Only once, in *Legat.*, does he equate "Israel" with a real social group, namely, his Jewish contemporaries. In all other cases, it is difficult to identify "Israel" decisively with any social group. In the works which concentrate upon Scriptural verses about the Biblical nation Israel (*Mos.* 1–2 and *QE* 1–2), the word "Israel" itself is conspicuously absent. Most

---

[17] See Danell, *Studies in the Name Israel*; Kuhn, "Ἰσραήλ, Ἰουδαῖος, Ἑβραῖος"; Gutbrod, "Ἰουδαῖος, Ἰσραήλ, Ἑβραῖος"; Neusner, "Israel: Judaism and Its Social Metaphors"; idem, *Judaism and Its Social Metaphors.*

probably, Philo avoids this term here because for him "Israel" has a different connotation, namely, as the group of people that sees or sees God.

With these considerations in mind, we can now turn to passages in which Philo speaks about "Israel seers" to try and identify a referent for them. I shall use the word "referent" to describe the social, ethnic, or political group[s] Philo may have in mind when he uses various terms or expressions for "Israel seers." Our task, then, is to determine which people Philo is referring to when he speaks about those who see who are "Israel."

Passages in Which Philo Mentions "Israel Seers"

In all, fifty-four passages describe "Israel" with expressions for seers that may refer to people and not abstractions like the soul or mind.[18] Besides these passages, four others include expressions for seers that may or may not be related to the etymology of "Israel": *Somn.* 1.117, *Somn.* 2.271, *Mos.* 2.271, and *Spec.* 1.54. Since these passages are not clearly related to the etymology, I am simply noting them but not including them in this study.[19]

To describe the "Israel seers" in these passages, Philo uses the following expressions: ὁ [or τὸ] ὁρῶν, the one that sees (15 passages); [ὁ or τὸ] ὁρῶν [τὸν] θεόν, [the] one that sees God (15); τὸ ὁρατικὸν γένος, the race/class that can see (15); ὁ βλέπων, the one that sees (5); ὁ [or τὸ] ὁρατικός [όν], the one that can see (3); and οἱ ὀξὺ καθορῶντες, those who see sharply (2).[20] Philo's most frequent expressions, then, for those who

---

18 For expressions that include abstractions, see n. 1. Also, in three cases (*Leg.* 3.186, *Conf.* 146, and *Somn.* 2.172–73—see above, nn. 6 and 7), even though the expression for seers itself does not include an abstraction, the passage directly links the expression with an abstraction, and so these passages are not counted among the fifty-four. In some other cases, Philo's expressions for seers may be part of an interpretation about the soul or mind, but the link between the expression and the abstraction is unclear. See, e.g., the discussion below of *Migr.* 18 and n. 25.
19 *Somn.* 1.117 and *Somn.* 2.271 are discussed in Chapter Two as comprising Category D—the unclear references. In Somn. 1.117, "Israel" is not explicitly interpreted but serves as an implied contrast to "those who are blind in the eyes of the soul rather than of the body and do not know the rays of virtue" (my translation). *Somn.* 2.271, which interprets Num. 21:17, mentions οἱ φιλοθεάμονες, those who are fond of contemplating, but it is unclear whether these people are intended to correspond to "Israel," which is cited in the verse. *Mos.* 2.271 speaks of the Biblical nation as "the whole people who until recently had been the most sharp-sighted of all the nations" (my translation). Similarly, *Spec.* 1.54 describes apostates—i.e., "members of the nation [who] betray the honour due to the One"—as choosing "darkness in preference to the brightest light and [blindfolding] the mind which had the power of keen vision." In the two latter cases, it is not certain whether the characterizations are related to the etymology for "Israel" or are instead simply metaphorical descriptions.
20 For a list of passages that use ὁρῶν, ὁρῶν θεόν, and ὁρατικὸν γένος, see above, nn. 6

see who are equated with "Israel" are ὁ [or τὸ] ὁρῶν, [ὁ or τὸ] ὁρῶν [τὸν] θεόν, and τὸ ὁρατικὸν γένος.

A few observations about this tally are in order. First, with regard to the counting, since one passage (*Leg.* 3.172) has two different expressions for "Israel seers" (ὁ τὸν θεὸν ὁρῶν and ὁ βλέπων τὸν ὄντα), the number of passages presented above totals fifty-five. In one passage, *Mut.* 81, ὁ ὁρῶν τὸν θεόν appears twice, but the passage is counted only once since the expression is the same. Similarly, in *QE* 2.47, the phrase "the seeing one" —presumably ὁ ὁρῶν—appears twice but the passage is counted only once.

Second, occasionally the terms or expressions listed above appear with variations. In *Leg.* 3.172, for example, ὁ βλέπων, the one that sees, has as an object ὁ ὤν, the One who is. In *Migr.* 54, τὸ ὁρατικὸν γένος has as an object ὁ [τὸ] ὤν [ὄν], the One who (or that, n.) is. Finally, in *Mos.* 2.196, the phrase τὸ ὁρατικὸν γένος is amplified as τὸ ὁρατικὸν καὶ ἐπιστημονικὸν γένος, the race/class able to see and know.

Last, in several QGE passages, the Greek is uncertain, since the passages in question do not have parallel Greek fragments. I have assumed that the Greek phrase ὁρῶν θεόν is behind the translation of "seeing God" in *QG* 3.49, and that ὁ [or τὸ] ὁρῶν and οἱ ὁρῶντες are behind the translations of "one who sees" in *QG* 4.233 and "the seeing one(s)" in *QE* 2.38 and 47.

QE 2.46 is one passage with a parallel Greek fragment in which the expression ὁρατικὸν γένος does occur. In the LCL edition, Ralph Marcus translates this phrase as "contemplative nation." He also uses "contemplative nation," "seeing nation," or the word "contemplative" alone in several other passages. Since the use of ὁρατικὸν γένος is attested to in one passage, and since Philo frequently uses this expression in his other writings, I am assuming that ὁρατικὸν γένος also underlies the other instances in which "contemplative [or seeing] nation" occurs in the English and similarly, that ὁρατικός is the Greek behind "contemplative," when this word appears alone.

Since the Greek is uncertain in a number of cases, the frequency with which some of the expressions occur, as reported above, may not be accurate. The questionable QGE passages are listed in the notes.[21]

As always, in the following discussion, brackets within translations include my own adaptations to translations from the LCL edition. Also, for

---

and 7. βλέπων occurs in *Leg.* 2.46; *Leg.* 3.81, 172 (this passage has ὁ ὤν, the One who exists, as an object); *Migr.* 224; *Somn.* 1.114. ὁρατικός occurs in *Mut.* 258 (here the word appears in the dative singular and may be either masculine or neuter); and *Plant.* 46 (here the word appears in the plural as ὁρατικοί). In *QE* 1.12, the word ὁρατικός may appear, but the Greek is uncertain. The phrase οἱ ὀξὺ καθορῶντες occurs in *Agr.* 81 and *Fug.* 19.

[21] See above, nn. 6 and 7.

convenience, the exegetical series to which each passage belongs is indicated in parentheses next to the name of the passage. Only *Legat.* 4 comes from a non-exegetical work.

Passages in Which a Referent for "Israel Seers" Can Be Determined

Of all the passages which have expressions for "Israel seers," we can identify only two with a real social group. These passages are *Mos.* 2.196, in which the phrase τὸ ὁρατικὸν καὶ ἐπιστημονικὸν γένος is the Biblical nation, and *Legat.* 4, in which "Israel," the ὁρῶν θεόν, denotes the Jews. In both cases, only the context of the passage allows us to identify a referent for these expressions, as is explained below.

Mos. 2.196 (Exposition)

Of primary interest in this passage is the phrase τὸ ὁρατικὸν καὶ ἐπιστη-μονικὸν γένος, the race/class that can see and know. Since Philo is clearly narrating the history of the Biblical nation in his two treatises on Moses, this phrase cannot be construed as any other group. We have observed, however, that throughout these two treatises, Philo refrains from calling the nation "Israel." Strictly speaking, then, we cannot say that the ὁρατικὸν καὶ ἐπιστημονικὸν γένος is "Israel," as he understands the term; instead, it is the Biblical nation Israel.

In *Mos.* 2.196, Philo paraphrases the incident narrated in Lev. 24:10–16, quoted below, about the blasphemer. The larger context of the passage, *Mos.* 2.192–208, is a discussion of oracles given in question and answer exchange between God and Moses. Philo presents the incident from Leviticus to illustrate this kind of oracle. Our specific concern, however, is with the way he narrates the episode leading up to the oracle (*Mos.* 2.193–96).

Lev. 24:10–11 describes the incident as follows: "Now an Israelite woman's son, whose father was an Egyptian, went out among the people of Israel; and the Israelite woman's son and a man of Israel quarrelled in the camp, and the Israelite woman's son blasphemed the Name and cursed."

In retelling this episode, Philo elaborates upon the background of the blasphemer. He writes, "A certain base-born man, the child of an unequal marriage, his father an Egyptian, his mother a Jewess, had set at naught the ancestral customs of his mother and turned aside, as we are told, to the impiety of Egypt and embraced the atheism of the people" (*Mos.* 2.193).

Based upon the brief account in Leviticus of the man's pedigree—he is described as the son of an Israelite woman and an Egyptian father—Philo characterizes the man as baseborn and the offspring of unequals. He also elaborates that the man rejected the ancestral customs (πάτρια ἔθη) from his mother's side in favor of the atheistic impiety of his father's people. It is interesting that Philo depicts the mother's heritage as one of "ancestral customs." This expression denotes a traditional framework of practices, one which Philo does not mention in other passages where he discusses the "Israel seers."

It is also noteworthy that while the Bible talks of the mother as an Israelite woman (γυνὴ Ἰσραηλῖτις), Philo describes her as a Jewess (Ἰουδαία). Since he uses "Hebrews" for the Biblical people throughout the two treatises on Moses, we might expect him to do so here as well, especially because he seems to reserve the term "Jew" for his contemporaries.

Philo goes on to describe the wrong-headed beliefs of the Egyptians, who revere earth as a god. He writes,

> For the Egyptians almost alone among the nations have set up earth as a power to challenge heaven. Earth they held to be worthy of the honours due to a god, and refused to render to heaven any special tribute of reverence, acting as though it were right to shew respect to the outermost regions rather than to the royal palace. (*Mos.* 2.194)

Changing from the aorist to the present tense, Philo then goes on to explain that the Egyptians revere the earth because, unlike other countries which are watered by rain from heaven, the land of Egypt is watered by the yearly flooding of the Nile. The Egyptians therefore regard the river with the kind of reverence owed to a god (*Mos.* 2.195).

After this brief digression from the story, Philo describes the encounter between the blasphemer and the Israelite:

> And, lo, this half-bred person, having a quarrel with someone of [the race/class able to see and know, τὸ ὁρατικὸν καὶ ἐπιστημονικὸν γένος], losing in his anger all control over himself, and also urged by fondness for Egyptian atheism, extended his impiety from earth to heaven, and with soul and tongue and all the organism of speech alike accursed, foul, abominable, in the superabundance of his manifold wickedness cursed Him, whom even to bless is a privilege not permitted to all but only to the best, even those who have received full and complete purification. (*Mos.* 2.196)

Eschewing speculation about the nature of the quarrel, Philo expands instead upon the character of the half-Egyptian man, telling that he loses control of himself because of his anger and also that he is zealous for Egyptian atheism. What makes his transgression especially outrageous is that he dares to curse God when even to bless Him is reserved for only the best and purest. It is unclear whether Philo means by this last characterization to describe only the priests or whether he may also include others who have purified themselves properly. In any event, the person from the race/class that is able to see and know stands in sharp contrast to the half-

Egyptian man, who yields to his passions and not only denies God but also blasphemes Him.

It is striking that this passage has the only occurrence of the expression ὁρατικὸν γένος in the treatises on Moses and indeed in any of the Exposition treatises. Philo does not explicitly develop the theme of seeing God here, but the ability to see and know God does contribute to the meaning of the discussion, because Philo portrays the Egyptians as lacking this ability. Although the phrase ὁρατικὸν καὶ ἐπιστημονικὸν γένος does not specify an object, it is implicit that what the γένος sees and knows is God. In fact, Philo uses the Biblical incident—which is rather spare in detail—to set up a contrast between the γένος that is able to see and know God, on the one hand, and the Egyptians, on the other, who are characterized by impiety and denial of God, and at least one of whom shows a lack of control.

On the most obvious level of this retold narrative, the ὁρατικὸν καὶ ἐπιστημονικὸν γένος seems to be the Biblical nation. By calling the mother a "Jewess," however, rather than a "Hebrew," by elaborating upon the beliefs of the Egyptians—among whom he and probably most of his readers dwell in Alexandria—and by portraying the son of a mixed marriage as rejecting his mother's "ancestral practices," Philo may be using this incident to reflect contemporary issues as well. I shall address this possibility in my conclusions to this chapter.

Legat. 4 (Non-Exegetical)

This is another passage in which we can identify "Israel," the one that sees God, with a real social group, i.e., the Jews. Philo explains that "Israel" means "one that sees God" in his prologue to this treatise, which tells about the travels of an Alexandrian Jewish embassy to Caligula and the events that lead up to it. This is the only extant non-exegetical work in which Philo uses the word "Israel," and he mentions it here only once, along with the etymology. Much of the treatise describes the suffering of Alexandrian Jewry and to some extent the travails of Palestinian Jewry as well. Because the larger context of the treatise is about the Jews, it is clear that Philo means to identify them with "Israel."

One of the chief purposes of the prologue is to argue for divine providence. Philo begins with the observation that people place more faith in fate than in nature, and he attributes this misplaced faith to reliance upon sense perception instead of intellect (*Legat.* 1–2). While the sight of the senses sees only what is near, the keener sight of reason sees into the future. People weaken reason's vision, however, through drink and other indulgence or, even worse, through ignorance (*Legat.* 2). Nonetheless

Philo argues that the current situation should convince even those who
have lost faith in God's providence:

> And yet the present time and the many important questions decided in it are
> strong enough to convince even those who have come to disbelieve that the Deity
> takes thought for men, and particularly for [the suppliants' race/class which has
> been allotted or which has allotted itself to] the Father and King of the Universe
> and the source of all things. (*Legat.* 3)

Here Philo claims that the current events display God's care not only
for all men but especially for the suppliants' race/class (τὸ ἱκετικὸν γένος),
which is His special portion. He continues, "Now this race is called in the
Hebrew tongue Israel, but expressed in [Greek], the word is 'he that sees
God' (ὁρῶν θεόν) and to see Him seems to me of all possessions, public or
private, the most precious" (*Legat.* 4).

At this point, Philo digresses to extol the vision of God:

> For if the sight of seniors or instructors or rulers or parents stirs the beholders to
> respect for them and decent behaviour and the desire to live a life of self-control,
> how firmly based is the virtue and nobility of conduct which we may expect to find
> in souls whose vision has soared above all created things and schooled itself to
> behold the uncreated and divine, the primal good, the [beautiful], the happy, the
> blessed, which may truly be called better than the good, more [beautiful] than the
> [beautiful], more blessed than blessedness, more happy than happiness itself, and
> any perfection there may be greater than these. (*Legat.* 5)

If the sight of human models inspires proper conduct, because God
exemplifies the highest excellence, it follows that vision of Him must call
forth well-founded virtue and excellence in the beholders. Here, Philo
describes God in such a way as to place Him above any philosophical
concept, like the Good (τὸ ἀγαθόν) or the Beautiful (τὸ καλόν).

Philo goes on to say that reason (ὁ λόγος) cannot succeed in ascending
to God, nor can it even find words to describe Him or His powers (*Legat.* 6).
In the rest of the prologue, Philo comments about God's powers (*Legat.* 6)
and about the beneficial aspects of His punitive powers in particular
(*Legat.* 7).

Since this treatise depicts the situation of the Jews, "Israel" must be
understood implicitly to refer to them. Besides using the designations
"Israel" and "one that sees God," Philo also describes them as "the suppliants' race/class which has been allotted or has allotted itself (προσκεκλήρωται) to God."[22] The notion that this race/class is God's special portion

---

22 *Legat.* 3 is the only passage in which Philo uses the expression "suppliants'
race/class" (ἱκετικὸν γένος). Once again, his use of γένος, race/class, as opposed to ἔθνος,
nation, is worth noting as typical, since he usually uses γένος rather than ἔθνος in
relation to "Israel." Throughout *Legat.*, Philo uses τὸ ἔθνος to refer to the Jews and

may come from Deut. 32:9 or from another Biblical verse that expresses the unique relationship between God and Biblical Israel.[23]

At present, however, our interest is in Philo's description of "Israel" as the ὁρῶν θεόν and his identification of "Israel" with the Jews. Calling the vision of God the most precious of all possessions, private or public, he emphasizes the significance of seeing God and associates those who can see Him with virtue and excellence. He does not, however, claim that "Israel" sees God because it is His special portion or that "Israel" is God's special portion because it sees Him. Instead, the two associations—the ability of "Israel" to see God and its status as God's special portion—stand side by side.

Finally, when Philo writes in *Legat.* 6 that reason cannot extend to rise up to God, he implies that philosophy alone is not enough. Indeed, in this prologue, Philo may be validating the Jewish way of life even above philosophy. I shall explore this possibility further in Chapter Five. For now, however, what is important is that Philo identifies "Israel," the one that sees God, with the Jews.

Passages in Which a Referent for "Israel Seers" Cannot Be Determined

We are able to identify Philo's expressions for seers with the Biblical nation in *Mos.* 2.196 and with the Jews in *Legat.* 4 only because the context of each treatise provides enough information. In all the other passages,

---

seems to mean by this specifically the Jews of Alexandria. He uses γένος to describe the Jews in *Legat.* 178, 201, and 346. In each of these three cases, he seems to mean the entire Jewish race (whether by birth or choice), as opposed to the Alexandrian Jewish ἔθνος.

Although the adjective ἱκετικός does not appear elsewhere, Philo does use the word ἱκέτης, suppliant, in a variety of ways to describe those who are suppliants of other people (e.g., the Jews in Egypt, *Mos.* 1.34–36; see also *Prob.* 64) and suppliants of God (e.g., *Migr.* 124, *Fug.* 56, *Spec.* 2.217). It is interesting that he describes two specific groups as suppliants: the Levites, as suppliants of God (*Ebr.* 94, *Somn.* 2.273), and proselytes, as suppliants of God (*Spec.* 1.309) and of the law (*Spec.* 2.118). Philo's use of ἱκέτης in general suggests that the designation "the suppliants' race/class" may be intended to emphasize that "Israel" or the Jews have a relationship to God which might be available to anyone who chooses to become His suppliant. Elsewhere in Philo's works, for example, the suppliant represents someone who has a direct relationship to God whether or not that person belongs to a particular ethnic group. Especially striking are *Virt.* 79 and 185, in which Philo suggests that the suppliant's direct relationship to God is more important than membership in the nation (i.e., Biblical Israel).

23 These verses are discussed in the next chapter. The language in Deut. 32:9, which says that Israel became the portion of God's inheritance (σχοίνισμα κληρονομίας), is somewhat similar to the wording here, which says that Israel was allotted or allotted itself (προσκεκλήρωται) to God. For Philo's use of the verb προσκληρόω in relation to the Jews, see Chapter Five.

however, in which Philo speaks about "Israel" as people who can see, we cannot decisively identify these people with a real social group.

To illustrate the nature of the difficulties in identifying "Israel" with a particular group, below are six representative examples from each of Philo's exegetical series: three from the Allegory (*Congr.* 51, *Migr.* 18, *Mut.* 189); one from the Exposition (*Praem.* 44); and two from QGE (*QE* 1.21 and *QE* 2.43). In a later section I shall review the overall characteristics of each series.

Congr. 51 (Allegory)

In this passage, Philo describes "Israel," the one that sees God, as the best race/class (τὸ ἄριστον γένος). We cannot, however, identify this γένος with a real social group for several reasons. First, Philo denies the historical dimension of the figures he is about to discuss. Second, he defines "Israel" solely on the basis of its ability to see God. Finally, his discussion of the group in the present tense contributes to the impression that any contemporary who can see God may belong to "Israel," regardless of descent.

The general theme of the treatise pertains to different kinds of learning. The immediate context of *Congr.* 51 (*Congr.* 43–53) describes the different kinds of learners exemplified by Nahor, the brother of Abraham; Milcah, Nahor's wife; and Reumah, his concubine. Rejecting the historical level of the story, Philo writes, "Now let no sane man suppose that we have here in the pages of the wise legislator a historical pedigree. What we have is a revelation through symbols of facts which may be profitable to the soul" (*Congr.* 44).

Philo introduces a reference to "Israel" when he describes Milcah and Reumah. Noting that Milcah stands for "queen," he likens her to knowledge of heaven, which is "queen of the sciences," since heaven is the best of created things (*Congr.* 50). This kind of knowledge is what the astronomers and Chaldeans pursue.

Before taking up the subject of Reumah, which means "the one [f.] who sees something" (ἡ ὁρῶσα τι)—an etymology no doubt derived from the Hebrew, ראו מה—he writes:

> Now to see the best, that is the truly existing, is the lot of the best [race/class], Israel, for Israel means [one that sees God]. The [race/class] that strives for second place sees the second best, that is the heaven of our senses, and therein the well-ordered host of the stars, the choir that moves to the fullest and truest music. Third are the sceptics, who do not concern themselves with the best things in nature, whether perceived by the senses or the mind, but spend themselves on petty quibbles and trifling disputes. These are the housemates of Reumah, who 'sees something,' even the smallest, men incapable of the quest for the better things which might bring profit to their lives. (*Congr.* 51–52)

By introducing the figure of "Israel," Philo sets up three groups of learners: Israel, Milcah, and Reumah. Israel, the best class, sees the best, i.e., God, "the truly existing (τὸ ὄντως ὄν)"; in second place is Milcah or the Chaldeans, who see the heavens; and last is Reumah or the sceptics, who "see something."

Clearly, here "Israel" is the best race/class because it can see God. Moreover, all three groups are defined by what they can see, not by ancestry. To be sure, Philo frequently uses the word "Chaldean" to describe astronomers, not necessarily a race defined by birth. The sceptics too are certainly not a group defined by descent. In addition, the present sense of the verbs in this passage further lends the impression that Philo is describing three kinds of contemporaries who are classed according to what they can perceive.

In this passage, then, "Israel" represents the class of people who can see God, regardless of ancestry. Although we cannot rule out the possibility that Philo may equate "Israel" with the Biblical nation or his contemporary Jews, nothing in the passage or in the larger context of the passage makes this equation definite. Moreover, Philo's earlier statement that the story presents facts about the soul and not a historical genealogy only reinforces the impression that "Israel" does not refer to the real historical nation—either in the past or present—but instead to a group defined solely by its ability to see God.[24]

Migr. 18 (Allegory)

This passage illustrates the difficulty in determining a referent for the phrase ὁρατικὸν γένος when the expression appears in an allegorical interpretation. The passage, Migr. 18, comments upon Gen. 50:24–25, which reads as follows:

> And Joseph said to his brothers, 'I am about to die, but God will visit you, and bring you out of this land which he swore to Abraham, to Isaac, and to Jacob.' Then Joseph took an oath of the sons of Israel, saying, 'God will visit you, and you shall carry up my bones from here.'

In Migr. 16, Joseph serves as an example of someone who has made a "truce with the body." Philo notes that while the body-loving and passion-loving parts of these people or types (he does not provide a clear subject)

---

[24] Examples of other passages in the Allegory where "Israel" appears to be understood primarily as one or a group that sees or sees God, but where we cannot rule out the possibility that it may also correspond to the Biblical nation or the Jews, are as follows: Post. 63; Deus 144; Sobr. 13; Conf. 148; Migr. 54, 113, 125; Her. 78; Fug. 19, 208; Mut. 258; Somn. 2.276, 279. Similarly, in the following passages about Jacob, it is unclear whether or not his identity as the one that sees God replaces or merely adds to his historical identity: Migr. 39, Mut. 81, Somn. 1.171–72.

are buried and forgotten, any virtue-loving tendency is preserved by memory. Joseph's bones, then, which the sons of Israel will carry out from Egypt, represent "those elements of such a soul as are left uncorrupted and worthy of being remembered" (*Migr.* 17, my translation).

One example of what renders this soul worthy of being remembered is Joseph's faith that God will save Israel from Egypt or ignorance. Philo writes, "These things were worthy of being remembered: the belief that 'God will visit' the race/class that can see and will not completely hand it over to ignorance, that blind mistress" (*Migr.* 18, my translation).

This exegesis, then, is an allegory of the soul—that is, the "Joseph soul," part of which loves the body and part of which loves virtue. Egypt, the land from which God will bring out the people, is interpreted symbolically as ignorance. Amid these symbols, Philo's exact understanding of the phrase ὁρατικὸν γένος is unclear. He may intend the phrase to symbolize what is good in the soul—i.e., the quality or nature of being able to see—and thus, Joseph's words express faith that God will preserve what is good in the soul from ignorance. On the other hand, he may also intend the ὁρατικὸν γένος to refer to the Biblical people or to a loosely defined group of those who see, whom God will save from ignorance. Since the phrase ὁρατικὸν γένος can be understood in a variety of ways, the identity of this γένος remains ambiguous.[25]

Mut. 189 (Allegory)

This passage shows how the expression ὁρατικὸν γένος can be used as an automatic substitute for the word "Israel" without emphasizing the meaning of a group that is able to see. The passage is part of an interpretation of Gen. 17:17, which describes Abraham's disbelief when God tells him that his wife will bear a son. Abraham says, "Shall a son be born to one of a hundred years and shall Sarah being ninety years bear a son?" (LCL translation). Philo tries to argue that rather than disbelief, what Abraham is expressing is a prayer that such an illustrious birth should take place only under the perfect numbers ninety and one hundred (*Mut.* 188).

The theme in the larger context of the passage (*Mut.* 188–92) is praise of the number one hundred as a perfect number, and Philo offers several examples of where the number one hundred appears in Scripture. In *Mut.* 189, he refers to Gen. 11:10, which says that Shem was a hundred years old when he begat Arphaxad. He writes,

---

[25] Examples of other passages in the Allegory in which expressions for the "Israel seers" are included in allegorical or symbolic interpretations, and it is difficult to know how to interpret these expressions, include the following: *Leg.* 2.34; *Leg.* 3.38, 81, 172, 212; *Sacr.* 134; *Post.* 92; *Agr.* 81; *Plant.* 46; *Conf.* 56, 91; *Migr.* 224; *Somn.* 1.114.

> To begin with Shem, the son of the just Noah, the ancestor of the [race/class that can see]; he is said to have been a hundred years old when he begat Arphaxad, the meaning of whose name is 'he disturbed affliction.' And surely it is excellent that the soul's offspring should harass and confound and destroy injustice, afflicted and full of evils as it is.

Philo mentions Shem because his age of one hundred at the birth of Arphaxad illustrates the larger theme he is discussing. Reference to Shem as son of the just Noah and ancestor of the ὁρατικὸν γένος seems to be purely parenthetical. Indeed since Philo goes on to allegorize Arphaxad as the soul's offspring, it is not even clear whether he is talking about biological or symbolic relationships.

The phrase ὁρατικὸν γένος is similarly ambiguous. Serving as a replacement phrase for "Israel," it can be understood either as the Biblical nation or as a group of seers whose descent is irrelevant. In any case, reference to the ὁρατικὸν γένος is beside the main point—i.e., Shem's age of one hundred at the birth of Arphaxad—and the ability to see is not emphasized in the interpretation. It is therefore not clear whether the phrase is meant to describe a quality that "Israel" has or simply to substitute for the name.[26]

Praem. 44 (Exposition)

This passage illustrates yet again the difficulty in identifying a referent for "Israel" when the term appears to describe a group defined solely by its ability to see. The larger context of the passage (*Praem.* 36–46) is a description of the life of Jacob, "the practicer" (ὁ ἀσκητής), and his rewards, especially the reward—i.e., the vision of God—which he receives when his name is changed to "Israel." The portrayal of Jacob as a "practicer," the idea of patriarchal rewards as this treatise presents them, and the significance of Jacob's new name "Israel" as "one that sees God" are not found in the Bible, however, but only in Philo's interpretations. From the start, then, *Praem.* is not discussing the Biblical or historical reality of Jacob but rather his symbolic role in Philonic exegesis.

Unfortunately, this treatise does not provide sufficient information for us to determine how far Philo identifies the "practicer" of his interpretations with the Biblical or historical patriarch Jacob. In fact, *Praem.* does not even mention the Biblical figures by name.

Commenting that people vary in their methods of apprehending God (*Praem.* 40–46), Philo ends his account of the practicer's life by describing

---

[26] Other passages in the Allegory in which expressions for "Israel seers" may be substitute phrases, whose intrinsic meaning is not emphasized, include the following: *Leg.* 3.15, *Conf.* 159, *Fug.* 140, *Mut.* 109, and *Somn.* 2.23.

a superior mode of perception, i.e., the ability to see God through Himself. He writes,

> If any are able to grasp Him through Himself using no other reasoning as assistance towards the vision, let them be enrolled among the holy and genuine worshippers and friends of God in the true sense. Among them is he who in Hebrew is called Israel but in Greek, one who sees God (ὁρῶν θεόν), not what He is—for that is impossible, as I said—but that He is ... (*Praem.* 43–44, my translation)

With the words, "if any are able," Philo introduces a theoretical group that can perceive God through Himself. In this group he includes "Israel," the one that sees God. The rest of this passage describes more fully this superior mode of direct perception (*Praem.* 44–46). For our purposes, however, what is important is that Philo discusses the apprehension of God as an ongoing contemporary endeavor—not an event in the past—whether it be achieved through inference from creation (*Praem.* 41–43) or through direct perception (*Praem.* 43–46).

Because of the contemporary significance to Philo of seeing God and because of the meaning of its name, "Israel" here is primarily a symbol of one who sees God, and it is unclear whether or not it also represents the historical patriarch Jacob or the nation of his descendants. Complicating this determination is that the antecedent for ὁρῶν, one who sees, is vague and could represent either a singular or a collective entity. In addition, Philo discusses the various seekers after God in the present tense, further loosening the association between "Israel" and its historical namesakes. Finally, because the immediate context in *Praem.* does not discuss real social groups, we cannot conclusively identify any referent for "Israel," the one who sees God.[27]

QE 1.21 (QGE) [28]

In this passage, the phrase ὁρατικὸν γένος appears to serve as an automatic substitute for "Israel." The passage raises a question about Exod. 12:17, "I will bring out your force from Egypt." Philo asks why the verse says "your force" instead of "you." He answers as follows:

---

[27] The one other passage in the Exposition that mentions "Israel" and the etymology ὁρῶν θεόν is *Abr.* 57. Here too, Philo expounds upon seeing God, calling this "the height of happiness." It is difficult in this passage to discern whether Philo has in mind the Biblical nation and its Jewish descendants or any people who are able to see God.

[28] Although there is a Greek fragment for this passage, it does not include the relevant part which may have the phrase ὁρατικὸν γένος (race/class that can see). Again, since the fragment for *QE* 2.46 does attest to Philo's use of this phrase, I have assumed that he uses it in his other *QE* interpretations, and I have substituted this phrase in my translation of this passage and the next, where Marcus uses "seeing nation" and "contemplative race," respectively.

'Force' is the godly piety of the [ὁρατικὸν γένος]. Now so long as those who have this force dwell in cities and villages, the cities and villages act well and properly, for they are adorned at least with the virtue of others if not with their own. But when (these inhabitants) depart, the portion of common good fortune is changed. For good men are the pillars of whole communities, and they support cities and city-governments as [columns support] great houses. That is the literal meaning.[29]

According to this interpretation, God says that He will bring out "your force" rather than "you," because "force" refers specifically to the quality of piety which the ὁρατικὸν γένος has. Philo explains that this force is responsible for the "common good fortune" of a community, and he speaks of those who have this force as "good men," whose piety and virtue raise the standard of goodness within a particular community.

The Biblical verse, Exod. 12:17, does not mention "Israel" specifically, but it obviously refers to the historical nation. Although Philo uses ὁρατικὸν γένος here as an equivalent name for "Israel," it is unclear who the ὁρατικὸν γένος is. He uses this expression only in the opening statement. From there he goes on to generalize, using the present tense, about the importance of virtuous people to a community. The ability of the ὁρατικὸν γένος to see appears irrelevant to the meaning of the passage.

It may be that the first sentence—in which the phrase ὁρατικὸν γένος occurs—refers to the Biblical nation, while the rest of the exegesis is about virtuous people in general. On the other hand, the ὁρατικὸν γένος itself may encompass all the virtuous people discussed in the passage. Since both construals are possible, identification of the ὁρατικὸν γένος remains inconclusive, and we can only observe that the expression serves as a substitute name for "Israel," however "Israel" is understood.[30]

QE 2.43 (QGE)

In this second example from QGE, the phrase ὁρατικὸν γένος once again appears to be an automatic substitute for "Israel." Here too, however, we cannot identify this γένος conclusively with a real group. *QE* 2.43 is also one of four passages in which Philo uses the phrase ὁρατικὸν γένος in an interpretation of Exodus 24, which describes the establishment of the

---

[29] This translation is modified according to the suggestion of Petit, *Quaestiones*, OPA, 33:237. In the LCL edition, Marcus translates the second to last sentence as follows: "For good men are the pillars of whole communities, and they support cities and city-governments as if they were great houses."

[30] The "literal" interpretation cited here is followed by a "deeper meaning," which speaks of "force" as the godly piety of the soul. The "deeper sense" does not contribute to this investigation. Other examples from QGE in which ὁρῶν, ὁρῶντες, or ὁρατικὸν γένος may serve as automatic substitutes for "Israel" are *QE* 1.12; *QE* 2.38, 42, 43 (discussed below), 46, 47, and 76.

covenant between God and Israel. It is striking that Philo links election of the γένος with the giving of the law, since he does not usually link these two features in his other works.[31]

QE 2.43 comments upon Exod. 24:13, which says that Moses and Joshua went up to the mountain of God. Philo asks why Joshua accompanies Moses up the mountain when in Exod. 24:12, it says that God summons only Moses. His answer is as follows:

> The two [Moses and Joshua] are potentially one, since no one would say that those who are of like mind and like sentiments with one another are the same single (person) except in respect of another species. For 'Joshua' is to be interpreted as 'salvation.' But is being saved by God more appropriate to anyone else than the inspired soul, in which prophecy resounds, since even in (Moses') lifetime he was over the rulers and at (Moses') death he was his successor? Rightly, therefore, does he go up as an assurance of two most necessary things: one, of the election of the [ὁρατικὸν γένος], and the other, that the Law should be considered not as an invention of the human mind but as a divine command and divine words.

Philo's meaning here is obscure. The following is a possible construal: Moses and Joshua may be considered as one, since both have prophetic ability. This suggests that when God calls only Moses, Joshua is also included implicitly. Moreover, since Joshua leads the people both before and after Moses's death, his accompaniment of Moses to get the law assures those after Moses that the ὁρατικὸν γένος is indeed chosen and that the law has a divine and not a human origin.

Unfortunately, Philo's other writings do not provide further illumination about this passage. The other instances in which he refers to Joshua are not pertinent,[32] and he does not interpret Exod. 24:13 anywhere else.

Nevertheless, Philo's exegesis in *QE* 2.43 seems to understand God's giving the law to Moses in the company of Joshua as the election of the ὁρατικὸν γένος. The ability of this γένος to see does not contribute to the sense of the interpretation nor does this ability seem to be connected with the election of the γένος. The expression ὁρατικὸν γένος, then, appears to be merely a substitute for the name "Israel." That Philo does not explain this phrase suggests that he assumes its meaning is understood.[33]

---

[31] This observation will be discussed further in the conclusions to this chapter. Other QGE passages in which Philo describes "Israel" or the ὁρατικὸν γένος as chosen are *QG* 3.49; *QE* 2.38, 42, and 46. In *QG* 3.49, he seems to link chosenness with the commandment for circumcision; in the *QE* 2 passages, election is linked with the giving of the law.

[32] *Ebr.* 96; *Mut.* 121; *Mos.* 1.216; *Virt.* 55, 66–69.

[33] The end of *QE* 2.43 gives another explanation of why Joshua accompanies Moses, but this does not add to the present discussion.

The Members of "Israel"

As one can observe from the examples just discussed, when the larger context of a passage does not provide enough relevant information, it is difficult, if not impossible, to determine whom Philo has in mind when he speaks of "Israel" as the one that sees God or the race/class that can see. Since he provides no further guidance on this matter, one can only speculate about who these God-seers or seers may be. Four groups, listed below, suggest themselves as possibilities for who may belong to Philo's "Israel." These groups are composed of the following:

1) all respected philosophers, or philosophically-minded people, whether they are Jews or not;
2) a subset of the Jews who are philosophically-minded;
3) all Jews; or
4) all Jews, whether philosophers or not, and all respected non-Jewish philosophers.[34]

Let us consider each of these suggestions more carefully. (All the observations offered below about Philo's attitude toward the Jews are fully developed in Chapter Five.)

The first possibility—that "Israel" may consist of all respected philosophers or philosophically-minded people, whether Jewish or not—places importance upon philosophical sophistication but not ethnic affiliation. We have noted that Philo's very ideas about the vision of God are strongly influenced by his non-Jewish philosophical environment. Since he keeps his discussions about seeing God fairly separate from his discussions about Jewish beliefs and practices, it would seem that anyone—Jew or non-Jew—who is spiritually capable of seeing God might be eligible to belong to "Israel." Philo also speaks, however, about seeing God in elitist terms, often emphasizing how rare an experience this is and how few are able to attain it. These various observations suggest that "Israel" might encompass a philosophically knowledgeable elite of both Jews and non-Jews.

The second possibility—that Philo has in mind a philosophical elite consisting only of Jews—places importance upon both philosophical sophistication and ethnic affiliation. As we shall see, Philo believes the Jews are the only people who worship the true God. Though he does not say so, he may also think that only members of the people who worship God can be capable of seeing Him. In addition, we have observed that

---

[34] I am grateful to Prof. Alan Mendelson for pointing out that Philo would not include a thinker like Epicurus in the company of "Israel." I have therefore qualified my suggestions that non-Jewish philosophers might be part of Philo's "Israel" by speaking only of *respected* non-Jewish philosophers.

Philo speaks most frequently by far about "Israel seers" and about seeing God in the Allegory, a series probably directed to Jews who are quite familiar with Scripture and who are interested in its deeper spiritual meaning. Accordingly, one could argue that Philo envisages "Israel" to be this same Jewish elite.

Yet a third possibility is that Philo equates "Israel" with all Jews, a possibility that emphasizes ethnic affiliation only. In *Mos.* 2.196, for example, he clearly identifies the ὁρατικὸν γένος with the Biblical nation, and in *Legat.* 1–7, he implicitly equates "Israel," the one that sees God, with all Jews. In the latter passage, Philo also implies that the Jewish way of life is superior to philosophy alone, suggesting that the God whom the Jews see is superior to any philosophical concept and that a philosophical approach to God is not enough. One might therefore infer that Philo thinks that all Jews, through believing in and worshipping God, are able to see Him as well.

Finally, a fourth possibility is that Philo considers "Israel" to include all Jews and all respected philosophers, whether Jews or not. This possibility, which places importance upon either ethnic affiliation or philosophical sophistication, draws support from arguments presented for the first and third suggestions mentioned above, namely, that seeing God is a pursuit of philosophers, but Jews too have special access to Him because they believe in and worship Him. Indeed, in one passage (*Virt.* 65), Philo expresses this point of view quite directly. He writes, "What the disciples of the most excellent philosophy gain from its teaching, the Jews gain from their customs and laws, that is to know the highest, the most ancient Cause of all things and reject the delusion of created gods."

Of all the possibilities mentioned above, I believe the first to be the most likely—that Philo's "Israel" consists of all respected philosophers, whether Jewish or not. Philo does indeed emphasize again and again how difficult it is to see God and how few are able to achieve this vision (see, e.g., *Post.* 13–21, *Migr.* 46, *Praem.* 44). Although he may believe that Judaism embodies the best way of life through its beliefs and practices, he occasionally speaks disparagingly of other Jews who interpret the Scriptures literally.[35] This suggests that he does not view all Jews as equally sophisticated and therefore may not regard them all as equally capable of being part of the elite. In addition, if Philo believes that all Jews are capable of seeing God, it is surprising that he never mentions this in the Exposition, in which he talks at length about the Jews. The elitist nature of

---

[35] See, e.g., *Cher.* 42, *Det.* 22, *Migr.* 45, *Somn.* 1.39. See also Shroyer, "Alexandrian Jewish Literalists," esp. 271–79; and Wolfson, *Philo*, 1:57–66. Although Philo does not specifically call them "Jews," presumably he is speaking only about Jews.

being able to see God, then, seems to rule out the third and fourth possibilities suggested above, which would include all Jews.

As to the second suggestion, that "Israel" is comprised of an elite group of Jews alone, although this is certainly possible, nothing that Philo says about seeing God necessitates that one *must* be a Jew to achieve this vision. Indeed, as Philo portrays it, the goal of seeing God appears to be available to anyone able to strive toward it. Even though he may speak about the God who is seen in personal terms suggested by the Bible, God is still the Father and Maker of all, not simply the God of the Jews. In addition, although the Jews believe in and worship God, Philo speaks about seeing Him in different, more philosophical terms. Thus, believing in God and worshipping Him are not necessarily the same as seeing Him. On the basis of these various observations, then, Philo's vision of "Israel" would appear to be potentially universalist, encompassing all Jews and non-Jews who are spiritually capable.

In considering the proposal that "Israel" may in theory include non-Jews, one might reasonably ask why Philo speaks of "Israel" chiefly in works addressed to knowledgeable Jews, namely, the Allegory and QGE. If "Israel" is in fact meant to include "outsiders," then why does he mention this term only rarely in such works as the Exposition or his political treatises—works apparently intended, at least in part, for non-Jews?

In reply, I would only repeat my suggestion from the Introduction that Philo restricts his discussion of "Israel" to the Allegory and QGE because the designation "Israel" probably carries more meaning for "insiders" than it does for "outsiders." Indeed, we have seen that "Israel" is a self-referential term used by Jews generally to signify a person's own social set.

While Philo does not completely refrain, then, from speaking about "Israel"—or about seeing God—in the Exposition or his political treatise *Legat.*, neither does he emphasize these topics. In these works, he concentrates instead upon presenting a basic course to his less knowledgeable audience, reserving issues from "advanced Judaism" for his more sophisticated Jewish readers.

To be sure, it appears that Philo's aim is to bring Jews into the company of "Israel" and non-Jews into the community of Jews. Perhaps because he implicitly accepts that some non-Jews may already belong to "Israel," he presents this entity to his Jewish readers as an ideal toward which to strive.

Philo's Estimation of Non-Jewish Philosophers

If Philo does in fact believe that "Israel" may include some non-Jewish philosophers, then what may we deduce about his estimation of these non-Jewish philosophers in relation to the Jews? On this matter, we find different positions among his works.

We saw above that in at least one passage, *Virt.* 65, Philo seems to view the two groups equally, writing that "what the disciples of the most excellent philosophy gain from its teaching, the Jews gain from their customs and laws, that is to know the highest, the most ancient Cause of all things and reject the delusion of created gods."[36] Another perspective, however, can be found in *Legat.* 1–7, in which Philo seems to place the Jewish way of life above philosophy, implying that philosophy—or reason—alone is not enough to attain the vision of God.[37]

Since Philo can say contradictory things throughout his works, it is difficult to know how much weight to put upon either of these points of view. Indeed, one could argue that Philo's differing positions may be explained by the contexts in which each appears.

Philo's equation of Jews and non-Jewish philosophers in *Virt.* 65, for example, occurs in the Exposition, in which he apparently wishes to present Jews and their way of life in the best light in order to impress favorably those who may be interested in or hostile toward them. Accordingly, Philo may equate Jews and philosophers in this passage, not because he necessarily regards them as equal, but because he wishes to show that Judaism incorporates the best that philosophy has to offer. Similarly, one could also argue that in *Legat.*, he may wish to portray his suffering compatriots as superior even to philosophers in order to highlight more sharply the outrage of the persecution of the Jews. Since one can find rationales for either point of view—that Philo esteems Jews and non-Jewish philosophers equally or that he regards Jews more highly—any firm conclusion about what he really thinks eludes us.

---

[36] Other passages in which Philo highly praises non-Jewish sages include *Prob.* 74 and *Spec.* 2.44–48 (see, e.g., below, n. 39).

[37] This passage is discussed earlier in this chapter, and later, in Chapter Five. For another passage in which Philo holds the Jewish way of life superior to that of philosophers, see *Contempl.* 57–64, where he derisively compares the banquets described by Xenophon and Plato with the banquets of the Therapeutae, who live in contemplation of the truths of nature, "following the truly sacred instructions of the prophet Moses" (*Contempl.* 64). Strictly speaking, however, Philo's comparison here is between the philosophers and the Therapeutae, not all Jews.

"Other Seers" and "Israel"

It may be appropriate at this point to recall the "other seers," discussed at the beginning of this chapter, whom Philo mentions but whom we are unable to relate directly to "Israel." Some of these seers Philo characterizes rather generally as οἱ ὁρατικοί (those who can see) or οἱ φιλοθεάμονες (those who are fond of contemplating), and it is certainly possible that people so described might be considered part of "Israel." Conversely, Philo could just as easily apply the same general descriptions to "Israel" that he uses for these other seers.

The relationship between "Israel" and prophets (whom Philo describes as "seers") is somewhat different. To be sure, Philo would probably consider all prophets to be part of "Israel." The real question, perhaps, is whether or not he would consider all "Israel" to be prophets![38]

Especially pertinent is the question of the relationship between "Israel" and specific social groups like the Therapeutae, the Persian Magi, the Athenians, or Greek and foreign philosophers, whom Philo describes in one way or another as being able to see. Without a doubt, his treatise *On the Contemplative Life* portrays the Therapeutae as perfect candidates for inclusion in "Israel," even though Philo himself never describes them as such. Indeed a glance at the four groups suggested earlier as possibly comprising the members of "Israel" shows that the Therapeutae fit into each and every category.

In contrast, Philo's discussions of the Magi (*Prob.* 74) and the Athenians (*Prob.* 140) are just too brief to permit any judgments about their relationship to "Israel." Finally, even where he describes non-Jewish philosophers at some length (*Spec.* 2.44–48), he never calls them "Israel" or comments about them in relation to "Israel."[39] Since Philo never explicitly addresses whether or not non-Jews may belong to "Israel," our conclusion that they may belong can remain only speculative.

---

[38] On this question, see Wolfson, *Philo*, 2:46–52, 61.

[39] In this passage (*Spec.* 2.44–48), Philo pays tribute to "all who practice wisdom either in Grecian or barbarian lands" (*Spec.* 2.44). He describes them as "the best observers (θεωροί) of nature and all things in it" (my translation) and writes, "While their bodies are firmly planted on the land, they provide their souls with wings, so that they may traverse the upper air and gain full contemplation (περιαθρῶσι) of the powers which dwell there..." (*Spec.* 2.45). The context of this intriguing passage is a discussion of the Jewish holidays in general and, in specific, of the notion that every day is a holiday. As Philo portrays it, the life of these philosophers exemplifies a year-round holiday.

Although one might well imagine that such people might be considered part of "Israel," Philo does not call them "Israel" nor does he address the question of how the two groups might be related. It is also interesting that this passage has none of the vocabulary for seeing that Philo uses in passages explicitly about "Israel" (see n. 2).

One might well ask why in fact Philo does not address this question
directly. In the Introduction, I raised the issue of whether or not Philo is
being deliberately ambiguous by remaining silent about matters such as
the relationship between the terms "Israel" and "Jew." There I suggested
that he may keep his use of these two words separate because they hold for
him different, though perhaps overlapping, meanings. If this were true,
then he would have no reason to address why he does not use the words
interchangeably. What appears to us, his modern-day readers, as ambiguity or possibly even evasion may be perfectly understandable if we
acknowledge that his definitions of the terms "Israel" and "Jew" may differ from what we expect them to be. Philo's ambiguity on this matter may
thus be completely unintentional.

A similar discrepancy between what we expect and what Philo takes
for granted may contribute to our perplexity about who may belong to
"Israel." The identity of "Israel" may be self-evident to Philo in the same
way that today one might speak of an "intellectual elite" without concern
for defining who exactly belongs to this group. Membership is self-
selecting and requirements are obvious. Like this elite, "Israel" too may be
an unstructured sort of entity. God-seers need not apply to belong;
acceptance is automatic.[40]

Further Observations and Conclusions

The study of how Philo uses expressions for seers whom he equates with
"Israel" yields an interesting observation that reinforces our findings in
earlier chapters—namely, that different series of writings display
different patterns of use. Especially striking are where, whether, and how
Philo uses the word "Israel." Outside the Allegory, the word appears only
seven times.[41] Apart from two cases in which "Israel" occurs either in a
Biblical quotation (*QE* 2.37) or in a Biblical paraphrase (*QE* 2.30), each time
Philo uses "Israel" in works other than the Allegory, he also provides the
etymology to explain the meaning of the name. With two exceptions,
then, "Israel" never appears alone—i.e., without the etymology—in
Philo's other works. In *Mos.* 1–2 and *QE* 1–2, where he discusses verses
pertaining specifically to the Biblical nation and where we should
therefore expect him to use the word "Israel" in his commentary,
surprisingly he never does, preferring other terms instead.

Finally, in only two cases, *Mos.* 2.196 and *Legat.* 4, can we link Philo's
expressions for "Israel seers" with a real social group. In *Mos.* 2.196, "the

---

[40] Membership requirements for "Israel"—and for the Jews—are discussed further
in Chapter Six.
[41] *Abr.* 57; *Praem.* 44; *QG* 3.49; *QG* 4.233; *QE* 2.30, 37; *Legat.* 4.

race/class that can see and know" refers to the Biblical nation and perhaps its Jewish descendants, while in *Legat.* 4, Philo associates "Israel," the one that sees God, with his Jewish contemporaries. Both passages are found in works that are probably intended at least in part for "outsiders," and, as we shall see, Philo may have a special purpose here when he presents the past and present nation in this way.

Below is a summary, organized according to series, of how Philo uses "Israel," the etymology, the phrase ὁρατικὸν γένος, and other expressions for "Israel seers." The differences we can observe among his various writings can perhaps be best understood when we take into account Philo's different aims and audiences, as discussed in the Introduction.

The Allegory

Of all Philo's writings, either exegetical or non-exegetical, the Allegory displays the most frequent and varied use of all the terms for "Israel seers." The word "Israel" appears both in Biblical quotations and in the commentary. Philo uses it in relation to the etymology and thus to seeing but also in ways unrelated to seeing or to seeing God, as the previous chapter shows. The Allegory also has more variations on expressions for "Israel seers" than any other work, using the etymology ὁρῶν θεόν or a shorter term ὁρῶν or βλέπων, the phrase ὁρατικὸν γένος or simply ὁρατικός, and οἱ ὀξὺ καθορῶντες (those who see sharply).

Although I did not discuss expressions for seers which include an abstraction, like "the mind (or soul) that can see," it is worth noting that these expressions occur only in the Allegory. Only in the Allegory, moreover, do we find references to "Israel seers" within allegorical interpretations, as in the example of *Migr.* 18, presented earlier. Finally, in this series, Philo often links "Israel" explicitly with the kind of philosophical seeing he values so highly (as in *Congr.* 51, also discussed above). These features, many of which are unique to the Allegory, contribute to the impression that Philo composed this series for more sophisticated Jewish readers with an interest in allegorical interpretation.

Since Philo uses "Israel" in different ways throughout the Allegory, the appearance or non-appearance of the word in individual cases seems insignificant. It is interesting, however, that Philo does occasionally use expressions for seers to substitute for "Israel" in passages where vision is not clearly relevant to the interpretation.[42] Thus, even though this series

---

[42] For this use of the etymology or a shorter form, see, e.g., *Leg.* 3.15, 81; *Sobr.* 13. For ὁρατικὸν γένος, see, e.g., *Fug.* 140; *Mut.* 109, 189 (on this last passage, see earlier in the chapter). Cf. *Plant.* 46 and *Mut.* 258, in which ὁρατικός is used. These isolated occurrences, in which the terms seem to be mere exegetical nicknames and do not

displays a widely developed application of expressions for "Israel seers"—
as just described—the Allegory still has instances in which expressions
for seers seem to replace "Israel" mechanically, serving as exegetical
nicknames whose intrinsic meaning is irrelevant to the commentary.
Such instances may represent Philo's retention of earlier, traditional
material.

Of all the references to "Israel seers" in the Allegory, none can be
clearly or exclusively identified with either Biblical Israel or Philo's
Jewish contemporaries. Although such an identification cannot be ruled
out, these seers may also be understood as a group defined only by their
ability to see. If Philo's audience for the Allegory is indeed composed of
philosophically sophisticated Jews, then this emphasis upon the symbolic
meaning of "Israel," without concern for the literal, may offer these
readers just what they are seeking.

The Exposition

In the Exposition Philo uses "Israel" twice (*Abr.* 57 and *Praem.* 44), both
times with the etymology. These are the only two places in the series
where the etymology occurs. The phrase ὁρατικὸν γένος (race/class that
can see), or to be exact, τὸ ὁρατικὸν καὶ ἐπιστημονικὸν γένος (the race/class
that can see and know), appears once, in *Mos.* 2.196.

In the two passages in which "Israel" and the etymology appear, we
cannot conclusively identify a referent. Philo expounds upon the philosophical significance of seeing God in both passages, describing the
experience in *Abr.* 58 as the "height of happiness" (ἄκρον εὐδαιμονίας).
Because he depicts the vision of God as a universal philosophical goal,
when Philo explains "Israel" as "one that sees God," he seems to be speaking about anyone who can see God.

If Philo's readers in the Exposition are, as I suggest, not quite familiar
with Jewish beliefs, Scriptures, and practices, they may also vary in their
philosophical sophistication as well. One could speculate that Philo goes
out of his way in these two passages to elaborate upon the special kind of
seeing of which "Israel" is capable. His intent may be both to educate his
readers who are unfamiliar with philosophy and to acknowledge to his
more sophisticated ones that this type of philosophical contemplation is
highly valued among the Jews. He leaves the identity of "Israel" vague,
however, perhaps because he regards seeing God as reserved for an elite
and wishes instead to focus upon what is common to all Jews.

In contrast to the two passages mentioned above, in *Mos.* 2.196, it is

---

emphasize the ability to see, are similar to passages in *QE*, where expressions for
seers are automatic replacements for "Israel" throughout.

possible to identify the ὁρατικὸν καὶ ἐπιστημονικὸν γένος with the Biblical nation, because the treatise is narrating the history of this nation. Philo never actually uses the term "Israel" in either of his treatises on Moses but instead usually substitutes "Hebrews," or calls them the nation (τὸ ἔθνος) or the people (ὁ λαός). Since the ὁρατικὸν καὶ ἐπιστημονικὸν γένος is clearly the Biblical nation, the absence of the term "Israel" appears significant, confirming the impression that Philo reserves "Israel" to designate a different kind of entity.

If, however, Philo does understand "Israel" as the group that can see, which may not always coincide exactly with Biblical Israel or the Jews, his characterization of the Biblical nation as able to see is all the more noteworthy here. *Mos.* 2.196 is the only instance where Philo refers to the Biblical people with an expression that is clearly linked to the etymology for "Israel" and where the ability to see, which the expression suggests, contributes to the meaning of the discussion. If I am correct that the phrase ὁρατικὸν γένος has a history behind it, then in this passage, Philo is employing a traditional expression for the Biblical nation and amplifying it with the adjective ἐπιστημονικόν to emphasize his characterization.

Mos. 2.196, is unusual for another reason as well. This passage narrates the incident from Lev. 24:10–16 of the blasphemer, who is the son of an Israelite mother and an Egyptian father. Instead of calling the mother a "Hebrew"—the word he uses for the Biblical nation—Philo calls her a "Jewess" ('Ιουδαία). Moreover, he embellishes the Biblical tale by portraying Egyptian beliefs as impious and by declaring that the blasphemer abandons his mother's ancestral practices and acts without restraint.

These added features suggest that Philo may be using this passage to mirror his contemporary situation in Alexandria. Describing the nation as the γένος that can see and know, he highlights the difference between this enlightened race—presumably the Jews—and the unenlightened Egyptians, who still worship elements of creation rather than the Creator. By portraying the Egyptians in this way and by noting that the son of the mixed marriage departs from his mother's ancestral customs, Philo may wish to convey a subtle message to his Jewish readers about the dangers of mingling too closely with those from the outside culture.

Apart from these three passages, the Exposition has no other references to "Israel," "[the] one that sees God," or "the race/class that can see." Philo's sparse mention of these entities, however, may very well suit his purposes. In this series, he does not concentrate upon "Israel" and seeing God, perhaps—as I have suggested—because these subjects belong to a more sophisticated kind of Judaism. Instead, he focuses here upon the history, beliefs, and practices of all Jews, presenting their way of life as exemplary.

QGE

In QGE, the word "Israel" appears four times—twice in Philo's commentary (*QG* 3.49 and *QG* 4.233), both times with the etymology, and twice
in questions that either paraphrase (*QE* 2.30) or quote (*QE* 2.37) the Bible.
(In the latter two references, "Israel" appears without a corresponding
expression for seers.) In *QE*, "Israel" occurs only in two Biblical citations
(just noted); it is never used in the commentary. Expressions for seers
serve as substitute phrases in this work not only in the commentary (*QE*
1.12, 21; *QE* 2.42, 43, 46, 76), but also in two Scriptural quotations (*QE* 2.38
and 47). Since *QE* comments upon the Book of Exodus, which pertains
specifically to Biblical Israel's departure from Egypt and its journey
through the desert, it is especially surprising that the term "Israel" appears
so rarely there.

Philo's ten references in QGE to seers who are "Israel" are strikingly
different from those in his other exegetical writings for several reasons.
First, the ability to see is almost always incidental to the meaning of the
interpretation.[43] In two cases (*QG* 3.49 and *QG* 4.233), Philo mentions the
etymology or a shortened form as merely parenthetical information about
the meaning of "Israel," without at all developing the theme of seeing or
seeing God. In the eight remaining passages, listed above, in which
expressions for seers occur, these expressions appear to serve exclusively as
automatic substitutions for "Israel." Whether "Israel" or the substitute
expression refers to the Biblical nation or to a group defined only by the
ability to see is impossible to determine.

Second, contributing to the impression that the expressions for seers do
not emphasize the meaning of a group that is able to see or see God is that
Philo does occasionally comment in QGE about the vision of God as a contemporary philosophical pursuit or goal,[44] but never in passages in which
"Israel" or expressions for "Israel seers" occur. Instead, in this series, the
significance of the philosophical goal of seeing God is acknowledged
separately from discussions of "Israel seers." This separateness suggests
there may well indeed have been an earlier stage of use for both the
etymology of "Israel" and the phrase ὁρατικὸν γένος, wherein these

---

[43] The theme of seeing God is pertinent in *QE* 2.47, which interprets Exod. 24:17:
"Now the appearance of the glory of the Lord was like a devouring fire on the top of
the mountain in the sight of (ἐναντίον) the people of Israel." In the question, Philo
quotes the verse as follows: "The form of the glory of the Lord (was) like a fire burn-
ing before the sons of the seeing one." In the answer, however, Philo concentrates
upon the appearance of God rather than the ability of Israel to see Him. "The seeing
one" seems to be merely a substitute expression for "Israel."
[44] See, e.g., *QG* 2.34; *QG* 3.34; *QG* 4.1, 8, 21, 138, 196; *QE* 2.39, 51, 52. Especially striking
is *QE* 2.51: "For the beginning and end of happiness is to be able to see God."

expressions were not yet linked to the philosophical significance of seeing God.

A third distinctive feature of the QGE passages is that Philo characterizes as "literal" three interpretations which have expressions for "Israel seers" (QE 1.12, 21; QE 2.47). We should bear in mind, however, that what Philo calls "literal" does not always conform to the apparent sense of the Biblical narrative. Two of these passages (QE 1.12 and QE 2.47) may favor a construal of the seeing ones as Biblical Israel, because Philo uses the past tense and seems to follow the details of the Biblical narrative fairly closely. The other passage, QE 1.21, examined earlier, also presents a "literal" interpretation, but the discussion is in the present tense and does not clearly intend the Biblical nation. Despite the two instances which may favor an understanding of the group as Biblical Israel, none of these three passages provides enough information to identify conclusively the ones who can see.

A fourth notable feature of QGE is that five or half of the references to "Israel seers" occur in questions on Exodus 24, which describes events related to the giving of the law at Mount Sinai (QE 2.38, 42, 43, 46, 47). In his other writings, Philo devotes very little attention to this event or to specific verses in this Biblical chapter.[45]

Finally, in five passages in which Philo talks about "Israel" or those who can see, he also mentions them as the "chosen γένος" or refers to divine election of this γένος, an aspect he rarely alludes to in his other works.[46] Especially noteworthy is that these passages link election with circumcision (QG 3.49) and with the giving of the law as narrated in Exodus 24 (QE 2.38, 42, 43, 46). Although the Bible explicitly associates both circumcision and the giving of the law with the covenant between God and Israel, Philo rarely discusses either circumcision or the giving of the law and never associates these themes with the covenant or the idea that "Israel" is chosen.[47]

---

[45] For references to interpretations of verses from Exodus 24 in Philo's other works, see *Biblia Patristica: Supplement,* 67–68.

[46] The QGE passages in which Philo describes "Israel" as chosen are QG 3.49; QE 2.38, 42, 43, 46. Philo explicitly describes "Israel" as the chosen race/class in *Post.* 92 (τὸ ἐπίλεκτον γένος) and possibly in *Conf.* 56 (γένος τῶν ἐπιλέκτων). The latter passage is ambiguous about whether the γένος is part of or the same as "Israel." For two instances in which Philo uses the designation "chosen race/class" without the word "Israel," see QG 2.58, where "Israel" is not necessarily intended, and QG 2.65, where "Israel" is clearly intended, even though the word itself is not mentioned. For a discussion about how Philo interprets these phrases and also Biblical verses that depict the covenantal relationship between God and Israel, see the next chapter.

[47] See Gen. 17:11; Exod. 19:5, 24:7–8. Philonic passages outside QGE that mention circumcision are *Sobr.* 8, *Migr.* 92, *Somn.* 2.25, and *Spec.* 1.1–11. On the giving of the law generally, see *Decal.,* especially 1–49, and *Her.* 167–73. Most of Philo's discussions

In different ways, the abovementioned characteristics contribute to the impression that QGE is intended to reflect a wide range of Alexandrian Jewish approaches to the Bible. We have just noted that the focus in *QE* upon Exodus 24 and the affirmation of a link between the chosenness of "Israel" and the giving of the law—or in the case of *QG* 3.49, between chosenness and circumcision—are not typically Philonic features. The prevalence and acceptance here of so-called "literal" interpretations is another feature uncharacteristic of Philo in his other works. Finally, since the etymology and ὁρατικὸν γένος are not linked with the philosophical significance of seeing, Philo's use of these two expressions appears to reflect an earlier, traditional understanding. If one regards QGE, however, as a collection of various types of Alexandrian Jewish exegesis for a broad spectrum of Jewish readers, these atypical features become more understandable.

Non-Exegetical Works

Of all the non-exegetical works, only *Legat.* mentions "Israel" and the etymology. The phrase ὁρατικὸν γένος, race/class that can see, does not occur in any of the non-exegetical works.

In *Legat.* 4, Philo uses the word "Israel" and provides the etymology as an explanation of this name. Since he elaborates upon the philosophical importance of seeing God in this passage, "Israel," the ὁρῶν θεόν, or one that sees God, appears to indicate a group capable of this spiritual vision. Furthermore, since the treatise is about the contemporary political situation of the Jews in Alexandria and elsewhere, we can identify this group with Philo's Jewish contemporaries. In this passage, then, it would seem that Philo equates the one who sees God with the Jews. Moreover, he suggests here that the Jewish way is superior even to that of philosophy.

Why would Philo wish to equate "Israel" with all Jews in this political treatise, when he does not do so anywhere else? And why would he wish to emphasize that "Israel"'s vision and the Jews' way of life excels any other vision or way of life? Once again, a consideration of Philo's aims and audience may shed light upon these questions. In this treatise, Philo presents for all to know the story of his persecuted countrymen. Presumably he hopes to elicit sympathy, outrage, and finally admiration

---

about the episode at Sinai, narrated in Exodus 19–24, focus upon specific verses and laws rather than the significance of the event. See Jaubert, *La notion d'Alliance*, 375–442, and John J. Collins, "A Symbol of Otherness: Circumcision and Salvation in the First Century," *"To See Ourselves As Others See Us": Christians, Jews, "Others" in Late Antiquity,* Scholars Press Studies in the Humanities, ed. Jacob Neusner and Ernest S. Frerichs (Chico, California: Scholars Press, 1985), 163–86.

for them. Toward this end, perhaps, he presents his people as the finest
with respect to their minds, their virtuous behavior, and their worship of
the greatest Being.

Depending upon which Philonic work one reads, then, "Israel," the ὁρῶν
θεόν (one that sees God), or the ὁρατικὸν γένος (race/class that can see)
may be somewhat different for the reasons just described. However Philo
may understand "Israel" in his heart of hearts, though, it is certain that in
the Bible, "Israel" is the name of the nation chosen by God to be His
special people and to enter into a covenant with Him. Up to this point, we
have concentrated upon how Philo may redefine "Israel." Let us now
consider how he approaches the relationship between God and the nation
Israel as it is described in the Bible.

CHAPTER FOUR

PHILONIC INTERPRETATIONS
OF THE RELATIONSHIP BETWEEN GOD
AND BIBLICAL ISRAEL

Earlier chapters have shown that Philo's "Israel" is somewhat different from the nation Israel whose history is narrated in the Pentateuch. We shall now look at how Philo interprets the relationship between God and this nation as the Bible portrays it. Since Philo's exegetical efforts focus upon the Pentateuch, let us begin by considering how the Pentateuch presents this relationship and what some possible ramifications of this presentation might be. We shall then turn to Philo's interpretation of the Pentateuchal account by examining a selection of passages from his works.

The Relationship Between God and Israel
As Described in the Pentateuch

In the Book of Exodus (chapters 19–24), God establishes His covenant with the people of Israel at Mount Sinai, a covenant that fulfills His promises to Israel's ancestors—the patriarchs, Abraham, Isaac, and Jacob. The Bible does not provide a completely consistent account either of divine promises to the patriarchs concerning their descendant nation or of the covenant between God and Israel. Instead, Scripture unfolds details about these matters, repeating, reworking, omitting, and adding to these details as the narrative progresses.

To each of the patriarchs, Abraham, Isaac, and Jacob, God announces His intentions for their descendants, promising to make them a great and populous nation, to bless them, to give them the land of Canaan, and to establish His covenant with them.[1] At Sinai (Exodus 19–24), He enters into a covenant with the whole nation Israel. Subsequent parts of the Pentateuch and especially the Book of Deuteronomy refer to and develop various aspects of this covenant relationship.[2]

---

[1] These promises appear several times with variations. For God's promises to *Abraham*, see, e.g., Gen. 12:1–3, 7; 15:13–16, 18–21; 17:1–14, 16, 19–21; 18:18–19; 22:17–18; *Isaac*: Gen. 26:2–5, 24; *Jacob*: Gen. 28:13–15; 35:9–12. God also establishes a covenant with Abraham.

[2] For scholarly discussion about the covenant and related issues, see Klaus Baltzer,

Basically, the divine promises to the patriarchs and the covenant between God and Israel involve God's choice of one nation upon which He bestows His blessings. The covenant with the nation includes the added feature of a formal agreement entailing specific conditions for the people to follow, namely, obedience to God's commandments.[3] Israel receives God's laws and statutes with few, if any, explanations about their intrinsic worth or meaning. For the most part, these stipulations are delivered with divine authority and no other explicit rationale.

The Bible does not provide a consistent reason for God's choice of Israel or its ancestors. At times this choice remains unexplained; at other times, it seems to be based upon God's love; at still other times, God's choice of the nation is linked with His previous commitment to the patriarchs.

In Exod. 6:2–8, for example, God declares that He will bring the people of Israel out of Egypt to the land that He promised their forefathers, instructing Moses to tell the nation, "I will take you for my people, and I will be your God" (Exod. 6:7).[4]

Elsewhere, God stresses that the people must fulfill certain obligations: "And now, if you will obey My voice and keep My covenant, you shall be to Me a special people among all the nations; for all the earth is Mine, and you shall be to Me a royal priesthood and a holy nation" (Exod. 19:5–6, my translation). Similarly, in Lev. 26:3–13, God announces that if the people fulfill His commandments, He will uphold His covenant with

---

The Covenant Formulary in Old Testament, Jewish, and Early Christian Writings, trans. David E. Green (Philadelphia: Fortress Press, 1971); Walther Eichrodt, Theology of the Old Testament, trans. J. A. Baker, 2 vols., The Old Testament Library (Philadelphia: Westminster Press, 1961), esp. vol. 1; Delbert R. Hillers, Covenant: The History of a Biblical Idea, Seminars in the History of Ideas (Baltimore: Johns Hopkins Press, 1969); Jaubert, La notion d'Alliance, esp. 27–66; Jon D. Levenson, Sinai and Zion: An Entry into the Jewish Bible, New Voices in Biblical Studies, ed. Adela Yarbro Collins and John J. Collins (San Francisco: Harper & Row, 1985); Dennis J. McCarthy, Treaty and Covenant: A Study in Form in the Ancient Oriental Documents and in the Old Testament, 2nd ed., Analecta Biblica, 21 (Rome: Biblical Institute, 1978); George E. Mendenhall, Law and Covenant in Israel and the Ancient Near East (Pittsburgh: Biblical Colloquium, 1955); Gerhard von Rad, Old Testament Theology, trans. D. M. G. Stalker, 2 vols. (New York: Harper & Row, 1962 and 1965), esp. vol. 1; Harold Henry Rowley, The Biblical Doctrine of Election (London: Lutterworth Press, 1952); Seock-Tae Sohn, The Divine Election of Israel (Grand Rapids, Michigan: Eerdmans, 1991).

[3] Some divine blessings to the patriarchs also mention conditions but, aside from circumcision (Genesis 17), these conditions pertain generally to obedience to God's commands, which are not specified. See, e.g., Gen. 17:1, 18:19, 22:18, 26:5.

[4] As explained in the Note to the Reader, Bible translations are from the RSV (1952), unless otherwise indicated. Occasionally the Greek Bible, which Philo uses, differs significantly from the Hebrew text, upon which the RSV is based. In these instances, I have either modified the RSV translation to reflect the Greek and inserted the modification within brackets, or I have provided my own translations based upon the Greek.

them, declaring, "I will walk among you, and will be your God, and you shall be my people" (Lev. 26:12).

In other passages, particularly in Deuteronomy, Moses reminds the people of this relationship, highlighting different elements at different times. In one address to Israel, for example, he mentions divine love and divine promises to the nation's ancestors:

> For you are a people holy to the Lord your God; the Lord your God has chosen you to be [a special people to Him beyond all the nations] that are on the face of the earth. It was not because you [are] more in number than [all the nations] that the Lord [preferred] you and chose you, for you [are] the fewest of all [the nations]; but it is because the Lord loves you, and is keeping the oath which he swore to your fathers ... (Deut. 7:6–8)

In Deut. 9:5, Moses denies that God gives Israel the promised land because of the people's own inherent qualities. Instead he contends that God's behavior is motivated by the impiety of other nations and by His agreement with the patriarchs. Moses declares,

> Not because of your righteousness or the piety of your heart are you going in to possess their land, but because of the impiety of these nations the Lord will utterly destroy them from before you, and that He may establish His covenant which He swore to your fathers, to Abraham, to Isaac, and to Jacob. (Deut. 9:5, my translation)

Finally, while most of these passages depict God as initiating the relationship by selecting Israel or its ancestors, Deut. 26:16–19 suggests a mutual choice indicating the nation's obedience to divine commandments as a central component:

> On this day the Lord your God has commanded you to do all these ordinances and decrees and you shall keep and do them with all your heart and with all your soul. Today you have chosen God to be your God and to walk in His ways and keep His ordinances and decrees and obey His voice; and the Lord has chosen you today to be a special people to Him, just as He said to you, to keep all His commandments, and that you be above all the nations, as He has made you famous and an object of pride and glorified, that you be a holy people to the Lord your God, just as He has spoken. (Deut. 26:16–19, my translation)

The Pentateuch, then, portrays the link between God and Israel in different and somewhat inconsistent ways. It is not clear why God selects Israel above all the other nations and indeed His choice may appear somewhat arbitrary. Nonetheless, it *is* clear that God chooses Israel to enter into a special relationship with Him. Central to this relationship is the covenant, the agreement He makes with the people to be their God and to stand by them if they follow His commandments.

Potential Ramifications of the Pentateuchal Account

Certain features of the account outlined above are potentially offensive to different people for any number of reasons. Although Philo never cites specific charges concerning the Biblical claims, one may speculate about possible objections on the basis of how he presents Biblical Israel and indeed his own Jewish contemporaries.[5]

God's apparently arbitrary choice of Israel, for example, might be offensive to individuals—whether Jewish or not—whose conception of God is philosophical. The idea that the truly Existent might be swayed by favoritism would be incompatible with their beliefs about His rational nature, since favoritism suggests an emotional, i.e., non-rational, component. A related problem is how or why the universal God of all creation might be especially concerned about the welfare of one particular people. Yet another potentially troubling aspect of the covenant is that God requires specific practices, such as following dietary restrictions, which do not appear to have any rational basis. Finally, even for those not concerned about these various intellectual difficulties, the self-proclamation of one nation to be specially chosen by God can appear boastful and arouse hostility among other peoples.[6]

When Philo interprets Biblical verses that deal explicitly with divine promises to the patriarchs or with the covenant between God and Israel, he may be implicitly addressing some of these concerns. For one thing, he redefines or completely omits mention of the word "covenant," thereby eliminating the image of a preset agreement. He transforms the meaning of certain verses to suggest that God chooses not the nation Israel but any virtuous person or soul. God's choice then no longer appears arbitrary but instead can be understood to be based upon merit. Finally, Philo does not mention the particular statutes and commandments as conditions of the covenant but rather speaks generally about virtue and harmony in one's behavior. These various characteristics of Philo's approach are illustrated below.

Philonic Interpretations of the Relationship Between God and Biblical Israel

As is typical of his approach to most Biblical themes, Philo does not address the relationship between God and Israel in one place or in a uniform way. Even in his treatises on Moses, which retell in part the story

---

[5] Our present concern is with Philo's interpretations of the Biblical account. In the next chapter, we shall consider his remarks about the Jews and their ancestors.

[6] On some of these problems, see Attridge, *The Interpretation of Biblical History*, 149, esp. n. 1; Ephraim E. Urbach, *The Sages: Their Concepts and Beliefs*, trans. Israel Abrahams (Cambridge: Harvard University Press, 1987), 525–54.

of Israel's exodus from Egypt, Philo concentrates more upon the role of Moses than upon the nation. Where the Bible narrates the relationship between God and Biblical Israel as a series of encounters between God and the patriarchs and God and the nation, Philo deals with these encounters synchronically—not as a series of events but as separate passages in different exegetical contexts. To learn how he understands this relationship, then, requires that we examine his discrete treatments of individual passages. Before turning to this examination, however, let us briefly consider how Philo deals with two specific terms or notions which also merit our attention, namely, the idea of the covenant and the phrase "chosen people [or race/class]."

The Covenant. The Bible describes a variety of covenants—those that take place between people, between God and individuals, and between God and the nation Israel. The Greek Bible, upon which Philo bases his interpretations, translates the Hebrew word ברית, or covenant, as διαθήκη, a word which also carries the sense of a testament, will, or disposition.

While our chief interest is in the covenant between God and Israel, it is worth noting that even where he discusses other covenants, Philo never affirms the Biblical sense of διαθήκη as a mutual agreement with stated conditions. Often he interprets the term symbolically, without presenting a uniform understanding of what a covenant, especially God's covenant, is. Although he refers to two treatises of his own on the subject of covenants (*Mut.* 53; cf. *QE* 2.34), unfortunately, these works have not survived.[7]

While Philo occasionally speaks of God's covenants in the Allegory and QGE, he never mentions them in the Exposition.[8] Especially noteworthy is that despite the centrality of the covenant to the relationship between God and Israel in the Bible, Philo mentions this covenant only four times (*Sacr.* 57; *Det.* 67; *QE* 2.34, 106). In the two passages in which he expounds upon the term (*Sacr.* 57 and *QE* 2.106), he interprets it symbolically.

Given the predominance of the covenant theme in the Bible, Philo's sparse mention of it is surprising. Discussion of the covenant, however, is also rare in other literature from this period that may be intended for

---

[7] The word διαθήκη appears in the following Philonic passages: *Leg.* 3.85 (2); *Sacr.* 57 (2); *Det.* 67–68; *Her.* 313; *Mut.* 51, 52 (3), 53, 57, 58 (3), 263; *Somn.* 2.223 (2), 224 (2), 237; *Spec.* 2.16. In addition, covenants are spoken of in *QG* 3.40, 42, 60 and *QE* 2.34, 106. Except for *Spec.* 2.16, in which the word denotes a person's will, all the other references pertain to God's covenants with people, e.g., Noah, Abraham, Isaac, or the nation Israel. For a survey of how Philo interprets God's covenant, see Jaubert, *La notion d'Alliance*, 414–37.

[8] In the Exposition, the word διαθήκη appears once, in *Spec.* 2.16, where it refers to a person's will. See also Colson, *Philo*, LCL, 7:316, nn. 1 and a.

people unfamiliar with Jews and Judaism.[9] A possible reason for this lack of attention is that writers may feel the depiction of an exclusive, and apparently arbitrary, relationship between God and Israel or between God and the Jews could be offensive to outsiders. Perhaps this kind of sensitivity to his audience may explain why Philo does not discuss the covenant in the Exposition. Nevertheless, the fact that he understands the term in a variety of ways in his other writings and that he never affirms the Biblical sense of the covenant suggests that he may indeed not consider it central to the relationship between God and Israel. Without his treatises on the subject, however, we cannot draw any firm conclusions.

The "Chosen People." Besides the notion of the covenant, a phrase that also conveys God's relationship to Israel is "chosen people [or race/class]." The exact expression (τὸ γένος μου τὸ ἐκλεκτόν) appears in Isaiah 43:20 but not in the Pentateuch. Perhaps the phrase closest in meaning to this in the Pentateuch is λαὸς περιούσιος, a special or particular people (Exod. 19:5, 23:22; Deut. 7:6, 14:2, 26:18). Philo uses different Greek equivalents for the expression "chosen people [or race/class]" twice in the Allegory (Post. 92, Conf. 56) and once in the Exposition (Praem. 123);[10] and the English translation of QGE has the expression "chosen race" four times: QG 2.58, 65; QE 2.38, 42. Philo also speaks of God's choice of the people—without using an exact phrase for "chosen people [or race/class]"—two other times in the Exposition (Spec. 1.303, Virt. 184) and three more times in QGE (QG 3.49; QE 2.43, 46).

Despite these various references, however, it is not clear that Philo means to affirm that Israel is a people chosen by God. As we shall see, in the Allegory and the Exposition, he gives new meaning to God's selection of Israel, and in QGE, he uses the phrase "chosen race" as an automatic designation without necessarily intending its literal sense.

General Observations

To be consistent with the approach used throughout this study, we shall consider Philo's treatment of passages by series. Philo speaks about the

---

[9] Attridge, *The Interpretation of Biblical History,* 149, esp. n. 1. For a different perspective on the use or non-use of a word for "covenant" in the rabbinic tradition, see Alan F. Segal, "Covenant in Rabbinic Writings," *The Other Judaisms of Late Antiquity,* Brown Judaic Studies, ed. Jacob Neusner et al., no. 127 (Atlanta: Scholars Press, 1987), 148–65.
[10] *Post.* 92: τὸ ἐπίλεκτον γένος; *Conf.* 56: γένος τῶν ἐπιλέκτων; *Praem.* 123: λαὸς ἐξαίρετος. *Post.* 91–92 and *Praem.* 123 are examined further below. In *Conf.* 56, it is unclear whether the chosen ones are part of or equal to "Israel." This is because when Philo mentions the race/class of the chosen ones of Israel, γένος τῶν ἐπιλέκτων τοῦ Ἰσραήλ, he is interpreting the following phrase from Exod. 24:11: οἱ ἐπίλεκτοι τοῦ Ἰσραήλ, the chosen ones of Israel, which indicates only some members of Israel.

relationship between God and Biblical Israel—either through the interpretation of relevant passages or mention of the "chosen people [or race/
class]"—in all three exegetical commentaries. Although he also discusses
this relationship to some extent in his apologetic work *Hypoth.*, and may
allude to it indirectly in the political treatise *Legat.*, he does not deal there
specifically with passages about God's choice of Biblical Israel or about His
covenant with the people. (We shall examine Philo's remarks in these
other writings in the next chapter, when we turn to the relationship
between God and the Jews.)

One can certainly point to differences in Philo's approach among the
three exegetical series, and we shall see that these differences may be
explained by taking into account the possible aims and audience(s) for
each work. What is common to all Philo's writings, however, is that he
neither denies nor affirms the literal sense of passages about the relationship between God and Israel. Instead, he introduces a variety of new
meanings to this relationship: he interprets Scriptural terms as symbols,
he presents the relationship with God so that it appears available to any
virtuous person, or he sidesteps the significance of the relationship by
focusing upon other issues. (As always, bracketed portions in the Philonic
quotations offered below are my own adaptations to the LCL translation.)

The Allegory

In this section, we shall consider *Sacr.* 57, 87; *Post.* 91–92; and *Migr.* 53–61.
These passages illustrate how Philo changes the sense of Biblical verses
about the relationship between God and Israel by symbolically interpreting such terms as "covenant," "nation," and "Israel"; omitting details
about God's love, His commandments, and His promises to the patriarchs;
and using verses as prooftexts to legitimate points unrelated to the Biblical
context.

Sacr. 57

In this passage—the only one in the Allegory which expands upon God's
covenant with Israel—Philo understands "covenant" differently from the
Bible. In addition, he uses Deut. 9:5, which mentions the covenant, as a
prooftext to support a point unconnected to God's relationship with Israel.
Deut. 9:5, quoted below, explicitly speaks of God's covenant with Israel's
forefathers as a basis for His special favor to the people in bringing them
into the promised land:

> Not because of your righteousness or the piety of your heart are you going in to
> possess their land, but because of the impiety of these nations the Lord will utterly

destroy them from before you, and that He may establish His covenant which He swore to your fathers, to Abraham, to Isaac, and to Jacob. (my translation)

Philo cites this verse in *Sacr.* 57 in the context of a discussion about Cain as a self-lover (φίλαυτος, *Sacr.* 52) rather than a lover of God. The Biblical citation that serves as the basis for this discussion is Gen. 4:3, which says that Cain brought an offering to God "after some days." According to Philo, Cain is at fault for delaying to pay honor to God (*Sacr.* 52). Philo explains that there are three kinds of people who neglect this duty: those who have lost the feeling of gratitude for their well-being out of forgetfulness, those who ascribe their blessings to themselves rather than to God, and finally those who acknowledge that God is the cause of good things but think that they are worthy of His favors on account of their own virtue (*Sacr.* 54).

In elaborating upon this third type, Philo cites Deut. 9:5, giving a new sense to the idea of covenant:

[He that] thinks himself worthy of the possession and enjoyment of good may learn a better lesson from the oracle which says 'Not for thy righteousness nor for the holiness of thy heart dost thou go into the land to [inherit] it,' but first 'because of the iniquity of these nations,' since God visited their wickedness with destruction, and next 'that he might establish the covenant which he sware to our fathers.' Now the covenant of God is an allegory of His gifts of grace, and it may not be that any of His gifts should be imperfect. Thus, all the bounty of the Uncreated must be perfect and complete. But amongst all existing things the one that is complete is virtue and virtuous actions. (*Sacr.* 57)

Philo seems to be saying here that since all God's gifts are perfect, and among created things only virtue is perfect, virtue and virtuous actions must emanate from God's grace rather than from human will. Therefore, those people who think themselves worthy of divine blessings are mistaken because they themselves are not the source of their good behavior. (His argument would have been clearer perhaps had he added that perfect things can come only from God and nothing perfect can come from what is created.)

In any event, Philo is using Deut. 9:5 here because it emphasizes that God brings the people into the land *not because of their own righteousness.* Moreover, by explaining God's covenant with Israel's forefathers as a symbol of His grace, Philo changes the sense of the covenant as an agreement entailing mutual obligations between God and specific men, Israel's ancestors. Instead, according to this exegesis, God's covenant, grace, may be understood to extend to all creation.[11]

---

[11] This is the only passage in which Philo interprets Deut. 9:5. In *Mut.* 52, the term "covenant" is also explained as a symbol of God's grace. This passage interprets Gen. 17:2, a verse that speaks of God's covenant with Abraham.

Sacr. 87

In *Sacr.* 87, at the conclusion of this same discussion of Cain's sacrifice in Gen. 4:3, Philo illustrates God's readiness to accept true worshippers by using as prooftexts two other Biblical verses which describe the divine appointment of Israel. Here again he sidesteps the literal sense of verses that pertain specifically to God and the nation Israel by using these verses to highlight a different point. In the Biblical context of both passages, Exod. 6:7 and Lev. 26:12–13, God instructs Moses to declare to Israel that He will take them for His people and He will be their God.

As noted above, the Philonic passage is a discussion of Gen. 4:3, which reads as follows: "And it came to pass after some days that Cain brought of the fruits of the earth as an offering to God" (LCL translation). Based upon this verse, Philo finds two faults in Cain's behavior. First, as we saw in the discussion of *Sacr.* 57, the words "after some days" suggest to him that Cain delayed in giving thanks. Second, he also believes that Cain was wrong because he made an offering "of the fruits" but not of the *first* fruits (*Sacr.* 52).

Sacr. 87 comes at the end of a long and intricate discussion of Lev. 2:14 concerning the offering of first fruits. In *Sacr.* 76–87, Philo expounds upon what it means to offer first fruits that are new, roasted, sliced, and pounded. He concludes,

> When then you acknowledge as God wills these four things, the 'new,' that is the blossom or vigour; the 'roasted,' that is the fire-tested and invincible reason; the 'sliced,' that is the division of things into their classes; the 'pounded,' that is the persistent practice and exercise in what the mind has grasped, you will bring an offering of the first-fruits, even the first and best offspring of the soul.

After interpreting the offering of first fruits to be a matter of internal discipline of the mind or soul instead of an external ceremony, Philo now says, "Yet even if we are slow to do this, He Himself is not slow to take to Himself those who are fit for His service. 'I will take you,' He says, 'to be My people and I will be your God' [Exod. 6:7], and 'ye shall be to Me a people. I am the Lord' [Lev. 26:12–13]."

The point of these prooftexts is to stress that God responds readily to those who worship Him. In Exod. 6:7 and Lev. 26:12–13, God's words are intended for the people of Israel. In the Exodus context (Exod. 6:2–8), God mentions His covenants with Israel's forefathers, while in Leviticus (26:3–13), He presents Israel's obedience to His commandments as a condition of His fulfillment of promises to them.

As Philo uses the verses, however, both the historic identity of the nation Israel and the circumstances of God's adoption of this people disappear and become irrelevant. Instead, God's words now provide evidence of His immediate willingness to take to Himself true worshippers, understood to be those who offer "first fruits" in the way Philo describes earlier. By concentrating only upon the element of God's adoption of the people and using this element to support his own observation about God's readiness, Philo brackets entirely the original meaning of the verses.[12]

Post. 91–92

This passage provides an example of how Philo redefines the "chosen race." The passage interprets the following verses from Deuteronomy (32:8–9):

> 8When the Most High distributed nations,
> When he dispersed the sons of Adam,
> He set boundaries of nations
> According to the number of the angels of God,
> 9And Jacob His people became the Lord's portion,
> Israel became the lot of His inheritance.[13] (LCL translation)

Most important for our purposes are the last two lines, for they suggest that the people of Israel are uniquely linked with God.

The larger context of the interpretation in *Post.* (83–93) is a discussion about the danger of changing "the boundaries fixed for things by nature" (*Post.* 83) and by divine principles (*Post.* 89). In *Post.* 91, Philo offers the following interpretation of Deut 32:8 as an example of boundaries set by divine principles:

> When God divided and partitioned off the nations of the soul, separating those of one common speech from those of another tongue, and causing them to dwell apart; when He dispersed and put away from Himself the children of the earth, whom the lawgiver calls 'sons of Adam,' then did He fix the boundaries of the offspring of virtue corresponding to the number of the angels; for there are as many forms or 'nations' of virtue as there are words of God.

Without commenting upon the literal sense of the Biblical verses, Philo understands them to apply to the soul: the nations that God distributes become "nations of the soul" (τὰ τῆς ψυχῆς ἔθνη). The second reference to

---

[12] This is the only passage which mentions Exod. 6:7. The following passages also interpret Lev. 26:12: *Post.* 122, *Mut.* 265–66, *Somn.* 1.148, *Somn.* 2.248, *Praem.* 123. Except for *Praem.* 123, discussed below, these other exegeses focus upon the first part of the verse—"I shall walk among you"—and redefine those among whom or "in whom" God walks. *Praem.* 123 also interprets the second part of the verse: "You shall be a people to me."

[13] The Hebrew and Greek differ in the last part of Deut. 32:8. In the Hebrew, God sets the boundaries of nations "according to the number of the sons of Israel (למספר בני ישראל)"; in the Greek, it is "according to the number of the angels of God (κατὰ ἀριθμὸν ἀγγέλων θεοῦ)."

"nations" in verse 8 is construed as offspring (ἔκγονοι) or forms (εἴδη) of virtue. Here as elsewhere, Philo interprets angels as words of God.[14] Thus the angels or words of God are equal in number and correspond to the forms of virtue. Next, he interprets the sons of Adam as children of the earth, an interpretation presumably based upon the connection between the Hebrew words for Adam (אדם) and earth (אדמה) (cf. *Leg.* 1.90). Accordingly, God sets apart from Himself those who are concerned with earthly matters. The separation of earthly and godly pursuits is, of course, a common theme in Philo's work.

Philo then continues, incorporating Deut. 32:9:

> But what are the portions of His angels, and what is the allotted share of the All-Sovereign Ruler? The particular virtues belong to the servants, to the Ruler the chosen [race/class] of Israel. For he that sees God, drawn to him by surpassing beauty, has been allotted [or has allotted himself] as His portion to Him [who is seen]. (*Post.* 92)

This passage contrasts the portions of the angels with the portion of God. The angels or servants get the various forms or species of virtue (αἱ ἐν εἴδει ἀρεταί), while God the Master has for His own the "chosen race/class" of Israel (τὸ ἐπίλεκτον γένος Ἰσραήλ). Here Philo plays upon a double meaning of the word γένος. Although it can signify race or class, as we have seen, it also denotes the genus, or the general class, in contrast to the εἶδος, or species. Thus, the particulars of virtue belong to the subordinates of God, while the genus of virtue or the race/class, γένος, of Israel belongs to Him.

Then, using the etymology for Israel, Philo explains why "Israel" belongs to God: the one who sees God (ὁ ὁρῶν τὸν θεόν) belongs to the One who is seen (ὁ ὁρώμενος). Because the etymology assigns an active role to "Israel" as the one that sees, Philo's interpretation introduces a more reciprocal aspect to the relationship than is portrayed in the Bible. Whereas the Scriptural verse offers no apparent reason for God's appointment of Israel, Philo provides a rationale that makes God's choice seem less arbitrary.

In this interpretation, then, the literal meaning of a passage that might be construed as indicative of a special relationship between God and the nation Israel disappears completely. Philo retains the idea that Israel is chosen but interprets Israel as both generic virtue and the one that sees God. He does not deny that Israel is a real nation that is chosen; he simply ignores the issue.[15]

---

[14] See, e.g., *Conf.* 28, *Migr.* 173, *Somn.* 1.148.
[15] See *Plant.* 58–60 for another example of how Philo redefines Israel in an interpretation of the same passage, Deut. 32:7–9.

Migr. 53–61

The fairly intricate interpretation in this passage provides a good illustration of the different ways in which Philo changes the sense of Biblical verses about God's relationship to Israel. The passage interprets three relevant sections: Gen. 12:2, in which God promises Abraham that He will make him a "great nation" (*Migr.* 53); Deut. 4:6–7, which emphasizes that God is near to the nation, calling it "a wise and knowing people" (*Migr.* 56–58); and Deut. 7:7–8, which says that God chooses the people of Israel not because they are numerous but because He loves them and is keeping His oath with their forefathers (*Migr.* 59–61). In this passage, Philo changes the sense of "great nation"; provides a different basis from the Bible for calling it "a wise and knowing people"; redefines the "nation" to which God is near; and uses Deut. 7:7–8 as a prooftext for an observation unconnected to the Biblical context.

Migr. 53–61 is part of an extended allegory of the soul, in which Philo interprets God's directions to Abraham to leave his homeland (Gen. 12:1–3). In this particular section, Philo is interpreting Gen. 12:2, in which God promises Abraham, "And I will make of you a great nation (ἔθνος μέγα)."

Philo construes this blessing of a "great nation" to be "improvement of the doctrines of virtue toward number and greatness together" (*Migr.* 53, my translation). He focuses upon the phrase "great nation" to develop the idea that "great" signifies growth and improvement while "nation" denotes populousness or large number (*Migr.* 53). The ensuing treatment (through *Migr.* 69) expounds upon this theme of greatness and number, or quality and quantity, through exploration of other occurrences of words such as "great," "many," or "great nation" in other Biblical verses.

After *Migr.* 53, our particular interest is in *Migr.* 56–58, in which Philo interprets Deut. 4:6–7, and *Migr.* 59–61, in which he cites Deut. 7:7–8. Because this exegesis is fairly complicated, I have divided the discussion into two sections.

Migr. 56–58. In *Migr.* 56, Philo turns to Deut. 4:6–7 because this Biblical passage provides two examples of the phrase "great nation." In the Bible, the verses appear in the following context:

Addressing the Israelites, Moses declares,

> 5Behold I have shown you ordinances and decrees, as the Lord commanded me, that you should do so in the land which you are entering to possess. 6And you will observe and do them, because this is your wisdom and understanding in the eyes of all the nations, as many as will hear all these ordinances, and they will say, 'Behold this great nation is a wise and knowing people.' 7For what great nation is there that has God drawing near to it as the Lord our God [draws near to us] in all things for which we may call upon Him? (Deut. 4:5–7, my translation)

Although these verses do not mention God's choice of Israel as explicitly as some of the others considered so far, Deut. 4:7 does refer to the nation's special access to God.

As noted, Philo brings in this passage because it has the phrase "great nation," which occurs twice. According to the Bible, in the first occurrence (Deut. 4:6), the words "great nation" are attributed to "all the nations" that, impressed by Israel's observance of the Mosaic statutes, declare, "Behold this great nation is a wise and knowing people." The second occurrence (Deut. 4:7) is spoken by Moses, who associates the great nation, i.e., Israel, with God's nearness to it. In this second verse, Moses asks, "For what great nation is there that has God drawing near to it as the Lord our God [draws near to us]? ..."

Ignoring the context of the first occurrence, namely, that the words are spoken by all the nations in admiration of Israel's statutes, Philo links the declaration of these nations with Moses's question which follows. As we shall see below, he combines Deut. 4:6 and 7 and uses this combination in two different ways.

In addition, according to the Hebrew, Moses's question in Deut. 4:7 is "For what great nation is there (כי מי גוי גדול) that has [God] so near to it as the Lord our God is to us, whenever we call upon Him?" The implied answer is that only Israel is this great nation. The Greek, however, translates the Hebrew interrogative מי, "who" or "which," as ποῖον—a word that can also mean "what kind of."[16] Thus, in the Greek, Moses's question can be understood as "What kind of great nation is there?" rather than as "What great nation is there?" In answer to the latter question, one would name a particular nation; in answer to the former, one would name a quality.

To return to *Migr.* 56, we find a complicated exegesis that combines this different nuance of the Greek with Philo's concern to explore the meaning of "great nation" as implying both greatness and number. He writes,

> The beginning and end of the greatness and large number of the noble (οἱ καλοί) is the continuous memory of God and the calling down of help from Him against the familiar, confusing, and relentless battle of life, for it says, 'Behold this great nation is a wise and knowing people; for what kind of great nation is there that has God drawing near to it as the Lord our God [draws near to us] in all things for which we may call upon Him?' (*Migr.* 56, my translation)

In the first part of this passage, Philo associates "great nation" with the memory of God and the summoning of His help. Having already set aside the literal meaning of "great nation" by understanding "great" to

---

[16] This is the only instance in which the LXX translates מי as ποῖος. More commonly, it uses τίς or τις.

signify greatness and "nation" to signify populousness, he now ascribes these qualities to the noble. The great nation, then, consists of the noble ones instead of a particular ethnic group.

Next, when Philo quotes Deut. 4:6–7 as a prooftext that the memory of and calling upon God are associated with a great nation, he merges the two Biblical verses Deut. 4:6 and 7 into one. Here we see his first use of these combined verses. As noted above, in Deut. 4:6, when the nations behold Israel's observance of divine statutes, they comment, "Behold this great nation is a wise and knowing people." Philo turns their comment into an implied answer to Moses's question that immediately follows, namely, "What great nation is there? ..." Because the word ποῖον has a different sense, however, Philo understands the question to be "What kind of great nation is there?" He finds the answer in the preceding verse: "This great nation is a wise and knowing people..."

After focusing upon the quality of the great nation as a "wise and knowing people," Philo now turns to the issue of God's drawing near, and he poses another question based upon Deut. 4:7. In this passage he uses the combined verse Deut. 4:6–7 in a slightly different way. He writes,

> So far it has been shown that [at God's side a ready helpful power lies in wait to be of assistance] and that the Sovereign Ruler will Himself draw near for the benefit of those who are worthy to receive His benefits. *But who are they that are worthy to obtain these? Is it not clear that all the lovers of wisdom and knowledge are so?* For these are the wise and understanding people which was spoken of, each member of which is with good reason great, since he reaches out after great things; and after one most eagerly, never to be severed from God, the supremely Great, but without dismay stedfastly to abide His approach as He draws near. (*Migr.* 57–58, my emphasis)

In this part of his interpretation, Philo seems to understand Deut. 4:6–7 as follows: "This great nation consists of all wise and knowing people because what [other] kind of great nation is there that has God drawing near to it?" Thus, while the Deuteronomic passage uses "wise and knowing people" to *describe* the great nation—namely, the ethnic group Israel—in the eyes of other nations that behold their statutes, Philo uses the phrase "wise and knowing people" to *identify* who they are. Implicitly eliminating the ethnic identity of the people, he argues that the great nation is made up of "all the lovers of wisdom and knowledge."

Finally, Philo concludes by going one step further. He explains that wise and knowing people are great precisely because they strive after God and stand firm as He draws near: "This is the defining mark of the people that is 'great,' to draw nigh to God, or to be that 'to which God draws nigh'" (*Migr.* 59). Here he assigns the nation an active role—namely, to draw near to God—lending it a quality that may explain why God is near to it.

In *Migr.* 56–58, then, Philo transforms the meaning of Deut. 4:6–7 in several ways. By presenting the great nation as wise and knowing people, who are great because they strive toward God, Philo removes any ethnic associations from the great nation. To the question of who is worthy of God's assistance, he answers, "all lovers of wisdom and knowledge." He also ignores the Biblical connection between the nation's wisdom and the divine commandments and links the qualities of wisdom and knowledge instead with the striving toward God. In fact, the passage does not mention God's commandments at all.

Migr. 59–61. From this discussion, Philo goes on to develop the idea that number alone without greatness is not enough (59–69). The beginning of this argument is especially pertinent because it cites Deut. 7:7–8, a Biblical passage that explicitly describes God's selection of Israel. In the passage, Moses addresses Israel as follows: "It was not because you are more numerous than all the nations that the Lord preferred you and chose you, for you are the fewest compared with all the nations; but it is because the Lord loves you and is keeping the oath which He swore to your fathers..." (my translation).

Philo writes, "Now the world and the wise man, the world-citizen, is filled full of good things, many and great, but the remaining mass of men experiences evil things in greater number but fewer good things; for in the medley and confusion of human life the good is rare and scanty" (*Migr.* 59).

Continuing with the theme of "great nation" as signifying greatness and number, Philo notes that the good things that are both many and great are possessed by a select few. On the other hand, many people partake of evil things in plenitude but good things in scarcity, for in the mixture of human life, what is noble is sparse. He then brings in Deut. 7:7–8 as an example of the scarcity of the good among the many and interprets this verse on the level of the soul:

> And for this reason the sacred oracles contain this utterance: 'Not because ye are numerous beyond all the nations did the Lord prefer and choose you out; for ye surpass all the nations in fewness; but because the Lord loveth you.' For were a man to desire to distribute, as it were into nations, the crowd contained in a single soul, many disorderly companies would he find, commanded by pleasures or desires or griefs or fears or again by follies and wrongdoings, and the nearest kinsfolk of these, but one only well-ordered, of which right reason is the captain. (*Migr.* 60)

Philo omits the part of the verse that mentions God's promise to the nation's forefathers, and he does not refer in his interpretation to God's love, although he does include this part in the quotation. Instead he focuses upon the nation's small population: "For ye surpass all the nations in fewness." Philo then provides an allegory of the soul to emphasize the rarity of what is good. Even the soul is a mixture of good and bad, with the bad outnumbering the good. Only one element in the soul, right reason (ὁ ὀρθὸς λόγος), is well-ordered. In this interpretation of Deut. 7:7–8, then, right reason, the only good element among the elements of the soul, corresponds to Israel, the smallest among the nations.

Philo now shifts his interpretation away from the allegory of the soul. In *Migr.* 61–63, he argues that while human beings value the unjust multitude over the single just person, God prefers the few good to the many unjust. He adduces further prooftexts for this argument, but none pertains directly to the selection of Israel.

In *Migr.* 59–61, then, Philo eclipses any sense of God's selection of the ethnic group Israel by interpreting the nation as a symbol of right reason in the soul. Moreover, by arguing that God prefers the few good to the many evil, he suggests that divine choice is based upon virtue rather than, as the Bible implies, lineage.

The Allegory: A Summary

In these examples from the Allegory, Philo transforms or simply ignores the Biblical depiction of God's relationship with Israel. The Bible speaks of a historic nation Israel standing in a special covenantal relationship to God, bound by obedience to His ordinances, favored because of its fore-fathers, or chosen out of God's love. Philo, however, gives new meaning to terms such as "covenant" (*Sacr.* 57), "Israel" (*Post.* 91–92), "chosen race" (*Post.* 91–92), and "nation" (*Post.* 91–92, *Migr.* 53–61). He also ignores or omits reference to God's commandments (*Sacr.* 87, *Migr.* 56–58), His earlier promises to the patriarchs (*Sacr.* 87, *Migr.* 59–60), or His love (*Migr.* 59–60).

Instead, Philo provides the basis for a relationship with God other than through the covenant and, while retaining the notion that God chooses, he redefines who or what is chosen. In *Sacr.* 57, the relationship with God would seem to exist solely on account of divine grace: people cannot be responsible for their virtue, since virtuous behavior is a gift of God's covenant. Other passages, however, suggest that one earns special stand-ing with God through merit. Philo emphasizes, for example, that God responds to the devoted worshipper (*Sacr.* 87) and to those who draw near to Him—i.e., all wise and understanding people (*Migr.* 57–59). Redefining "Israel" as "the one that sees God," he also explains that the one that sees belongs to the one who is seen. This "chosen race of Israel," moreover, is virtue (*Post.* 91–92).

Finally, Philo uses verses about the divine election of Israel as prooftexts to support points unrelated to the Biblical context. In *Sacr.* 87, he uses Exod. 6:7 and Lev. 26:12–13 to demonstrate that God responds readily to the true worshipper, and in *Migr.* 60, he uses Deut. 7:7–8 to make the point that the good is rare.[17]

Generally speaking, then, in this series, Philo reworks the relationship between God and Israel to present the impression that God associates with virtue and with wise and knowing people, who reach out to Him and who see Him. This approach to the Bible appears consistent with his aims and audience in this series. If indeed Philo's readers are people like himself— philosophically sophisticated Jews who are also well-versed in Jewish tradition—then he has no need to emphasize Scripture's portrayal of God's covenantal relationship with a particular nation. Presumably his readers are members of this nation who are or who strive to be among those who can "see"—i.e., "Israel," as Philo understands the term. These readers wish to explore and achieve a deeper relationship between God and the soul. Through his various interpretations of the relationship between God and the nation Israel, Philo shows how Scripture points the way.

The Exposition

In the Exposition too, Philo changes the meaning of Biblical verses about the relationship between God and Israel—but in a somewhat different way. The Allegory frequently interprets individual terms and whole verses allegorically or else uses verses as prooftexts to support points unrelated to the Biblical context. The Exposition, in contrast, often universalizes the meaning of Scripture by applying to all good people what is said of Israel in particular.

As noted earlier, Philo does not mention covenants between people and God at all in this series, even to give them a new meaning. He does emphasize the importance of observing God's commandments, but he generalizes his discussion in two ways. First, he presents God's injunctions as exhortations calling for upright or virtuous behavior in general instead of as specific legal or ritual requirements that are part of an agreement. Second, he speaks as though these commandments were directed toward any virtuous person—not just toward a specific nation. These features may perhaps be accounted for when one considers that Philo may be writing for assimilated Jews or non-Jews unfamiliar with Jewish beliefs and practices.

---

[17] Another example from the Allegory in which Philo brackets the original meaning of a verse by using it as a prooftext is *Sobr.* 66, which comments on Exod. 19:6: "You shall be to me a royal priesthood and a holy nation." See also the interpretation of this verse in the Exposition passage *Abr.* 57, and below, n. 18.

To illustrate these various characteristics, I shall discuss *Spec.* 1.299–300, 303; *Praem.* 83–84, 123; and *Virt.* 184–86.[18]

Spec. 1.299–300, 303

These passages provide a good example of how Philo renders God's message to Israel applicable to a broader audience. In the larger context, *Spec.* 1.299–311, he expounds upon the exhortations addressed to Israel in Deut. 10:12–21. The Biblical passage opens as follows:

> And now, Israel, what does the Lord your God require of you, but to fear the Lord your God, to walk in all his ways, to love him, to serve the Lord your God with all your heart and with all your soul, and to keep the commandments and statutes of the Lord, which I command you this day for your good? (Deut. 10:12–13)

Philo presents these words of Moses as follows:

> [For God, he says, asks from you, O Mind, nothing] that is heavy or complicated or difficult, but only something quite simple and easy. And this is just to love Him as a benefactor, or failing this to fear Him at least as a ruler and lord, and to tread in every way that will lead thee to please Him, to serve Him not halfheartedly but with thy whole soul filled with the determination to love Him and to cling to His commandments and to honour justice. (*Spec.* 1.299–300)

Several points are of interest in this interpretation. First, Philo changes the addressee from Israel to the mind. He emphasizes that what God asks is not a burden but rather something simple. Considering his discussion in the Allegory, it is striking that here he retains the injunction to keep God's commandments. To this he adds that one should honor justice. Finally, while the Bible enjoins Israel equally to fear and love God, Philo places the love of God above fear of Him, implying that He is more kindly than stern.[19]

Another important difference between the Bible and Philo's discussion can be found later in this section (*Spec.* 1.303), where Philo interprets Deut. 10:15. This verse, which refers explicitly to God's choice of Biblical Israel's ancestors, reads as follows: "Yet the Lord deliberately chose your fathers to

---

[18]   Also of interest are *Abr.* 56–59 and *Virt.* 163–74. In *Abr.* 56–59, Philo refers to Exod. 19:6: "You shall be to Me a royal priesthood and a holy nation" (my translation). Philo explains that the name of the nation is "Israel," which means "one that sees God," and he goes on to elaborate about the vision of God. Here then, he introduces ambiguity about whether "Israel" is the historical nation or a group defined by its ability to see God, ignoring the idea that God chooses the nation Israel to be a special people to Him. In *Virt.* 163–74, Philo interprets Deut. 8:11–18, which refers to God's covenant with Israel. Philo omits mention of the covenant and interprets the verses as applying to people in general.

[19]   Philo also places love of God above fear of Him in *Deus* 69; cf. *Migr.* 21.

love them and chose their descendants after them, you above all nations, as on this day" (my translation). In contrast, Philo writes, "Yet out of the whole human race He chose as of special merit (ἀριστίνδην) and judged worthy of pre-eminence over all, those who are in a true sense men (οἱ πρὸς ἀλήθειαν ἄνθρωποι), and called them to service of Himself..." (*Spec.* 1.303). In this interpretation, God's apparently arbitrary choice of Israel's ancestors becomes His selection of "true persons" on account of their merit.

In this section of *Spec.* 1, then, Philo portrays Moses's address to the particular nation of Israel as an exhortation to the mind in general, and he depicts the specific obligations placed upon Israel as a way of life that should be attractive to any virtuous person. Like the Bible, Philo too enjoins observance of God's commandments. By adding, however, the words "to honor justice," one of the cardinal virtues, he conveys the sense that keeping the commandments is a matter of upholding virtue. Finally, Philo eliminates the seeming arbitrariness of God's selection of Israel's ancestors as Scripture presents it. Retaining the notion that God chooses a select group, he redefines this group and attributes God's choice to their merit.

Praem. 79–126

Some of the features noted above are also apparent in *Praem.* 79–126, in which Philo tells about the blessings—mentioned in Leviticus and Deuteronomy—which are bestowed upon those who obey the commandments. Especially noteworthy is that Philo emphasizes obedience to the commandments (*Praem.* 98, 101, 106, 110–11, 119, 126) and speaks about those who receive the attendant blessings as good or wise men in general rather than as members of Israel or as Jews (*Praem.* 112, 120). Below, we shall examine two sections of this long passage—*Praem.* 83–84 and 123.

Praem. 83–84

This first section comments upon Deut. 4:6–7, which Philo also interprets in *Migr.* 56–59, discussed above. In that passage from the Allegory, Philo omits the Biblical emphasis on the nation's obedience to the commandments. Here in *Praem.*, however, he acknowledges the importance of the commandments but generalizes the audience to whom the Biblical message is addressed.

Again, Scripture reads as follows:

> 5Behold I have shown you ordinances and decrees, as the Lord commanded me, that you should do so in the land which you are entering to possess. 6And you will observe and do them, because this is your wisdom and understanding in the eyes

of all the nations, as many as will hear all these ordinances, and they will say, 'Behold this great nation is a wise and knowing people.' 7For what great nation is there that has God drawing near to it as the Lord our God [draws near to us] in all things for which we may call upon Him? (Deut. 4:5–7, my translation)

Here Israel is distinguished, on the one hand, by its commandments (verse 6) and, on the other, by its special access to God (verse 7).

As noted above, the treatment of this passage in *Praem.* 83–84 is part of Philo's description of the rewards granted for obedience to the divine commandments. The first category of blessings is victory over one's enemies. Philo introduces this category (*Praem.* 80–81) with some general comments based upon Deut. 30:11–14 about how the commandments are not too burdensome and should be followed in words, thoughts, and deeds. In *Praem.* 82, he turns to Deut. 4:6 and writes,

Now when the commandments of the laws are merely spoken, they meet with little or no acceptance, but when consequent and concomitant deeds are added in all the habits of life, the commandments will shine around, as it were, brought up from deep darkness into light, through praise and acclamation. (my translation)

This comment that it is not enough simply to give lip service to the laws but that they should also be observed in practice may be a construal of the double injunction in Deut. 4:6 that Israel should observe the commandments and do them. From the redundancy of the two verbs, Philo may deduce that the first signifies speaking, while the second signifies acting. Whether or not this interpretation is prompted by the verbal redundancy, however, Philo's statement that the meaning of the laws is enhanced by their observance is quite significant. Indeed, he rarely emphasizes practice of the commandments, preferring instead to discuss their spiritual meaning.[20]

Philo continues,

For who even of those who are malicious in nature would not say, 'Surely this race/class (γένος) alone is wise and most knowing to whom it befell to leave the divine teachings not empty and void of the deeds akin to them, but who fulfilled the words with praiseworthy deeds'? (*Praem.* 83, my translation)

In the Bible, the observation "Surely this great nation is a wise and knowing people" is attributed to the other nations when they behold the ordinances which Israel obeys. Here, Philo comments that anyone, even a malicious person, would make such an observation.[21] He also suggests

---

[20] Cf. the often-quoted *Migr.* 93, in which Philo writes that observance of the laws is as important as their spiritual meaning.

[21] Perhaps since Philo is about to discuss victory over one's enemies as a reward for following the commandments, he wishes to suggest that obedience to the laws would stir admiration even among one's enemies. Thus he claims that the observation

that the nation continues to deserve admiration. Moreover, since Philo speaks in the past tense about the γένος that has fulfilled God's commandments, he appears to be talking about the Jews and their ancestors.

Finally, he concludes,

> Such a [race/class (γένος)] has its dwelling not far from God; it has the vision of ethereal loveliness always before its eyes, and its steps are guided by a heavenward yearning. So that if one should ask 'what manner of nation is great?' (ποῖον ἔθνος μέγα) others might aptly answer 'a nation which has God to listen to its [most reverent] prayers and to draw nigh when they call upon him with a clean conscience.' (*Praem.* 84)

Again, the Greek translation of the question in Deut. 4:7 can be understood either as "What kind of great nation is there?" or as "What great nation is there?" as the Hebrew intends. In *Migr.* 56–59, Philo answers this question with the words that precede in Deut. 4:6, namely, that the great nation is made up of wise and knowing people. Here, however, he divides the entire question posed in Deut. 4:7 into a question and an answer. Instead of "What kind of great nation is there that has God drawing near to it? ..." he asks, "What kind of nation is great?" His answer is based upon the rest of Deut. 4:7: the great nation is the one that has God drawing near to it whenever its members call upon Him.

In the question posed in Scripture, Moses implies that Israel is the great nation and he calls God "our God." Philo, however, stops short of identifying the nation. Instead he simply answers in the third person, amplifying the nature of the call and the intention of the callers. Thus he writes that the great nation is the one *whose most reverent prayers* reach God and whose members find Him near when they call upon Him *with pure conscience* (*Praem.* 84, my emphasis). Unlike the Scriptural verse, which gives the sense that God responds automatically to the nation Israel whenever its people summon Him, this interpretation suggests that He responds only when a call is motivated by genuine holiness and purity.

What is especially striking about this interpretation—at least compared with his treatment in the Allegory—is Philo's emphasis upon following the laws in practice. Here he upholds both characteristics of the great nation mentioned in the Bible—observance of the laws and nearness to God. While the original words in Deuteronomy are addressed to the historic people Israel, however, Philo derives from them a general lesson for all time: even one's "worst enemies" will admire the kind of people who uphold the laws. By using the past tense, he implies that up until now, these people have been the Jews and their ancestors.

---

made by the nations would be made even by a wicked person.

Besides using the Biblical phrase ἔθνος μέγα, great nation, Philo also uses the more ambiguous word γένος, race/class or kind, to describe the group that observes the commandments. Because he uses γένος sparingly in his exegetical works when he speaks about the real Biblical or contemporary nation, his choice of words here may underscore his emphasis in this passage that what is primarily important is practice of the laws and the worshipper's purity of intention rather than—as the Bible implies—membership in the historic nation Israel.

Praem. 123

At the end of this long passage in *Praem.* (79–126) about the blessings or rewards bestowed upon those who live virtuously and obey the commandments, Philo gives new meaning to the phrase "chosen people." In this larger section, he discusses the blessings in categories, grouping together, for example, the blessings of victory over enemies or blessings of different kinds of wealth. Beginning in *Praem.* 118, he turns to the blessings bestowed upon the body. Particularly relevant here is his interpretation of Lev. 26:12, quoted further below.

Although the blessings in the Biblical passages are directed toward the nation Israel, Philo again changes the recipient of these blessings to the more general "man of worth" (σπουδαῖος, *Praem.* 120). In *Praem.* 120–22, he explains that bodily health is bestowed upon the man of worth particularly for the sake of the mind, that it may enjoy peacefulness and devote itself to contemplation of wisdom and holy thoughts. At this point, he brings in Lev. 26:12: "I shall walk among you (ἐν ἡμῖν) and I shall be God to you and you shall be My people" (my translation).

Philo transposes the meaning of this verse to the level of the mind (νοῦς, *Praem.* 120; διάνοια, *Praem.* 123). Likening the mind to God's house, he elaborates upon the metaphor of God walking, understanding ἐν ἡμῖν, among you, as "in you." It is the mind of the good man, he declares,

> in which God, so says the prophet, 'walks' as in a palace, for in truth the wise man's mind is a palace and house of God. This it is which is declared to possess personally the God who is the God of all, this again is the chosen people (λαὸς ἐξαίρετος), the people not of particular rulers, but of the one and only true ruler, [a holy people of a holy ruler]. (*Praem.* 123)

By identifying the "chosen people" as the mind of the man of worth, Philo completely changes the original meaning of a verse that describes God's choice of the nation Israel to be His people. The universal "God of all" becomes the personal God of the mind of the man of worth, not of a specific nation. Moreover, unlike a specific people, the mind is not subject to any particular ruler, but to God alone. In changing the recipient of the

blessings from the nation Israel to the man of worth and in understanding the "chosen people" to be the mind of such a man, Philo shows his
readers that the particular teachings of Judaism carry universal import.

Virt. 184–86

In this passage, Philo conveys a similar message to his audience. The
larger context in *Virt.* (175–86) is a discussion of repentance or conversion
(μετάνοια). As part of this discussion, Philo emphasizes that even one
worshipper may be equal in worth to a whole nation. To argue this point,
he again changes the sense of a Biblical passage (Deut. 26:17–18) that
expresses the relationship between God and the nation Israel.

Although Philo begins the section by speaking about μετάνοια as
repentance (*Virt.* 175–79), he then turns to a different aspect of μετάνοια,
i.e., the change from revering created things to honoring God (*Virt.* 180).
Here he speaks about proselytes (*Virt.* 181–82). In *Virt.* 183, Philo goes on to
emphasize, on the basis of Deut. 30:11–14, that what is required is not
beyond one's reach. The Deuteronomy passage is as follows:

> For the Lord your God will again rejoice in you for good, just as He rejoiced in
> your fathers, if you will listen to the voice of the Lord your God, to observe and do
> all His commandments and His ordinances and His decrees that are written in
> the book of this law, if you turn to the Lord your God with all your heart and with
> all your soul. For this commandment which I command you today is not excessive
> nor is it far from you... The word is very near you, in your mouth and in your
> heart and in your hands, that you may do it. (Deut. 30:9–11, 14, my translation)

Philo understands "mouth, heart, and hands" to signify "words,
thoughts, and deeds," explaining, "For the mouth is a symbol of speech,
the heart [a symbol] of thoughts and intentions, and the hands [a sym-
bol] of action and in these lies happiness" (*Virt.* 183). He elaborates, "For
when thoughts correspond to words and actions correspond to intentions,
life is praiseworthy and perfect, but when they are at strife with each
other, it is imperfect and a matter for reproach" (*Virt.* 184). In praising the
harmony of words, thoughts, and deeds, Philo does not specify the commandments, which are central to the original context in Deuteronomy.
Instead, it would seem that this harmony is achieved through unspecified
means.

Philo then modifies Deut. 26:17–18. The Biblical verses read, "Today
you have chosen God to be your God and to walk in His ways and keep
His ordinances and decrees and obey His voice; and the Lord has chosen
you today to be a special people (λαὸς περιούσιος) to Him, just as He said to
you (καθάπερ εἶπεν σοι), to keep all His commandments..." (my translation).

In *Virt.* 184–85, Philo writes,

If someone does not neglect this harmony [among thoughts, words, and deeds],
he will be well-pleasing to God, becoming at the same time God-loving and God-
beloved. Wherefore in full accord with these words, this oracle was delivered:
'Today you have chosen God to be God to you, and the Lord has chosen you today to
be a people to Him.' Beautiful is the mutuality of the choice, with a person, on the
one hand, hastening to serve the Existent, and, on the other, God hastening
immediately to take to Himself the suppliant and to anticipate the intention of the
one who sincerely and honestly comes to His service.' (my translation)

Comparing Philo's Scriptural quotation with the original verses, we can
see that he makes three omissions: the condition of obedience to the
commandments, the reference to God's earlier promise (καθάπερ εἶπεν
σοι), and the adjective περιούσιος, special, that modifies λαός, people.[22] As
to the first, by using this passage as a prooftext for what happens when
one's thoughts, words, and deeds are in agreement, Philo ignores the
condition of obedience to the commandments, changing it to achievement of harmony among thoughts, words, and deeds. Without explaining how one ought to achieve this harmony, he argues that when
someone does arrive at this state, that person will "be well-pleasing to God,
becoming at the same time God-loving and God-beloved." Thus, instead of
mentioning obedience, Philo instead stresses the immediately reciprocal
nature of the relationship between God and anyone who achieves harmony in his or her behavior. In keeping with his earlier claim that God's
requirements are not burdensome, perhaps he prefers to present these
requirements as somewhat general than to call attention to the specific
obligations of the commandments.

Second, by omitting mention of God's promise, Philo eliminates the
sense that His action is part of a standing agreement between God and a
particular people. The third modification, omission of the word for
"special" to describe the people, may or may not be significant.

The real point of the interpretation, however, seems to be what Philo
says next. He continues, "And the true servant and suppliant, even though
in actual number he be but one, is in real value, what God's own choice
makes him, the whole people, in worth equal to a complete nation"
(*Virt.* 185).[23]

---

[22] Further discrepancies—which are not immediately relevant to the present discussion—can be found in other manuscripts of this passage. See David T. Runia, "Underneath Cohn and Colson: The Text of Philo's *De Virtutibus*," *SBL 1991 Seminar Papers*,
SBL Seminar Paper Series, ed. Eugene Lovering, Jr., no. 30 (Atlanta: Scholars Press),
126.
[23] In the LCL edition, F. H. Colson notes that the phrase καθάπερ αὐτὸς αἱρεῖται,
which he translates, "what God's own choice makes him," is obscure, and he suggests
several possible emendations. See LCL, 8:276–77, n. 3 and 448, note on *Virt.* 185.

This exegesis is based upon a point of grammar in Deut. 26:17–18, namely, that the pronoun "you" in these verses is singular. Because Moses's words are addressed to a singular "you," and because a singular "you" is said to choose and be chosen, Philo derives the lesson that an individual suppliant is of equal value to a whole nation. He concludes, "Against the worth of a whole nation the wise man can hold his own, protected by the impregnable wall of godliness" (*Virt.* 186).

Significantly, Philo does not acknowledge the literal sense of the Biblical verses that God and the people of Israel choose each other, and he omits reference to the nation's agreement to obey God's commandments. Instead, he changes the sense of a passage that describes the exclusive relationship between God and the historical nation to give the impression that such a relationship can be achieved by any genuine suppliant, a wise man, who seeks to please God and to serve Him.

The Exposition: A Summary

In this series, Philo presents the relationship between God and Biblical Israel as one that is accessible to any virtuous person. He changes the addressee of Moses's exhortations from Israel to the mind (*Spec.* 1.299) and the recipient of God's blessings from Israel to the man of worth (*Praem.* 120). God does indeed have special relationships with people; the "chosen," however, are not a particular historical or contemporary nation but the mind of the man of worth (*Praem.* 123), those who are people in truth (*Spec.* 1.303), or the true suppliant (*Virt.* 185–86).

Although Philo notes that obedience to the commandments is important, he stresses that what God requires is easy and not too demanding (*Spec.* 1.299–300, *Praem.* 80–81, *Virt.* 183). Indeed, obeying these commandments is similar to achieving harmony in words, thoughts, and deeds (*Praem.* 81, *Virt.* 184). Even one's "worst enemies" must acknowledge the wisdom of those who fulfill these ordinances (*Praem.* 83). By changing the meaning of passages about Biblical Israel so they might apply to all virtuous people and by presenting God's commandments as exhortations to virtue and harmony—which are easy to follow—Philo depicts Judaism as a way of life that his readers might want to consider.

QGE

In this series, Philo does not directly interpret any verses, such as those quoted at the beginning of the chapter, about the relationship between God and Israel. He does, however, mention God's covenants with Abraham, Isaac, and the nation Israel, and he comments about the covenant in passing when speaking of the ark of the covenant. In addition, the English translation uses the phrase "chosen race" several times, and some passages refer to the election of Israel or the ὁρατικὸν γένος (the race/class that can see).[24]

As we saw in the last chapter, Philo comments more here than in his other exegetical works on verses from Exodus 24, in which God establishes His covenant with the people of Israel. Out of seven references in QGE to the "chosen race" or to the election of the race, four occur in his discussion of Exodus 24. Finally, Philo links election with the commandment for circumcision and with the giving of the law, both of which the Bible associates with God's covenants, first with Abraham, and then with Israel. Unfortunately, the meaning of the relevant passages in this series is fairly obscure. Before examining two sample passages (QG 3.49 and QE 2.42), I shall first review briefly Philo's comments about the covenant with Israel and about the "chosen race."

The Covenant in QGE

Philo cites the covenant between God and Israel twice: first, in relation to Exod. 24:7, in which Moses takes "the book of the covenant" and reads it "to the ears of the people" (QE 2.34) and second, in relation to Exod. 27:21, which speaks of the ark of the covenant (QE 2.106). In his interpretation of Exod. 24:7 (QE 2.34), Philo focuses upon what Scripture means when it says, "reading to the ears." He quickly dismisses the topic of the divine covenant, noting that he has spoken of this "in detail" elsewhere.[25]

Philo's interpretation of the covenant in QE 2.106 is somewhat obscure, although it is clear that he gives it a different sense from the Bible.[26]

---

[24] For references, see below under "The 'Chosen Race'" and also n. 27. When quoting from LCL, I use the expression "chosen race," as Marcus translates it, since we have so few Greek fragments to verify Philo's original language. See, however, the discussion of QE 2.42 and n. 31 below.

[25] This is presumably a reference to Philo's two treatises about covenants, which have not survived; cf. Mut. 53.

[26] QE 2.106 is quoted below. For a discussion of this passage, see Jaubert, La notion d'Alliance, 429–31. The text of the passage is as follows:

Why does He say that they shall light the lamps 'outside the veil which is over the covenant'?

May it not be because the things within (the veil) were incorporeal and intelligible and had no need of sense-perceptible light, for they were themselves their own light and more luminous stars than those which are seen? But the one within the veil he calls 'of testimony,' symbolically indicating that the covenant of God is the only true one, and that those which (men) write in testaments are permanent and secure in themselves and are similar. And this is the measure of all things in common, the ideas and intelligible forms. Now external things are also secure but still not in the same way, since they have a sense-perceptible and

Indeed none of Philo's discussions of the covenant in QGE (the others are in *QG* 3.40, 42, and 60) affirms the Biblical sense of divine covenants or treats them as historical agreements.

The "Chosen Race" in QGE

The expression "chosen race" appears four times in the English translation of QGE: *QG* 2.58, 65; *QE* 2.38, 42. *QG* 3.49 also refers to the election of Israel and *QE* 2.43 and 46 mention the election of the ὁρατικὸν γένος, the race/class that can see.[27] In one instance, *QG* 2.58, it is not clear whom Philo means when he uses the phrase "chosen race," but he seems to be speaking about vegetarians. As to the other passages in which this phrase occurs, Philo appears to use "chosen race" as an automatic designation, similar to the way he uses ὁρατικὸν γένος (race/class that can see), as discussed in the previous chapter. Unlike ὁρατικὸν γένος, the phrase "chosen race" does not seem to be a literal equivalent for the word "Israel." Nevertheless, Philo's use of this phrase does have a mechanical quality to it, and he never enters into what it means to be chosen. Regardless of how he understands chosenness, however, it is not clear that Philo is talking about either the real Biblical nation or its Jewish descendants.

In our earlier analysis of *QE* 2.43, we saw that Philo associates the election of the ὁρατικὸν γένος with the giving of the law. He explains that

---

changeable nature and do not have permanence in themselves as do incorporeal things, and they make use of external bonds, some of which are in themselves altogether eternal, but others only dissolve during long periods.

[27] Of these seven passages, three have parallel Greek fragments: *QG* 2.65; *QE* 2.38, 46. Although Marcus's translation from the Armenian uses the phrase "chosen race" in *QG* 2.65 and *QE* 2.38, the Greek for these passages differs from the Armenian and has no parallel phrase. In the English, *QG* 2.65 mentions "the chosen and God-beloved race." The Greek has only ὁ θεοφιλὴς λαός, the God-beloved people. See Petit, *Quaestiones*, OPA, 33:120.

The Greek for *QE* 2.38 has no phrase that corresponds to "chosen race." In the English translation, this phrase appears in the answer. It is interesting that this passage interprets Exod. 24:11, which mentions the ἐπίλεκτοι τοῦ Ἰσραήλ, the chosen ones of Israel. (Cf. *Conf.* 56; see above, n. 10.) The English translation mentions "the chosen seeing ones" in the question—a phrase that presumably corresponds to οἱ ἐπίλεκτοι ὁρῶντες, where "Israel" is understood as ὁρῶντες, based upon the etymology. The Greek fragment, however, does not include the question. See Petit, *Quaestiones*, OPA, 33:264–65.

QE 2.46 does not have the expression "chosen race," either in the English or the Greek, but instead speaks of the election of the race/class that can see (ἡ τοῦ ὁρατικοῦ γένους ἐκλογή) and includes the words τὸ γένος εἵλετο, he chose the race/class. Again, the Greek differs from the Armenian. As noted in the previous chapter, this is the only passage with a Greek fragment that attests to Philo's use of the expression ὁρατικὸν γένος in QGE. See LCL, suppl. 2:90–91 and Petit, *Quaestiones*, OPA, 33:268.

Joshua accompanies Moses up the mountain "as an assurance ... of the election of the [ὁρατικὸν γένος]." Here Philo does not elaborate upon divine election but simply takes it for granted. The same is true for all the other passages in which he mentions either the "chosen race" or the election of the race.

The following two passages illustrate some of the features discussed above: *QG* 3.49 shows how Philo links the election of "Israel" with the commandment for circumcision, and *QE* 2.42 shows how the phrase "chosen race" seems to be an automatic designation.

QG 3.49[28]

In this interpretation, Philo understands the command for circumcision as a sign of the divine election of Israel. He also draws parallels between the election of Israel and creation (cf. *QE* 2.46). His exact understanding of "Israel," however, is not clear, and his explanation for the link between chosenness and circumcision is vastly different from the Biblical depiction of circumcision as a sign of the covenant.

Basing himself upon Gen. 17:12, in which God commands Abraham that all males should be circumcised on the eighth day, Philo asks why circumcision is commanded for the eighth day. After describing various qualities associated with the number eight, he explains why this number is linked with circumcision:

> This nation of ours to which a commandment was given to circumcise on the eighth day is called in Chaldean "Israel" and in Armenian, "one that sees God." He [God?] wishes that it [the nation?] participate in the naturally righteous things and that which is according to election. That which is according to the principle of creation is through the first hebdomad, which is right after creation [and] which the Generator and Creator had shown clearly to the world [as] the celebration of creation, having completed it in six days. On the other hand, that which is according to election came about by means of the group of eight which is a second hebdomad's beginning. As the ogdoad is the hebdomad and one, so the well-ordered γένος is always [a] γένος and [has] received in addition that which is election by means of nature and according to the will and the goodness of the Father.[29]

Although the thought in this passage is somewhat obscure, Philo seems to be saying that the number eight signifies two groups of seven (hebdomads), since eight encompasses one group of seven and the beginning of a second group of seven. The first hebdomad is associated with creation,

---

[28] The Greek fragment for this passage does not parallel the section under discussion.
[29] I am indebted to Prof. Sze-kar Wan for his assistance with this translation from the Armenian. Bracketed suggestions and minor modifications for the sake of clarity are my own. Use of the word γένος is explained in n. 30.

while the second is associated with the election of Israel. Seven is associated with creation because God completed creation in six days and celebrated this completion on the seventh.

No direct explanation is given for the link between election and the second group of seven. An implicit assumption, however, seems to be that circumcision signifies election. Since circumcision is commanded for the eighth day, that is, the beginning of the second hebdomad, this second hebdomad thereby represents election. Moreover, the passage seems to contend that the fact that circumcision is commanded for the eighth day shows—through these two symbolic groups of seven—that Israel is naturally righteous, having been created that way, and is also chosen by God, as signified through the command for circumcision.[30]

An interesting question about this passage is how Philo understands "Israel." He writes that the nation which was commanded to circumcise is called "Israel," which means "one that sees God." This comment, however, seems merely to provide an explanation of the name and adds nothing to the meaning of the passage. Because Philo uses the past tense and because, according to the Bible, Israel is indeed the descendant nation of Abraham to whom the commandment was given, the most reasonable way to construe "Israel" here is as the Biblical nation. Philo's concern with this nation, however, does not have to do with its historical or contemporary reality or with the meaning of its election. Instead, he focuses upon the symbolic importance of the eighth day when circumcision is commanded.

QE 2.42 [31]

The meaning of this interpretation, which speaks about the "chosen γένος" in the context of the giving of the law, is similarly obscure. Nonetheless this passage shows that for Philo the phrase "chosen γένος" seems to be an automatic designation. Even if Philo may intend to speak of the Biblical people by using this designation, he does not elaborate upon the implications of their being chosen.

---

[30] The next part of this interpretation—which is not directly relevant to the present discussion—seems to play upon Philo's various understandings of the word γένος as a genus or idea and as a race/class. In several places, Philo speaks about a γένος (i.e., genus or idea) as incorruptible, in contrast to a species, which is corruptible. (See *Cher.* 5–7, *Post.* 105, *Her.* 118, *Mut.* 78–80, *QG* 3.53; cf. *Leg.* 1.22–23 and *Leg.* 2.12–13.) When he writes, therefore, that the γένος will always be a γένος, presumably he is playing upon the different nuances of the word. That is, the well-ordered γένος (i.e., race or class) will always be incorruptible γένος (genus or idea), never corruptible species.

[31] Because this passage has the phrase "contemplative race," I am assuming the original Greek expression is ὁρατικὸν γένος (race/class that can see) and have substituted γένος for "race" in the phrase "chosen race."

The passage is based upon Exod. 24:12, which reads, "The Lord said to Moses, 'Come up to me on the mountain, and wait there; and I will give you the tables of stone, with the law and commandments, which I have written for their instruction" (LCL translation).

In connection with the latter part of this verse, Philo asks, "Does God write the Law?" After addressing the issue of anthropomorphism and how God might be said to "write," Philo offers the following interpretation:

> In the second place, this world is a great city and is a legal one. And it is necessary for it to use the best law of state. And it is fitting that it should have a worthy author of law and legislator, since among men He appointed the ὁρατικὸν γένος in the same manner (as the Law) for the world. And rightly does He legislate for this γένος, also prescribing (its Law) as a law for the world, for the chosen γένος is a likeness of the world, and its Law (is a likeness of the laws) of the world.

In answer to the question, "Does God write the Law?" this exegesis seems to argue that it is fitting that the best law should have a worthy author and therefore this author must be God. Philo associates the law for the ὁρατικὸν γένος with the law for the world. He writes, moreover, that the chosen γένος is a likeness of the world and, as the translation suggests, its law is a likeness of the laws of the world.

To some extent, these ideas are reminiscent of passages in the Exposition treatises *Opif.* and *Abr.*, in which Philo claims that the particular or special laws are copies of the natural law which was immanent in creation.[32] In *QE* 2.42, he does not use specific terms to distinguish between the particular laws and nature, even though Exod. 24:12 pertains to what he elsewhere does call the particular laws. If the concepts of natural and particular laws do underlie this passage, however, the reasoning here may be that the law for the ὁρατικὸν γένος, which would correspond to the particular laws, represents the law for the world, which would correspond to the natural law. Alternatively, perhaps Philo is suggesting that the ὁρατικὸν γένος itself is a law for the world, just as the patriarchs represent "laws endowed with life and reason" (*Abr.* 5).

In any case, Philo uses the phrase ὁρατικὸν γένος as a periphrasis for "Israel," and he also calls this group the "chosen γένος." He does not, however, develop the idea either that the γένος can see or that it is chosen. Instead, both expressions appear to substitute for the word "Israel," whose identity he implicitly takes for granted. Since he provides no conclusive

---

[32] In *Opif.* 1–3, Philo simply distinguishes between the law (νόμος) and the world (κόσμος). In *Abr.* 3–5, he uses designations such as special laws (νόμοι ἐπὶ μέρους), enacted ordinances (τεθειμένα διατάγματα), and laws laid down (κείμενοι νόμοι), on the one hand, and, on the other, nature (φύσις), unwritten law (ἄγραφος νομοθεσία), and laws endowed with life and reason (ἔμψυχοι καὶ λογικοὶ νόμοι).

information to identify this γένος with a particular entity, the modern reader cannot determine whether Philo means the historical people Israel and their descendants or a group defined only by the ability to see, or whether he equates the two.

Because the rest of this passage is uncertain and obscure, I shall not attempt further to make sense of it. For now, what is important is that the designations "ὁρατικὸν γένος" and "chosen γένος" appear to be part of a common exegetical parlance, since Philo does not explain them specifically and seems to assume their meaning is understood.

QGE: A Summary

The brief information provided by QGE regarding the relationship between God and Biblical Israel is consonant with our previous findings that this commentary has features uncharacteristic of Philo's other works. Here, for example, Philo associates the chosenness of Israel with circumcision and the giving of the law, a connection which the Bible makes but which Philo himself does not make elsewhere. Adding to our earlier observations is that Philo seems to use the phrase "chosen race" as an automatic designation. His use of this phrase, moreover, and his discussion of the election of the race seem to presuppose an understanding of what election means and who the "chosen race" is.

Once again, then, one might conjecture that the atypical features in this series may reflect the opinions of a broader community of Alexandrian Jewish exegetes than Philo's own likeminded associates. Even though not all segments of this community may share the same outlook on Scripture, the meaning of a certain exegetical vocabulary is assumed and understood.

Philonic Interpretations of the Relationship Between God and Biblical Israel: A Summary

When viewed through Philonic lenses, the covenant between God and Biblical Israel—based upon obedience to divine commandments, God's earlier promises to the nation's ancestors, or divine love—becomes something quite different. Philo never affirms that God chooses the nation Israel to enter into a covenant with Him. Although he never rejects this meaning, he transforms it in different ways. Aside from this general observation, one can also point to differences among the three series, differences which may be attributable to Philo's different aims and audiences for each work.

In the Allegory, "Israel," the nation, the "chosen people [or race/class]," and the covenant serve as symbols. Here Philo ignores such elements as God's commandments, His previous commitment to the patriarchs, or His love of the nation. In fact, by using relevant verses as prooftexts, he completely sidesteps the literal meaning of these verses. In this series, presumably Philo wishes to uncover the deeper meaning of Scripture for those like himself, who can or who want to "see" it. He therefore has no need to dwell upon the literal meaning of Scripture or its ramifications.

In the Exposition, Philo presents the relationship between God and Biblical Israel as available to anyone who chooses to turn to God and live virtuously. Here the "chosen people" become the mind of the worthy person, and any true suppliant is equal in worth to a whole nation. Philo does enjoin following the commandments, but his exhortations are not restricted to the nation Israel. This approach, which portrays a relationship to God as accessible to all, is well-suited to an audience of "outsiders," i.e., people who are not familiar with Judaism or who may be put off by its claims to an exclusive relationship with God or by the seeming burden of its laws.

Finally, QGE imparts very little information on this subject. One can, however, notice that certain features are not typical of Philo's other works, such as use of the phrase "chosen race" as an automatic designation; assumption of a connection between chosenness and circumcision or chosenness and the giving of the law; and attention to parts of the Bible like Exodus 24 upon which Philo does not otherwise concentrate. Again, such features may reflect the concerns of other Jewish exegetes, and this series may be intended for a broader exegetical community than Philo's own particular circle.

Whatever factors may influence Philo's presentation of the relationship between God and Biblical Israel, he does introduce to this relationship a range of new meanings. If, however, he does not affirm that Israel stands in a covenantal relationship with God and if the relationship portrayed in the Bible is applicable to any good person or virtuous soul, then how does Philo view Israel's descendants, the Jews, and their relationship to God? This is the question to which we now turn.

CHAPTER FIVE

THE RELATIONSHIP BETWEEN GOD
AND THE JEWS

Our investigation so far has shown that, on the one hand, Philo does not necessarily identify "Israel"—the one that sees God or the race/class that can see—with the real Biblical nation or its Jewish descendants and, on the other hand, that he does not explicitly affirm that God chose the Biblical nation Israel to participate in His covenant and to be His "special people." One might well ask, then, what being a Jew means to Philo. More specifically, what, if anything, is distinctive about the relationship between God and the Jews? To answer this question, we must take into account what Philo writes about the Biblical nation and his Jewish contemporaries in all his works. Thus, while the previous chapter examines how Philo explicitly interprets the Biblical depiction of the relationship between God and Israel, this one will consider how he implicitly interprets this depiction in his various observations about God and the Jews, past and present.

The discussion will begin with some general observations about Philo's vocabulary and the works in which he speaks about the Jews before and contemporary to him. (Following Philo's practice, I shall use the word "Jews" for both the past and present people; whenever necessary, I shall distinguish between the Biblical nation and his own contemporaries.) After careful examination of five features that, according to him, characterize the relationship between God and the Jews, I shall analyze four Philonic passages to see how he presents these features within specific contexts.

Philo's Discussion of the Jews: General Observations

Philo discusses the Jews most extensively in one exegetical series, the Exposition; his two political treatises, *Flacc.* and *Legat.*; and his apologetic work, the *Hypothetica.* He also mentions the Jews sporadically in two philosophical treatises, *Prob.* and *Aet.*[1] Of the remaining works, the Allegory never alludes to the Jews by name and speaks only rarely and

---

[1] Philo refers to the nation itself in *Prob.* 75, but most of his references to the Jews in the philosophical works are primarily to Moses, whom he calls "the lawgiver of the Jews" (*Prob.* 29, 43, 68; *Aet.* 19). In *Prob.* 57, Philo mentions the legislation of the Jews.

in passing about members of the Jewish community.[2] The English translation of QGE mentions the Jews only once, but in the Armenian, the word is "Hebrews."[3]

For the most part, Philo refers to the people of his time as the Jews (οἱ Ἰουδαῖοι), the nation of Jews (τὸ Ἰουδαίων ἔθνος), or simply "the nation" or "our nation" (τὸ or ἡμέτερον ἔθνος). Sometimes too, he speaks of the Jews as a polity (πολιτεία) or a γένος (see, eg., above, p. 59). As for the Biblical nation, Philo calls them the Hebrews (οἱ Ἑβραῖοι) or the people (ὁ λαός).

Occasionally, Philo also uses the term "Jews" to refer to the Biblical people alone or else to refer to the nation as a continuous entity from Biblical times to his own. For example, he writes that the Jews were strangers in Egypt (Mos. 1.34) even though, strictly speaking, he is talking about the Hebrews of Biblical times. He also describes the mother of a son by mixed marriage as a Jewess (Ἰουδαία) rather than a Hebrew in relating an episode from Lev. 24:10–16.[4] Finally, he calls Moses "the legislator of the Jews" (ὁ τῶν Ἰουδαίων νομοθέτης)[5] and describes Abraham as "the founder of the whole Jewish nation" (ὁ τοῦ σύμπαντος Ἰουδαίων ἔθνους ἀρχηγέτης, Mos. 1.7), using the term "Jew" to denote the nation from the past up to his own time.

The Hypothetica, only fragments of which survive, has no proper name for the nation either before or during Philo's time; instead it uses ὁ λαός (the people) for the Biblical people (Hypoth. 6.1, 2) or τὸ ἔθνος (the nation) for the past and present people (Hypoth. 6.1). Otherwise in this work, Philo speaks of both past and present people using a third person plural pronoun.

To some extent, Philo's presentation of the Jews—both before and contemporary to him—is influenced by a desire to portray them in the best possible light, since all the works which mention them extensively appear to be intended for a mixed audience of Jews and non-Jews. It is striking that Philo does not discuss the real Biblical or Jewish nation in works most likely intended for a sympathetic Jewish audience—i.e., the Allegory and QGE.[6] Keeping in mind that Philo probably wants to portray the Jews to their best advantage, I shall focus not only upon what he says

---

[2] See, e.g., Migr. 89–93 and Somn. 2.123–24.

[3] QG 3.48 (see LCL, suppl. 1:243, note d). In the context of the passage, "Jews" makes more sense than "Hebrews," since Philo is speaking about his contemporaries who practice circumcision. On Philo's use of "Hebrews," see Chapter One.

[4] Mos. 2.193. For a discussion of this passage, see Chapter Three.

[5] Mos. 1.1; Prob. 29, 43, 68; Aet. 19.

[6] As I have argued earlier, Philo probably does not discuss the nation in these works because his readers are already familiar with Jewish beliefs and practices and are instead interested in exploring the manifold meanings of Scripture. For further discussion about Philo's different audiences, see the Introduction.

about the relationship between God and the Jews but also upon how his presentation enhances the impact of his remarks.

Five Features That Characterize the Relationship Between God and the Jews

Throughout his writings about the Jews, Philo inserts various observations about their relationship to God. Occasionally, he comments only once without elaboration,[7] or else he contradicts, or at least tempers, a remark about the Jews by making a similar observation in another place about all people.[8] Despite the apparently desultory nature of his remarks, however, we can identify five features—listed further below—that, according to Philo, characterize the relationship between God and the Jews.

Philo himself of course never lists these observations systematically.[9] Instead, he incorporates his perspective while commenting upon Scripture, reworking the original material to suit his editorial aims. In the Exposition and *Hypothetica*, Philo's editorial insertions appear within his rewritten version of the Pentateuch and his descriptions of contemporary Jewish observances. In *Flacc.* and *Legat.*, he inserts his remarks either before or amid his portrayal of recent political events affecting Jews in Alexandria and elsewhere.

Since Philo presents his ideas about the relationship between God and the Jews not in isolation but rather within an ongoing discourse, I shall select as significant only those characteristics which he 1) mentions more than once and 2) does not contradict elsewhere.[10] According to

[7] Comments that occur only once without elaboration are found in *Abr.* 98, *Mos.* 2.189, and *Virt.* 77. In *Abr.* 98, Philo claims that the nation of Abraham and Sarah's descendants receives the office of prophecy for all humanity. (This passage is discussed later in this chapter and in n. 60.) In *Mos.* 2.189, he describes oracles that God directs toward all humanity and particularly toward "the race/class that worships Him for whom He opens up the road which leads to happiness" (my translation; see below, n. 60). Finally, in *Virt.* 77, Philo describes the nation as holding "the highest rank under the command of the Creator and Father of all." This depiction may be based upon perceived military imagery in Deut. 33:2–3.

[8] Compare, e.g., *Mos.* 1.279, in which Philo writes of the Hebrews that they are "near of kin to God" (ἀγχίσποροι θεοῦ), and *Spec.* 4.14, in which he says the same thing about people in general (ἄνθρωπος ἀγχίσπορος θεοῦ). See LCL, 6:420, note b; cf. also *Virt.* 79.

[9] For one of the few instances where Philo presents a list of ideas, see *Opif.* 170–72, in which he summarizes the five lessons taught by Moses in the creation account. Goodenough calls this list "the first creed of history" (*Introduction to Philo Judaeus*, 37). Cf. Wolfson, *Philo*, 1:164–65; Mendelson, *Philo's Jewish Identity*, 29–49.

[10] Also significant would be a characteristic mentioned only once but with some elaboration; Philo, however, does not provide any such instances. Since he offers no further explanation about the one-time comments cited in n. 7, it is difficult to evaluate their significance in his overall thought.

these criteria, one can distinguish from among all his writings the following five features that characterize the relationship between God and the Jews:

1) The Jews believe in the one true God and worship Him by following specific laws and customs.
2) The Jews serve as priestly intercessors between God and the whole world.
3) The Jews have been allotted or have allotted themselves to God.
4) The Jews are especially beloved by God or are especially God-loving.
5) The Jews are particular beneficiaries of God's providence.

It is especially noteworthy that Philo does not speak about the Jews as being able to see God, an ability he associates predominantly with "Israel."[11]

Closer examination of the five features listed above reveals that each one has a basis in Scripture and, more specifically, is linked either to divine promises made to the patriarchs about their descendant nation or to the covenant between God and the people Israel. As we shall see, however, Philo's presentation of these features differs significantly from the Biblical sources.

The Biblical Sources Behind Philo's Discussion and Their Potential Ramifications

As noted in the last chapter, the Bible presents the relationship between God and Israel by describing God's promises to the patriarchs about their descendants and by telling of His covenant with the nation Israel itself, a covenant which entails the condition of obedience to His commandments. It is not clear why God chooses Israel or its ancestors. One explanation is that He loves the people (e.g., Deut. 7:7–8); another is that He chooses them because of His previous commitment to the patriarchs (e.g., Deut. 4:31, 7:7–8, cf. 10:15). Sometimes God's choice is simply unexplained (e.g., Exod. 19:3–6, Deut. 26:16–19).

It was also noted that the Biblical portrayal may be offensive to different people for a variety of reasons. Philosophically inclined individuals, for example—whether Jews or non-Jews—might be troubled by the apparent

---

[11] In *Mos.* 2.196 and *Legat.* 4, Philo applies language he uses for "Israel" to the Jews. See the discussion of these exceptional passages in Chapter Three. In addition, Philo uses the metaphor of sight in *Mos.* 2.271 and *Spec.* 1.54. In *Mos.* 2.271, he notes that before their worship of the golden calf, the people had been the most sharp-sighted (ὀξυωπέστατος) of all the nations. In *Spec.* 1.54, he says that members of the nation who give up honor of the One—i.e., apostates—"have chosen darkness in preference to the brightest light and blindfolded the mind which had the power of keen vision (τυφλὴν ἀπεργαζόμενοι διάνοιαν ὀξὺ καθορᾶν δυναμένην)." Neither passage quite says, however, that the Biblical nation or Philo's Jewish contemporaries can "see God."

arbitrariness of God's choice of Israel, since they would expect Him to act in accordance with reason. A related difficulty is why or how the Father and Maker of all creation might show special attention to one particular people. In addition, many of the commandments—which God requires as part of His covenant—such as the dietary laws, do not have obvious, rational explanations. Finally, even for those not troubled by these various intellectual problems, the claim of one nation to be specially chosen by God might appear boastful and cause resentment among other peoples.

In the previous chapter, we saw that Philo may implicitly address some of these concerns in his interpretations of relevant Biblical verses and of concepts like "covenant" or "chosen race." He accomplishes this by re-defining or omitting reference to the covenant, by presenting the relation-ship between God and "Israel" as applicable to any virtuous person or soul, or by describing God's commandments as exhortations to people to behave virtuously in general.

In the same way that Philo transforms the meaning of specific Biblical verses about God's choice of Israel, so too does he rework and reapply general themes derived from these verses to depict the relationship between God and the Jews in a favorable, i.e., inoffensive, manner. Thus, in his comments about the relationship between God and the Jews, Philo omits mention of the covenant, never presenting Jewish laws and prac-tices as a condition of a preset agreement. Instead of giving the impression that the Jews have an exclusive relationship with God, Philo portrays them as showing universal concern for all humanity in their worship of Him. Finally, as he presents it, the relationship between God and the Jews appears accessible to any virtuous person who turns to belief in the truly Existent.

These various Philonic modifications of Biblical themes are illustrated in the following consideration of the five characteristics listed earlier.[12]

1. *The Jews believe in the one true God and worship Him by following specific laws and customs.*

Philo discusses Jewish laws and practices at length in his Exposition treatises, especially in *Decal.-Spec.* 4, and he occasionally observes that the ancestral customs of the people set them apart from other nations (*Mos.*

---

[12] It should be remembered, of course, that Philo inherits a tradition of exegesis and does not approach his Biblical sources in a vacuum. (See, e.g., the Introduction, esp. n. 49.) Some references to other interpretations are cited in nn. 16, 22, 35, and 38. While it is not my purpose to trace the relationship between these interpretations and those of Philo, I offer these references to illustrate how various exegetes in antiquity approached similar Scriptural problems.

1.278, *Spec.* 4.179). Throughout these discussions and elsewhere, the notion that the Jews believe in the one true God is certainly implicit. In three passages (*Spec.* 2.165–67, *Virt.* 64–65, and *Legat.* 115), however, Philo connects the Jews' belief in God with their laws and customs, asserting explicitly that the Jews believe in God and worship Him via these laws and customs.

The three passages appear within different contexts. *Spec.* 2.165–67 and *Virt.* 64–65 are from the Exposition, while *Legat.* 115 is part of Philo's political treatise about the embassy to Gaius. *Spec.* 2.165–67—analyzed in more detail later in this chapter—occurs in a passage in which Philo describes the Sheaf Feast. The larger context of the treatise is a discussion of the Jewish holidays in general. Philo notes that the Jewish nation chooses (ἑλόμενον, *Spec.* 2.166) worship only of the Uncreated and Eternal and that it serves the truly existing God through its prayers, holidays, and first-fruit offerings.

Virt. 64–65 occurs in a passage in which Philo praises Moses for asking God to choose his successor rather than choosing the person himself. Here Philo writes that the person selected will lead not an ordinary nation, but the one that makes supplication to the truly Existent, the Maker and Father of all. Moreover, through their laws and customs, the Jews gain knowledge of God, a knowledge which others gain through the most excellent teachings of philosophy.

Finally, *Legat.* 115 explains that the emperor Gaius dislikes the Jews because they refuse to worship him. Instead, trained by parents, teachers, and their laws and unwritten customs, they recognize the one God who is Father and Maker of all.

To find the Biblical roots of these statements, one need not search far. Most obviously, in the Book of Exodus, chapters 19–24, when God establishes His covenant with the people of Israel, their obedience to His commandments is part and parcel of His covenant. God charges, "If you will obey My voice and keep My covenant, you shall be to Me a special people among all the nations" (Exod. 19:5, my translation). This charge is followed by recitation of the Ten Commandments and a variety of other laws pertaining to social and ritual matters (Exodus 20–23). Indeed, God's commandments to Israel, which apply to a wide range of domains, are presented as an integral part of His covenant with the nation throughout subsequent parts of the Pentateuch as well. Thus, according to the Bible, Israel's observance of God's laws represents the people's side of an agreement which He initiates with them.

When Philo, however, mentions the Jews' belief in God and their worship of Him through their laws and customs, he departs from the Biblical portrayal in important ways, emphasizing some details, while omitting others. Thus, for example, he does not say that the Jews practice God's commandments as part of a covenantal relationship which God initiates. In fact, instead of proclaiming that God chooses the Jews, he declares the Jews have chosen Him (*Spec.* 2.166).

Nor in these passages does Philo speak of the laws as God's commandments. Instead he refers to them simply as laws (νόμοι) and customs (ἔθη) (*Virt.* 65, *Legat.* 115). These laws and customs, moreover, are not an end in themselves but rather are the means through which the Jews serve God (*Spec.* 2.167) and indeed through which they come to know Him (*Virt.* 64–65, *Legat.* 115). Accordingly, Jewish laws and customs appear not as part of a preset agreement handed down by the Lord, but instead as a path which leads the Jews to Him. Implicitly, anyone may follow this path, not only the Jews. In addition, at the end of this path is not just the God of the Jews, but the Father and Maker of all (*Spec.* 2.165, *Virt.* 64, *Legat.* 115), the Uncreated and Eternal (*Spec.* 2.166), the God of the philosophers (*Virt.* 65).

2. *The Jews serve as priestly intercessors between God and the whole world.*

Philo writes that the Jews serve as priests or intercessors for all humanity in *Abr.* 98, *Mos.* 1.149, *Spec.* 1.97, and *Spec.* 2.162–67.[13] This priestly role is also suggested but not stated directly in *Spec.* 4.180 and *Legat.* 3.[14] As to the larger contexts of these remarks, in recounting Biblical history in the Exposition, even before the nation appears on the scene, Philo mentions that it is destined to become the priesthood and to offer prayers for the world (*Abr.* 98, *Mos.* 1.149). Later, while describing the special practices of the Jews, he portrays their high priest both as a national figure and as one who prays on behalf of all people and indeed of the whole universe (*Spec.* 1.97).[15] Philo's most extended statement of the nation-as-priest theme appears in a discussion of the Sheaf Feast in *Spec.* 2.162–67, in which he asserts that not only do the Jews act as the priesthood for all other nations, but they also serve to correct the false worship of these other nations.[16]

---

[13] *Abr.* 98 and *Spec.* 2.162–67 are analyzed in the last section of this chapter.

[14] Both of these passages are discussed in the last section of this chapter. Cf. *Mos.* 2.189, in which Philo calls the Biblical—and perhaps contemporary—nation the race/class that worships Him (τὸ θεραπευτικὸν αὐτοῦ γένος). On *Mos.* 2.189, see above, n. 7, and below, n. 60.

[15] It should be noted that this remark refers only to the Jewish high priest and not to the whole nation. Philo arrives at the idea that the high priest serves a universal role based upon the symbols of the universe represented by his special garments. See also *Mos.* 2.117–35.

[16] In general, Philo seems to speak about the Jews as priests in a metaphorical sense, meaning, that is, that they serve as representatives for all humanity in the worship of God. *Spec.* 2.162–67, however, pertains to a real priestly ritual, namely, the offering of first fruits. See also *Spec.* 1.168 and 190, which describe sacrifices made on behalf of

Although Philo frequently portrays the Jews as worshippers of God whose practices and customs are a means for serving Him, what distinguishes them from other people is that they *alone* serve God[17] and that they serve Him on behalf of all humanity. Related to this theme is Philo's denunciation of all forms of false worship. Under this rubric he includes, for example, worship of the four elements and parts of nature (*Decal.* 53–65, *Spec.* 1.13–20); idols (*Decal.* 66–76, *Spec.* 1.21–27); animals (*Decal.* 76–80); and mythic gods (*Spec.* 1.28–29, *Spec.* 2.164) (cf. also *Spec.* 1.325–45). In contrast to people who hold these false beliefs, the Jews are distinguished by their faith in the one true God. In fact, they play a role in correcting this false worship of other nations (*Spec.* 2.162–67).

A basis for the idea that Israel is a nation of priests can certainly be found in the Bible, for example, in Gen. 12:2–3, Exod. 19:6, or Lev. 20:26. While these various Biblical passages, however, may—in one way or another—represent the entire nation as priestly, none of them claims directly and unambiguously that the people serve as priests on behalf of the whole world. Indeed all these statements emphasize the exclusive relationship between God and Israel, without clearly specifying its role vis-à-vis other peoples.[18]

A strong possibility for the Scriptural support behind Philo's claim that the nation serves as the priesthood for all humanity can be found among the divine promises to the patriarchs. In Gen. 12:1–3, for example, God tells Abraham to leave his homeland, and He blesses him as follows: "And I will make of you a great nation, and I will bless you, and make your name great, so that you will be blessed.[19] I will bless those who bless you, and him who curses you I will curse; and in you all the families of the earth shall be blessed" (Gen. 12:2–3).

The latter part of this verse—"in you all the families of the earth shall be blessed (καὶ ἐνευλογηθήσονται ἐν σοὶ πᾶσαι αἱ φυλαὶ τῆς γῆς)"—is ambiguous.[20] Because the verb ἐνευλογηθήσονται is in the passive voice,

the Jewish nation and the whole world. Cf. BT Sukkah 55b.
[17]   *Spec.* 2.165–67, *Spec.* 4.179–82, *Legat.* 115–18.
[18]   Only later in the Bible, in Second Isaiah, is this role discussed. See, e.g., Isaiah 42:1–7, 49:6. See also Robert Martin-Achard, *A Light to the Nations: A Study of the Old Testament Conception of Israel's Mission to the World*, trans. John Penney Smith (Edinburgh: Oliver and Boyd, 1962), esp. 8–31. For a somewhat different perspective, see Harry M. Orlinsky, "Nationalism-Universalism and Internationalism in Ancient Israel," *Translating & Understanding the Old Testament: Essays in Honor of Herbert Gordon May*, ed. Harry Thomas Frank and William L. Reed (Nashville: Abingdon Press, 1970), esp. 227–28.
[19]   καὶ ἔσῃ εὐλογητός. In the Hebrew, the last part of the verse says, "So that you will be a blessing (וֶהְיֵה ברכה)."
[20]   This clause or a similar one is repeated in Gen. 18:18, 22:18, 26:4, and 28:14, where the verb ἐνευλογέομαι is always in the passive (ἐνευλογηθήσονται). In the Hebrew

and because the meaning of the prepositional phrase ἐν σοί (in you) is not precise, it is unclear what role Abraham or his descendants will play in transmitting blessings to the families of the earth. Also, it should be noted that the pronoun σύ, you, is singular.

One way of understanding the clause quoted above is that the blessings bestowed upon Abraham may spread through a kind of "trickle-down effect" to his descendants and all other nations. In other words, Abraham will serve as a source of blessings, but just how these blessings will be spread remains vague.[21] The clause may also, however, be understood to suggest that all the families of the earth will be blessed *by* Abraham and perhaps by his descendants. This sense may imply that Abraham's heirs will play a direct role in conferring blessings upon other peoples.[22]

Philo's claim that the Jews serve as priests for the whole world is more in accord with this latter construal. While the verse does not declare that the nation will actively bless others, the ambiguity of the words certainly permits this interpretation. Of the two possibilities just mentioned—namely, that Abraham will be a source of blessings but just how is unclear or that he or his descendants will actively spread the blessings themselves—the second understanding might be more palatable to outsiders. This is because unlike the first construal, the second portrays Abraham and his descendants as actively "sharing the wealth."

Besides this divine promise to Israel's ancestors,[23] other passages addressed to the nation itself can be understood to portray them as priests. For example, in Exod. 19:6, God proclaims to Israel, "You shall be to Me a

---

for these verses, the verb ברך is sometimes in the נפעל (וְנִבְרְכוּ, Gen. 12:3, 18:18, 28:14) and sometimes in the התפעל (וְהִתְבָּרְכוּ, Gen. 22:18, 26:4). While the נפעל can be translated in either a passive or reflexive sense, the התפעל is translated only as reflexive or reciprocal: "They shall bless themselves." (Ephraim A. Speiser, ed., *Genesis*, vol. 1 of *The Anchor Bible*, ed. William Foxwell Albright and David Noel Freedman [Garden City, New York: Doubleday, 1964], 86.) This further ambiguity in the Hebrew contributes to the different ways these verses have been understood. See below, n. 22.

[21] Philo interprets Gen. 12:3 along these lines in *Migr.* 118–26. Cf., e.g., *Migr.* 121: "For in truth the righteous man is the foundation on which mankind rests. All that he himself has he brings into the common stock and gives in abundance for the benefit of all who shall use them." Here, the righteous man is a source of blessings but does not seem to confer them directly upon the people.

[22] For various interpretations of this verse, see Ben Sira 44:21, Acts 3:25, Gal. 3:8. The first two interpretations understand God's blessing to apply to Abraham's descendants, even though the pronoun in the phrase ἐν σοί is singular. Rabbinic and other Jewish interpretations are collected by Menahem M. Kasher, *Encyclopedia of Biblical Interpretation: A Millennial Anthology*, trans. Harry Freedman (New York: American Biblical Encyclopedia Society, 1955), 2:118–19. See also Martin-Achard, *A Light to the Nations*, 33–37, and Jaubert, *La notion d'Alliance*, 56–57.

[23] The promise is repeated to Isaac (Gen. 26:4) and Jacob (Gen. 28:14). See above, n. 20.

royal priesthood[24] and a holy nation" (my translation). Here God actively and explicitly chooses Israel to serve Him. Indeed, this characterization of the nation as a "royal priesthood" comes at the beginning of the pivotal event at Sinai when the exclusive bond is forged between God and the whole people (Exodus 19–24). Exod. 19:6, however, defines Israel's role only in relation to God and does not mention other nations. God says, "You shall be *to Me* a royal priesthood and a holy nation" (my emphasis). When Philo claims that the Jews serve as the priesthood for all humanity, then, he goes beyond and extends the divine directive quoted here.[25]

Lev. 20:26 is another verse that depicts Israel as a consecrated people. Here, God says, "You shall be holy to Me, because I the Lord your God am holy, who has separated you from all the nations to be Mine" (my translation, cf. Lev. 19:2). This verse emphasizes God's singling out of the nation Israel to be holy to Him. As in the previous example, however, even though the Bible characterizes Israel as consecrated and holy, it stops short of declaring, as Philo does, that Israel serves a role for the whole world.[26]

When Philo proclaims then that the Jews act as priests for all humanity, he is significantly recasting the meaning of divine promises to the nation's ancestors and the covenant relationship between God and Israel. Instead of repeating Biblical claims that God bestows His blessings upon one nation, appointing it as His exclusive servant, Philo stresses that that nation serves a role for other peoples, indeed for the whole world. When he claims that the Jews correct the error of the other nations that worship falsely, he implies that other nations too can serve God once they recognize the folly of their ways. By presenting the Jews as the representative priesthood for all people, then, Philo transforms what in the Bible is part of an exclusive relationship with God into a role that benefits all humanity and that conceivably is available to anyone who turns to belief in Him.

3. *The Jews have been allotted or have allotted themselves to God.*

In four places (*Spec.* 4.159, 180; *Virt.* 34; *Legat.* 3), Philo writes that the Jews have been allotted or have allotted themselves (προσκεκλήρωνται) to God.[27]

---

[24] βασίλειον ἱεράτευμα. Cf. the Hebrew, ממלכת כהנים, a kingdom of priests.

[25] On this verse, see also Martin-Achard, *A Light to the Nations*, 37–40.

[26] Besides these examples, Philo derives from Exod. 12:6 that the whole nation serves as priests for one day, i.e., during the Pascha feast. In this interpretation, however, he does not mention the nation's role on behalf of all humanity. See *QE* 1.10, *Mos.* 2.224, *Decal.* 159, *Spec.* 2.145–46.

[27] *Spec.* 4.180 and *Legat.* 3 are analyzed in the last section of this chapter and are therefore not quoted in the notes. Philo does not speak about the nation in the same way in these four passages. In *Spec.* 4.159, for example, he does not mention the

Each reference appears as a passing remark, upon which he never elaborates. In all these passages, the remark falls in a context in which Philo is distinguishing the Biblical nation or the Jews from foreigners or from all other people. In *Spec.* 4.159, for example, he says that all members of the nation are assigned to God, in the context of explaining why a foreigner cannot be their ruler.[28] The reference in *Spec.* 4.180 appears in a passage in which he compares the contemporary Jewish nation to an orphan, in contrast to other nations which always have allies. In *Virt.* 34, Philo describes the people as allotted to God in recounting the reason for the Midianites' hostility toward the Biblical nation, narrated in Num. 25:1–18 and 31:1–18.[29] Finally, in *Legat.* 3, he notes that the Jews are allotted to God in the context of arguing that God extends His providence to all people, especially the Jews.[30]

It is particularly striking that in all these references, Philo always uses the verb προσκληρόω, allot, in a form that can express either the middle or passive voice, leaving some ambiguity as to whether the people have allotted themselves to God or God has allotted them to Himself.[31] Had Philo wished to be explicit on this matter, he certainly could have been. Indeed although the verb προσκληρόω is fairly rare among Greek writers in antiquity, Philo uses it the most frequently and in the most varied forms.[32] Occasionally, for example, he uses προσκληρόω in the active voice

---

nation by name but seems to mean the past and present people. In *Spec.* 4.180, he does name the Jews explicitly (*Spec.* 4.179), referring to the contemporary nation. *Virt.* 34 speaks about the Hebrews, i.e., the Biblical nation; and *Legat.* 3 mentions "Israel," which, as we have seen, Philo implicitly identifies with the Jews.

[28] This passage is based upon Deut. 17:15: "One from among your brethren you shall set as king over you; you may not put a foreigner over you, who is not your brother." In *Spec.* 4.159, Philo writes, "For he assumed with good reason that one who was their fellow-tribesman and fellow-kinsman related to them by the tie which brings the highest kinship, the kinship of having one citizenship and the same law and [one God to whom all who belong to the nation have been allotted or have allotted themselves (προσκεκλήρωνται)] would never sin in the way just mentioned."

[29] *Virt.* 34: "They [the Midianites] were hostile toward the Hebrews, for no other reason than that they reverence and honor the most supreme and eldest cause, being dedicated (προσκεκληρωμένοι) to the Creator and Father of the universe" (my translation).

[30] Again, Philo does not use the word "Jews" explicitly in *Legat.* 3, although they are the implicit referent. See the discussion of *Legat.* 1–7 in the last section of this chapter.

[31] For a discussion of a similar ambiguity in Acts 17:4, see Werner Foerster, "προσκληρόω," *TDNT*, 3:766. In two out of the four passages cited above (*Spec.* 4.159 and *Legat.* 3), Colson, in the LCL edition, opts for the sense that God assigns the people to Himself, translating the verb in the active voice with God as the subject.

[32] Philo uses προσκληρόω thirty-six times. Results of a search through the TLG database show that the word also appears once in each of the following sources: Clement of Alexandria, Dio Cassius, Diodorus Siculus, Eusebius, Pseudo-Lucian, Josephus, and the New Testament (Acts 17:4); and three times in John Chrysostom.

to describe a subject that devotes itself to something.[33] At the same time, he also speaks about God in the active voice as assigning something to Himself.[34] Since Philo uses the verb in the active voice elsewhere, and since he chooses the middle or passive voice each time he speaks about the Jews being allotted to God, he may wish to remain purposely ambiguous about who allots them to Him—God or the people themselves.[35]

Several Scriptural passages support, at least indirectly, the idea either that Israel is especially assigned to God or that God assigns Israel to Himself. Examples of these verses include Exod. 4:22, 19:5; Lev. 20:26; and Deut. 32:8–9. The previous section, for example, cites Lev. 20:26, in which God says He has separated Israel from all other peoples to be His own. Similarly, in Exod. 19:5, God proclaims Israel to be His own special people (λαός περιούσιος). In Exod. 4:22, God calls Israel His firstborn son (υἱὸς πρωτότοκός μου Ἰσραήλ). Although this specific verse does not describe God as choosing Israel, one finds throughout the Bible the notion that the firstborn or first fruits belong to God or that He has taken them for Himself.[36]

Other passages as well could be cited as examples in which God expressly "chooses" Israel or in which He describes Israel as belonging to Him (e.g., Deut. 7:6, 14:2). Perhaps the most relevant in this case, however, is Deut. 32:8–9. Here it says,

> 8When the Most High distributed nations,
> When He dispersed the sons of Adam,
> He set boundaries of nations
> According to the number of angels of God,
> 9And Jacob His people became the Lord's portion;
> Israel became the lot of His inheritance.[37] (LCL translation)

This passage is especially attractive as a possible source for Philo's claims that Israel is assigned to God. For one thing, Deut. 32:9 is vague about who assigns Israel to Him, even though Deut. 32:8 suggests that God is the active agent. Thus, verse 8 says that "the Most High distributed

---

[33] E.g., *Mut.* 127, *Abr.* 198, *Decal.* 108.

[34] E.g., *Cher.* 85, *Sacr.* 119, *Somn.* 2.227.

[35] Cf. *Spec.* 1.114, in which the same ambiguity pertains to the high priest, described as προσκεκληρωμένος, allotted, to God. For rabbinic discussions about the mutuality of choice between God and Israel, see Urbach, *The Sages*, 530–31.

[36] Firstborn: Exod. 13:11–13, 34:19; Numbers 3:13, 8:17; et al. First fruits: Exod. 23:19, 34:26; et al. The injunctions about the firstborn and first fruits are probably based upon the same principle, i.e., that the first produce (of the womb or the earth) belongs to God. See Baruch A. Levine, "Firstborn" and "First Fruits," *Encyclopedia Judaica* 6:1306–08, 1312–14.

[37] The Greek for Deut. 32:8 differs somewhat from the Hebrew. See Chapter Four, n. 13.

nations," while verse 9 says that "Israel became the lot of His inheritance."[38] Moreover, in *Post.* 92, Philo interprets this verse by commenting that the one who sees God (i.e., Israel) is assigned (προσκεκλήρωται) to the One who is seen. Although we cannot conclusively identify "Israel" with the Jews in *Post.* 92, it seems possible, nevertheless—since Philo uses the verb προσκληρόω in this interpretation—that he may have Deut. 32:8–9 in mind when he uses the same verb elsewhere to describe the Biblical or contemporary nation as being dedicated to God.

Whatever specific verse(s) he may have in mind, however, Philo's formulation downplays or alters the declaration that God actively chooses or describes Israel as His special people, an assertion which may offend his readers. Furthermore, if one were to understand from the ambiguity of the verb that the Jews have allotted themselves to God, one might conclude that anyone who chooses may do the same. Indeed Philo contends explicitly in several places that anyone who wishes may turn to belief in and worship of the true God.[39] As a result, allotment to God need not be seen as the exclusive domain of the Jews.

4. *The Jews are especially beloved by God or are especially God-loving.*

Philo talks about the Jews—either the Biblical nation or their descendants—as beloved by God or God-loving (θεοφιλής) in *Abr.* 98; *Mos.* 1.147, 255; and *Hypoth.* 6.7.[40] In *Abr.* 98, he proclaims that the nation of Abraham and Sarah's descendants is the one most beloved by God or most God-loving (θεοφιλέστατον) and that it has received the offices of priesthood and prophecy for all humanity. In *Mos.* 1.147, he mentions that some people join the Hebrews in leaving Egypt, attracted by the divine favor or God-loving quality (τὸ θεοφιλές) of the nation. *Mos.* 1.255 describes the Biblical nation as θεοφιλεῖς, those beloved by God or God-loving, in telling how they sing a song of thanks to Him upon finding a well on the border of the land they are about to possess. Finally, in *Hypoth.* 6.7, Philo suggests that the Biblical nation may conquer the land (Canaan) not by force but by winning the respect of its inhabitants, a feat which would show that

---

[38] In the Allegory, Philo interprets these verses in *Post.* 91–92 and *Plant.* 58–60. For a discussion of *Post.* 91–92, mentioned immediately below, see Chapter Four. Cf. also Ben Sira 17:17.

[39] *Decal.* 58; *Spec.* 1.16–20, 51; *Virt.* 102, 177–79; et al.

[40] *Abr.* 98 is discussed in the last section of this chapter. As explained below, θεοφιλής can mean either beloved by God or God-loving. Both understandings are possible in the first three passages. In *Hypoth.* 6.7, however, the passive meaning, i.e., beloved by God, makes more sense than the active meaning, since the passage describes the respect of the nation's enemies for the nation, and it would seem that these enemies would be more impressed by God's love of the nation than by its love of Him.

even the people's enemies acknowledge them as most beloved of God (θεοφιλέστατοι).

We can find Biblical support for the notion that the Jews are beloved by God in several passages, which either declare or suggest that God loves or favors Israel especially (Deut. 4:37, 7:7–8, 10:15; Exod. 4:22; et al.). Many of these passages appear in contexts which cite the covenant relationship between God and the people. Philo, however, recasts the claim that God loves Israel, in a way that would not offend his readers. For one thing, he never refers explicitly to the covenant between God and the nation, thereby eliminating any sense of a preset relationship. Instead, to express God's love for the people, he uses the word θεοφιλής, which is quite common in Greek and can be used to describe people, places, and things.[41]

Also, since Philo's contemporary Greek-speaking world had various conceptions of divinity, the word θεοφιλής, i.e., "God-beloved" or "god-beloved," could connote different meanings to different people. Finally, θεοφιλής can also be understood in an active sense, i.e., as God-loving. Thus the word introduces an ambiguity as to whether the people are beloved by God or are God-loving themselves. When Philo calls the nation θεοφιλής, beloved of God or God-loving, or even θεοφιλέστατος, most beloved of God or most God-loving, then this description is qualitatively different from a declaration that the God of all creation favors one particular people, namely, the Jews.

In addition, apart from the flexibility or indeed ambiguity of the word's applications and connotations, in two of the four passages cited above, the divine favor of the Jews is acknowledged by *outsiders*—i.e., the "mixed multitude," who join the people when they leave Egypt (*Mos.* 1.147), and the inhabitants of Canaan—the people's very enemies!—who Philo suggests may willingly yield their land to the Hebrews (*Hypoth.* 6.7). By ascribing to outsiders this observation about the Biblical nation, Philo portrays the nation as worthy of admiration by other people. In a third case (*Abr.* 98), Philo simply asserts that the people are the most beloved of God (or most God-loving), without further discussion. Finally, the fourth passage (*Mos.* 1.255) describes the people as θεοφιλεῖς when they sing a song—presumably of thanks—to God. Accordingly, they are shown as appreciating God's favor or celebrating their devotion to Him. If in fact the word denotes that they are favored by God, then they do not take His favor for granted.

---

[41] Philo, for example, also uses this word to describe Moses, Jacob, Noah, the soul, God-beloved people in general, and God-beloved beliefs and practices. See also Yehoshua Amir, "Die Umformung des εὐδαίμων in den θεοφιλής bei Philon," *Die hellenistische Gestalt*, 207–19.

As he does with the other features under discussion, then, in this case too, Philo manages to preserve features from the relationship between God and Israel as it is portrayed in the Bible. At the same time, however, he shears these features of their possible offensiveness. By not mentioning the covenant, by using the familiar word θεοφιλής—which can carry different meanings and associations—and by attributing to outsiders the observation that the Jews are θεοφιλεῖς, he tempers the Scriptural claim that the universal God Himself declares His special love to Israel.

5. *The Jews are particular beneficiaries of God's providence.*

Philo mentions that his Jewish contemporaries benefit from God's providence (πρόνοια, *Flacc.* 170, *Legat.* 3), His help (ἐπικουρία, *Flacc.* 191), and His pity and compassion (ἔλεος καὶ οἶκτος, *Spec.* 4.179–82). In *Flacc.* and *Legat.*, his observations pertain to God's watchfulness over the specific current affairs of the nation. Indeed the purpose of these works seems to be to demonstrate that God helps the Jews, especially in times of trouble.[42] In *Spec.* 4.179–82, Philo does not refer to specific circumstances but rather observes generally that the Jews are the object of God's concern.[43]

Unlike the other features mentioned above whose roots we can trace primarily to Biblical tradition, the idea that the Jews are particular beneficiaries of God's providence brings Philo's Biblical and Jewish background into conflict with his philosophical background. Indeed belief in divine providence, which can be found in the writings of Plato (esp. *Laws*, Book 10), became more prominent under the influence of the Stoics. The latter attributed all the workings of the universe to providence, or God's reason, understood to operate through the law of nature for the benefit of humanity.[44]

---

[42] Herbert Box, ed., *Philonis Alexandrini: In Flaccum* (London: Oxford University Press, 1939), xxxviii; Colson, *Philo*, LCL, 10:xiv–ix and 186, note a; Goodenough, *The Politics of Philo Judaeus*, 10–13, 19; Massebieau, "Le classement des oeuvres de Philon," 65–78; Morris, "The Jewish Philosopher Philo," 859–64; Smallwood, *Philonis Alexandrini*, 40 and 324, n. 373.

[43] *Spec.* 4.179–82 and *Legat.* 3 are analyzed in detail in the last section of this chapter. Besides the explicit declarations cited here, *Mos.* 1.147 and 255, mentioned in the previous section, may imply that the Biblical nation benefits from God's providence. In *Mos.* 1.147, if τὸ θεοφιλές is to be understood as "divine favor" rather than "the God-loving quality" of the people, then the "divine favor" may refer to God's role in the circumstances of the nation's departure, His punishment of Israel's enemies in Egypt, and thus His concern for and involvement in the fate of the nation. *Mos.* 1.255 notes that God gives the people the land and leads them in their migration.

[44] For the philosophical background of Philo's position on providence and related issues, see Dillon, *The Middle Platonists*, 44–45, 80–81, 166–68; A. A. Long, *Hellenistic Philosophy: Stoics, Epicureans, Sceptics*, 2nd ed. (London: Duckworth, 1986), 112, 169–70;

One problem with this philosophical conception of an impersonal, all-embracing providence is that it cannot offer a convincing rationale for ethical behavior. It is not clear, for example, that providence is concerned with the individual. In addition, if everything is in God's hands, one may wonder whether or not individuals in fact have free will to choose between good and evil.

In grappling with these dilemmas, Philo was not alone among the thinkers of his time. As John Dillon writes,

> Philo is neither a determinist nor a believer in absolute free will... The Platonist position maintained the autonomy of the will, in order to preserve the basis of ethical judgments. In his assertion of our free will, Philo is really concerned above all to assert our liability to praise and blame. But yet every Platonist wished to maintain the doctrine of God's Providence. Without that, one would fall into Epicurean atheism... The Platonists are thus caught in what is, if not a contradiction, at least a profound tension between free will and determinism. If Philo's various stances appear contradictory, therefore, the contradiction is at least not peculiar to himself, but one common to all Platonists.[45]

Philo's comments about divine providence, then—whether for all people in general or for the Jews in particular—are marked by a certain vagueness about the role of human behavior in influencing providence. Although he acknowledges that the Jews benefit from God's special attention, he is somewhat unclear about what entitles them to this special attention. Despite his somewhat contradictory remarks, however, he does seem to lean toward the idea that if one believes in God, then one benefits from His providence. A brief consideration of Philo's general statements about divine providence may help to put in perspective his specific comments about the Jews.

Philo frequently emphasizes that God cares for and watches over all creation.[46] Indeed he understands God's providence as a necessary corollary to His role as Creator, calling it a law of nature that the maker cares for what has been made.[47]

Divine care can be both directive and protective. God's providence is directive, for example, in that it can influence events in the lives of individuals and nations alike and can affect the course of nature.[48] Philo also speaks of God's providence as protective, however, e.g., when he says

---

David Winston, "Freedom and Determinism in Greek Philosophy," *SP* 2 (1973): 40–50; Wolfson, *Philo*, 1:297–99; 2:283–86.

[45] Dillon, *The Middle Platonists*, 168.

[46] *Abr.* 71, *Mos.* 1.149, *Spec.* 1.209, *Spec.* 2.260, *Virt.* 216.

[47] *Opif.* 8–9, 171–72; *Spec.* 3.189; *Praem.* 42; cf. *Ebr.* 13.

[48] For examples of God's providence as directive, see *Ios.* 99, 236; *Mos.* 1.67, 85, 132, 162, 211; *Mos.* 2.3, 5, 6, 261; *Flacc.* 125; *Legat.* 220, 336.

that proselytes, orphans, and widows are objects of His pity and compassion or when he mentions the help which God can give.[49]

Beyond claiming that God cares for and directs human affairs, Philo does not make explicit what people can do to secure this watchful attention. In some passages he suggests that God extends His providence to those who act virtuously and believe in Him, as in the case of the patriarchs.[50] He also devotes a treatise to rewards and punishments (*Praem.*, cf. *Mos.* 2.52–65), using examples from Scripture to illustrate how God rewards righteousness and punishes evil. Finally, Philo states that divine providence is the best incentive for piety (*Opif.* 8–9), implying perhaps—though not necessarily—that the pious stand to benefit especially from divine concern.

In spite of these examples, however, Philo stops short of stating explicitly that piety or virtue is a *guarantee* that one will win God's protective care. Instead, in discussing the benefits of keeping the first five commandments, he argues that "virtue is its own reward."[51] Moreover, in his treatise on divine providence he writes that God's reasons for acting are completely different from human ones and we cannot expect to understand His actions (*Prov.* 35–36, 54).[52]

In sum, then, although Philo believes that God rewards the virtuous and punishes the wicked, he does not view divine providence as a predictable or guaranteed response to virtuous behavior. Instead of explaining providence from the perspective of human activity, he understands it as a necessary outcome of God's role as Creator, arguing that the maker cares for what is made.[53]

The ambiguity found in Philo's statements about the relationship between divine providence and human behavior in general is also reflected in his remarks about the Jews as special beneficiaries of this providence. In *Legat.* 3, for example, it would seem that the Jews are simply one

---

[49] *Mos.* 1.12, 17; *Mos.* 2.58; *Spec.* 1.308; *Flacc.* 191; cf. *Opif.* 9–10.

[50] *Abr.* 90, 235; *Ios.* 37; *Mos.* 1.148–49.

[51] *Spec.* 2.257–62. In part, this argument may be attributed to the fact that, except for the fifth commandment, the first four do not explicitly mention rewards. Virtue as its own reward, however, is a common Stoic notion, which Philo may adopt apart from its suitability to this particular Scriptural context. See also Wolfson, *Philo*, 2:285.

[52] Regarding Philo's treatise *On Providence*, Dillon (*The Middle Platonists*, 167–68) writes that Philo is "essentially appropriating a standard Stoic treatise on providence (the analogies with Cicero, *De Natura Deorum* II are very close), and fitting it into his Platonic metaphysical scheme. A reading of this treatise by itself would lead one to the conclusion that Philo was a determinist."

[53] For other views on providence from antiquity, see Attridge, *The Interpretation of Biblical History*, 71–107, 154–65. Attridge shows, for example, that Josephus links πρόνοια with divine retribution. See also Johannes Behm, "προνοέω, πρόνοια," *TDNT*, 4:1009–17; Urbach, *The Sages*, 255–85.

illustration of God's concern for all of creation. There Philo observes that God extends providence to all people and particularly to the Jews, calling them the suppliants' race/class (τὸ ἱκετικὸν γένος) and pointing out that they have been allotted or have allotted themselves (προσκεκλήρωται) to God. Although one might infer that God takes special care of the Jews *because* they are the suppliants' race/class or because they are allotted to Him, Philo himself does not make this explicit.

In another example, Philo concludes his treatise on Flaccus as follows: "These things Flaccus too suffered, becoming the surest proof that the nation of the Jews was not deprived of the help which comes from God" (*Flacc.* 191, my translation). On the one hand, this statement may mean that help from God, which is available to all creation, was also available to the Jews during the events described in the treatise. On the other hand, it may also mean that help from God, which is always or usually extended to the Jews, was not withheld—as some may think—during the aforesaid events. Indeed the latter construal is the more likely since earlier in the work, Philo has none other than Flaccus himself declare:

> King of gods and men ... so then Thou dost not disregard the nation of the Jews, nor do they misreport Thy Providence, but all who say that they [the Jews] do not find in Thee a Champion and Defender, go astray from the true creed. I am a clear proof of this, for all the acts which I madly committed against the Jews I have suffered myself. (*Flacc.* 170)

The same perspective that God is especially concerned about the Jews is expressed in *Legat.* 196, in which Philo prays to God for help and mentions that God "often saved the nation when in helpless straits."

In these examples from Philo's two extant historical works, he declares without further explanation that the Jews have God as their Protector. It is generally accepted that his purpose in these historical or political writings is to present current events as a demonstration that God cares especially for the Jews.[54] This assertion then is his starting point, which he seeks to prove but not necessarily to explain or rationalize.

In contrast, in *Spec.* 4.179–82, Philo sets forth a variety of reasons to account for God's special care for the nation. This passage claims that the Jews receive God's pity and compassion because they are set apart from other people and dedicated to God; because their ancestors are exceptionally virtuous; and implicitly because, like their ancestors, they too live according to a high standard of virtue. Unlike *Legat.* 3, quoted earlier, here Philo does link God's special care for the Jews with their devotion to Him. Moreover, in contrast to the idea that God's actions are beyond human understanding and therefore perhaps beyond human influence, this

---

54 See above, n. 42.

perspective suggests that people *can* make themselves worthy and earn God's concern, as the Jews have done.

It was noted earlier that Philo's apparent inconsistency about whether or not people's behavior can influence God's providence reflects a philosophical dilemma of his time. Besides the philosophical issues, however, Philo is also heir to a Biblical tradition which teaches that the nation Israel and its Jewish descendants are the beneficiaries of God's special concern. Indeed this notion is integral to the divine promises and the covenant theology discussed earlier. From the Biblical perspective, then, God's benevolent protection represents both the fulfillment of His earlier promises as well as His side of an ongoing agreement with Israel. According to this agreement—particularly as it is developed in the Book of Deuteronomy and related Biblical books—if the people of Israel follow God's commandments, He will cause the nation to prosper. If they fail to live up to the commandments, the nation will suffer.[55]

Influenced by philosophical issues regarding free will and divine providence, however, Philo transforms the idea that God's protective care for the Jews is part either of promises to their ancestors or of a prior agreement He has with the nation. Instead, his point seems to be that God's providence is available to everyone, and particularly to those who believe in Him as Creator and Provider. It would appear, then, that anyone who believes in God might be eligible for His special providence, not only Jews. God therefore does not guarantee His protection to the Jews by previous commitment. Instead He shows them His care both because this follows from His role as Creator of the universe and because they believe in and worship Him.

The foregoing discussion illustrates how—in various ways—Philo subtly reinterprets Biblical motifs associated with divine promises and the covenant between God and Israel, to render these motifs less offensive to his readers and to portray the Jews favorably. To be sure, his presentation is at times shaped by his philosophical concerns—as in the case of divine providence—or by earlier exegetical approaches—as may be the case in his interpretation of God's promise to Abraham in Gen. 12:3.[56]

Whatever may influence Philo's positions, however, he seems to enhance his presentation of the Biblical motifs by carefully selecting the contexts in which to discuss them. Four passages cited in the above

---

[55] Exod. 23:20–33; Deut. 7:12–16, 28; et al. See also Chapter Four, n. 2, and Ernest Wilson Nicholson, *Deuteronomy and Tradition* (Philadelphia: Fortress Press, 1967); Moshe Weinfeld, *Deuteronomy and the Deuteronomic School* (Oxford: Clarendon Press, 1972).

[56] See above, n. 22.

discussions are particularly good illustrations both of what Philo says about the relationship between God and the Jews and of how and where he chooses to say it. These passages—*Abr.* 98, *Spec.* 2.162–67, *Spec.* 4.179–82, and *Legat.* 1–7—are analyzed below.[57]

Passages in Which Philo Speaks About the Relationship Between God and the Jews

Abr. 98

In *Abr.* 98, Philo describes the Jews as the most God-beloved or God-loving nation (ἔθνων τὸ θεοφιλέστατον) and claims that they are assigned the offices of priest and prophet for the whole world. The larger passage (*Abr.* 89–98) also portrays Abraham as benefitting from God's protection. As we shall see, this passage is especially noteworthy because Philo introduces his observations when Abraham and Sarah are in an Egyptian setting and also because he includes some details from different sections of the Biblical account but omits others.

Abr. 89–98 relates the story told in Gen. 12:10–20 of Abraham and Sarah in Egypt. According to the Bible, Abraham and Sarah go to Egypt to get away from a famine (Gen. 12:10—the verse mentions only Abraham). Fearing for his life because Sarah is so beautiful that the Egyptians would kill him to get her, Abraham asks her to claim she is his sister, not his wife (Gen. 12:11–13). When they come to Egypt, Pharaoh, taken by her beauty, brings Sarah into his house and treats Abraham well, thinking he is her brother (Gen. 12:14–16). God afflicts Pharaoh's house with plagues, however, whereupon Pharaoh confronts Abraham about his deception and then sends him and Sarah on their way (Gen. 12:17–20).[58]

Introducing the theme of divine providence, Philo transforms this Biblical episode from a story about Abraham's deception into one about God's protection of Abraham's marriage. This protection, moreover, is a *reward* to Abraham for rejecting the beliefs of his fatherland, Chaldea, and turning to God (*Abr.* 90). In fact, Philo completely omits the detail that Abraham asks Sarah to misrepresent their relationship. Instead, he portrays the king of Egypt as licentious because he wishes to shame the wife

---

[57] Another passage of interest is *Mos.* 1.147–49, which discusses several themes related to this chapter. For example, the passage mentions the θεοφιλές (divine favor or God-loving quality) of the Biblical nation and describes it as "destined to be consecrated above all others and to offer prayers for ever on behalf of the whole human race." The theme of divine providence is also pertinent because Philo notes that God, "who presides over and takes charge of all things," appoints Moses as leader of the people as a reward for Moses's virtuous qualities.

[58] The Greek adds that Lot was sent with them.

of a stranger (*Abr.* 94). While the Septuagint simply says, "And they led her into Pharaoh's house," Philo adds that Sarah, having no one to protect her in the foreign country, joins her similarly helpless husband in fleeing to God for help (*Abr.* 95). Then God, who shows mercy to those who are maltreated, afflicts Pharaoh with terrible plagues (*Abr.* 96).

After describing the plagues which God inflicts upon Pharaoh (*Abr.* 96) and upon Pharaoh's household for failing to decry the outrage (*Abr.* 97), Philo concludes the story as follows:

> Thus the chastity of the woman was preserved, while the nobility and piety of the man was evidenced by God, Who deigned to grant him this signal boon, that his marriage, which would have been in almost immediate danger of violation, should remain free from harm and outrage, that marriage from which was to issue not a family of a few sons and daughters, but a whole nation, and that the nation dearest of all to God [or most God-loving], which, as I hold, has received the gift of priesthood and prophecy on behalf of all mankind. (*Abr.* 98)

At first glance, it is somewhat surprising to find Philo's comments about the nation in this context, since Gen. 12:10–20 does not mention Abraham and Sarah's descendants at all. Earlier in the Genesis chapter, however, when God tells Abraham to leave his homeland, He blesses him as follows:

> Go from your country and your kindred and your father's house to the land that I will show you. And I will make of you a great nation, and I will bless you, and make your name great so that you will be blessed. I will bless those who bless you, and [those who curse] you I will curse; and [in] you all the families of the earth shall be blessed. (Gen. 12:1–3)

Philo's comments about the nation in *Abr.* 98 may well be based upon this blessing. When he writes that Abraham and Sarah will produce "not a few sons and daughters, but a whole nation," he probably derives this idea from the promise quoted above, or perhaps from subsequent promises, that God will make Abraham a great nation.[59] Of special interest to us, however, are Philo's observations that the nation is the most God-beloved or God-loving (θεοφιλέστατον) and that it has been granted the offices of priesthood and prophecy on behalf of all humanity. It is worth noting that he prefaces his remarks that the nation has received these offices by saying, "it seems to me," or "as I hold" (μοι δοκεῖ), implying that this is his own opinion, rather than an objective fact.

The idea that Abraham's descendants are to serve as the priesthood for the whole world is most probably connected to the latter part of Gen. 12:3, as discussed earlier. As to Philo's description of the nation as most God-beloved or God-loving, this may simply be a general observation about

---

[59] E.g., Gen. 15:5, 17:4–6, 18:18, 22:17.

God's attitude toward Abraham's descendants or their attitude toward Him, since none of the relevant Biblical promises to the patriarchs specifically mentions His love for the people or their love for Him.

Although Philo refers to the qualities just mentioned elsewhere in his works, that the nation serves as prophet for all people is a characteristic he mentions only here. Since he makes this observation only once and offers no further elaboration, it is difficult to know precisely what associations lie behind this comment or to evaluate how seriously he takes the role of the nation as prophet in his overall thinking about the Jews. Perhaps the most likely explanation is that Philo is basing this comment—like the one about the nation serving as the priesthood for all—upon the blessing given in Gen. 12:3, "In you all the families of the earth shall be blessed." Since both priests and prophets serve as intercessors between God and humanity, theoretically either figure may convey blessings. Thus Philo may perhaps understand from this verse that God assigns to Abraham's descendants both roles, those of priest and prophet.[60]

---

[60] Although this explanation for Philo's comment is probably the most likely, others are also possible. For example, in *Her.* 78, Philo links "Israel," the one that sees God, with prophets, who, he points out, were once known as seers. This association of the nation with prophecy through the etymology for Israel, however, is quite indirect, especially since Philo does not use the name "Israel" for the real nation either before or during his time, nor does he speak of them as "seers."

Another possibility is that he associates the office of prophecy with the nation because from this nation came the historical Biblical prophets. Philo, however, rarely mentions these prophets. Moreover, it is not clear that he believes prophecy is limited only to Jews (see, e.g., *Her.* 259–60).

Yet another possible explanation for the assertion that the nation serves as prophet for the world may be found in Philo's comment in *Spec.* 4.192 that "the true priest is necessarily a prophet" (ὁ πρὸς ἀλήθειαν ἱερεὺς εὐθύς ἐστι προφήτης). Since he understands the nation to be the priest for all humanity, he may think that it is necessarily also the prophet. As is the case with many Philonic statements, however, the observation in *Spec.* 4.192 can probably be explained by the specific context in which it appears and therefore may not be representative of his thinking in general. (See, e.g., LCL, 8:436, note on *Spec.* 4.190.)

Finally, yet another comment which may shed light on Philo's depiction of the nation as prophet for all humanity can be found in *Mos.* 2.189, in which he describes different kinds of divine oracles. There he writes of the divine utterances that

> some are spoken by God in His own Person with His prophet for interpreter, in some the revelation comes through question and answer, and others are spoken by Moses in his own person, when possessed by God and carried away out of himself. The first kind are absolutely and entirely signs of the divine excellences, graciousness and beneficence, by which He incites all men to noble conduct, and particularly the [race/class] of His worshippers (τὸ θεραπευτικὸν αὐτοῦ γένος), for whom He opens up the road which leads to happiness. (*Mos.* 2.188–89)

In this passage, Philo says that many of God's directives delivered through the

182 CHAPTER FIVE

Although his remark that the nation serves as priest and prophet for all humanity may be based upon God's blessing in Gen. 12:1–3, it is noteworthy that Philo never explicitly mentions this or any other of God's blessings to Abraham, here or anywhere else in *Abr.* A brief review of these omissions will illustrate the extent to which Philo reworks the Biblical narrative.

Among the more significant of God's blessings to Abraham are those expressed in Gen. 17:1–14, concerning the everlasting covenant. In that passage, God changes the patriarch's name from Abram to Abraham and promises,

> No longer shall your name be Abram, but your name shall be Abraham, for I have made you the father of a multitude of nations. I will make you exceedingly fruitful; and I will make nations of you, and kings shall come forth from you. And I will establish my covenant between me and you and your descendants after you throughout their generations for an everlasting covenant, to be God to you and to your descendants after you. And I will give to you, and to your descendants after you, the land of your sojournings, all the land of Canaan, for an everlasting possession; and I will be their God. (Gen. 17:5–8)

To confirm this covenant, God establishes the commandment of circumcision as a sign throughout the generations (Gen. 17:9–14). Other Biblical passages in which God mentions His intentions for Abraham's descendants include Gen. 18:17–19, when He is about to destroy Sodom and Gomorrah, and Gen. 22:15–18, following the binding of Isaac.[61] Although Philo includes all these episodes in the treatise on Abraham, in none of his retellings does he refer to the divine blessings, nor does he mention circumcision as a sign of the covenant.

As suggested earlier, Philo may omit these details in order to avoid presenting the relationship between God and the Jews as the result of a preset agreement meant only for Abraham's descendants. Such a presentation might offend his non-Jewish readers and encourage complacency

---

prophet Moses are intended especially for the γένος that worships Him. It does not say that this γένος *mediates* God's message, but rather that it receives His words through His prophet Moses. (For a different perspective, see Wolfson, *Philo*, 2:51–52.) Although in this context the γένος probably signifies the Jewish nation—past and present—it is worth noting that Philo also describes the sect of the Therapeutae as the θεραπευτικὸν γένος (*Contempl.* 11.)

[61] Abraham's descendants are also mentioned in Gen. 12:7, in which God promises to give them the land of Canaan. Philo, however, does not allude to this part of the verse either in this treatise or elsewhere. In general, he allegorizes God's promise to give the land of Canaan to Abraham's descendants. See, e.g., *Her.* 96–99, 313–16, and *Somn.* 2.255–58 on Gen. 15:18; and *QG* 3.45 on Gen. 17:8. See also Jaubert, *La notion d'Alliance*, 414–18. Other relevant verses may be cited from Genesis 15, but with the exception of *Abr.* 262, which comments on Gen. 15:6, Philo does not mention this Biblical chapter in the present treatise.

in his Jewish readers, who may feel they need do nothing to earn God's favor (cf. *Spec.* 1.54, *Spec.* 4.182, *Virt.* 187–98).

So far we have discerned Philo's editorial hand in his added remarks— e.g., that the nation descended from Abraham and Sarah is the most God-beloved or God-loving and that it has received the offices of priest and prophet for all humanity—and in his omissions—e.g., of God's blessings to Abraham. It is also striking that Philo chooses the story about Abraham and Sarah in Egypt in which to include his observations about their descendant nation. Not only does the Biblical account of Abraham and Sarah's sojourn in Egypt (Gen. 12:10–20) make no mention of Abraham's heirs, but also Philo leaves out God's promises about Abraham's descendants from two Biblical episodes which he recounts *before* he tells of this sojourn.[62]

It seems therefore that Philo may have a special purpose when he inserts his comment about the nation specifically at the point when Abraham and Sarah are in Egypt. Indeed he may include his observations at this point specifically to convey a message to his readers, i.e., fellow Jews—who might be tempted to stray from their ancestral beliefs or to intermarry or betray their marriages while living among the Egyptians—and non-Jews—who may be attracted to or put off by Jewish beliefs.

These readers might derive from Philo's version of Abraham and Sarah's sojourn in Egypt at least the following two lessons: First, God rewards those who believe in Him, whether they are newcomers or prospective newcomers to belief in God, as some of his non-Jewish readers may be, or whether they are "strangers in a strange land," as his fellow Jews may perceive themselves. One can learn this lesson from the way God preserves Abraham's marriage in Egypt as a reward to him for turning his back on the misconceptions of his homeland, Chaldea, in order to follow God (*Abr.* 90) and from the way He helps Sarah, who also flees to God for help once she is in Egypt (*Abr.* 95).

Second, the nation whose ancestral purity God preserves is a venerable and philanthropic one indeed, since it is His most beloved of nations and serves the roles of priest and prophet on behalf of all humanity (*Abr.* 98). For his fellow Jews, then, Philo presents the nation as one whose purity is well worth preserving, while for all his readers he depicts the nation's role on behalf of all people as both magnanimous and longstanding.

---

62 These two episodes are Abraham's departure from Haran (Gen. 12:1–3, cf. *Abr.* 60–80) and the change of Abram's name to Abraham (Gen. 17:5; cf. *Abr.* 81–83). In presenting Abraham's change of name before his and Sarah's sojourn in Egypt, Philo departs from the Biblical arrangement of these incidents.

Spec. 2.162–67

In this section, Philo declares that the Jews believe in the one God and serve Him through specific practices. The passage also elaborates upon the role of the Jews as priests for the whole world. What is especially noteworthy about Philo's discussion is its explicitly apologetic nature, for here Philo directly answers the charge that the Jews are antisocial.

The passage discusses the Sheaf Feast, based on Lev. 23:10–14, and forms part of a larger discourse about the Jewish holidays in general, which Philo talks about under the heading of the Second Commandment. As he does with some of the other holidays,[63] Philo provides both a national and a universal significance for this feast. Noting that the Jews bring to the altar a sheaf from both the Jewish homeland and the whole earth,[64] he explains that they offer these as a thanksgiving on their own behalf and on behalf of the whole human race (*Spec.* 2.162).

Philo elaborates on this practice as follows:

> The reason of this is that the Jewish nation is to the whole inhabited world what the priest is to the State. For the holy office in very truth belongs to the nation because it carries out all the rites of purification and both in body and soul obeys the injunctions of the divine laws, which restrict the pleasures of the belly and the parts below it and the horde... (*Spec.* 2.163)

This passage is an interesting contrast to other passages (e.g., *Abr.* 98 and *Mos.* 1.149), which may derive the characterization of the nation as priests from God's blessings to the patriarchs or from the divine covenant with Israel. In those passages, Philo is describing the Biblical nation and its promise for the future. In *Spec.* 2.163, however, he is describing his Jewish contemporaries, and he attributes their priestly role to their observance of the laws. Here, then, their priestly office seems to follow upon rather than precede their observance.

In addition, Philo explains that the laws restrict the pleasures of the body, the irrational senses, and the wild impulses of the soul (*Spec.* 2.163). Thus, in contrast to the Bible, which usually sets forth the commandments on divine authority with no other explanation, in this passage Philo tries to show that these laws serve a purpose.

By commenting that the Jews are considered priests for the world because they observe the laws and by providing a rationale for these laws,

---

[63] See, e.g., *Spec.* 2.150 on the "Crossing-Feast" and *Spec.* 2.188 on the "Trumpet Feast."

[64] This passage contrasts with *Somn.* 2.75, in which Philo interprets Lev. 23:10 as meaning that the sheaf should come only from the land which God gives the people, i.e., Canaan. Cf. Belkin (*Philo and the Oral Law*, 218), who ignores the contradiction between the two interpretations on this point. See also Heinemann, *Philons griechische und jüdische Bildung*, 125.

Philo completely reworks the idea that the Jews have a special relationship with God based upon a prior pact which stipulates the nation's obedience to the laws as a condition. Furthermore, according to his portrayal,
it would seem that anyone who follows the laws automatically becomes a
member of the community of priests: "[T]he legislation is in a way a
lesson on the priestly office and one who lives according to the laws is
naturally (εὐθύς) considered a priest or rather a high priest in the
judgment of truth..." (*Spec.* 2.164, my translation).

Philo adds another point. The world is filled with false deities, created
by humans, and different nations worship different gods (*Spec.* 2.164). By
honoring the true God, however, the Jews correct the error made by those
who worship false deities. Philo writes,

> But if He exists Whom all Greeks and barbarians unanimously acknowledge, the
> supreme Father of gods and men and the Maker of the whole universe, whose
> nature is invisible and inscrutable not only by the eye, but by the mind ... then it
> was the duty of all men to cleave to Him and not to introduce new gods staged as by
> machinery to receive the same honours. [Since they slipped in regard to the most
> essential particular, the failure of others was corrected, most properly speaking, by
> the Jewish nation] which passed over all created objects because they were created
> and naturally liable to destruction and chose the service only of the Uncreated and
> Eternal... (*Spec.* 2.165–66)

Philo's claim that the God worshipped by Jews is acknowledged by all
other people is surprising, and it is hard to know quite what he has in
mind.[65] In any event, by portraying the Jews as the ones who rectify the
mistake of all the nations, he enhances the role of the Jews as priests for
the world.

Philo's explicitly apologetic motive behind this characterization becomes apparent in his conclusion. He writes,

> And therefore it causes me to wonder how some dare to charge with inhumanity
> the nation which exercises to such a great extent sociability and goodwill toward
> all people everywhere, inasmuch as it celebrates its prayers and holidays and first
> fruit offerings on behalf of the human race generally and worships the truly
> existent God on its own behalf and on behalf of others who have shunned their
> obligatory service. (*Spec.* 2.167, my translation)

Although Philo notes elsewhere that the Jews serve as the priesthood for
the human race, and although he also denounces false worship in several
places throughout his works, this is the only passage in which he makes
explicit the claim that the Jews not only represent all humanity but also
correct its errors. Moreover, although he frequently portrays the Jews and

---

[65] See LCL, 7:408, note a. In the French translation, Suzanne Daniel suggests that
Philo is talking about the God of the philosophers and the supreme God of popular
religions, *De Specialibus Legibus I–II, OPA*, 24:332, n. 3.

their practices as characterized by humanity and goodwill[66]—perhaps implicitly answering charges to the contrary—he rarely refers directly as he does here to accusations of inhumanity against the nation (cf. *Virt.* 141). This then is one of the few explicitly apologetic passages in the Exposition.

Finally, it is worth asking why Philo chooses the Sheaf Feast as a context in which to emphasize the priestly role of the Jews, since the Bible mentions the sheaf offering very briefly and does not comment there upon a universal role for the people.[67] It may be helpful to recall that Philo presents this interpretation about the Jews as the universal (in contrast to the national) significance of the holiday. The main focus of the occasion is the offering of the sheaf from the first fruits, an act involving priestly ritual. The Jews carry out this offering with first fruits both from their own homeland and from the whole earth. Finally, this is the first offering of first fruits in the holiday cycle. Although the holiday may elsewhere appear to be fairly minor, then, it provides Philo with a suitable context in which to highlight the role of the Jews as representative priests for all people.

Spec. 4.179–82

In this passage, Philo argues that the Jews receive God's compassion (ἔλεος καὶ οἶκτος), asserts that they are allotted or allot themselves to God, and implicitly calls to mind an association to them as priests for the whole world. He also notes that the nation benefits from God's special concern *because* it has been allotted or has allotted itself to Him and that this allotment, in turn, results from the virtue of the nation's ancestors and implicitly the virtue of the nation itself.

Philo's comments appear within the context of a discussion based upon Deut. 10:17–18 about God's justice toward the proselyte,[68] orphan, and widow. Since these verses are basically about the disadvantaged in general,[69] the context itself arouses sympathy, even before one reads his specific remarks.

---

[66] *Spec.* 1.324; *Spec.* 2.79, 104, 107, 110, 138, 141, 183; *Spec.* 4.24, 71; *Virt.* 51–174.

[67] On this question, see also LCL, 7:406, note a; and Heinemann, *Philons griechische und jüdische Bildung*, 125–26. In the Bible, the sheaf offering is not itself called a feast, and in rabbinic tradition, this does not constitute a full holiday. See also Daniel in *De Specialibus Legibus I–II, OPA*, 24:330, n. 3.

[68] The term προσήλυτος appears in Deut. 10:18. Philo uses ἔπηλυς, ἐπηλύτης, and ἐπήλυτος synonymously with προσήλυτος, understanding these terms to mean someone who has come over to the Jewish polity. The issue of the proselyte is addressed in the next chapter.

[69] Cf. *Spec.* 1.308, in which Philo describes these individuals as "those most helplessly in need."

After describing the situation of each figure—the proselyte, orphan, and widow—Philo compares the Jews to an orphan because they have no allies:

> One may say that the whole Jewish [nation] is in the position of an orphan compared with all the nations on every side. They when misfortunes fall upon them which are not by the direct intervention of heaven are never, owing to international intercourse, unprovided with helpers who join sides with them. But the Jewish nation has none to take its part, as it lives under exceptional laws which are necessarily grave and severe, because they inculcate the highest standard of virtue. But gravity is austere, and austerity is held in aversion by the great mass of men because they favour pleasure. (*Spec.* 4.179)

Philo claims that while other nations always have allies, the Jews stand alone. Moreover, they stand alone because they live virtuously according to their laws, in contrast to most other people, who are pleasure-loving. It is interesting that he attributes the isolation of the Jews to the severity of their laws and that he claims these laws inculcate the highest standard of virtue. From this perspective, the isolation of the Jews appears to be to their credit.

In *Spec.* 4.180, Philo observes that although the Jews have no allies among the nations, they do enjoy God's special solicitude:

> Nevertheless as Moses tells us the orphan-like desolate state of his people is always an object of pity and compassion to the Ruler of the Universe [to whom it has been allotted or has allotted itself (ᾧ προσκεκλήρωται)], because it has been set apart (ἀπενεμήθη) out of the whole human race as a kind of first fruits to the Maker and Father.

As was mentioned earlier, because Philo uses the verb προσκληρόω, allot, in a form that can be either middle or passive, it is unclear whether God allots the Jews to Himself or the Jews dedicate themselves to Him. In this passage, however, since he uses the passive to say that the Jews are set apart (ἀπενεμήθη), it is quite possible that προσκεκλήρωται also has a passive sense here.

This image of the Jewish nation assigned to God as a kind of first fruits calls to mind the theme of the people as priests, through a series of associations that would be familiar to most readers of the Bible, though not necessarily to Philo's readers of this work. These associations pertain to the Biblical injunctions that the firstborn and first fruits are set aside and dedicated to God and that the priestly tribe Levi is set aside to serve God in place of all the firstborn of Israel. Num. 3:11–13 describes this appointment of Levi as follows:

> Behold, I have taken the Levites from among the people of Israel instead of every first-born that opens the womb among the people of Israel. The Levites shall be mine, for all the first-born are mine; on the day that I slew all the first-born in

the land of Egypt, I consecrated for my own all the first-born in Israel, both of men and of beast; they shall be mine. I am the Lord.[70]

The portrayal of the Jews set apart as a kind of first fruits is reminiscent of the priestly tribe of Levi set apart instead of the firstborn of Israel. Moreover, in Exod. 4:22, God describes Israel itself as His firstborn son. Philo's statement in *Spec.* 4.180, then, indirectly evokes the idea that Israel, God's firstborn, is set apart out of the whole human race as the first fruits or as the priestly Levites for the world, in the same way that the tribe of Levi is set apart from the whole nation Israel as the firstborn or priestly tribe.

In the next section (*Spec.* 4.181), Philo remarks that God cares especially for the Jews on account of the righteousness of their ancestors, even though the descendants may be sinners:

> And the reason is the highly prized qualities of righteousness and virtue of the founders of the nation, qualities which persist like imperishable plants bearing ever-blooming fruit, salutary to the descendants and beneficial toward all things, even though the descendants may be sinners, but only with regard to curable matters, not completely incorrigible ones. (*Spec.* 4.181, my translation)

As we have observed, several Scriptural passages note that God's covenantal commitment to the nation Israel derives from His promises to their ancestors.[71] The Bible, however, gives no rational explanation for God's choice of these ancestors, though occasionally it says that He chooses Abraham, Isaac, and Jacob out of love. When Philo attributes God's choice of the patriarchs to their righteousness and virtue, then, he subtly changes the Biblical depiction. Moreover, since God's choice is based upon virtue, it appears less arbitrary.

In addition, this explanation for God's choice enables Philo to argue that noble lineage in itself is not enough. He warns,

> Yet let no one think that good lineage is a perfect blessing and then neglect noble actions, but reflect that greater anger is due to one who while his parentage is of the best brings shame upon his parents by the wickedness of his ways. Guilty is he who, having for his own models of true excellence to copy, reproduces nothing that serves to direct his life aright and keep it sound and healthy. (*Spec.* 4.182)

In these comments we can discern Philo's awareness of his audience. For Jews who may have strayed, he suggests that they still have a chance to be redeemed on account of the righteousness of their ancestors. He stresses, however, that it is not enough to be born a Jew; one must emulate the ancestors by living virtuously. Moreover, by acknowledging that virtuous behavior is what is really important, Philo can also argue—as he does

---

[70] Cf. Deut. 18:1–5 and refs. given in n. 36.
[71] E.g., Deut. 7:7–8, 8:18, 9:5, 29:13; cf. Deut. 4:37.

elsewhere—that the essential elements of kinship are not blood but pious beliefs and noble behavior. Therefore people without noble lineage who turn to a life of piety and virtue, i.e., proselytes, deserve to be embraced by the Jewish community.[72] Finally, by emphasizing that the nation is set apart for God on account of the virtue of its ancestors, Philo may also be addressing concerns of either Jews or non-Jews regarding God's apparently arbitrary choice of Israel as depicted in Scripture. If indeed these ancestors are virtuous, then His choice of them is merited.

Legat. 1–7

This passage, analyzed in part in Chapter Three, is unique in Philo's writings because it is the only place where he links "Israel," the one that sees God, with the Jews. In addition, Philo combines philosophical themes, such as the vision of God and the nature of God's powers, with claims based upon Jewish tradition about the relationship between God and the nation. Specifically, he notes that the people are particular beneficiaries of divine providence, that they are allotted or have allotted themselves to God, and that they are the suppliants' race/class (τὸ ἱκετικὸν γένος), a characterization which calls to mind their intercessory role as priests for all people.

We have already seen that Philo does not connect the ability of "Israel" to see God—which is implied by the meaning of its name, ὁρῶν θεόν—with any of the abovementioned claims about the relationship between God and the Jews. In other words, it is not *because* they see God that the Jews are the suppliant γένος, that they have been allotted or allot themselves to God, or that they benefit from His providence.[73] Nor does Philo allege that the Jews can see God *because* of these other characteristics of their relationship to Him. We shall now turn again to the prologue in *Legat.* to examine the effect created when Philo brings together these various elements from philosophy and Jewish tradition.

It was mentioned that one of the main purposes of this introductory passage is to argue that God extends providence to all people and especially toward the Jews. Unfortunately, since the work is incomplete, we cannot see how Philo applies these arguments to the political situation he is describing. Nonetheless, he most likely intended to show how the

---

[72] For Philo's comments on kinship, see *Abr.* 31, *Mos.* 2.171, *Spec.* 1.317, *Spec.* 2.73. On proselytes: *Spec.* 1.51–52; *Virt.* 102–4, 179; cf. *Virt.* 189 and 198. These topics will be discussed in the next chapter.
[73] Goodenough, in contrast, does attribute the intercessory role of the Jews to their "mystic powers of vision" (*The Politics of Philo Judaeus*, 13).

unfolding of events—perhaps the downfall of the oppressors—substantiates his contention that the Jews enjoy God's special protection.[74]

To review briefly the entire passage, Philo begins by observing that people have more confidence in fate than in nature, and he attributes this misplaced confidence to reliance upon sense perception instead of intellect (*Legat.* 1–2). Whereas the sight of the senses perceives only what is near, the keener sight of reason sees into the future. People confuse reason's vision, however, through drink and other indulgence or, even worse, through ignorance (*Legat.* 2). Nonetheless Philo argues that the situation at hand should convince even those who have given up on God's providence:

> And yet the present time and the many important questions decided in it are strong enough to convince even those who have come to disbelieve that the Deity takes thought for (προνοεῖν) men, and particularly for [the suppliants' race/class (τὸ ἱκετικὸν γένος) which has been allotted or has allotted itself (προσκεκλήρωται) to] the Father and King of the Universe and the Source of all things. (*Legat.* 3)

This passage presents without elaboration some of the features discussed above of the relationship between God and the Jews. Philo asserts, for example, that God, who cares for all people, takes special thought for the Jews, whom he does not name but calls "the suppliants' γένος which has been allotted or has allotted itself" to Him. By describing them in this way, he implies that the nation may receive God's special attention *because* it serves Him and is allotted to Him. Moreover, the designation "suppliants' γένος" suggests that this γένος serves an intercessory role for all people, though Philo does not explicitly mention this role.

In *Legat.* 4, Philo declares that the name of the suppliants' γένος is "Israel," which means "one that sees God." He then argues that seeing Him necessarily evokes a high standard of virtue and excellence in the beholders and that He who is seen is better than any philosophical concept, like the Good or the Beautiful (*Legat.* 5).

In *Legat.* 6–7, Philo turns to different issues. First he mentions that it is impossible for reason to approach God as He is and that it is difficult to find words even for God's powers, which he then describes as "the creative, the kingly, the providential, and ... the others all that are both beneficial and punitive..." (*Legat.* 7).

Here, Philo reflects upon the role of God's punitive powers, considering them to be part of His beneficial powers. He explains that

> the punitive powers are to be classed among the beneficial ones, not only because they are part of laws and ordinances—for law is naturally made complete by two elements, reward of the good and punishment of the wicked—but also because

---

[74] See n. 42.

punishment admonishes and chastens often even those who have gone astray, but if not, most certainly their associates;[75] for punishments of others improve the multitude through fear that they may suffer similar things. (*Legat.* 7, my translation)

What is especially striking about this prologue is that Philo introduces philosophical motifs at the beginning of a work about the political situation of the Jews. These motifs include the description of "Israel" as the one that sees God; the very idea of seeing God as inspiring virtuous behavior; the inaccessibility of God even to reason; God's powers; and the importance to laws of rewards and punishments.

Philo elaborates frequently upon some of these philosophical motifs in the Allegory and QGE—those exegetical writings in which he never talks about the real nation. In the Exposition, however, especially where he does mention the Jews, he rarely discusses these motifs. Since he seems to keep discussion of these philosophical motifs separate from discussion of the Jewish nation—at least in his exegetical works—it is surprising to find even a summary of various philosophical themes at the beginning of this political treatise.

Why does Philo begin *Legat.* in this way? As we have noted, in all likelihood, he intends this prologue to show his readers—both Jews and Gentiles—that God watches out especially for the Jews, perhaps by punishing those who mistreat them, as one can see from the current events. He may also wish to reinforce his own faith amid the anguish he has been suffering with his people. When he introduces philosophical motifs, however, Philo vindicates his people's way of life from a perspective other than that of current events.

By implicitly linking the Jews with "Israel," the one that sees God, Philo presents them as embodying the highest philosophical goal, i.e., seeing God. When he contends that reason cannot attain this goal, however, he implies that philosophy alone is not enough. As the suppliants' γένος which is dedicated to God, "Israel" or the Jews exemplify something greater than philosophy, i.e., worship of God through observance of His special laws. Laws, moreover, are made complete by providing for rewards and punishments, and these rewards and punishments come from God through His powers. In thus arguing that God protects the Jews and punishes their enemies, Philo validates the Jewish path, even above the philosophical one.[76]

---

[75] πλησιάζοντες. This could also be translated, "those who are close to sinning," as Smallwood notes (*Philonis Alexandrini*, 157, n. 7), citing Hans Leisegang in *JBL* 57 (1938): 383; but see *Spec.* 4.223 for a thought similar to the one expressed by the translation given here.

[76] Cf. *Virt.* 65, in which Philo seems to equate Judaism with philosophy. (These two

In different ways, then, the various passages discussed above express Philo's ideas about the relationship between God and the Jews, past and present. Philo's observations are connected with the Biblical depiction of the relationship between God and Israel. As he does in his explicit interpretations of that depiction, here too in his comments about God's relationship to the Jews and their ancestors—which are implicit interpretations of the Biblical depiction—Philo modifies Biblical notions to suit his aims and audiences. According to these implicit interpretations, it would seem that anyone who chooses may achieve the same standing with God as the Jews have.

Conspicuously absent from Philo's discussion about the Jews is any reference to their ability to see God. Accordingly, one might assume that God's relationship with them is somewhat different from the one He has with "Israel." In the next chapter, we shall have an opportunity to compare the two relationships when we consider what Philo says about newcomers to God, or proselytes.

---

passages, *Legat.* 1–7 and *Virt.* 65, are discussed in Chapter Three.) For another perspective on *Legat.* 1–7, see Wayne A. Meeks, "The Divine Agent and His Counterfeit in Philo and the Fourth Gospel," *Aspects of Religious Propaganda in Judaism and Early Christianity*, ed. Elisabeth Schüssler Fiorenza, University of Notre Dame, Center for the Study of Judaism and Christianity in Antiquity, no. 2 (Notre Dame, 1976), 49–54.

CHAPTER SIX

PROSELYTES IN RELATION TO
GOD, JEWS, AND "ISRAEL"

Having established that Philo links "Israel" with the ability to see God and associates the Jews with a very different set of characteristics, we are now prepared to test whether or not our distinction between "Israel" and the Jews remains valid when Philo talks about proselytes. To do this, we shall examine the relationship between proselytes and God and compare this relationship to the one God has with "Israel," on the one hand, and with the Jews, on the other. Finally, we shall also consider whether proselytes become members of "Israel," the Jews, or both. Although Philo himself does not usually address these issues directly, his discussions about proselytes and other matters do permit us to draw some relevant conclusions.

A few preliminary remarks regarding the complex issue of proselytes and conversion in antiquity are perhaps in order. Solutions to the questions of who was considered a Jew and how one became a Jew are far from uniform. In an article entitled "Crossing the Boundary and Becoming a Jew," Shaye J. D. Cohen describes the situation in antiquity as follows:

> A gentile who was accepted as a proselyte by one community may not have been so regarded by another. Nor should we assume that the proselytes of one community were necessarily treated like those of another, because the Jews of antiquity held a wide range of opinions about the degree to which the proselyte became just like the native born.[1]

---

[1] Shaye J. D. Cohen, "Crossing the Boundary and Becoming a Jew," *HTR* 82 (1989): 14. For other discussions of proselytes during this period and related topics, see idem, "Conversion to Judaism in Historical Perspective: From Biblical Israel to Postbiblical Judaism," *Conservative Judaism* 36 (1983): 31–45; Bernard J. Bamberger, *Proselytism in the Talmudic Period* (Cincinnati: Hebrew Union College Press, 1939); Johannes Behm and Ernst Würthwein, "μετανοέω, μετάνοια," *TDNT*, 4:975–1008; C. H. Cave, "Gentiles and Judaism: 'God-Fearers' and Proselytes," in Emil Schürer, *History of the Jewish People*, rev. and ed. Geza Vermes et al. (Edinburgh: T. & T. Clark, 1986), 3:1:150–76; Louis H. Feldman, *Jew and Gentile in the Ancient World: Attitudes and Interactions From Alexander to Justinian* (Princeton: Princeton University Press, 1993); Karl Georg Kuhn, "προσήλυτος," *TDNT*, 6:727–44; Scot McKnight, *A Light Among the Gentiles: Jewish Missionary Activity in the Second Temple Period* (Minneapolis: Fortress Press, 1991); Arthur Darby Nock, *Conversion: The Old and the New in Religion from Alexander the Great to Augustine of Hippo* (Oxford: Oxford University Press, 1933), esp. 1–16; George Foote Moore, *Judaism in the First Centuries of the Christian Era: The Age of the Tannaim* (New York: Schocken Books, 1958), 1:323–53; Alan F. Segal, "The Costs of Proselytism and Conversion," *SBL 1988 Seminar Papers*, SBL Seminar Paper Series, ed. David J. Lull, no.

Diversity is apparent not only concerning the broader issues of who was considered a Jew and how one became a Jew, but also among the terms used by different communities both for individuals and for the process of turning to Judaism. In some communities, for example, we find terms in Greek and Hebrew for "God-reverers" or "God-fearers" (e.g., θεοσεβεῖς; σεβόμενοι or φοβούμενοι τὸν θεόν; יי ירא; ירא שמים שמים), whose precise standing with the Jewish community is unclear. Rabbinic literature has references to the גר תושב, or resident alien, another figure who, while apparently sympathetic to Judaism, was not considered a Jew. The Rabbis also speak of different kinds of proselytes. Besides the גר צדק (the true or righteous proselyte), they mention proselytes who came over to Judaism out of different motives, some considered honorable, some not.[2]

Finally, variety also exists among words describing the activity of these different figures in relation to Jews and Judaism. Thus terms like μετάνοια, repentance or conversion; 'Ιουδαΐζειν, to act like a Jew (Esther 8:17; cf. the Hebrew, התיהד); and התגייר , to become a proselyte, may express a range of behavior from acting like a Jew to becoming one.[3]

Sometimes variations occur even in the way just one word is used. A term like μετάνοια, for example, has more than one meaning—even in Philo's works alone. Whereas Philo may use μετάνοια to denote repentance or conversion—in the sense of turning from polytheistic belief to belief in the one God—in the New Testament, μετάνοια signifies "conversion" as a complete and irreversible religious transformation.[4]

The unmistakable diversity of terms and positions regarding who was considered a Jew and how one became a Jew would seem to reflect a rather fluid situation among the various communities in antiquity. Non-Jews, it appears, might express an interest in Judaism in any number of ways without becoming a Jew.

---

27 (Atlanta: Scholars Press, 1988), 336–69; idem, *Paul the Convert*, 72–75.

[2] On these various figures, see, e.g., Bamberger, *Proselytism in the Talmudic Period*, 133–40; Cave, "Gentiles and Judaism," 165–72; Cohen, "Crossing the Boundary," 31–33; Feldman, *Jew and Gentile*, 342–82; idem, "Proselytes and 'Sympathizers' in the Light of the New Inscriptions From Aphrodisias," *Revue des études juives* 148 (1989): 265–305; Kuhn, "προσήλυτος," 730–44; Saul Lieberman, *Greek in Jewish Palestine: Studies in Life and Manners of Jewish Palestine in the II–IV Centuries C.E.* (New York: Feldheim, 1965), 77–84; McKnight, *A Light Among the Gentiles*, 90–101, 110–14; Moore, *Judaism*, 1:323–41.

[3] On 'Ιουδαΐζειν, see Amir, "The Term 'Ιουδαϊσμός," 36. Shaye Cohen reviews various uses of 'Ιουδαΐζειν in an unpublished paper entitled "The Polemical Uses of 'Ιουδαῖος and 'Ιουδαΐζειν in Early Christian Writings," delivered at the 1991 SBL Conference. On התגייר, see Kuhn, "προσήλυτος," 736–37.

[4] Philo's notions about μετάνοια are discussed later in this chapter (see also below, n. 31). For New Testament understandings of this term, see Behm, "μετανοέω, μετάνοια," *TDNT*, 4:999–1006.

Recognizing that the relationship between proselyte and Jew in antiquity is far from clear, I shall concentrate here exclusively upon Philo's approach to the proselyte—which in itself can be somewhat ambiguous—without trying to compare his discussions with those of other communities. Let us begin this consideration of Philo with some general observations.

Philo's Presentation of Proselytes: General Observations

Vocabulary and Definitions

In sixteen passages, Philo uses the words, προσήλυτος, ἔπηλυς, ἐπηλύτης, and ἐπήλυτος to describe proselytes or incomers.[5] (For convenience, I shall refer to the last three terms as "ἔπηλυς and its variations.") In *Spec.* 1.51, he provides an etymological explanation for προσήλυτοι, noting that they are so-called "because they have *come to* (προσεληλυθέναι) a new and God-loving polity" (my emphasis).

In *QE* 2.2, in which Philo uses both προσήλυτος and ἔπηλυς, he explains different nuances of the word ἔπηλυς as follows:

> [S]ome call strangers (ξένοι) 'incomers' (ἐπήλυδες). But strangers are also those who come of their own accord to the truth, in the same way as those who sojourned in Egypt. For the latter are incomers to the land, the former to laws and customs. But the common name of 'incomers' is ascribed to both.[6]

With their basic meaning of "one who comes to," then, προσήλυτος and ἔπηλυς and its variations may be understood in a number of ways. These words can denote, for example, a person of foreign birth; one who dwells with temporary or inferior status among a foreign population; one who joins a new people, adopting their beliefs and practices; or all the foregoing. Although we are interested only in those passages in which Philo understands προσήλυτος or ἔπηλυς and its variations as meaning one who joins a new people and adopts their beliefs and practices, he does occasionally use these words in other ways as well. I shall discuss these cases presently.

---

[5] Some passages use more than one of these words. The passages are as follows: *Cher.* 108, 119–21; *Somn.* 1.160; *Somn.* 2.273; *Mos.* 1.7, 147; *Spec.* 1.51–53, 308–9; *Spec.* 2.118–19; *Spec.* 4.176–78; *Virt.* 102–4, 182, 219; *Praem.* 152; *QE* 2.2; *Flacc.* 54.

[6] This is my translation based upon the Greek fragment. The Armenian adds a negative so that the sentence reads, "[S]trangers are also those who have come of their own accord to the truth *not* in the same way as those who sojourned in Egypt" (my emphasis). Both ways of reading the passage can make sense. Without the negative, the passage emphasizes the commonality that all incomers share; with the negative, the passage emphasizes the difference between what each incomer comes to.

In ten passages in which Philo uses προσήλυτος or ἔπηλυς and its variations, he elaborates upon these terms and it is usually clear that he means by them a person who leaves behind old beliefs and practices as well as a community of family and friends to adopt new beliefs and practices and to join a new community.[7] In one passage (*Somn.* 2.272–73), Philo describes proselytes simply as μετανάσται καὶ πρόσφυγες, emigrants and refugees. The interpretation makes sense, however, only if one understands proselytes as emigrants and refugees who come to God, not merely emigrants and refugees who leave one physical home for another.[8]

Of the ten passages in which Philo does define the proselyte in some way, eight assert that he or she[9] leaves behind something old *and* comes over to something new, while two mention only the coming over to something new, although the abandonment of the old may also be implied. The dual activity of leaving behind the old and taking on the new appears especially important, since the old ways and the new are presented as fundamentally incompatible.[10]

Unfortunately Philo never provides the same list twice of what is left and what is adopted, nor does even one specification appear consistently in every list. Nonetheless we may observe generally that the proselyte abandons belief in and worship of many gods to adopt belief in and worship of the one God. More specifically, Philo mentions that proselytes leave behind mythical inventions, polytheistic beliefs, ancestral customs, family, friends, and country and come over to the one true God, truth, piety, virtue, the laws, and a new polity. Although he does not do so in every case, Philo most frequently cites the turning to God—whether it be to honor of, worship of, or belief in Him.[11]

---

[7] These ten passages are as follows: *Somn.* 1.160–62; *Spec.* 1.51–53, 308–9; *Spec.* 2.116–19; *Spec.* 4.176–78; *Virt.* 102–4, 180–82, 219; *Praem.* 152; and *QE* 2.2. *Spec.* 2.116–19, which explains a Biblical law about buying houses within a city (Lev. 25:29–31), understands the proselyte in two senses, as one who comes over to the laws and as a newcomer to the land.

[8] Philo's use of migration or pilgrimage vocabulary to describe the proselyte is discussed further below. See also nn. 28 and 29.

[9] I use both genders advisedly. As I argue later in the chapter, Tamar might serve as an example of a female proselyte. Although Philo does not call her one explicitly, he employs the same language for her as he does for the proselyte.

[10] On the importance of the dual activity of leaving old ways and adopting new ones, see Nock, *Conversion*, 7, 13–14. The two passages which mention only the coming over to something new are *Spec.* 2.116–19 and *Praem.* 152. In *Spec.* 2.118, Philo describes the ἐπηλύται as suppliants and refugees to the *laws*, while in *Praem.* 152, he says that the ἔπηλυς comes of his own accord to *God*. On *Spec.* 2.116–19, see also above, n. 7.

[11] Of the ten passages listed in n. 7, only *Spec.* 2.116–19 does not mention God. I shall discuss the turning to God in more detail further below.

It is worth noting that Philo mentions the adoption of new laws or customs only twice.[12] Because he speaks of these laws or customs in only a general way, we do not have sufficient evidence to be able to identify the legal requirements for either becoming a proselyte or maintaining one's status as a member of the community. Moreover, on the basis of what Philo tells us, we are unable to discern whether or not or to what degree the proselyte is accepted by the new community which he or she joins.

Perhaps the most we can say then about Philo's understanding of the proselyte is that he or she abandons old polytheistic beliefs and practices, leaving behind a community of family and friends, and comes over to belief in and worship (loosely defined) of the one true God, becoming part of a new community. For the rest of this discussion, I shall use the term "proselyte" to denote this meaning. It is significant that, according to this description, becoming a proselyte has both religious and social dimensions.

As to the interchangeability of προσήλυτος and ἔπηλυς or its variations, Philo always uses the word προσήλυτος only when it occurs in Biblical passages he is discussing.[13] More frequently, he uses ἔπηλυς and its

---

[12] *Spec.* 2.118 and *QE* 2.2 (the latter passage is quoted earlier); cf. *Somn.* 1.162. On the debate over whether or not circumcision is required of proselytes, see below, n. 21.

[13] *Cher.* 108 (Lev. 25:23), 119–21 (Lev. 25:23); *Somn.* 2.273 (Deut. 26:13); *Spec.* 1.51–53 (Lev. 19:33–34), 308–9 (Deut. 10:17–19); *QE* 2.2 (Exod. 22:20). In the Septuagint, προσήλυτος is a translation for גר from the Hebrew Bible. Both Biblical terms are ambiguous. In the Hebrew Bible, the word גר seems to carry at least two different senses: It can refer to a foreigner or sojourner, as in the case of Abraham among the Hittites (Gen. 23:4); Moses in Midian (Exod. 2:22, 18:3); Israel in Egypt (Exod. 22:20, 23:9; Lev. 19:34; Deut. 10:19); or Israel in relation to God (Lev. 25:23, 1 Chron. 29:15). At the same time, גר also designates foreigners who live among the Israelites, not merely as sojourners but as a class of people with certain rights—i.e., resident aliens (Exod. 12:49, 22:20; Lev. 22:18; Num. 35:15; Deut. 24:14). Although the Pentateuch does not give conclusive evidence to support understanding the גר as a religious convert, in some other parts of the Bible, the גר and other designations may indeed indicate people who adopt Israelite beliefs and practices (Isa. 14:1, 56:3 and 6; Zech. 2:15; Esther 9:27; Ezra 6:21; Neh. 10:29). Developments in the meaning of the term no doubt reflect changing realities among the people of Israel after the exile. See Cohen, "Conversion to Judaism"; Yehezkel Kaufmann, *History of the Religion of Israel*, vol. 4: *From the Babylonian Captivity to the End of Prophecy*, trans. C. W. Efroymson (New York: Ktav, 1977), 42–46, 136–39, 233, 341–43; T. M. Mauch, "Sojourner," *Interpreter's Dictionary of the Bible*, 4:397–99; Theophile James Meek, "The Translation of *Ger* in the Hexateuch and Its Bearing on the Documentary Hypothesis," *JBL* 49 (1930): 172–80.

The Septuagint translators, responding perhaps to the different nuances associated with גר, generally use either of two different words for it: πάροικος or προσήλυτος. The two terms, however, do not correspond exactly to the two different senses of גר mentioned above—i.e., sojourner and resident alien. For example, although προσήλυτος usually designates resident aliens among the Israelites, it also describes the people of Israel as sojourners in Egypt (Exod. 22:20, 23:9; Lev. 19:34; Deut. 10:19) or in relation

variations, whether the word προσήλυτος appears in a related Scriptural text or not. In one Biblical quotation, in fact, he substitutes ἐπήλυτος for προσήλυτος, which is found in the Septuagint.[14]

It may be that Philo prefers ἔπηλυς and its variations to προσήλυτος because these words are more familiar to his readers. προσήλυτος appears almost exclusively in Jewish and Christian writings, while ἔπηλυς and its variations can be found in classical Greek writings, in which these terms denote a foreigner and indicate only a civic standing.[15] By using ἔπηλυς and its variations to signify one who abandons polytheism to come over to belief in God, then, Philo adds a religious connotation to these words.[16]

Philo does, however, also use προσήλυτος and ἔπηλυς and its variations without a religious connotation in three passages. In *Flacc.* 54, he cites a proclamation of Flaccus against the Jews, which denounces them as foreigners and aliens (ξένοι καὶ ἐπήλυδες). Here, Philo's use of ἔπηλυς reflects Roman classification of his Jewish contemporaries. Similarly, in *Cher.* 108 and 119–21, προσήλυτος, ἔπηλυς, and ἐπήλυτος denote simply a foreigner or sojourner. In these passages, which discuss the Israelites as sojourners in relation to God, Philo's use of the terms is based upon the understanding of προσήλυτος in the Septuagint verse Lev. 25:23. Because none of these three passages are about proselytes, they are not relevant to the present study.

In two places, *Mos.* 1.7 and 147, Philo uses ἐπηλύτης ambiguously, so that the word can denote a foreigner, a proselyte, or both.[17] Since these two

---

to God (Lev. 25:23). Although the Greek translators of the Bible may have understood προσήλυτος as one who has left behind old beliefs and practices to adopt new ones, we cannot determine this on the basis of the Septuagint alone. For a different view, see W. C. Allen, "On the Meaning of προσήλυτος in the Septuagint," *The Expositor* 4 (10) (1894): 264–75. See also Kuhn, "προσήλυτος," 727–31 and K. L. and M. A. Schmidt, "πάροικος," *TDNT*, 5:841–48.

It is interesting that in *Conf.* 82, Philo uses the word γειώρας in quoting Exod. 2:22, even though the Septuagint translates גּר as πάροικος. For a possible explanation, see Suzanne Daniel, *De Specialibus Legibus I–II, OPA,* 24:221–22.

[14] *Spec.* 4.177, quoting Deut. 10:17–18. This passage is discussed later in the chapter.

[15] Allen, "On the Meaning of προσήλυτος," 264–65; Daniel, *De Specialibus Legibus I–II, OPA,* 24:221–22; Kuhn, "προσήλυτος," 728.

[16] See *QE* 2.2 (quoted earlier), in which Philo explicitly presents the double sense of ἔπηλυς.

[17] In *Mos.* 1.7, Philo describes Abraham as an ἐπηλύτης. The passage, however, is actually about Moses. Philo writes, "He [Moses] is the seventh generation from the first, who being an ἐπηλύτης became the founder of the whole Jewish nation" (my translation). Since Philo elsewhere describes Abraham as both a sojourner (μέτοικος, *Mos.* 2.58) and a proselyte (*Somn.* 1.160–62, *Virt.* 219), we cannot determine which meaning he has in mind here, and either or both would certainly make sense.

Although Philo does not elaborate upon the ἐπηλύται in *Mos.* 1.147, the context favors the sense of "proselyte." This passage describes as follows the group that

passages at least allow for a broader understanding of the ἐπηλύτης as a proselyte, I shall include them in this study. Of the sixteen passages which have the words προσήλυτος or ἔπηλυς and its variations, then, thirteen are about or may be about proselytes.[18]

Contexts in Which Philo Discusses Proselytes

All thirteen passages just mentioned are found only in Philo's exegetical works and most are from the Exposition. Specifically, ten passages appear in the Exposition, two in the Allegory, and one in Questions and Answers. Philo does not mention proselytes at all in his non-exegetical works.[19]

Philo's two references to the proselyte in the Allegory (*Somn.* 1.160–62, *Somn.* 2.272–73) occur only in symbolic interpretations. Although we can gain some information from these instances about how Philo understands the proselyte, in the Allegory this figure has primarily a symbolic importance. The Exposition, in contrast, always discusses proselytes as

---

accompanies the Hebrews out of Egypt:

> They [the Hebrews] were accompanied by a promiscuous, nondescript and menial crowd, a bastard host, so to speak, associated with the true-born. These were the children of Egyptian women by Hebrew fathers into whose families they had been adopted and also those who, [admiring the men's quality of being God-beloved or God-loving, became ἐπηλύται and such as were changed (μετεβάλοντο)] and brought to a wiser mind by the magnitude and the number of the successive punishments.

This passage delineates three groups who join the Hebrews in their departure from Egypt: those born of a mixed marriage, those who become ἐπηλύται, and those who are changed. Although Philo does not define ἐπηλύται per se, the context certainly suggests that these are proselytes, i.e., people who leave behind their backgrounds to join the Hebrews, by departing both from Egypt and from their beliefs and practices. Indeed the only distinction between the second and third groups—i.e., the ἐπηλύται and the changed ones—seems to be their different motives for joining the Hebrews. The ἐπηλύται join them out of a positive motive, namely, admiration of the people's quality of being God-beloved or God-loving. (On the ambiguity of τὸ θεοφιλές, see Chapter Five.) In contrast, the ones who are changed join out of a negative motive, namely, the fear instilled by the punishments inflicted upon the Egyptians. Since Philo, however, does not state explicitly, as he does elsewhere, that the ἐπηλύται abandon their old beliefs to adopt those of the Hebrews, it is still possible to view them simply as a group of foreigners or newcomers to the Hebrews without the sense necessarily that they adopt new beliefs and practices. For other discussions of this passage, see Amir, "Philon und die jüdische Wirklichkeit seiner Zeit," 26; and McKnight, *A Light Among the Gentiles*, 93–96. Regarding those who are changed, see further below in the chapter and n. 27.

[18] These thirteen passages are *Somn.* 1.160–62; *Somn.* 2.272–73; *Mos.* 1.7, 147; *Spec.* 1.51–53, 308–9; *Spec.* 2.116–19; *Spec.* 4.176–78; *Virt.* 102–4, 180–82, 212–19; *Praem.* 152; *QE* 2.2.

[19] As noted earlier, in *Flacc.* 54, he uses the term ἔπηλυς with a non-religious meaning.

real people—never as symbolic figures—either in the past or in Philo's present.[20] The Exposition is also where we find most of the passages, discussed further below, which do not mention proselytes explicitly but pertain to them or to positive Gentile attitudes towards the Jews.

Finally, in the one passage about proselytes in QGE (*QE* 2.2), Philo uses the term προσήλυτος in a symbolic interpretation of Exod. 22:20, in which he mentions circumcision. His comments, however, do not address the practical issue of whether or not circumcision is required of proselytes, and it is difficult to know how to apply his remarks to real proselytes.[21] The same passage also sets forth two ways of understanding ἐπήλυδες, as incomers to the land or to laws and customs. Philo's remarks about proselytes in this passage, however, are either too ambiguous or spare to permit us to draw any firm conclusions about real proselytes.

In seven of the thirteen passages under consideration, Philo discusses

---

[20] The Exposition passages are as follows: *Mos.* 1.7, 147 (but see n. 17 concerning the ambiguity in these two passages); *Spec.* 1.51–53, 308–9; *Spec.* 2.116–19; *Spec.* 4.176–78; *Virt.* 102–4, 180–82, 212–19; *Praem.* 152. By "real" proselytes, I mean potentially real, since we do not have evidence to determine whether or not Philo's Alexandrian Jewish community included such individuals.

[21] These problems have not prevented many scholars from trying, however! The passage itself reads as follows:

[Exod. 22:20] Why does (Scripture) in admonishing, 'Thou shalt not oppress a sojourner,' add, 'For ye were sojourners in the land of the Egyptians'?

(Scripture) first makes it clearly apparent and demonstrable that in reality the sojourner is one who circumcises not his uncircumcision but his desires and sensual pleasures and the other passions of the soul. For in Egypt the Hebrew nation was not circumcised but being mistreated with all (kinds of) mistreatment by the inhabitants in their hatred of strangers, it lived with them in self-restraint and endurance, not by necessity but rather of its own free choice, because it took refuge in God the Saviour, Who sent His beneficent power and delivered from their difficult and hopeless situation those who made supplication (to Him). Therefore (Scripture) adds, 'Ye yourselves know the soul of the sojourner.' But what is the mind of the sojourner if not alienation from belief in many gods and familiarity with honouring the one God and Father of all?

(The remaining part of this passage, in which Philo offers two definitions for the ἔπηλυς, is quoted at the beginning of the chapter.) This passage seems to have a purely exegetical purpose. When Philo describes the Hebrews as uncircumcised but living in self-restraint, for example, he may be answering the exegetical question, "In what way were the Hebrews 'proselytes' in Egypt?" Nonetheless, he sidesteps the issue of whether or not proselytes are required to be circumcised. Similarly, his remark that the real proselyte circumcises his desires, etc., also does not address the issue of physical circumcision. For a variety of approaches to this controversial passage, see Belkin, *Philo and the Oral Law*, 44–48; Borgen, *Paul Preaches Circumcision*, 16–18, 86–90; Collins, "A Symbol of Otherness," 173–75, 184; N. J. McEleney, "Conversion, Circumcision, and the Law," *New Testament Studies* 20 (1974): 319–41; Moore, *Judaism*, 1:327–28; J. Nolland, "Uncircumcised Proselytes?" *Journal for the Study of Judaism* 12 (1981): 173–94; Wolfson, *Philo*, 1:369–71.

proselytes in connection with Biblical verses that are explicitly about the προσήλυτος.[22] With one exception (*Praem.* 152),[23] these Biblical verses describe rights or treatment of the proselyte by the community. Of the six remaining Philonic passages, three describe Abraham as an ἐπηλύτης or ἐπήλυτος (*Somn.* 1.160, *Mos.* 1.7, *Virt.* 219); one uses ἐπηλύται to refer to a group that leaves Egypt with the Hebrews (*Mos.* 1.147);[24] one explains a Biblical law as applying to ἐπηλύται (*Spec.* 2.116–19);[25] and one mentions ἐπηλύται in a discussion of μετάνοια, or conversion (*Virt.* 182).

Passages Related to Proselytes Which Do Not Mention Them Explicitly

Besides the thirteen passages in which Philo explicitly uses προσήλυτος or ἔπηλυς and its variations to signify one who leaves behind a social and religious background to adopt a new community and belief in and worship of the one God, he also discusses matters related to proselytes in several other places without using an explicit word for them. Occasionally, for example, he describes people in ways that suggest they may be proselytes, without calling them "proselytes"; he discusses themes related to the proselyte's experience, like migration, repentance, nobility of birth, or kinship; and he speaks of non-Jews who wish to join the Jewish community or who admire the Jews. These topics are considered briefly below.

People Who May Be But Are Not Called "Proselytes"

In three passages (*Virt.* 220–22, *Mos.* 1.147, and *Spec.* 2.256), Philo writes about people who may be proselytes without so naming them. For example, in *Virt.* 220–22, he presents Tamar as someone who leaves behind belief in and worship of many gods in order to worship the one God.[26] In *Mos.* 1.147, in which Philo does in fact mention ἐπηλύται, he also speaks of others who "have been changed" (μετεβάλοντο). This passage, which describes the "mixed multitude" that departs from Egypt with the Hebrews, may imply that these people who have been changed or

---

[22] *Somn.* 2.272–73 (Deut. 26:13); *Spec.* 1.51–53 (Lev. 19:33–34), 308–9 (Deut. 10:17–19); *Spec.* 4.176–78 (Deut. 10:17–19); *Virt.* 102–4 (Lev. 19:33–34); *Praem.* 152 (Deut. 28:43); *QE* 2.2 (Exod. 22:20).

[23] *Praem.* 152 comments on Deut. 28:43, which reads, "The stranger (προσήλυτος) among you will mount higher and higher and you will descend lower and lower."

[24] See n. 17.

[25] See n. 7.

[26] See Madeleine Petit, "Exploitations non-bibliques des thèmes de Tamar et de Genèse 38: Philon d'Alexandrie, textes et traditions juives jusqu'aux Talmudim," *Alexandrina: Hellenisme, judaïsme et christianisme à Alexandrie, Mélanges offerts au P. Claude Mondésert, S.J.* (Paris: Éditions du Cerf, 1987), 77–115.

"turned around" join the Hebrews out of fear. Since he does not elaborate further about them, however, a more precise understanding of their status with the Hebrew nation eludes us.[27]

Philo also refers to individuals who become disciples of Moses (φοιτητὴς γενόμενος Μωυσέως) in the context of explaining the punishment for denying the true God and worshipping lifeless things, i.e., for breach of the first commandment (*Spec.* 2.256). It is tempting to understand these individuals as proselytes, since Philo often notes that proselytes leave a background which denies God and worships lifeless things. The Greek wording, however, may simply mean one who *is* a disciple of Moses. Moreover, if Philo does mean one who *becomes* a disciple of Moses, he may have in mind Jews, not necessarily outsiders, who have become earnest followers of Moses's teachings.

Themes Related to Proselytes

Besides alluding to people who sound like proselytes, Philo discusses several themes related to the abandonment of one's old religious and social background and the adoption of new religious beliefs and practices and a new social community. Examples include pilgrimage or migration motifs; μετάνοια, repentance or conversion; εὐγένεια, nobility of birth; and συγγένεια, kinship.

Pilgrimage or Migration Motifs. Philo frequently uses similar terms to describe Abraham's migration from Chaldea and the proselyte's "migration." As someone who leaves behind his family and background of false beliefs to discover the one true God, Abraham serves as a prototype of the proselyte.[28] Philo also uses similar language for proselytes and those who make a pilgrimage to the temple. Indeed migration or pilgrimage vocabulary in general is quite prevalent in his discussion of proselytes.[29]

---

[27] See n. 17. The LCL translates μετεβάλοντο as "converted," where I have used "changed" or "turned around." While all these meanings may be equivalent, I have not used "converted," so as to avoid the issue of whether or not formal procedures are involved—an issue which "converted," because of its contemporary usage, may implicitly raise.

[28] Compare *Spec.* 1.52, a passage about proselytes, with God's charge to Abraham in Gen. 12:1. In *Virt.* 212–19, Philo presents Abraham's migration from Chaldea as his search for God and calls Abraham "a standard of nobility for all proselytes" (οὗτος ἅπασιν ἐπηλύταις εὐγενείας ἐστὶ κανών, *Virt.* 219). In general, Abraham's migration from Chaldea is an important motif in Philo's writings, serving as the focus of his Allegory treatise *Migr.* For other symbolic interpretations of Abraham's migration, see *Ebr.* 94, *Her.* 287–89, *Somn.* 1.160–62, *Abr.* 60–80. See also Wilfred Lawrence Knox, "Abraham and the Quest for God," *HTR* 28 (1935): 55–61.

[29] Compare *Spec.* 1.52 and *Spec.* 1.68, both of which echo God's charge to Abraham in

μετάνοια. With its root meaning of "afterthought," in the sense of "rethinking," μετάνοια is an ambiguous term which can mean reconsideration, improvement, repentance, or conversion.[30] Philo devotes a whole section in his treatise *On the Virtues* to μετάνοια (*Virt.* 175–86). In the latter part of this section (*Virt.* 182), he refers to proselytes and clearly understands μετάνοια to include a kind of religious change, which involves turning from false beliefs to belief in the one true God. In the opening section (*Virt.* 175–77), however, the term may also mean simply repentance.

Philo also discusses μετάνοια in relation to Enoch (*Abr.* 17–26 and *Praem.* 15–21), where he appears to be speaking about improvement or repentance rather than conversion. Improvement or repentance, however, does share common traits with conversion in that both concepts involve a move to something better. They differ in that conversion entails complete abandonment of one's background, while improvement or repentance does not. Repentance, in fact, may signal the return to an earlier state of virtue. In any case, although Philo links proselytes with μετάνοια in *Virt.* 182, his use of the term μετάνοια is not restricted to describing the change undertaken by proselytes.[31]

εὐγένεια and συγγένεια. Philo devotes another section of his treatise *On the Virtues* to εὐγένεια, or nobility of birth (*Virt.* 187–227). Here he emphasizes that true nobility depends not upon noble ancestry but upon individual virtue. In this section and elsewhere he makes the related argument that kinship (συγγένεια) consists not simply in blood relationships but in similarity of conduct and shared beliefs.[32] As we shall see, these various remarks, in which Philo places more value upon noble behavior than upon ancestry or blood relationships, reflect an openness to outsiders who may wish to adopt Jewish beliefs and practices.

Gen. 12:1. Many passages describe proselytes as emigrants (μετανάσται), refugees (πρόσφυγες), or ones who set out for a beautiful home (καλὴν ἀποικίαν στειλάμενοι). See, e.g., *Somn.* 1.160; *Somn.* 2.273; *Spec.* 1.51–52, 308–9; *Spec.* 2.116–19; *Spec.* 4.176–78; *Virt.* 102–4, 219. For reflections on Philo's use of migration imagery in relation to proselytes, see Amir, "Philon und die jüdische Wirklichkeit seiner Zeit," 24–25.

[30] See Behm and Würthwein, "μετανοέω, μετάνοια," *TDNT*, 4:975–1008.

[31] For Philo's use of μετάνοια, see Jon Nelson Bailey, "*Metanoia* in the Writings of Philo Judaeus," *SBL 1991 Seminar Papers*, SBL Seminar Paper Series, ed. Eugene H. Lovering, Jr., no. 30 (Atlanta: Scholars Press, 1991), 135–41; Alain Michel, "La *métanoia* chez Philon d'Alexandrie: De Platon au Judéo-Christianisme en passant par Cicéron," *Augustinus* 32 (1987): 105–20; Winston, "Judaism and Hellenism," 4–7.

[32] *Mos.* 2.171, *Spec.* 1.317–18, *Spec.* 2.73 (see also the note to this passage in LCL, 7:625), *Virt.* 195. Cf. Josephus, *Contra Apionem* 2:210.

Interested Non-Jews

Finally, Philo also mentions non-Jews who may wish to join the Jewish community or who admire the Jews. Commenting on Deut. 23:8–9 in *Virt.* 108, for example, he discusses how Jews should treat settlers (μέτοικοι, *Virt.* 105) who come from nations that had been inhospitable to the Hebrews and who may wish "to pass over into the polity of the Jews" (μεταλλάξασ-θαι πρὸς τὴν Ἰουδαίων πολιτείαν).[33] He also refers to non-Jews who respect and honor Jewish laws (*Mos.* 2.17–44) and notes that Jews welcome such admirers "no less than their own countrymen" (*Legat.* 211).

Now that we have considered Philo's discussion of proselytes in passages in which he mentions them explicitly and in which he speaks about topics related to them, let us turn our attention specifically to his depiction of the relationship between proselytes and God. For the sake of precision and consistency in method, the observations in this section will be based only upon passages which have an explicit word for "proselyte." We shall consider the other related passages later, when we turn to the broader question of where proselytes fit in with "Israel" and the Jews.

The Relationship Between God and Proselytes According to Philo

Philo does not frequently comment about the relationship between God and proselytes. Moreover, the occasional observations he does make may not accurately reflect his position on this issue, for a variety of reasons explained below. I shall, however, consider everything that Philo says about God and proselytes and then evaluate the evidence.

   To begin with the proselyte's side of the relationship, Philo most frequently speaks of him or her as turning to God.[34] Specifically, he talks

---

[33] Deut. 23:8–9 reads as follows: "You shall not abhor an Edomite, for he is your brother; you shall not abhor an Egyptian, because you were a sojourner (πάροικος) in his land. The children of the third generation that are born to them may enter the assembly of the Lord." It is interesting that Philo uses μέτοικος instead of πάροικος, which appears in the LXX. The word μέτοικος seems to denote a resident alien rather than a temporary sojourner, as πάροικος implies. Perhaps Philo is speaking about a figure similar to one denoted by the rabbinic term גר תושב.

[34] In these passages about proselytes, Philo often speaks of God in different ways: e.g., *Somn.* 1.161: the Cause of all things (ὁ πάντων αἴτιος); *Spec.* 1.52: the one God (ὁ εἷς θεός); *Spec.* 1.53, 309: the truly Existing (ὁ ὄντως ὤν or τὸ ὄντως ὄν); *Spec.* 1.309, *Praem.* 152: God (θεός); *Spec.* 4.178: the One worthy of honor (ὁ εἷς τίμιος or τὸ ἓν τίμιον); *Virt.* 102: the one and truly existing God (ὁ εἷς καὶ ὄντως ὢν θεός); *Virt.* 181: the existing God (ὁ ὢν θεός); *Virt.* 214: the One who alone is eternal and father of all intellectual and sensible things (ὁ εἷς, ὃς ἐστιν ἀίδιος μόνος καὶ ὅλων πατὴρ νοητῶν τε αὖ καὶ αἰσθητῶν); *QE* 2.2: God the savior (ὁ σωτὴρ θεός); the One and father of all (ὁ εἷς καὶ πατὴρ τῶν ὅλων). Cf. *Virt.* 221: the one Cause (ὁ εἷς αἴτιος). (Translations are mine.) See also Anthony J.

of the proselyte as coming to the honor (τιμή) of God (*Spec.* 1.52, *Spec.* 4.178, *Virt.* 181, *QE* 2.2); reverence (σεβασμός) of God (*Virt.* 102); worship (θεραπεία) of God (*Somn.* 1.161); and God alone, without a noun preceding (*Praem.* 152). He also describes proselytes as becoming suppliants and worshippers (ἱκέται τε καὶ θεραπευταί) of God (*Spec.* 1.309, cf. *Virt.* 221). Among these various elements, then, Philo cites honor of God most frequently.

In addition, in *Virt.* 212–19, Philo presents in various ways the search for God by Abraham, who serves as a standard of nobility for proselytes. For example, he speaks of Abraham as wishing to know God, seeking Him, gaining clearer visions (τρανότεραι φαντασίαι) of Him, believing in Him,[35] yearning for kinship with Him, and striving to become His familiar. Apart from the reference to Abraham gaining clearer visions, Philo never mentions proselytes as seeing God or coming to a vision of Him.[36]

Besides the comments just described, which pertain to Philo's very definition of the proselyte as one who comes over to belief in and worship of God and to a new community, Philo also makes the following observations:

1) A proselyte requires God's powers of governance and kindness (*Somn.* 1.160–62).

2) Proselytes are among those chosen for high merit to the temple ministry (*Somn.* 2.272–73).

3) Abraham, a standard of nobility (εὐγένεια) for all proselytes, receives sovereignty among his neighbors by the election of the virtue-loving God, who rewards all lovers of piety with powers to benefit those around them (*Virt.* 218–19).

Guerra, "The One God Topos in *Spec. Leg.* 1.52," *SBL 1990 Seminar Papers*, SBL Seminar Paper Series, ed. David J. Lull, no. 29 (Atlanta: Scholars Press, 1990), 148–57. For a list of the different ways in which Philo speaks about God in general, i.e., in passages that are not only about proselytes, see Drummond, *Philo Judaeus*, 2:63.

[35] Gen. 15:6 provides a textual basis for speaking of Abraham as believing in God. The verse begins, "And he believed God..."

[36] Philo does elsewhere speak of Abraham as seeing God but not in passages that depict him as a proselyte. Philo uses metaphors about light in *Virt.* 179 and 221, passages which are related to proselytes but do not mention them specifically. In *Virt.* 179, he writes about those who come to "embrace the rulership of One instead of many" (my translation) that "we must rejoice with them, as if, though blind at the first they had recovered their sight and had come from the deepest darkness to behold the most radiant light" (LCL translation). In *Virt.* 221, he writes that Tamar, "emerging as if from deep darkness, was able to see a little ray of truth." *Spec.* 1.51–53, a passage about proselytes, immediately follows a long passage (*Spec.* 1.32–50) about the search for God and Moses's request to see Him (based upon Exod. 33:13–23), but Philo does not make any connection between proselytes and seeing God.

4) God welcomes virtue that comes from ignoble birth (*Praem.* 152).

5) Proselytes benefit from God's πρόνοια, or protective concern (*Spec.* 1.308–9 and *Spec.* 4.176–78).

All these statements, except for the last, are in some way problematic. The first two remarks, for example, occur in allegorical interpretations and may not apply to real proselytes. At the least, however, these observations convey Philo's symbolic associations to the relationship between God and proselytes. Unfortunately, it is often impossible to know how much Philo separates symbol from reality. In fact, this is the very problem we face in trying to determine the social identity of "Israel," the one that sees God.

The third and fourth observations cited above are general lessons which—though they are derived from God's behavior toward proselytes— may also apply to a larger group. The third observation, for example, is based upon a Biblical verse about Abraham (Gen. 23:6), whom Philo presents as a standard of nobility for all proselytes. Although Philo writes that Abraham receives sovereignty among his neighbors by the election of God, when he says that God rewards all lovers of piety with powers to benefit their neighbors, he generalizes beyond Abraham to a larger group—namely, lovers of piety. Since lovers of piety may encompass more than just proselytes, we cannot determine whether Philo's comments apply only to proselytes or extend to the larger group. Similarly, the fourth observation—that God welcomes virtue that comes from ignoble birth—may also include virtuous people from base backgrounds who are not necessarily proselytes.

Given these considerations, then, the fifth observation, namely, that proselytes benefit from God's πρόνοια, carries the most weight, since it clearly refers only to real proselytes. Also significant is that this comment appears twice, whereas the others occur only once. We shall therefore focus now only upon the last observation, which concerns God's πρόνοια toward proselytes.

God's πρόνοια Toward Proselytes

Both passages which allude to God's πρόνοια toward proselytes, *Spec.* 1.308–9 and *Spec.* 4.176–78, comment on the same Biblical text, Deut. 10:17–19, which reads as follows:

17For the Lord your God is God of gods and Lord of lords, the great, the mighty, and the terrible God who is not partial and takes no bribe. 18He executes justice for the [προσήλυτος], the orphan, and the widow, and loves the [προσήλυτος], giving him food and clothing. 19Love the [προσήλυτος], therefore; for you were [προσή-λυτοι] in the land of Egypt.[37]

Spec. 1.308–9. In *Spec.* 1.308–9, Philo comments on these verses as part of an exhortation based upon Deut. 10:12–14:1 (*Spec.* 1.299–318). He remarks that despite God's mighty powers, He cares for even the neediest. Philo writes,

> Yet vast as are his excellences and powers, he takes pity and compassion on those most helplessly in need, and does not disdain to give judgement to strangers (προσήλυτοι) or orphans or widows. He holds their low estate worthy of His providential care (πρόνοια),[38] while of kings and despots and great potentates, He takes no account. (*Spec.* 1.308)

Philo goes on to account for why each figure in this group deserves God's πρόνοια. Regarding proselytes, he observes,

> He cares for the proselytes (ἐπήλυτοι) for this reason: after abandoning the ancestral customs in which they were raised, customs loaded with false inventions and vanity, after becoming genuine lovers of modesty and truth, they migrated to piety. Suppliants and worshippers of the truly Existing as He deserves, they partake in His πρόνοια suited to them, as it is fitting, finding the fruit of taking refuge in God to be the help that comes from Him. (*Spec.* 1.309, my translation)

Philo then explains that orphans and widows have no one else to take care of them since they have lost parents and husbands respectively. He writes,

> [I]n this desolation no refuge remains that men can give; and therefore they are not denied the hope that is greatest of all, the hope in God, who in the graciousness of His nature does not refuse the task of caring for and watching over them in their desolate condition. (*Spec.* 1.310)

It is significant that Philo's explanation for why proselytes receive God's πρόνοια is different from the one he gives for orphans and widows. The latter two groups have God's protection because they have no human protectors and therefore are not denied hope altogether. In the case of proselytes, however, God's πρόνοια seems to be a reward to them for giving up their old ways, since Philo writes that they partake of God's πρόνοια, finding His help to be the *fruit* (καρπός) of taking refuge in Him. Thus, God's protection appears as a benefit proselytes gain from turning to Him.

---

[37] This translation from the RSV uses the word "sojourner" where I have substituted προσήλυτος. Like the Septuagint, the RSV adds "sojourner" before the orphan and widow in verse 18, although the Hebrew omits the גר from this group.

[38] The critical edition of Philo (Cohn and Wendland, *Philonis Alexandrini*, 5:74) lists the following two manuscript variants to προνοίας: προνομίας (privilege) and προνομίας προνοίας (the privilege of [God's] protection).

Spec. 4.178–82. Here Philo comments on the same passage, Deut. 10:17–19, quoted earlier, to illustrate that great questions are to be judged by higher rather than lesser officials and also that great questions are not necessarily limited to those in which both disputants are distinguished, rich, or powerful (*Spec.* 4.171–72). In this passage, Philo does not mention God's πρόνοια specifically but speaks about His administration of justice, in keeping with the wording of the Bible. The sense of the passage, nonetheless, is that God offers special protection to certain groups. Philo notes that

> lowliness and weakness are attributes of the widow, the orphan and the incomer (ἐπήλυτος). It is to these that the supreme king who is invested with the government of all should administer justice, because according to Moses [even God,] the ruler of the Universe, has not spurned them from His jurisdiction. (*Spec.* 4.176)

After alluding to Deut. 10:17–18 (in *Spec.* 4.177), Philo explains why each figure—the ἐπήλυτος, the orphan, and the widow—is deserving of God's justice. God executes justice for the ἐπήλυτος, he observes,

> because he has turned his kinsfolk, who in the ordinary course of things would be his sole confederates, into mortal enemies, by coming as a pilgrim to truth and the honouring of One who alone is worthy of honour, and by leaving the mythical fables and multiplicity of sovereigns, so highly honoured by the parents and grand-parents and ancestors and blood relations of this immigrant to a better home. (*Spec.* 4.178)

Philo next remarks that orphans and widows benefit from God's justice since they too have no one to protect them, having lost parents and husbands, respectively (*Spec.* 4.178). This passage, then, differs from *Spec.* 1.308–9, in which Philo notes that proselytes receive God's πρόνοια not because they are without allies—like the orphan and widow—but because they adopt God and gain His providence as their reward.[39]

It is interesting that Philo goes on to compare the Jews to orphans, explaining that Jews too have no other allies, since the pleasure-loving masses are put off by the austerity of their laws. Because of their isolation, the Jews too then are an object of pity and compassion to God. Thus, in the same section, Philo groups proselytes, orphans, widows, and Jews as beneficiaries of God's protection, observing that no one else will take their side.

---

[39] The different contexts of the two passages probably account for their different explanations about God's πρόνοια toward proselytes. *Spec.* 4.176–78 comments on Deut. 10:17–19 to support the point that God has compassion for those in need. Philo therefore underscores proselytes' neediness, which stems from their isolation. His remarks in *Spec.* 1.308–9, however, belong to a running commentary on Deut. 10:12–14:1 and are not ostensibly intended to support a particular argument. Philo can therefore highlight a different point here, namely, that proselytes are rewarded when they turn to God.

Although Philo does speak of proselytes and Jews in the same section, he still distinguishes between them, giving different explanations for their respective situations: proselytes are alone because they leave their customary protectors, while Jews are alone because their laws are considered too severe. Since, according to Philo, the hallmark of the proselyte is that he or she leaves old ways for new ones, it makes sense that he would mention the abandoning of their backgrounds as the primary reason for proselytes' isolation, and this, to be sure, is reason enough. Even though Philo accounts for the isolation of proselytes and Jews differently, however, it would be a mistake to conclude that he sees them as completely separate groups. Indeed by becoming Jews, proselytes would seem to incur isolation for two reasons: not only do they abandon their families, but they also adopt laws too severe for most people!

The question of precisely how proselytes and Jews are related brings us to the larger issue of whether proselytes become members of "Israel," the Jews, or both. Now that we have examined the relationship between proselytes and God, we can compare this to the relationship God has with "Israel," on the one hand, and the Jews, on the other. Among other factors, this comparison will help us to determine where proselytes stand in relation to "Israel" and the Jews.

Proselytes, Jews, and "Israel"

In examining Philo's treatment of "Israel" and the Jews in previous chapters, we were able to identify at least three features that distinguish these entities from one another:

1) Philo speaks about "Israel" and the Jews in different writings;

2) he uses different words with different connotations to describe "Israel" and the Jews as collectivities; and

3) he portrays in different ways the relationship between each entity and God.

The evidence suggests that for Philo, the Jews are a clearly identifiable social group, while "Israel" seems to represent a more loosely defined entity. Although the two groups may be identical or may overlap, their precise relationship remains ambiguous.

Before turning to proselytes, I shall first briefly review the features which distinguish "Israel" and the Jews. In addition to the three noted above, I shall also consider what might constitute membership requirements for each group. Because Philo does not address this issue directly, my remarks about membership requirements are necessarily speculative. After considering the differences between "Israel" and the Jews in these four areas, I shall then examine where proselytes stand in relation to these areas to see where they might fit in with "Israel" and the Jews.

1) *Writings in Which Philo Speaks About "Israel" and the Jews*

Philo discusses "Israel" and the Jews in different works, with apparently different purposes. He mentions "Israel" most frequently in the Allegory, occasionally in QGE, and twice in the Exposition. In contrast, he speaks of the Jews only in the Exposition and non-exegetical writings. Only in his political treatise *Legat.* does Philo talk about "Israel" and the Jews in the same work.

Among the exegetical writings, I shall concentrate here upon the Allegory and Exposition since these two series provide more extensive evidence than QGE of his use of the two terms. I have hypothesized that readers of the Allegory may be Jews like Philo himself who are interested in the deeper meaning of Scripture, while readers of the Exposition may also include Jews or non-Jews who know little about Jewish beliefs and practices.[40]

If these speculations are correct, it makes sense that Philo would not speak about Jews in the Allegory, since his fellow Jews would already be quite familiar with Jewish history, beliefs, and practices. It also makes sense that he would elaborate in the Allegory upon "Israel" as an ideal entity that sees God, since his readers would associate the term "Israel" with their own heritage and take pride in the identification of "Israel" with the highest goal of philosophy.

As for the Exposition, if Philo is indeed writing for those unfamiliar with Jewish ways, it is understandable that he would focus here upon the real Jewish community in order to educate his readers. Furthermore, since the term "Israel" might not have the same resonances as it would for more knowledgeable Jews, it is understandable that he would not go out of his way to emphasize "Israel" as embodying the ideal of seeing God.

Finally, in the political treatise *Legat.*, Philo's purpose seems to be to present the Jewish nation in the best possible light for a variety of readers—Jews and non-Jews. To this end, when he mentions "Israel" in his introduction, implicitly identifying "Israel" with the Jews, he may wish to portray the Jews as having achieved the philosophical ideal represented by the etymology "one that sees God."

---

[40] For more information about Philo's different audiences, see the Introduction.

2) *Philo's Characterizations of "Israel" and the Jews as Collectivities*

To describe "Israel" and the Jews as collectivities, Philo uses different words with different connotations. He most frequently calls "Israel" a γένος, but the Jews and their forbears, the Hebrews, usually either an ἔθνος or a λαός and occasionally a πολιτεία or a γένος. In contrast, Philo never calls "Israel" a λαός or πολιτεία. In the few passages in which he does use ἔθνος with "Israel," whether or not "Israel" is a nation is not pertinent to the interpretation.[41]

Although γένος can refer to a race defined by birth, the term is ambiguous and can also describe a class defined by acquired qualities, a genus as opposed to individual species, an abstract nature or kind, or an ideal as opposed to a real entity. Indeed, Philo seems to take advantage of this ambiguity in some passages where the γένος "Israel" may be understood in different ways at the same time. When he calls "Israel" a γένος, then, the question is moot whether "Israel" is a race into which one is born, a class defined by acquired characteristics, or an idea in the intelligible world.

In contrast to the ambiguity of γένος, the words ἔθνος and λαός denote only a nation or people. When Philo calls the Hebrews or Jews an ἔθνος or λαός , it is clear that he is speaking about a real social group. Even when he calls them a γένος (*Virt.* 206, *Legat.* 178), it is evident from the context that he means a race defined by birth and perhaps too a social or political entity. (Later in this chapter, I shall address the implications of Philo's use of πολιτεία, polity, to describe the Jews.)

3) *Relationship Between God and "Israel" and Between God and the Jews*

Philo characterizes in different ways the relationship God has with "Israel," on the one hand, and the Jews, on the other. Based upon its etymology, ὁρῶν θεόν (one that sees God), he associates "Israel" with seeing God and the ability to see Him. Although Philo occasionally describes "Israel" as worshipping God, these descriptions are rare and he never specifies how "Israel" worships Him. Indeed, though he sometimes mentions other qualities of "Israel" in relation to God, the ability to see Him is by far the most predominant characteristic.[42] Moreover, this characteristic pertains to both sides of the relationship: "Israel" sees God and God grants "Israel" the ability to see Him.

---

41 See Chapter One, n. 67.
42 Philo mentions "Israel" as worshipping God in *Sacr.* 120, *Plant.* 60, *Praem.* 44, and *Legat.* 3. For additional descriptions of "Israel," see Chapter One under the discussion of γένος and Chapter Two under "Category B."

In contrast, Philo never speaks directly about the Jews as seeing God.[43] Instead, he presents them as the only ones who believe in God and notes that they worship Him by following specific laws and customs. In addition, he writes that the Jews act as priests for the whole world, are allotted to God, are God-beloved or God-loving, and benefit from His πρόνοια, or watchful concern.

4) *Membership Requirements for "Israel" and the Jews*

The different relationships God has with "Israel" and with the Jews carry implications for what might constitute each group's membership requirements. According to Philo, seeing God, which "Israel" represents, is an intellectual activity. One sees God with the eye of the mind or soul. Philo's description of the experience, moreover, is imprecise. Indeed, he depicts seeing God in such different ways that he seems at times to be describing a general belief in or awareness of God—i.e., seeing that God is—while at other times, he seems to be describing a specific experience, a mystical transport. Philo also portrays seeing God as an ability or an achievement. Accordingly, people may strive to develop their capacity to see Him, may attain different kinds of vision, and may achieve vision of Him in different ways. Occasionally, however, Philo also emphasizes that no one can see God without His help. Along these lines, he sometimes speaks of seeing Him as a reward, most saliently in the case of Jacob and the change of his name to "Israel."

In contrast to the vision of God, with which "Israel" is associated, Jewish worship, honor, and service of God are not achievements or rewards but consist in very specific practices—prayers, festivals, first fruit offerings, laws, and customs. Not only do Jews know and serve God, then, they serve Him in particular ways, and their practices reinforce their belief in Him. Unlike the vision of God—which may be an ability, achievement, or reward—Jewish worship and belief are rooted in a deliberate commitment and the choice to live a certain kind of life.

Philo himself does not explicitly draw a connection between the vision of God and Jewish worship of Him. We may speculate that seeing God *may* lead one to worship Him in the Jewish way and worshipping God in the Jewish way *may* lead one to be able to see Him. Despite these possibilities, however, Jewish worship of God and the vision of Him are not *necessarily* connected. We therefore cannot determine precisely the relationship between those who see God—"Israel"—and those who worship Him in the Jewish way—the Jews. Although the two entities may overlap or be one and the same, the exact connection between them remains unclear.

---

[43] See Chapter Five, n. 11.

If we turn now to the question of membership requirements for "Israel" and the Jews, it would seem that "Israel," as the ὁρῶν θεόν (one that sees God) or ὁρατικὸν γένος (race/class that can see), can include anyone who sees God. Seeing God, however, is by its very nature an elusive ideal, an experience difficult to maintain and impossible to achieve without God's help. If "Israel" is indeed the entity that sees God or the race/class that can see, not only would one become a member of "Israel" by virtue of spiritual ability or divine will, but the membership of "Israel" itself may be constantly fluctuating. Thus one does not "convert" to "Israel"; rather one strives both to belong to and remain among those who can see.

The Jews, on the other hand, are a political and social group. One becomes a member of the Jewish people by being born a Jew. Although one can reject his or her heritage, it seems nevertheless that he or she remains a Jew. At the same time, however, Philo describes the relationship between God and the Jews in such a way as to suggest that it may be available to anyone who wishes to participate, regardless of birth. For example, the Jews worship God by following specific laws and practices. The adoption of these laws and practices is the result of choice, not ability or divine will, as in the case of seeing God. Philo notes in fact that even some of his non-Jewish contemporaries choose to honor Jewish practices (*Mos.* 2.17–44).

In addition, the relationship between God and the Jews is marked by four other characteristics: the Jews serve as priests for the whole world; they are allotted to Him; they are God-beloved or God-loving; and they benefit from His πρόνοια. As Philo presents these features, they would appear to be accessible to anyone who believes in the true God.

Besides the factor of birth, then, membership in the Jewish nation also involves belief in and worship of the one God. Moreover, this belief and worship necessarily entail rejection of belief in and worship of many gods since the two stances are contradictory. Thus, if one is not born a Jew, one can achieve the same relationship Jews have with God by deliberately choosing to abandon old ways and adopt new ones.

Philo underscores the general point that one can overcome the conditions of one's birth in several passages in which he discusses noble birth (εὐγένεια) and kinship (συγγένεια). Because the Jews are a people or nation into which one is born, these comments about noble birth and kinship pertain directly to the situation of one who is not born a Jew but becomes one. Moreover, Philo's characterization of the Jews as a polity (πολιτεία) emphasizes that they are a group defined not only by birth but also by shared laws. Let us briefly consider Philo's comments about noble birth and kinship and his use of the term πολιτεία to describe the Jews.

Nobility of Birth. As noted earlier, Philo devotes a whole section (*Virt.* 187–227) to εὐγένεια, or noble birth, in which he argues that nobility consists in virtue rather than good parentage. He provides examples of εὐγένεια from humanity in general and from the Jews in particular (*Virt.* 206). Among the Jews, Philo cites two figures whom he considers proselytes—Abraham and Tamar.[44] These two figures serve as illustrations of εὐγένεια since they come from ignoble backgrounds and not only are virtuous but also turn to belief in God. The turning to God, of course, is a key characteristic of the proselyte.

The Basis of Kinship. Related to the theme that nobility is based upon virtue rather than birth are several remarks scattered throughout the Exposition in which Philo claims that kinship consists not only in blood relationships but in similarity of behavior and pursuit of the same goals, especially worship of God.[45] Philo applies these reflections specifically to proselytes in a passage concerning the Biblical exhortation (Lev. 19:34) to love the proselyte as oneself. He explains this injunction as follows:

> And surely there is good reason for this [injunction to befriend proselytes]; they have left, he says, their country, their kinsfolk and their friends for the sake of virtue and religion. Let them not be denied another citizenship or other ties of family and friendship, and let them find places of shelter standing ready for refugees to the camp of piety. For the most effectual love-charm, the chain which binds indissolubly the goodwill which makes us one is to honor the one God. (*Spec.* 1.52)[46]

The Jews as a πολιτεία. Philo's remarks about noble birth and ties of kinship are related to the problem of membership in the Jewish nation because they address the issue of overcoming one's birth. The Jews, however, are not only a nation into which one is born, they also constitute a polity (πολιτεία) characterized by shared laws. Philo uses πολιτεία in relation to the Jews to refer both to the laws of Moses as a form of government and to the community of people who live according to this form of government.[47] Although he sometimes uses πολιτεία with reference to the

---

[44]   As I have discussed, although Philo does not call Tamar a proselyte explicitly, he seems to consider her one implicitly.

[45]   See n. 32.

[46]   By indicating "he says" (φησί), Philo ascribes his own portrayal of proselytes to Moses himself! See also *Virt.* 179, which expresses a sense of kinship toward people who turn to the worship of God, ostensibly proselytes.

[47]   For Philo's various other uses of πολιτεία, see Chapter One, and Kasher, "The Term *Politeia* in Philo and Josephus." Passages in which Philo uses πολιτεία in relation to the Jews include *Mos.* 2.211; *Decal.* 98; *Spec.* 1.60, 63, 314, 319; *Spec.* 2.123; *Spec.* 3.24, 51; *Spec.* 4.55, 100, 105; *Virt.* 87, 127, 175; *Flacc.* 53.

Jews without naming them explicitly, in *Virt.* 108 and *Legat.* 194, he does specifically mention "the polity of the Jews" (ἡ Ἰουδαίων πολιτεία).

In the Exposition, when Philo describes the Jewish community as having or being a πολιτεία, he seems to mean either Moses's legislation or the people living under this legislation. In his political treatises *Flacc.* and *Legat.*, however, he appears to use πολιτεία more broadly to include both the ancestral customs of the Jews—presumably embodied in Moses's legislation and in the interpretation of this legislation—and their contemporary political organization (see, e.g., *Flacc.* 53). I shall focus, however, upon Philo's use of πολιτεία only in the Exposition since that is where he discusses proselytes. Indeed, in discussing proselytes, he does not introduce contemporary political issues at all.

Beyond speaking about πολιτεία as the form of government defined by the laws of Moses or the people living under this form of government, Philo also identifies πολιτεία as an element that brings the people together. Commenting, for example, upon the Biblical law (Deut. 17:15) which prohibits a foreigner from being chosen to rule so as to avoid the possibility that the foreigner might mistreat the native-born, he writes,

> For he [Moses] assumed with good reason that one who was their fellow-tribes-man and fellow-kinsman related to them by the tie which brings the highest kinship, that of having one citizenship (πολιτεία) and the same law and one God ... would never sin in the way just mentioned. (*Spec.* 4.159; cf. *Mos.* 1.241 and *Spec.* 2.73)

In sum, then, the Jews are characterized not only by their common ancestry but also by their shared πολιτεία of laws promulgated by Moses. As a community living under these laws, they themselves constitute a πολιτεία. Finally, while Philo speaks of the Jews as being or having a πολιτεία, he never describes "Israel" in this way.

We have just considered the various differences between "Israel" and the Jews with respect to four issues:

1) where Philo speaks about each group;

2) how he characterizes each collectivity;

3) how he describes the relationship of each to God; and

4) what might constitute membership requirements for each group.

We are now ready to examine what Philo says in each of these four areas about proselytes, so that we may ascertain whether they are newcomers to "Israel," to the Jews, or to both.

1) *Writings in Which Philo Discusses Proselytes*

We have seen that Philo talks of proselytes as real people only in the Exposition, which is also the only exegetical series in which he discusses the Jews.[48] In this series, moreover, he almost never mentions "Israel." By contrast, in the Allegory—in which Philo does refer frequently to "Israel"—he rarely talks of proselytes, and when he does, he presents them as symbolic figures, never linking them with "Israel." Since Philo discusses real proselytes and Jews, but not "Israel," in the same works, it stands to reason that he sees proselytes as coming over to the Jews but not necessarily to "Israel."

The observation that Philo talks of Jews and proselytes as real people only in the Exposition also supports the hypothesis that his intended audience in this series may include non-Jews whom he hopes to bring into the Jewish community. Indeed the Exposition discusses the actual situation of proselytes, describing, among other things, their rights and their acceptance by this community. Moreover, almost all of Philo's remarks that pertain to proselytes but do not mention them directly appear in the Exposition. Most significant, in addressing these various topics, this series expresses an open and welcoming attitude toward proselytes and other potential incomers.

2) *Philo's Characterization of the Collectivity Which Proselytes Join*

Philo never directly states that proselytes become members of "Israel" or the Jews. In his essay on εὐγένεια, or noble birth, however, he cites among his examples of Jews (*Virt.* 206) Abraham and Tamar, both of whom he also describes as proselytes—either explicitly, as in the case of Abraham, or implicitly, as in the case of Tamar. Philo's use of the particular proselytes Abraham and Tamar as Jewish examples suggests that he sees proselytes in general as part of the Jewish community.

In addition, we have seen that Philo most frequently speaks of "Israel" as a γένος (race/class) and of the Hebrews and Jews as an ἔθνος (nation) or λαός (people) and sometimes as a πολιτεία (polity) or a γένος. When discussing proselytes, he does not specify that they enter an ἔθνος, λαός, or γένος. He does write, however, that they come over to a new πολιτεία (*Spec.* 1.51, *Virt.* 219; cf. *Virt.* 175). Since Philo uses this word in connection with the Jews but not with "Israel," we may logically assume that he views proselytes as joining the πολιτεία of the Jews, i.e., the community of

---

[48] As mentioned earlier, Philo's discussion of the proselyte in *QE* 2.2 provides too little information for one to evaluate how he regards this figure.

people who live according to the constitution of Moses. Moreover, in *Spec.* 1.51, he notes that proselytes are so-called because they have come to "a new and God-loving polity" (φιλοθεὸς πολιτεία). Later, in *Spec.* 1.314, he describes his own community—implicitly the Jews—with the same words, "God-loving polity."[49]

Although Philo usually mentions the πολιτεία of Moses without explicitly naming Jews or any other group, as noted earlier, he does call the Jews a πολιτεία in *Virt.* 108. There he takes up the case of settlers (μέτοικοι) from nations originally hostile to the Jews—or more precisely, to their ancestors, the Hebrews—who may wish to become part of "the polity of the Jews." This example is especially significant, since it pertains specifically to the case of outsiders who want to join the Jewish community. On the basis, then, of this and the other evidence concerning how Philo describes the collectivity which proselytes join, we can reasonably assume that he identifies this collectivity as the Jews but not necessarily as "Israel."

3) *Relationship Between Proselytes and God*

When we recall what Philo says about the relationship between proselytes and God, we see that here too his comments are more compatible with what he says about Jews than about "Israel." Again, the hallmark of the proselyte is that he or she abandons polytheistic beliefs and worship to adopt belief in and worship of the one God. In return, proselytes enjoy God's πρόνοια, or protective care.

Among the new things that proselytes adopt are laws and—especially —honor, worship, or belief in the one God. The Jews, of course, are the ones who honor and worship God through observance of specific laws.

---

[49] In *Virt.* 175, Philo introduces his section on μετάνοια—i.e., repentance or conversion—as follows:

> Our most holy Moses, who so dearly loved virtue and goodness and especially his fellow men, exhorts everyone everywhere to pursue piety and justice, and offers to [μετανοῦντες] in honor of their victory the high rewards of membership in [the best polity (πολιτεία ἡ ἀρίστη)] and of the felicities both great and small which that membership confers.

Here μετανοῦντες can refer either to penitents or to proselytes, an observation which becomes clear as Philo develops the theme of μετάνοια in the treatise. Though he does not specify that "the best polity" refers to the Jews, this identification is implicit since he is talking about the πολιτεία of Moses, and the Jews are the very community which lives according to his πολιτεία. Philo also uses the phrase ἡ ἀρίστη πολιτεία in *Spec.* 3.167, where it signifies the best form of government, and in the following passages, where it signifies democracy: *Agr.* 45, *Deus* 176, *Abr.* 242, *Spec.* 4.237 (see also the note to this passage in LCL, 8:437); cf. *Conf.* 108 and *Virt.* 180.

Philo never discusses "Israel" as observing laws. Although he occasionally mentions that "Israel" worships God,[50] he much more frequently characterizes the relationship between "Israel" and God in terms of its seeing
Him. Philo never claims, however, that proselytes can see God or that
they come over to a vision of Him. Indeed, on the basis of how proselytes
and "Israel" each relate to God according to Philo, we cannot determine
what relationship, if any, proselytes have to "Israel."

As to Philo's other observations about the relationship between God and
proselytes, his clearest statement is that proselytes benefit from God's
πρόνοια. He presents πρόνοια both as a reward to proselytes and as a
demonstration of God's justice and kindness toward those who need help
the most. In one passage (*Spec.* 4.176–82), he also includes Jews among
this group that needs God's help. Besides this instance, Philo proclaims
elsewhere that the Jews are beneficiaries of God's πρόνοια, as we saw in
Chapter Five. Although he does mention once in *Legat.* that "Israel"
enjoys God's πρόνοια, in that context, he implicitly identifies "Israel" with
the Jews. This is, moreover, the only passage in which Philo mentions
God's πρόνοια in relation to "Israel." Indeed, if it is true that Philo sees
"Israel" as a rather loosely defined group—"not a social entity in an
everyday sense," as Jacob Neusner has put it[51]—its members would not
need this kind of divine protection, removed as they would be from
worldly affairs.

Philo's depiction of the relationship between God and proselytes, then,
links them by association with the Jews but not with "Israel." Just as
proselytes come over to laws and worship of the one God, enjoying His
πρόνοια in return, so too are the Jews the very people who worship God
through observance of laws and who benefit from His special protection.

4) *Proselytes' Fulfillment of "Membership Requirements"*

Philo presents both "Israel" and the Jews as theoretically open groups,
displaying in different ways a sense of universalism. Since "Israel"
represents those who can see God, an achievement which depends upon
spiritual capacity, it would seem that anyone—Jew or non-Jew—may
strive to join "Israel" by developing this capacity. The Jews, in contrast,
are a nation defined by birth, a shared constitution of laws, and belief in
the one God. As a social community, Jews worship God through specific
practices and, in addition, they serve as the priesthood for all humanity,
are allotted to God, are God-beloved or God-loving, and enjoy His πρόνοια.

[50] See above, n. 42.
[51] Neusner, *Judaism and Its Social Metaphors*, 221.

If a person is not born a Jew, he or she may still become one. To do so, that person must necessarily give up his or her background of incompatible beliefs and practices and adopt new ones.

We have seen that Philo depicts proselytes as people who abandon their backgrounds of false beliefs, false worship, family, and friends to adopt honor of the one God, laws, and a new polity. As such, they most certainly fulfill what seems to be required for becoming a Jew, though not necessarily for becoming a member of "Israel."

In sum, then, Philo's discussion of proselytes lends support to our distinction between "Israel" and the Jews. Although he presents both entities as potentially open to outsiders, proselytes are to be associated with the Jews, but not necessarily with "Israel." Like the vision of God itself, "Israel" appears to be an elusive and changeable entity, able to encompass whoever is spiritually qualified, regardless of ancestry. The Jews, however, are defined by birth and belief in and worship of the one God. If one is not born into the nation, one may become a Jew—not on the basis of spiritual ability, as in the case of "Israel"—but through a deliberate choice. By leaving their past to join a new polity, proselytes exercise just such a choice.

SUMMARY AND CONCLUSIONS

This investigation began with the aim of understanding the place of Judaism in Philo's thought. In pursuit of this understanding, we have focused upon how Philo discusses two kinds of relationships to God: first, the quest to see God or the goal of seeing Him, and second, the covenant between God and Biblical Israel and its Jewish descendants. Within this framework, I have used the terms "particularism" and "universalism," defined in specific ways.

While guided by a concern with these broad and important issues, our search has involved the close scrutiny of many seemingly disparate details. Since we have investigated such various topics as Philo's use of the word γένος, the source of his etymology for "Israel," his interpretation of Deut. 32:8–9, and his understanding of proselytes, it may be useful first to summarize our findings and then to consider the larger picture to which these discrete topics contribute. Before we turn to this summary, however, our study has yielded two somewhat general observations which deserve emphasis—one pertaining to Philo's exegetical background, the other, to method.

At various points in this investigation, we have noted that Philo is heir to a long tradition of Jewish exegesis. This observation is particularly striking when we consider his use of the expressions ὁρῶν θεόν (one that sees God) and τὸ ὁρατικὸν γένος (the race/class that can see). As discussed in Chapter Two, we have scarce evidence of these expressions in other sources. Nonetheless, the appearance of a fuller form of the etymology, ἀνὴρ ὁρῶν θεόν (a man who sees God), in just one other work—the *Prayer of Joseph*, which is probably contemporary to Philo—is enough to suggest that he may have drawn his etymology for "Israel" from a traditional exegetical vocabulary. Moreover, differences in the way he uses the two expressions even within his own writings suggest that behind each expression lies an interesting evolutionary history. One can only regret the paucity of extant evidence from what must have been for centuries a thriving community of Alexandrian Jewish exegetes.

With regard to method, we have consistently observed significant variations in the way Philo treats a number of topics throughout his different writings. Perhaps the most salient example of these variations is that among the exegetical works, only the Exposition speaks of the Jews by name, mentioning "Israel" only twice. While one can do no more than speculate about why variations occur from one work to the next, the variations themselves are clearly significant. All too often, however, passages from Philo are studied without regard to where they fit in his overall works and how their contexts may influence his presentation. It is hoped therefore that the evidence presented in this study will highlight the methodological importance of taking into account that Philo may be adapting his remarks to suit a particular audience or literary genre.[1]

Summary of Findings

We have seen that Philo distinguishes implicitly between "Israel" and the Jews, using the terms Ἰσραήλ and Ἰουδαῖος in different ways and in separate contexts. As the ὁρῶν θεόν, the one that sees God, or the ὁρατικὸν γένος, the race/class that can see, "Israel" seems to represent a loosely defined entity—not a readily identifiable social group but rather a class of individuals characterized by their spiritual capability. The Jews, in contrast, constitute the real nation that believes in and worships the one God of all creation through observance of specific laws and customs.

The grounds for distinguishing between "Israel" and the Jews in Philo's works can be summarized as follows:

1) Philo generally speaks of "Israel" and the Jews in different series of works, which are probably intended for different audiences.
2) To describe "Israel" and the Jews as collectivities, Philo uses different words with different connotations.
3) Philo portrays the relationship between God and "Israel" and between God and the Jews in different ways.
4) "Membership requirements" for "Israel" and the Jews appear to be different.

Let us examine these four observations more closely.

1) *Philo generally speaks of "Israel" and the Jews in different series of works, which are probably intended for different audiences.* Of Philo's three exegetical commentaries, only the Exposition discusses the Jews explicitly, while it cites "Israel" but twice. The Allegory, in contrast, frequently refers to "Israel." QGE uses the word occasionally, preferring instead a periphrasis like τὸ ὁρατικὸν γένος, the race/class that can see. The two words, "Israel" and "Jew" appear together only once in the same work, in the political treatise *Legat.*

I have suggested that in his exegetical writings, Philo speaks of the Jews only in the Exposition to educate readers who may not be familiar with Jewish history, beliefs, and practices and to appeal to those who may be

---

[1] Cf. Goodenough, *Introduction to Philo Judaeus*, 20–21.

alienated from or hostile toward the Jews. In this series, he mentions "Israel" only twice because the term probably carries no resonance for "outsiders." Philo's non-use of the word "Israel" in the Exposition treatises on Moses, in which he narrates the Biblical nation's exodus from Egypt, is particularly striking and seems to confirm the impression that "Israel" stands for a somewhat different entity from the Biblical nation or the Jews.

Since his audience in the Exposition may not be prepared to grasp the significance of "Israel," Philo may reserve his discussion of this entity for the Allegory, with its more knowledgeable Jewish readers. This audience can appreciate the double association of "Israel" with the Biblical patriarch and his descendant nation, on the one hand, and the experience of seeing God, on the other. Likewise, Philo need not speak of the Jews here, because his readers would already be quite familiar with the people and their ways.

In QGE, which seems to be a collation of interpretations from a broad spectrum of the Alexandrian Jewish community, two features of Philo's discussion of "Israel" are especially noteworthy. First, as we have just observed, though Philo does occasionally mention "Israel" explicitly, he seems to prefer the substitute expression τὸ ὁρατικὸν γένος, the race/class that can see. Second, when using this phrase or the etymology ὁρῶν θεόν, one that sees God, Philo does not directly link either expression with the philosophical significance of seeing God. QGE, then, may provide evidence of a common, traditional use of these expressions—a use one might expect in this series, which encompasses a wide range of interpretations for a variety of Jewish readers.

Finally, in his political treatise *Legat.*, Philo's aim seems to be to present the Jews in the most favorable light for a mixed audience of Jews and non-Jews. That he speaks of "Israel" and the Jews together only here may indicate his wish to impress his readers by depicting the Jews as those who embody the ideal of seeing God, which "Israel" represents.

2) *To describe "Israel" and the Jews as collectivities, Philo uses different words with different connotations.* He most frequently characterizes "Israel" as a γένος but calls the Jews—and their ancestors, the Hebrews—generally an ἔθνος or a λαός, and occasionally a πολιτεία or a γένος.

Philo uses the word γένος in a variety of ways so that it may mean a race defined by common birth, a class defined by shared characteristics, an abstract nature or kind, a collective genus as opposed to individual species, or an idea in the intelligible world. Thus, when he describes "Israel" as a γένος, it is unclear whether he means a race of people with common descent, a class of people with a shared quality, or a nebulous ideal. In contrast, on the few occasions when he uses γένος to describe the Jews, he is evidently speaking about a race of people who share common descent and who also constitute a political entity.

Philo's more frequently used words for the Jews—ἔθνος (nation) and λαός (people)—clearly designate them as a nation, whether its members belong through birth or choice. Finally, πολιτεία, or polity—a word Philo uses in connection with the Jews but not with "Israel"—denotes, among other things, a constitution of laws or a group of people living under such a constitution.

When considered from the perspective of how Philo uses these various words, "Israel" does not emerge as a clearly defined social group, but rather as a class that represents the ideal of seeing God. The Jews, on the other hand, are an acknowledged community, whose members share in common either their origins or a constitution of laws, or both.

3) *Philo portrays the relationship between God and "Israel" and between God and the Jews in different ways.* Philo most frequently associates "Israel" with seeing God. For him, seeing God represents the height of human happiness, achievement of the philosophical goal, attainable only through the sight of the mind with the help of God. Philo's notions about seeing God are strongly influenced by the Platonic tradition, which emphasizes the superiority of the sense of sight and proclaims belief in a transcendent One.

The source of Philo's association between seeing God and "Israel" is its etymology ὁρῶν θεόν, or one that sees God. This etymology and the related phrase τὸ ὁρατικὸν γένος, the race/class that can see, may have belonged to a body of traditional Jewish exegesis which Philo inherited. Originally the etymology may have been based upon Jacob's encounter with his adversary, narrated in Genesis 32; and the phrase τὸ ὁρατικὸν γένος may have been an adaptation to the etymology, intended to describe the nation Israel as a collectivity. In time, however, both expressions may have evolved in meaning to encompass the philosophical kind of seeing and to separate from their original identification with the historical patriarch and nation. As Philo uses these expressions, the precise identity of the seers they denote almost always remains uncertain.

In contrast to "Israel," who sees God, the Jews constitute the community of people—past and present—who believe in and worship God by observing specific laws and customs. In addition, they serve as the priesthood for all humanity, have been allotted or have allotted themselves to God, are God-beloved or God-loving, and benefit from His πρόνοια, or protective concern.

By depicting the Jews in this way, Philo implicitly transforms several themes from the Bible which pertain to the covenant relationship between God and Biblical Israel. Moreover, in the case of divine πρόνοια, he also adapts philosophical beliefs—in addition to the Biblical notions—to suggest that the Jews enjoy God's special care because they believe in Him. As explained in Chapter Five, Philo presents the relationship between God and the Jews as one that is available or accessible to anyone who chooses to believe in and worship the Creator and Father of all. Similarly, Philo transforms the sense of Biblical verses and terms like "covenant" or "chosen people" so that the relationship depicted in the Bible between God and Israel also appears potentially open to everyone. According to his presentation, then, the relationship between God and the Jews is not necessarily limited to those born into the historical nation.

4) *"Membership requirements" for "Israel" and the Jews appear to be different.* Since Philo does not directly address who may belong to "Israel" or how one becomes a Jew, one can only speculate about "membership requirements" for these two entities. Because the distinguishing mark of "Israel" is its ability to see God, it would seem that anyone who qualifies—whether Jew or non-Jew—may be considered part of "Israel." Indeed, Philo speaks quite admiringly of non-Jews like the Persian Magi and other unnamed sages from Greek and foreign lands. Although he never calls these people "Israel" or speaks of them as seeing God per se, his description of them would lead one to think that they meet the requirement for belonging, namely, that they have the spiritual ability to apprehend the existing God.

Though Philo is also not explicit about what is required to become a Jew, we saw in Chapter Six that he associates proselytes with Jews, but not necessarily with "Israel." The hallmark of the proselyte, moreover, is that he or she abandons belief in and worship of many gods, leaving behind a community of family and friends, to adopt belief in and worship of the one true God, becoming part of a new social community. In general, Philo does not provide enough information for us to determine what, if any, legal requirements the proselyte must fulfill. Despite what he does not say, however, it is clear that he considers the Jews to be an open group which gladly welcomes newcomers and that it is the Jewish community which proselytes join.

Particularist or Universalist?

Taking into account all the information just presented, let us now return to the questions posed at the outset of this study. Focusing upon two kinds of relationships to God—the quest to see Him or the goal of seeing Him and the covenant between Him and Biblical Israel and the Jews—I have asked whether Philo believes all people can participate in these relationships or only some people. Further, if only some can participate, must they be Jews? Within this framework, I have defined universalism as the position that anyone can participate in either relationship and particularism as the position that only Jews can participate.

Let us begin with the particularist stance. Our study suggests that Philo does *not* believe only a Jew can see God. Certainly, as those who believe in the one God—as opposed to many gods or no gods—Jews stand a better chance of being able to "see" Him. Philo does, however, speak of non-Jews such as the Persian Magi and other unidentified Gentile sages in a way that suggests they too may be capable of seeing God. In one passage, in fact, he equates Jewish laws and customs with the teachings of Greek philosophy, in that both lead to knowledge of "the highest, the most ancient cause of all things and [rejection of] the delusion of created gods" (*Virt.* 65). On the question of who can see God, then, Philo is not a particularist, in the sense that he believes both Jews and non-Jews are potentially capable of seeing Him. I shall return to this observation below.

As to whether only Jews may participate in the covenant relationship with God, we have seen that Philo transforms this relationship in several ways. While he does not affirm that God and Biblical Israel are bound by a covenant, he seems nevertheless to believe that this nation and its Jewish descendants do have a special standing with God. He expresses this idea by maintaining that the Jews believe in God and worship Him through their laws and customs, that they serve as priests for all humanity, that they are allotted to God, are God-beloved or God-loving, and benefit from His πρόνοια, or protective concern. Moreover, in his implicit and explicit interpretations of Scripture, Philo depicts the relationship between God and Biblical Israel and its Jewish descendants as a relationship available and accessible to all who choose it. To confirm this impression, he also exhibits a welcoming attitude and openness toward proselytes.

Since Philo transforms the covenant yet still presents the relationship between God and the Jews as distinctive, perhaps at this point we should shift the terms of the discussion to reflect his position more accurately. Instead of speaking about who Philo believes can see God or who can participate in His covenant, it is probably more appropriate to speak of who he believes may belong to "Israel" and/or the Jews. Because Philo does not appear to restrict membership either in "Israel" or the Jewish community only to those who are born as Jews, we cannot call him a particularist.

Before we leave the matter here, however, it may be useful to reconsider the view of Alan Mendelson, who, as we saw in the Introduction, emphasizes Philo's particularism above any universalist tendencies.

Indeed, Mendelson argues that "even as Philo proclaims the openness of the Jews to other peoples, we can detect a counter-current of exclusiveness which undermines the very concept he espouses."[2] How can we reconcile Mendelson's view of Philo's exclusiveness with our own conclusion that Philo is not a particularist?

As we approach this question, two points are especially germane. First, Mendelson evaluates Philo not from the perspective of his thought but rather in the context of his social environment, examining how Egyptians and Greeks regard Jews and how Philo in turn regards Egyptians and Greeks. Mendelson observes that "Philo's attitude toward pagan religion is condescending and dismissive" and that he has an "underlying contempt for the customs of other peoples."[3] From the evidence Mendelson adduces and indeed from what we ourselves have found, we can hardly disagree with this assessment.

Second, although we have rejected the notion that Philo is a particularist, we have not yet established him as a universalist. For us to do so would require that Philo allow any and all people to belong either to "Israel" or to the Jews. In fact, however, this is not the case.

Indeed a prerequisite for anyone who belongs to either entity is belief in the existence of the one true God. Obviously, to be able to see God and thus to be a member of "Israel," one must also believe that God exists. In fact, as we have noted, Philo occasionally describes seeing God as seeing *that* He is, not *what* He is. Similarly, to worship God—as the Jews do—one again must believe that He exists. In virtually all his descriptions of proselytes who join the Jewish πολιτεία (polity), Philo emphasizes that they must leave behind a background of false belief and worship to adopt belief in and worship of the one true God.

Although Philo may envision "Israel" and the Jews, then, as potentially open to all people, in his view, neither entity can encompass all people as they are. To be sure, he speaks quite disparagingly of polytheists, idolaters, and atheists—that is, people who believe in many gods, created gods, or no god. For Philo to embrace such individuals as part of "Israel" or the Jews, these individuals would first have to relinquish their wrong beliefs and adopt the monotheistic premise.

Because Philo would exclude from "Israel" and the Jews those who do not believe in the one God, we cannot consider him a universalist, according to our working definition. At the same time, however, neither is he a particularist, since he depicts both entities as potentially open to non-Jews.

---

[2] Mendelson, *Philo's Jewish Identity*, 113.
[3] Ibid., 130 and 138.

Our conclusion that Philo is neither a particularist nor a universalist highlights some of the difficulties inherent in using these terms, difficulties alluded to briefly in the Introduction, which now merit further comment. Jon D. Levenson, one scholar who has reflected upon the ambiguities of "universalism," offers some insightful observations about the use of this term. Levenson notes that all religious traditions, like other aspects of human culture, are particular. He further observes that "while no religion is universal, some aspire to be. In this sense, a 'universal religion' may mean simply one that accepts proselytes, that is, one that is willing or eager to extend its particularity indefinitely."[4]

Paradoxically, then, universalism may be seen as a concern "to extend [one's] particularity indefinitely." In contrast, as Levenson remarks, "Those who think outsiders can have a proper relationship with God *as they are* will feel less of an impulse to make them into insiders"[5] (my emphasis). One might easily consider this latter attitude to be universalist, in the sense that it affirms that all people may have a valid relationship with God, even though His relationship with "insiders" and with "outsiders" may not be identical. This stance does not evince the desire "to extend [one's] particularity indefinitely," nor does it imply a rejection of those outside one's own group. Instead it affirms and accepts people as they are. The line between "particularism" and "universalism" can be a faint one indeed![6]

In aspiring to encompass all people, then—either within "Israel" or the Jewish community—Philo is a potential universalist. Those who do not believe in the one God, however, might view him as wishing to impose upon others notions which are quite particular. Whether one perceives

---

[4] Jon D. Levenson, *The Universal Horizon of Biblical Particularism*, Jewish Perspectives (New York: American Jewish Committee, 1985), 2.

[5] Ibid., 5.

[6] Cf. the distinction between universalism and mission pointed out by Martin-Achard, *A Light to the Nations*, 3. Also pertinent is the following observation by Joseph R. Rosenbloom in *Conversion to Judaism: From the Biblical Period to the Present* (Cincinnati: Hebrew Union College Press, 1978), 31: "[T]he exilic literature was filled with statements indicating the universality of Judaism. This universality had its particularistic side in that non-Jews were expected to formally align themselves with Judaism through an act which long after the biblical period was to be called 'conversion.'" Other relevant discussions can be found in Sandra B. Lubarsky, *Tolerance and Transformation: Jewish Approaches to Religious Pluralism* (Cincinnati: Hebrew Union College Press, 1990), esp. 1–27; Orlinsky, "Nationalism-Universalism and Internationalism in Ancient Israel," 206–36; Alan F. Segal, *Rebecca's Children: Judaism and Christianity in the Roman World* (Cambridge: Harvard University Press, 1986), 163–81; Ephraim E. Urbach, "Self-Isolation or Self-Affirmation in Judaism in the First Three Centuries: Theory and Practice," *Jewish and Christian Self-Definition*, vol. 2: *Aspects of Judaism in the Greco-Roman Period*, ed. E. P. Sanders et al. (Philadelphia: Fortress Press, 1981), 269–98.

Philo to be a universalist or a particularist will obviously depend upon how one understands these two terms. To a non-Jewish sage—who, because of his philosophical understanding, would be eligible to be part of "Israel"— Philo might well appear to be a universalist. He would certainly not appear so, however, to an idolater—who, because of his wrong beliefs, would be excluded from both "Israel" *and* the Jews!

The Place of Judaism in Philo's Thought

In presenting "Israel" and the Jews, Philo depicts relationships with God in which potentially all people might participate. If, however, a non-Jew may have a legitimate relationship with God by "seeing" Him or belonging to "Israel," then why, according to Philo, should that individual also become a Jew? Moreover, why should a Jew who is able to see God remain a Jew?

As we approach these questions, let us not forget that while seeing God may be a matter only of spiritual capacity, relating to God as a Jew has both religious and social dimensions. By becoming a Jew, the proselyte leaves both an old religion and a social community to adopt both a new religion and a new community—the only community, in fact, that believes in and worships the one God. What further distinguishes this community is that its members serve as the priesthood for all humanity, have been allotted or have allotted themselves to God, are God-beloved or God-loving, and benefit particularly from His πρόνοια, or protective concern.

Today, perhaps, these characteristics may not strike us as especially compelling reasons for becoming or remaining a Jew. This is predominantly because in our times people may believe in and worship the one God within a variety of religious and social communities.

To arrive at a truly fair assessment, then, we must remember first and foremost to view Philo's presentation of Judaism within its proper historical context. In Philo's time, after all, Judaism was the only monotheistic religion. He shows no familiarity with the beginnings of Christianity. Instead, he depicts his environment as filled with all kinds of idolaters, polytheists, and atheists. His claim that the Jews were the only nation to believe in the one true God was a meaningful one indeed, a claim that surely did distinguish them as a people apart.

Despite this observation, however, if Philo does allow for a legitimate relationship with God outside Judaism, then how shall we assess the place of Judaism in his thought? Let us recall that though Philo himself does not use the word "Judaism" ('Ιουδαϊσμός), it was in use during his time. Yehoshua Amir has observed that for Jews of the Hellenistic period, this term encompassed both a legal aspect and a philosophical one. The legal aspect was expressed in the Greek terms νόμος (law) and πολιτεία. Amir notes that "Judaism did not consist in any one particular law but rather in a system of laws which made up a single entity. That is what the Jews termed with the lofty appellation πολιτεία (*politeia*), meaning 'constitution' in general, or even 'state.'"[7]

To illustrate the second aspect of Judaism, the philosophical one, Amir focuses upon Philo. He comments,

> Philo's attempt to interpret the Torah of Moses as a philosophical system which fulfills and complements all the true discoveries of Greek philosophy is but the crowning achievement of the prolonged effort of the Hellenistic Jews to present the Jewish tradition in intellectual terms borrowed from Greece, as a theoretical system which provided ultimate answers to ultimate questions.[8]

To be sure, Philo's presentation of Judaism as a kind of philosophy may well deserve to be called the "crowning achievement" of Hellenistic Jewish efforts. It is clear from his works, however, that for him, being a Jew is not only a matter of believing in a certain philosophy, it also involves a way of life embodied by a very particular community. To him, the Jewish πολιτεία refers both to the laws of this community and to the community itself.

In assessing the place of Judaism in Philo's thought, then, we can conclude that as a philosophy, "Judaism" represents one approach— indeed probably the best approach—to belief in the one God. Without a doubt, belief in God is supremely important in all Philo's writings. Judaism, however, is not the only path to this belief for, as he notes, "the disciples of the most excellent philosophy" also gain knowledge of "the highest, the most ancient Cause of all things" (*Virt.* 65).

Philo's own commitment to being a Jew—so apparent from his works and the little we know of his life—thus cannot be fully explained by his thought. Instead, his commitment seems rooted in his existence, in his involvement with the Jewish community and its way of life. Because he believes that one need not be a Jew to embark upon the path to God, Philo is potentially universalist in his thought, as we have seen. In his life, however, his participation in and concern for the political and social community of the Jews are unmistakably particular.

In his *Introduction to Philo Judaeus*, Erwin R. Goodenough recommends that the newcomer to Philo begin by reading his two political treatises, *Flacc.* and *Legat.* As Goodenough suggests,

---

7   Amir, "The Term Ἰουδαϊσμός," 41.
8   Ibid.

The first treatises of Philo which one should read seem to me to be the two, in the first of which he defends the Jews of Alexandria for their relations with Flaccus, and in the second for their refusing, even to Gaius' face, to accept the emperor's divinity... Not only are they Philo's most vividly written treatises, but in them Philo speaks more in the first person than in any others, and the reader of Philo's other works should always have in mind that they were written by a man who could write these.[9]

It is striking that this suggestion is made by a scholar who perhaps more than anyone else emphasizes the importance of what he calls a "distinctly non-Jewish type of salvation" in Philo's thought.[10] Good-enough's suggestion highlights that Philo's thought must be seen as only one part of a whole. In Philo's thought, then, one might say that Judaism as a philosophy holds the foremost place, though not to the exclusion of other philosophies which believe in the one true God.

Judaism, however, is more than a philosophy, and being a Jew encompasses more than adherence to Jewish beliefs and practices. Commitment to the Jewish πολιτεία is clearly important. Even to Philo, who represents "the crowning achievement" of the attempt to depict Judaism as a philosophy, being a Jew involves not only belief in but also worship of God through specific laws and customs. Moreover, the Jewish πολιτεία signifies not just these laws and customs but also the body politic of Jews, to whom he was so devoted.

The place of Judaism, then, cannot be measured in Philo's thought alone. For a complete understanding, one must also consider his life.

---

[9] Goodenough, *Introduction to Philo Judaeus*, 30–31.
[10] Goodenough, *By Light, Light*, 254.

BIBLIOGRAPHY

The Bibliography consists of all works cited in this book. Texts, translations, and indices of Philo's works are listed separately. Primary sources other than Philo's works are listed only when a specific edition has been mentioned.

Texts, Translations, and Indices
of Philo's Works

Arnaldez, Roger, Claude Mondésert, and Jean Pouilloux, eds. *Les oeuvres de Philon d'Alexandrie*. 36 vols. Paris: Éditions du Cerf, 1961–92. Individual volumes cited in the book are listed in this section under the name of the editor of each volume.

Berkowitz, Luci and Karl A. Squitier, with technical assistance from William A. Johnson. *Thesaurus Linguae Graecae: Canon of Greek Authors and Works*. 2nd ed. New York: Oxford University Press, 1986. Compact disc accessible on IBYCUS personal computer.

Biblia Patristica: Supplément, Philon d'Alexandrie. Paris: Éditions du Centre National de la Recherche Scientifique, 1982.

Box, Herbert, ed. *Philonis Alexandrini: In Flaccum*. London: Oxford University Press, 1939.

Cohn, Leopold, Paul Wendland, Siegfried Reiter, and Hans Leisegang, eds. *Philonis Alexandrini: Opera Quae Supersunt*. 7 vols. Berlin: Reimer, 1896–1930; repr., Berlin: de Gruyter, 1962–63.

Colson, F. H., G. H. Whitaker, and Ralph Marcus, trans. *Philo in Ten Volumes (and Two Supplementary Volumes)*. The Loeb Classical Library. Cambridge: Harvard University Press, 1929–62.

Daniel, Suzanne, ed. and trans. *De Specialibus Legibus I–II*. Vol. 24 of *Les oeuvres de Philon d'Alexandrie*. 1978. See Arnaldez, Roger et al., eds.

Kahn, Jean-George, ed. and trans. *De Confusione Linguarum*. Vol. 13 of *Les oeuvres de Philon d'Alexandrie*. 1963. See Arnaldez, Roger et al., eds.

Lewy, Hans, ed. "Philo: Selections." In *Three Jewish Philosophers*, 7–112. New York: Harper & Row, 1965.

Mayer, Günter. *Index Philoneus*. Berlin: de Gruyter, 1974.

Petit, Françoise, ed. *Quaestiones in Genesim et in Exodum: Fragmenta Graeca*. Vol. 33 of *Les oeuvres de Philon d'Alexandrie*. 1978. See Arnaldez, Roger et al., eds.

Smallwood, E. Mary, ed. and trans. *Philonis Alexandrini: Legatio ad Gaium*. 2nd ed. Leiden: E. J. Brill, 1970.

Winston, David, ed. *Philo of Alexandria: The Contemplative Life, The Giants, and Selections*, with a Preface by John Dillon. The Classics of Western Spirituality. New York: Paulist Press, 1981.

Other Works Cited

Allen, W. C. "On the Meaning of προσήλυτος in the Septuagint." *The Expositor* 4 (10) (1894): 264–75.

Amir, Yehoshua. "Authority and Interpretation of Scripture in the Writings of Philo." *Mikra: Text, Translation, Reading and Interpretation of the Hebrew Bible in Ancient Judaism and Early Christianity*, ed. Martin Jay Mulder, 421–53.

Compendia Rerum Iudaicarum ad Novum Testamentum, sec. 2, vol. 1. Assen/Maastricht: Van Gorcum, 1988.

——. "Explanation of Hebrew Names in Philo." *Tarbitz* 31 (1962): 297 (Hebrew).

——. *Die hellenistische Gestalt des Judentums bei Philon von Alexandrien.* Forschungen zum jüdisch-christlichen Dialog, ed. Yehuda Aschkenasy and Heinz Kremers, no. 5. Neukirchen-Vluyn: Neukirchener Verlag, 1983.

——. "Mose als Verfasser der Tora bei Philon." See Amir, Yehoshua. *Die hellenistische Gestalt,* 77–105.

——. "Philo and the Bible." *Studia Philonica* 2 (1973): 1–8.

——. "Philon und die jüdische Wirklichkeit seiner Zeit." See Amir, Yehoshua. *Die hellenistische Gestalt,* 3–51.

——. "The Term Ἰουδαϊσμός : A Study in Jewish-Hellenistic Self-Identification." *Immanuel* 14 (1982): 34–41.

——. "Die Umformung des εὐδαίμων in den θεοφιλής bei Philon. See Amir, Yehoshua. *Die hellenistische Gestalt,* 207–19.

Armstrong, A. Hilary. "Gotteschau (Visio beatifica)." In vol. 12 of *Reallexicon für Antike und Christentum: Sachwörterbuch zur Auseinandersetzung des Christentums mit der antiken Welt,* ed. Theodor Klauser, 1–19. Stuttgart: Hiersemann, 1983.

Attridge, Harold W. *The Interpretation of Biblical History in the* Antiquitates Judaicae *of Flavius Josephus.* Harvard Theological Review; Harvard Dissertations in Religion, ed. Caroline Bynum and George Rupp, no. 7. Missoula, Montana: Scholars Press, 1976.

Bailey, Jon Nelson. "*Metanoia* in the Writings of Philo Judaeus." In *Society of Biblical Literature 1991 Seminar Papers,* 135–41. Society of Biblical Literature Seminar Paper Series, ed. Eugene H. Lovering, Jr., no. 30. Atlanta: Scholars Press, 1991.

Baltzer, Klaus. *The Covenant Formulary in Old Testament, Jewish, and Early Christian Writings,* trans. David E. Green. Philadelphia: Fortress Press, 1971.

Bamberger, Bernard J. *Proselytism in the Talmudic Period.* Cincinnati: Hebrew Union College Press, 1939.

Behm, Johannes. "προνοέω, πρόνοια." In vol. 4 of *Theological Dictionary of the New Testament,* 1009–17.

Behm, Johannes and Ernst Würthwein. "μετανοέω, μετάνοια." In vol. 4 of *Theological Dictionary of the New Testament,* 975–1008.

Belkin, Samuel. "Interpretation of Names in Philo." *Horeb* 12 (1956): 3–61 (Hebrew).

——. *Philo and the Oral Law: The Philonic Interpretation of Biblical Law in Relation to the Palestinian Halakah.* Harvard Semitic Series, vol. 11. Cambridge: Harvard University Press, 1940.

Bethge, Hans-Gebhard, and Bentley Layton, trans. "On the Origin of the World." In *The Nag Hammadi Library,* 3rd ed., ed. James M. Robinson, 170–89. San Francisco: Harper & Row, 1988.

Bloch, Renée. "Israélite, juif, hébreu." *Cahiers Sioniens* 5 (1951): 11–31, 258–80.

Borgen, Peder. "Aristobulus and Philo." See Borgen, Peder. *Philo, John and Paul,* 7–16.

——. *Bread From Heaven: An Exegetical Study of the Concept of Manna in the Gospel of John and the Writings of Philo.* Supplements to Novum Testamentum, vol. 10. Leiden: E. J. Brill, 1965.

——. *Paul Preaches Circumcision and Pleases Men and Other Essays on Christian Origins.* Relieff, no. 8. Trondheim: Tapir, 1983.

——. *Philo, John and Paul: New Perspectives on Judaism and Early Christianity.* Brown Judaic Studies, ed. Jacob Neusner, no. 131. Atlanta: Scholars Press, 1987.

———. "Philo of Alexandria." In *Jewish Writings of the Second Temple Period: Apocrypha, Pseudepigrapha, Qumran Sectarian Writings, Philo, Josephus,* ed. Michael E. Stone, 233–82. Compendia Rerum Iudaicarum ad Novum Testamentum, sec. 2, vol. 2. Philadelphia: Fortress Press, 1984.

———. "Philo of Alexandria: A Critical and Synthetical Survey of Research since World War II." In *Aufstieg und Niedergang der römischen Welt: Geschichte und Kultur Roms im Spiegel der neueren Forschung.* Pt. 2, vol. 21, sec. 1: *Religion (Hellenistisches Judentum in römischer Zeit: Philon und Josephus),* ed. Wolfgang Haase, 98–154. Berlin: de Gruyter, 1984.

———. "'There Shall Come Forth a Man': Reflections on Messianic Ideas in Philo." In *The Messiah: Developments in Earliest Judaism and Christianity,* ed. James H. Charlesworth, 341–61. Minneapolis: Fortress Press, 1992.

Boyarin, Daniel. *Intertextuality and the Reading of Midrash.* Bloomington, Indiana: Indiana University Press, 1990.

Bréhier, Émile. *Les idées philosophiques et religieuses de Philon d'Alexandrie.* 2nd ed. Études de Philosophie Mediévale, ed. Étienne Gilson, no. 8. Paris: J. Vrin, 1925.

Buffière, Félix. *Les mythes d'Homère et la pensée grecque.* Paris: Société d'Édition "Les Belles Lettres," 1956.

Burkert, Walter. *Ancient Mystery Cults.* Cambridge: Harvard University Press, 1987.

Casanowicz, Immanuel M. *Paronomasia in the Old Testament.* Jerusalem: Makor, 1970; reprint of 1892 dissertation.

Cave, C. H. "Gentiles and Judaism: 'God-Fearers' and Proselytes." In vol. 3, pt. 1 of Emil Schürer, *The History of the Jewish People in the Age of Jesus Christ,* rev. and ed. Geza Vermes, Fergus Millar, and Martin Goodman, 150–76. Edinburgh: T. & T. Clark, 1986.

Chadwick, Henry. "Philo." In *The Cambridge History of Later Greek and Early Medieval Philosophy,* ed. A. Hilary Armstrong, 137–57. Cambridge: Cambridge University Press, 1970.

Charlesworth, James H., ed. *Old Testament Pseudepigrapha.* 2 vols. Garden City, New York: Doubleday, 1985.

Cohen, Naomi G. *Philo Judaeus: His Universe of Discourse.* Beiträge zur Erforschung des Alten Testaments und des antiken Judentums, ed. Matthias Augustin and Michael Mach, vol. 24. Frankfurt am Main: Peter Lang, 1995.

Cohen, Shaye J. D. "Conversion to Judaism in Historical Perspective: From Biblical Israel to Postbiblical Judaism." *Conservative Judaism* 36 (1983): 31–45.

———. "Crossing the Boundary and Becoming a Jew." *Harvard Theological Review* 82 (1989): 13–33.

———. "The Polemical Uses of Ἰουδαῖος and Ἰουδαΐζειν in Early Christian Writings." Paper presented at the Annual Meeting of the Society of Biblical Literature, Kansas City, November 1991.

Collins, John J. "A Symbol of Otherness: Circumcision and Salvation in the First Century." In *"To See Ourselves As Others See Us": Christians, Jews, "Others" in Late Antiquity,* 163–86. Scholars Press Studies in the Humanities, ed. Jacob Neusner and Ernest S. Frerichs. Chico, California: Scholars Press, 1985.

Dahl, Nils A. *Das Volk Gottes. Eine Untersuchung zum Kirchenbewusstsein des Urchristentums.* Oslo: Jacob Dybwad, 1941.

Dalbert, Peter. *Die Theologie der hellenistisch-jüdischen Missions-Literatur unter Ausschluss von Philo und Josephus.* Theologische Forschung, no. 4. Hamburg: Herbert Reich Evangelischen Verlag, 1954.

Danell, G. A. *Studies in the Name Israel in the Old Testament.* Uppsala: Appelbergs boktrychkeri-A.-B., 1946.

Daniel, Suzanne. "La Halacha de Philon selon le premier livre des 'Lois Speciales.'" In *Philon d'Alexandrie*, 221–40. Colloques Nationaux du Centre National de la Recherche Scientifique. Paris: Centre National de la Recherche Scientifique, 1967.

Darnell, D. R. and D. A. Fiensy. "Hellenistic Synagogal Prayers." In vol. 2 of *Old Testament Pseudepigrapha*, ed. James H. Charlesworth, 671–97. Garden City, New York: Doubleday, 1985.

Dawson, David. *Allegorical Readers and Cultural Revision in Ancient Alexandria*. Berkeley: University of California Press, 1992.

Deissmann, Adolf. "Papyrus Onomasticon Sacrum." Chapter in vol. 1 of *Veröffentlichungen aus der Heidelberger Papyrus-Sammlung*, 86–93. Heidelberg: Carl Winter, 1905. Papyrology on Microfiche, ser. 2, vol. 31. Missoula, Montana: Scholars Press, n.d.

Delling, Gerhard. "The 'One Who Sees God' in Philo." In *Nourished With Peace: Studies in Hellenistic Judaism in Memory of Samuel Sandmel*, ed. Frederick E. Greenspahn, Earle Hilgert, and Burton L. Mack, 28–41. Scholars Press Homage Series. Chico, California: Scholars Press, 1984.

Dexinger, Ferdinand. "Ein 'messianisches Szenarium' als Gemeingut des Judentums in nachherodianischer Zeit?" *Kairos* 17 (1975): 249–78.

Dillon, John. *The Middle Platonists, 80 B.C. to A.D. 220*. Ithaca: Cornell University Press, 1977.

———. "A Response to Runia and Sterling." *The Studia Philonica Annual* 5 (1993): 151–55.

———. "Self-Definition in Later Platonism." In *Jewish and Christian Self-Definition*. Vol. 3: *Self-Definition in the Greco-Roman World*, ed. Ben F. Meyer and E. P. Sanders, 60–75. Philadelphia: Fortress Press, 1982.

———. *The Transcendence of God in Philo: Some Possible Sources*. Protocol of the Colloquy of the Center for Hermeneutical Studies in Hellenistic and Modern Culture, ed. Wilhelm Wuellner, no. 16. Berkeley: Center for Hermeneutical Studies, 1975.

Dodd, Charles Harold. "Hellenism and Christianity." *Harvard Divinity School Bulletin* (1937): 24–44.

Drummond, James. *Philo Judaeus; or, The Jewish Alexandrian Philosophy in Its Development and Completion*. 2 vols. London: Williams and Norgate, 1888.

Eichrodt, Walther. *Theology of the Old Testament*, trans. J. A. Baker. 2 vols. The Old Testament Library. Philadelphia: Westminster Press, 1961.

Empson, William. *Seven Types of Ambiguity*. 3rd ed. New York: New Directions, n.d.

Feldman, Louis H. *Jew and Gentile in the Ancient World: Attitudes and Interactions From Alexander to Justinian*. Princeton: Princeton University Press, 1993.

———. "Proselytes and 'Sympathizers' in the Light of the New Inscriptions From Aphrodisias." *Revue des études juives* 148 (1989): 265–305.

Fiensy, David A. *Prayers Alleged To Be Jewish: An Examination of the Constitutiones Apostolorum*. Brown Judaic Studies, ed. Jacob Neusner, no. 65. Chico, California: Scholars Press, 1985.

Foerster, Werner. "προσκληρόω." In vol. 3 of *Theological Dictionary of the New Testament*, 765–66.

Fraser, P. M. *Ptolemaic Alexandria*. 3 vols. Oxford: Clarendon Press, 1972; repr., 1984.

Friedmann, Meir, ed. *Seder Eliahu Rabbah and Seder Eliahu Zuta*. Vienna: n.p., 1902.

Georgi, Dieter. *The Opponents of Paul in Second Corinthians*. Philadelphia: Fortress Press, 1986.

Ginzberg, Louis. *The Legends of the Jews.* 7 vols. Philadelphia: Jewish Publication Society, 1909–38.

Goodenough, Erwin R. *By Light, Light: The Mystic Gospel of Hellenistic Judaism.* New Haven: Yale University Press, 1935.

——. *An Introduction to Philo Judaeus.* Oxford: Basil Blackwell, 1962. Reprinted by Brown Classics in Judaica, ed. Jacob Neusner. Lanham, Maryland: University Press of America, 1986.

——. "Philo's Exposition of the Law and His De Vita Mosis." *Harvard Theological Review* 26 (1933): 109–25.

——. *The Politics of Philo Judaeus: Practice and Theory.* New Haven: Yale University Press, 1938.

——. "Problems of Method in Studying Philo Judaeus." *Journal of Biblical Literature* 58 (1939): 51–58.

Goulet, Richard. *La philosophie de Moïse: essai de reconstitution d'un commentaire philosophique préphilonien du Pentateuque.* Histoire des doctrines de l'antiquité classique, no. 11. Paris: Librairie Philosophique J. Vrin, 1987.

Grabbe, Lester L. *Etymology in Early Jewish Interpretation: The Hebrew Names in Philo.* Brown Judaic Studies, ed. Jacob Neusner, no. 115. Atlanta: Scholars Press, 1988.

Guerra, Anthony J. "The One God Topos in *Spec. Leg.* 1.52." In *Society of Biblical Literature 1990 Seminar Papers,* 148–57. Society of Biblical Literature Seminar Paper Series, ed. David J. Lull, no. 29. Atlanta: Scholars Press, 1990.

Gunkel, Hermann. *The Legends of Genesis: The Biblical Saga and History,* trans. W. H. Carruth. N.p., 1901; repr., New York: Schocken Books, 1964.

Gutbrod, Walter. "Ἰουδαῖος, Ἰσραήλ, Ἑβραῖος in Greek Hellenistic Literature." In vol. 3 of *Theological Dictionary of the New Testament,* 369–75.

Hagner, Donald A. "The Vision of God in Philo and John: A Comparative Study." *Journal of the Evangelical Theological Society* 14 (1971): 81–93.

Hamerton-Kelly, Robert G. "Sources and Traditions in Philo Judaeus: Prolegomena to an Analysis of His Writings." *Studia Philonica* 1 (1972): 3–26.

Hanson, Anthony T. "Philo's Etymologies." *Journal of Theological Studies* 18 (1967): 128–39.

Hay, David M. "Philo's References to Other Allegorists." *Studia Philonica* 6 (1979–80): 41–75.

——. "References to Other Exegetes in Philo's *Quaestiones.*" See Hay, David M., ed. *Both Literal and Allegorical,* 81–97.

——, ed. *Both Literal and Allegorical: Studies in Philo of Alexandria's* Questions and Answers on Genesis and Exodus. Brown Judaic Studies, ed. Ernest S. Frerichs., no. 232. Atlanta: Scholars Press, 1991.

Hecht, Richard D. "Philo and Messiah." In *Judaisms and Their Messiahs at the Turn of the Christian Era,* ed. Jacob Neusner, William Scott Green, and Ernest S. Frerichs, 139–68. Cambridge: Cambridge University Press, 1987.

Heinemann, Isaak. *Philons griechische und jüdische Bildung: Kulturvergleichende Untersuchungen zu Philons Darstellung der jüdischen Gesetze.* Breslau: Marcus, 1932; repr., Hildesheim: Olms, 1962.

——. *Ways of the Aggadah.* Jerusalem: Magnes Press, 1954 (Hebrew).

Hilgert, Earle. "The *Quaestiones*: Texts and Translations." See Hay, David M., ed. *Both Literal and Allegorical,* 1–15.

Hillers, Delbert R. *Covenant: The History of a Biblical Idea.* Seminars in the History of Ideas. Baltimore: Johns Hopkins Press, 1969.

Holladay, Carl A. *Fragments from Hellenistic Jewish Authors.* Vol 3: *Aristobulus.* SBL Texts and Translations 39; Pseudepigrapha Series 13, ed. Martha Himmelfarb. Atlanta: Scholars Press, 1995.

Jaubert, Annie. *La notion d'Alliance dans le judaisme aux abords de l'ère chrétienne.* Patristica Sorbonensia, no. 6. Paris: Éditions du Seuil, 1963.

Jonas, Hans. *Gnosis und Spätantiker Geist.* Pt. 2/1: *Von der Mythologie zur mystischen Philosophie.* Forschungen zur Religion und Literatur des Alten und Neuen Testaments, no. 63 (n.s. 45). Göttingen: Vandenhoeck & Ruprecht, 1954.

Kahn, Jean-George. "Did Philo Know Hebrew?" *Tarbitz* 34 (1965): 337–45 (Hebrew).

——. "Israel–Videns Deum." *Tarbitz* 43 (1971): 285–92 (Hebrew).

Kasher, Aryeh. "The Term *Politeia* in Philo and Josephus." Appendix in *The Jews in Hellenistic and Roman Egypt: The Struggle for Equal Rights*, 358–64. Texte und Studien zum Antiken Judentum, ed. Martin Hengel and Peter Schäfer. Tübingen: J. C. B. Mohr (Paul Siebeck), 1985.

Kasher, Menahem M. *Encyclopedia of Biblical Interpretation: A Millennial Anthology*, translated under Harry Freedman, ed. 9 vols. New York: American Biblical Encyclopedia Society, 1953–79.

Kaufmann, Yehezkel. *History of the Religion of Israel.* Vol. 4: *From the Babylonian Captivity to the End of Prophecy*, trans. C. W. Efroymson. New York: Ktav, 1977.

Kirk, Kenneth E. *The Vision of God: The Christian Doctrine of the Summum Bonum.* New York: Harper & Row, 1931.

Kittel, Gerhard. *Theological Dictionary of the New Testament*, trans. and ed., Geoffrey W. Bromiley. 10 vols. Grand Rapids, Michigan: Eerdmans, 1964–76.

Knox, Wilfred Lawrence. "Abraham and the Quest for God." *Harvard Theological Review* 28 (1935): 55–61.

Kugel, James. "Two Introductions to Midrash." *Prooftexts* 3 (1983): 131–55.

Kuhn, Karl Georg. "Ἰσραήλ, Ἰουδαῖος, Ἑβραῖος in Jewish Literature after the OT." In vol. 3 of *Theological Dictionary of the New Testament*, 359–69.

——. "προσήλυτος." In vol. 6 of *Theological Dictionary of the New Testament*, 727–44.

Lactantius. *De Mortibus Persecutorum*, ed. J. L. Creed. Oxford: Oxford University Press, 1984.

Lamberton, Robert and John J. Keaney, eds. *Homer's Ancient Readers: The Hermeneutics of Greek Epic's Earliest Exegetes.* Princeton: Princeton University Press, 1992.

Lampe, Geoffrey William Hugo. *A Patristic Greek Lexicon.* Oxford: Clarendon Press, 1961.

Lease, G. "Jewish Mystery Cults Since Goodenough." In *Aufstieg und Niedergang der römischen Welt: Geschichte und Kultur Roms im Spiegel der neueren Forschung.* Pt. 2, vol. 20, sec. 2: *Religion (Hellenistisches Judentum in römischer Zeit: Allgemeines)*, ed. Wolfgang Haase, 858–80. Berlin: de Gruyter, 1987.

Leisegang, Hans. *Der heilige Geist: Das wesen und werden der mystisch-intuitiven Erkenntnis in der Philosophie und Religion der Griechen.* Leipzig: B. G. Teubner, 1919.

Levenson, Jon D. *Sinai and Zion: An Entry into the Jewish Bible.* New Voices in Biblical Studies, ed. Adela Yarbro Collins and John J. Collins. San Francisco: Harper & Row, 1985.

——. *The Universal Horizon of Biblical Particularism.* Jewish Perspectives. New York: American Jewish Committee, 1985.

Levine, Baruch A. "First Fruits." In vol. 6 of *Encyclopedia Judaica*, 1312–16.

——. "Firstborn." In vol. 6 of *Encyclopedia Judaica*, 1306–12.

Lewy, Hans. *Sobria Ebrietas: Untersuchungen zur Geschichte der antiken Mystik.* Beihefte zur Zeitschrift für die neutestamentliche Wissenschaft und die Kunde der älteren Kirche, no. 9. Giessen: Alfred Töpelmann, 1929.

Lieberman, Saul. *Greek in Jewish Palestine: Studies in Life and Manners of Jewish Palestine in the II–IV Centuries C.E.* New York: Feldheim, 1965.

Long, A. A. *Hellenistic Philosophy: Stoics, Epicureans, Sceptics.* 2nd ed. London: Duckworth, 1986.

Louth, Andrew. *The Origins of the Christian Mystical Tradition From Plato to Denys.* Oxford: Clarendon Press, 1981.

Lubarsky, Sandra B. *Tolerance and Transformation: Jewish Approaches to Religious Pluralism.* Cincinnati: Hebrew Union College Press, 1990.

Mack, Burton L. "Exegetical Traditions in Alexandrian Judaism: A Program for the Analysis of the Philonic Corpus." *Studia Philonica* 3 (1974–75): 71–112.

———. "Imitatio Mosis: Patterns of Cosmology and Soteriology in the Hellenistic Synagogue." *Studia Philonica* 1 (1972): 27–55.

———. *Logos und Sophia: Untersuchungen zur Weisheittheologie im hellenistischen Judentum.* Studien zur Umwelt des Neuen Testaments, ed. Karl Georg Kuhn, vol. 10. Göttingen: Vandenhoeck & Ruprecht, 1973.

———. "Philo Judaeus and Exegetical Traditions in Alexandria." In *Aufstieg und Niedergang der römischen Welt: Geschichte und Kultur Roms im Spiegel der neueren Forschung.* Pt. 2, vol. 21, sec. 1: *Religion (Hellenistisches Judentum in römischer Zeit: Philon und Josephus),* ed. Wolfgang Haase, 227–71. Berlin: de Gruyter, 1984.

———. "Weisheit und Allegorie bei Philo von Alexandrien: Untersuchungen zur Traktat *De Congressu eruditionis.*" *Studia Philonica* 5 (1978): 57–105.

Mantel, Hugo D. "Did Philo Know Hebrew?" *Tarbitz* 32 (1962): 98–99 (Hebrew).

Martin-Achard, Robert. *A Light to the Nations: A Study of the Old Testament Conception of Israel's Mission to the World,* trans. John Penney Smith. Edinburgh: Oliver and Boyd, 1962.

Massebieau, M. L. "Le classement des oeuvres de Philon." *Bibliothèque de l'École des Hautes Études: Sciences religieuses* 1 (1889): 1–91.

Mauch, T. M. "Sojourner." In vol. 4 of *Interpreter's Dictionary of the Bible,* 397–99.

McCarthy, Dennis J. *Treaty and Covenant: A Study in Form in the Ancient Oriental Documents and in the Old Testament.* 2nd ed. Analecta Biblica, 21. Rome: Biblical Institute, 1978.

McEleney, N. J. "Conversion, Circumcision, and the Law." *New Testament Studies* 20 (1974): 319–41.

McKnight, Scot. *A Light Among the Gentiles: Jewish Missionary Activity in the Second Temple Period.* Minneapolis: Fortress Press, 1991.

Meek, Theophile James. "The Translation of *Ger* in the Hexateuch and Its Bearing on the Documentary Hypothesis." *Journal of Biblical Literature* 49 (1930): 172–80.

Meeks, Wayne A. "The Divine Agent and His Counterfeit in Philo and the Fourth Gospel." In *Aspects of Religious Propaganda in Judaism and Early Christianity,* ed. Elisabeth Schüssler Fiorenza, 43–67. Notre Dame: University of Notre Dame Press, 1976.

Mendelson, Alan. *Philo's Jewish Identity.* Brown Judaic Studies, ed. Jacob Neusner, no. 161. Atlanta: Scholars Press, 1988.

———. *Secular Education in Philo of Alexandria.* Monographs of the Hebrew Union College, no. 7. Cincinnati: Hebrew Union College Press, 1982.

Mendenhall, George E. *Law and Covenant in Israel and the Ancient Near East.* Pittsburgh: Biblical Colloquium, 1955.

Michaelis, Wilhelm. "ὁράω." In vol. 5 of *Theological Dictionary of the New Testament,* 315–67.

Michel, Alain. "La *métanoia* chez Philon d'Alexandrie: De Platon au Judéo-Christianisme en passant par Cicéron." *Augustinus* 32 (1987): 105–20.

Miles, John A., Jr. "Radical Editing, *Redaktionsgeschichte* and the Aesthetic of Willed Confusion." In *Traditions in Transformation: Turning Points in Biblical Faith*, ed. Baruch Halpern and Jon D. Levenson, 9–31. Winona Lake, Indiana: Eisenbrauns, 1981.

Moore, George Foote. *Judaism in the First Centuries of the Christian Era: The Age of the Tannaim.* 2 vols. New York: Schocken Books, 1958.

Morris, Jenny. "The Jewish Philosopher Philo." In vol. 3, pt. 2 of Emil Schürer, *The History of the Jewish People in the Age of Jesus Christ, (175 B.C.–A.D. 135)*, rev. and ed. Geza Vermes, Fergus Millar, and Martin Goodman, 809–89. Edinburgh: T. & T. Clark, 1987.

Myre, André. "La loi de la nature et la loi mosaïque selon Philon d'Alexandrie." *Science et Esprit* 28 (1976): 163–81.

Neumark, Hermann. *Die Verwendung griechischer und jüdischer Motive in den Gedanken Philons über die Stellung Gottes zu seinen Freunden.* Dissertation, Würzburg, 1937.

Neusner, Jacob. "Israel: Judaism and Its Social Metaphors." *Journal of the American Academy of Religion* 50 (1978): 331–61.

———. *Judaism and Its Social Metaphors: Israel in the History of Jewish Thought.* Cambridge: Cambridge University Press, 1989.

Nicholson, Ernest Wilson. *Deuteronomy and Tradition.* Philadelphia: Fortress Press, 1967.

Nikiprowetzky, Valentin. "Brève note sur le *Commentaire Allégorique* et l'*Exposition de la Loi* chez Philon d'Alexandrie." In *Mélanges bibliques et orientaux en l'honneur de M. Mathias Delcor*, ed. André Caquot, S. Légasse, and M. Tardieu, 321–29. Kevelaer: Butzon & Bercker, 1985.

———. *Le commentaire de l'Écriture chez Philon d'Alexandrie: Son caractère et sa portée; Observations philologiques.* Arbeiten zur Literatur und Geschichte des hellenistischen Judentums, ed. K. H. Rengstorf, no. 11. Leiden: E. J. Brill, 1977.

Nock, Arthur Darby. *Conversion: The Old and the New in Religion from Alexander the Great to Augustine of Hippo.* Oxford: Oxford University Press, 1933.

Nolland, J. "Uncircumcised Proselytes?" *Journal for the Study of Judaism* 12 (1981): 173–94.

Orlinsky, Harry M. "Nationalism-Universalism and Internationalism in Ancient Israel." In *Translating & Understanding the Old Testament: Essays in Honor of Herbert Gordon May*, ed. Harry Thomas Frank and William L. Reed, 206–36. Nashville: Abingdon Press, 1970.

Pascher, Joseph. ἡ βασιλικὴ ὁδός : *Der Königsweg zu Wiedergeburt und Vergottung bei Philon von Alexandreia.* Studien zur Geschichte und Kultur des Alterums, vol. 17, nos. 3–4. Paderborn: Schoningh, 1931; repr., [1968].

Pépin, Jean. *Mythe et allégorie: les origines grecques et les contestations judéo-chrétiennes.* Rev. ed. Paris: Études augustiniennes, 1976.

Petit, Madeleine. "Exploitations non-bibliques des thèmes de Tamar et de Genèse 38: Philon d'Alexandrie, textes et traditions juives jusqu'aux Talmudim." In *Alexandrina: Hellenisme, judaïsme et christianisme à Alexandrie, Mélanges offerts au P. Claude Mondésert, S.J.*, 77–115. Paris: Éditions du Cerf, 1987.

"Philo and Middle Platonism." In a Special Section of *The Studia Philonica Annual* 5 (1993): 95–155.

Rabbe, Paul R. "Deliberate Ambiguity in the Psalter." *Journal of Biblical Literature* 110 (1991): 213–27.

Rahlfs, Alfred, ed. *Septuaginta: Id est Vetus Testamentum graece iuxta LXX interpretes*, 8th ed. 2 vols. Stuttgart: Württembergische Bibelanstalt, 1965, ©1935.

Rainey, Anson F. "Hebrews." In *Harper's Bible Dictionary*, ed. Paul J. Achtemeier, 378–80. San Francisco: Harper & Row, 1985.

Rokeah, David. "A New Onomasticon Fragment from Oxyrhynchus and Philo's Etymologies." *Journal of Theological Studies* 19 (1968): 70–82.

Rosenbloom, Joseph R. *Conversion to Judaism: From the Biblical Period to the Present.* Cincinnati: Hebrew Union College Press, 1978.

Rowley, Harold Henry. *The Biblical Doctrine of Election.* London: Lutterworth Press, 1952.

Runia, David T. *Exegesis and Philosophy: Studies on Philo of Alexandria.* Variorum Collected Studies. Hampshire, Great Britain: Variorum, 1990.

———. "How to Read Philo." *Nederlands Theologisch Tijdschrift* 40 (1986): 185–98. See also Runia, David T. *Exegesis and Philosophy*, Study II.

———. "How to Search Philo." *The Studia Philonica Annual* 2 (1990): 106–39.

———. *Philo of Alexandria and the Timaeus of Plato.* Philosophia Antiqua, ed. W. J. Verdenius and J. C. M. van Winden, vol. 44. Leiden: E. J. Brill, 1986.

———. Review of *La philosophie de Moïse*, by Richard Goulet. In *Journal of Theological Studies* 40 (1989): 588–602. See also Runia, David T. *Exegesis and Philosophy*, Study VII.

———. "Underneath Cohn and Colson: The Text of Philo's *De Virtutibus*." In *Society of Biblical Literature 1991 Seminar Papers*, 116–34. Society of Biblical Literature Seminar Paper Series, ed. Eugene H. Lovering, Jr., no. 30. Atlanta: Scholars Press, 1991.

———. "Was Philo a Middle Platonist? a Difficult Question Revisited." *The Studia Philonica Annual* 5 (1993): 112–40.

Sacchse, E. "Die Etymologie und älteste Aussprache des Namens ישראל." *Zeitschrift für die alttestamentliche Wissenschaft* 34 (1914): 1–15.

Sanders, E. P. "The Covenant as a Soteriological Category and the Nature of Salvation in Palestinian and Hellenistic Judaism." In *Jews, Greeks and Christians: Religious Cultures in Late Antiquity*, ed. Robert Hamerton-Kelly and Robin Scroggs, 11–44. Leiden: E. J. Brill, 1976.

Sandmel, Samuel. *Philo of Alexandria: An Introduction.* New York: Oxford University Press, 1979.

———. "Philo's Knowledge of Hebrew." *Studia Philonica* 5 (1978): 107–11.

———. *Philo's Place in Judaism: A Study of Conceptions of Abraham in Jewish Literature.* Augmented ed. New York: Ktav, 1971.

Schmidt, K. L. and M. A. "πάροικος, παροικία, παροικέω." In vol. 5 of *Theological Dictionary of the New Testament*, 841–53.

Schürer, Emil. The history of the Jewish people in the age of Jesus Christ (175 B.C.–A.D. 135). A New English Version, rev. and ed., Geza Vermes, Fergus Millar, and Martin Goodman. 3 vols. in 4. Edinburgh: T. & T. Clark, 1973–87.

Segal, Alan F. "The Costs of Proselytism and Conversion." In *Society of Biblical Literature 1988 Seminar Papers*, 336–69. Society of Biblical Literature Seminar Paper Series, ed. David J. Lull, no. 27. Atlanta: Scholars Press, 1988.

———. "Covenant in Rabbinic Writings." Chapter in *The Other Judaisms of Late Antiquity*, 148–65. Brown Judaic Studies, ed. Jacob Neusner, no. 127. Atlanta: Scholars Press, 1987.

———. "Heavenly Ascent in Hellenistic Judaism, Early Christianity, and their Environment." In *Aufstieg und Niedergang der Römischen Welt: Geschichte und Kultur Roms im Spiegel der neueren Forschung*. Pt. 2, vol. 23 sec. 2: *Religion (Vorkonstantinisches Christentum: Verhältnis zu römischem Staat und heidnischer Religion [Forts.])*, ed. Wolfgang Haase, 1333–94. Berlin: de Gruyter, 1980.

——. *Paul the Convert: The Apostolate and Apostasy of Saul the Pharisee*. New Haven: Yale University Press, 1990.

——. *Rebecca's Children: Judaism and Christianity in the Roman World*. Cambridge: Harvard University Press, 1986.

Shroyer, Montgomery J. "Alexandrian Jewish Literalists." *Journal of Biblical Literature* 55 (1936): 261–84.

Siegfried, Carl. *Philo von Alexandria als Ausleger des alten Testaments: an sich selbst und nach seinem geschichtlichen Einfluss betrachtet*. Jena: Hermann Dufft, 1875.

Smith, Jonathan Z. "Prayer of Joseph." In vol. 2 of *Old Testament Pseudepigrapha*, ed. James H. Charlesworth, 699–714. Garden City, New York: Doubleday, 1985.

——. "The Prayer of Joseph." In *Religions in Antiquity: Essays in Memory of Erwin Ramsdell Goodenough*, ed. Jacob Neusner, 253–94. Studies in the History of Religions (Supplements to *Numen*), no. 14. Leiden: E. J. Brill, 1968.

Smith, R. Payne, ed. *Thesaurus Syriacus*, 1:163. Cited by E. Mary Smallwood, ed. and trans. *Philonis Alexandrini: Legatio ad Gaium*, 153–54. See in this Bibliography under Texts, Translations, and Indices of Philo's Works.

Sohn, Seock-Tae. *The Divine Election of Israel*. Grand Rapids, Michigan: Eerdmans, 1991.

Speiser, Ephraim A., ed. *Genesis*. Vol. 1 of *The Anchor Bible*, ed. William Foxwell Albright and David Noel Freedman. Garden City, New York: Doubleday, 1964.

Stanford, William B. *Ambiguity in Greek Literature: Studies in Theory and Practice*. Oxford: Basil Blackwell, 1939; repr., New York: Johnson Reprint Corporation, 1972.

Stein, Edmund. *Die allegorische Exegese des Philos aus Alexandreia*. Beihefte zur Zeitschrift für die alttestamentliche Wissenschaft, no. 51. Giessen: Alfred Töpelmann, 1929.

——. "Zur apokryphen Schrift 'Gebet Josephs.'" *Monatsschrift für Geschichte und Wissenschaft des Judentums* 81 (1937): 280–86.

Sterling, Gregory E. "Philo's *Quaestiones*: Prolegomena or Afterthought?" See Hay, David M., ed. *Both Literal and Allegorical*, 99–123.

——. "Platonizing Moses: Philo and Middle Platonism." *The Studia Philonica Annual* 5 (1993): 96–111.

Stern, David. "Midrash and Indeterminancy." *Critical Inquiry* 15 (1988): 132–61.

Sternberg, Meir. *The Poetics of Biblical Narrative: Ideological Literature and the Drama of Reading*. Bloomington, Indiana: Indiana University Press, 1985.

Strathmann, Hermann. "πόλις, κτλ." In vol. 6 of *Theological Dictionary of the New Testament*, 516–35.

Strauss, Leo. *Persecution and the Art of Writing*. New York: Free Press, 1952; repr., Chicago: University of Chicago Press, 1988.

Tcherikover, Victor. "Jewish Apologetic Literature." *Eos* 48/3 (1956): 169–93.

Tobin, Thomas H. *The Creation of Man: Philo and the History of Interpretation*. Catholic Biblical Quarterly Monograph Series, no. 14. Washington D.C.: The Catholic Biblical Association of America, 1983.

——. "Tradition and Interpretation in Philo's Portrait of the Patriarch Joseph." In *Society of Biblical Literature 1986 Seminar Papers*, 271–77. Society of Biblical Literature Seminar Papers Series, ed. Kent Harold Richards, no. 25. Atlanta: Scholars Press, 1986.

——. "Was Philo a Middle Platonist? Some suggestions." *The Studia Philonica Annual* 5 (1993): 147–50.

Tomson, Peter J. "The Names Israel and Jew in Ancient Judaism and in the New Testament."*Bijdragen* 47 (1986): 120–40, 266–289.
Urbach, Ephraim E. *The Sages: Their Concepts and Beliefs*, trans. Israel Abrahams. Cambridge: Harvard University Press, 1987.
———. "Self-Isolation or Self-Affirmation in Judaism in the First Three Centuries: Theory and Practice." In *Jewish and Christian Self-Definition*. Vol. 2: *Aspects of Judaism in the Greco-Roman Period*, ed. E. P. Sanders with A. I. Baumgarten and Alan Mendelson, 269–98. Philadelphia: Fortress Press, 1981.
Vanderlinden, E. "Les divers modes de connaissance de Dieu selon Philon d'Alexandrie." *Mélanges de Science Religieuse* 4 (1947): 285–304.
Völker, Walther. *Fortschritt und Vollendung bei Philo von Alexandrien: Eine Studie zur Geschichte der Frömmigkeit.* Texte und Untersuchungen zur Geschichte der altchristlichen Literatur 49:1. Leipzig: J. C. Hinrichs, 1938.
von Rad, Gerhard. *Old Testament Theology*, trans. D. M. G. Stalker. 2 vols. New York: Harper & Row, 1962 and 1965.
Walter, Nikolaus. *Der Thoraausleger Aristobulos: Untersuchungen zu seinen Fragmenten und zu pseudepigraphischen Resten der jüdische-hellenistischen Literatur.* Texte und Untersuchungen zur Geschichte der altchristlichen Literatur, vol. 86. Berlin: Akademie Verlag, 1964.
Wan, Sze-kar. "Philo's *Quaestiones et solutiones in Genesim et in Exodum*: A Synoptic Approach." Th.D. dissertation, Harvard University, 1992.
Weinfeld, Moshe. *Deuteronomy and the Deuteronomic School.* Oxford: Clarendon Press, 1972.
Winston, David. "Freedom and Determinism in Greek Philosophy." *Studia Philonica* 2 (1973): 40–50.
———. "Judaism and Hellenism: Hidden Tensions in Philo's Thought." *The Studia Philonica Annual* 2 (1990): 1–19.
———. *Logos and Mystical Theology in Philo of Alexandria.* Cincinnati: Hebrew Union College Press, 1985.
———. "Response to Runia and Sterling." *The Studia Philonica Annual* 5 (1993): 141–46.
———. "Was Philo a Mystic?" *Studies in Jewish Mysticism*, ed. Joseph Dan and Frank Talmage, 15–39. Cambridge: Association for Jewish Studies, 1982.
———, ed. *The Wisdom of Solomon.* Vol. 43 of *The Anchor Bible*, ed. William Foxwell Albright and David Noel Freedman. Garden City, N.Y.: Doubleday, 1979.
Wlosok, Antonie. *Laktanz und die philosophische Gnosis: Untersuchungen zu Geschichte und Terminologie der gnostischen Erlösungsvorstellung.* Abhandlung der Heidelberger Akademie der Wissenschaften, Philosophisch-historische Klasse, no. 2. Heidelberg: Carl Winter, Universitätsverlag, 1960.
Wolfson, Harry A. *Philo: Foundations of Religious Philosophy in Judaism, Christianity, and Islam.* 2 vols. Cambridge: Harvard University Press, 1975; repr., 1982.
Wong, C. K. "Philo's Use of *Chaldaioi.*" *The Studia Philonica Annual* 4 (1992): 1–14.
Zeitlin, Solomon. "The Names Hebrew, Jew and Israel: A Historical Study." *Jewish Quarterly Review* 43 (1952–53): 365–79.

INDICES

Index of Passages

References to passages are listed in two separate indices under 1) Bible, Apocrypha/Pseudepigrapha, New Testament; and 2) Philonic Works. References to other ancient sources are included in the Index of Subjects under the author or title.

Bible, Apocrypha/Pseudepigrapha, New Testament

Biblical passages shown below are listed as they are discussed in this book and may be cited from the Hebrew Bible or the Greek, depending upon the context of the discussion. Occasionally verse numbers differ slightly in the Hebrew and Greek. Biblical books in this index follow the order of the Jewish Bible.

BIBLE

Genesis

2:8	19n.36
4:3	135, 136
11:10	110
12-13	60n.97
12:1	202n.28, 203n.29
12:1-3	128n.1, 139, 167, 180, 182, 183n.62
12:2	139
12:3	168n.20, 168n.21, 178, 180, 181
12:7	78, 79, 128n.1, 182n.61
12:10-20	179, 180, 183
15:4	87, 88
15:5	88n.79, 180n.59
15:6	182n.61, 205n.35
15:13-16	128n.1
15:18	182n.61
15:18-21	128n.1
17:1	78, 79, 129n.3
17:1-14	128n.1, 182
17:2	135n.11
17:4-6	180n.59
17:5	183n.62
17:5-8	182
17:8	182n.61
17:9-14	182
17:11	125n.47
17:12	155
17:16	128n.1
17:17	110
17:19-21	128n.1
18:1-3	86-87, 88
18:17-19	182

18:18	167n.20, 180n.59
18:18-19	128n.1
18:19	129n.3
22:15-18	182
22:17	180n.59
22:17-18	128n.1
22:18	129n.3, 167n.20
23:4	197n.13
23:6	206
25:8	56
25:23	56n.90
26:2-5	128n.1
26:4	167n.20, 168n.23
26:5	129n.3
26:24	128n.1
28:13-15	128n.1
28:14	167n.20, 168n.23
32	90, 97, 98, 223
32:25-33	74, 78, 79, 96
32:29	71
32:31	71, 72, 73
35:9-12	128n.1
35:29	56, 57
46:1	62n.2
49:33	56
50:24-25	109

Exodus

1:9	50n.69
2:22	197n.13, 198n.13
2:23	65
3:6	79
3:14	84
4:22	171, 173, 188

APOCRYPHA/PSEUDEPIGRAPHA

NEW TESTAMENT

Index of Passages

Philonic Works

Philonic treatises are listed in alphabetical order of their abbreviations. For a list of abbreviations, which also shows the series or category to which treatises belong, see p. xvii. References to discussion of whole treatises are included in the Index of Subjects under the treatise abbreviation.

Abr. *(De Abrahamo)*

3-5	157n.32
5	157
17-26	203
56-59	33, 145n.18
57	44, 48n.61, 49, 49n.67, 112n.27, 120n.41, 122, 144n.17
57-58	79, 80
57-59	89n.83
58	122
60-80	183n.62
69-71	79
77-80	89n.83
80	80
81-83	183n.62
89-98	179-80
90	183
95	183
98	162n.7, 166, 172, 173, 179-83, 184
119-23	87n.75, 89n.81, 89n.83, 89n.84
119-30	98n.15
122	79
251	46n.50

Cher. *(De Cherubim)*

108	195n.5, 197n.13, 198
119-21	195n.5, 197n.13, 198

Conf. *(De Confusione Linguarum)*

36	64
56	53, 125n.46, 133, 133n.10, 154n.27
70	52n.78, 54n.85
72	49, 66
82	198n.13
92	66n.14
92-93	63n.4
93	64

95-97	80
146	74-76, 95n.7, 101n.18

Congr. *(De Congressu Quaerendae Eruditionis Gratia)*

43-53	108
50	108
51	53, 108-9, 121
51-52	108
86	63n.5

Contempl. *(De Vita Contemplativa)*

11	77n.49, 94, 98n.15, 182n.60
57-64	118n.37
85-87	59

Decal. *(De Decalogo)*

1-49	125n.47
53-65	167
66-76	167
76-80	167

Det. *(Quod Deterius Potiori Insidiari Solet)*

67	132
67-68	132n.7
94	64, 65
158-60	79

Deus *(Quod Deus Immutabilis Sit)*

69	145n.19
121	64
144-45	63n.4
145	65
148	50n.67

Ebr. *(De Ebrietate)*

77	64
82	63n.3, 66
82-83	79
94	107n.22

Index of Greek Terms

Page numbers in bold print refer to especially significant discussions. Under Ἰσραήλ (Israel), continuation pages in parentheses indicate that after its initial appearance, the Greek term is discussed in its English translation. Definite articles have been omitted. ¯

Index of Modern Scholars

Index of Subjects

Abraham
and Chaldea, 47, 60, 202
and circumcision, 153, 155, 182
and covenant, 128n.1, 135n.11, 153,
182
and divine blessings, 167-68, 180,
182
as founder of the Jewish nation,
161
in Philo and the Rabbis, 3
Philonic interpretations about, 56-
58, 86-87, 88, 110, 179-83
and proselytes, 198n.17, 201, 202,
205, 206, 214, 216
as a seer, 93
See also Patriarchs
Aet., 58, 160
Alexander the Great, 1
Allegorical interpretation, 2, 22, 109-
10, 121, 139, 143, 206
Allegory (Philonic exegetical series)
audience, 18-19, 55-56, 89-90, 116,
121-22, 144, 159, 210, 222
Biblical Israel in, 44, 158-59
Chaldean in, 47, 108-9
characteristics of, 18-19, 89
chosen people, race/class, or entity
in, 133, 137-38, 143, 158-59
covenant in, 134-35, 143, 158-59
divine election in, 136-39, 140, 142-
43, 144
etymology of "Israel" in, 49, 108,
121, 121n.42, 138
great nation in, 139-42
Hebrews in, 46
"Israel" in, 26, 40, 44, 48, 49, 55,
117, 210, 221, 222
"Israel seers" in, 108-11, 115-16,
121-22
Jews and, 26, 40, 44, 45, 55, 160-61,
210, 222
nation in, 50
people in, 50
polity in, 51
proselytes in, 199, 216
race/class in, 52-54
race/class that can see in, 99, 109-
11, 121
seeing God in, 89-90, 116
Ambiguity, 25-29
and audience, 28-29

and polysemous words, 26, 28
purpose of, 27-29
See also "Israel," ambiguity of, in
Philo; Philo, and ambiguity
Aristeas, Letter of, 24
Aristobulus, 24
Aristotle, 82
Athenians, as seers, 94, 119
Audience(s), Philo's adaptations of
discussions for
in presentation of a half-Egyptian
man, 105, 123
in presentation of "Israel seers,"
122
in presentation of Jews, 118, 126-27,
161, 172, 173, 178, 182-83, 188-89,
191, 192, 210
in presentation of the relationship
between God and Biblical Israel,
144, 152, 158-59, 172, 173, 178, 188-
89, 192
in presentation of seeing God, 89-
90, 117, 122, 126-27, 191, 210
in use of Egyptian setting, 183
in use of "Israel" and Jews, 28-29,
55-56, 117, 126-27, 191, 210, 221-22
in use of the race/class that can see,
99
See also under individual series; Philo

Balaam, oracles of, 48-49
Bible. *See* Septuagint

Chaldean
in the Allegory, 47, 108-9
in the Exposition, 47, 48
in non-exegetical works, 60
in QGE, 47
Chosen people, race/class, or entity,
133, 134, 224
in the Allegory, 133, 137-38, 143,
158-59
distribution of references throughout
Philo's works, 133
in the Exposition, 133, 149-50, 152,
159
Greek terms for, 133, 133n.10
and "Israel," 53, 63n.3, 106-7,
125n.46
as mind of a worthy person, 149-50,
152, 159

Jews *(cont'd)*
Philo's positive presentation of, 123, 126-27, 161-62, 164, 178, 185-86, 210
as a polity, 52, 59, 213, 214-15, 217, 230
as priesthood for all humanity, 163, 166-69, 179, 180, 184-86, 186, 187-88, 189, 190, 212
as prophet, 179, 180-81, 181n.60
and proselytes, 13, 208-9, 216-17, 218, 219, 224
in QGE, 44, 45, 56, 161
relationship with God, 13, 34-35, 162-63, 164, 166, 192, 211-12, 213, 218, 223-24, 225, 228
and seeing God, 163, 163n.11, 189, 192, 212, 225
and terminology, 5n.4, 12n.22, 14, 45, 160-61
and worship of God, 116, 163, 164-66, 184, 212, 213, 223, 230
Josephus, 38, 170n.32, 203n.32
Judaism
Greek term for, 3, 3n.2
and Hellenism, 1
legal aspect of, 229
as only first-century monotheistic religion, 13, 228
Philo's estimation of, 228-30
Philo's presentation of, 116, 118, 126-27, 150, 191
philosophical aspect of, 229-30
and proselytes, 13, 193-94
social aspect of, 214-15, 228, 230
Judaisms, 38-39

Kinship, 34, 42, 53, 170n.28, 189, 189n.72, 203, 213, 214, 215

Lactantius, 20n.42
Land, in Philo, 182n.61, 184, 184n.64, 186
Law
as divine, 114, 157
giving of the, 125, 125n.47, 154
See also Commandments; Divine election, and giving of the law, in QGE; Jews, laws and customs of
Legat., 18, 20-21, 117, 134, 162, 174, 210, 229-30
audience, 20-21, 126-27, 210, 222
Jews in, 40, 44, 58-59, 106n.22, 160, 162
only treatise that has "Israel" and Jews together, 12-13, 26, 36n.20, 44, 60, 100, 210, 221

polity in, 59, 215
purpose of, 20-21, 174, 191, 210, 222
Levites
as priests, 187-88
as suppliants, 107n.22
Literal sense, 17, 19, 27, 65, 116, 133, 134, 138, 152, 159
See also QGE, literal interpretations in

Magi, 93, 119, 224, 225
Method, 14-16, 220-21
and ambiguity in Philo, 25-26
and analysis of passages, 15-16, 86-88
and categorization of Philo's use of "Israel," 62-63
and other scholarly approaches, 43
and seeing God in Philo, 86-90
and selection of passages, 14, 15, 17-18, 91-92, 101-2, 162, 204
Middle Platonism, 22, 82
Monotheism, 13, 167, 226, 228
Mos. 1-2, 19n.39, 45n.49, 46, 89n.83, 103, 104, 105, 131-32
absence of "Israel" in, 27, 28, 48, 100, 103, 120, 123, 222
Moses
addresses to Biblical Israel, 130, 145, 146, 148
as a Chaldean, 60n.97
disciples of, 5n.4, 40, 202
and divine authority of the Bible, 17
and divine providence, 179n.57
as lawgiver of the Jews, 58, 160n.1, 161
in *Mos.* 1-2, 132
as a national or universal figure, 4
Philonic interpretations about, 84, 114, 165
and request to see God, 79, 84
as a seer, 93
Mystery language, 22-23, 41, 79, 81
Mysticism, 5, 10

Nation
in the Allegory, 50
in the Exposition, 51
in non-exegetical works, 58, 59
and people, 50-51, 56n.90
in QGE, 54-55
Neopythagorean writings, 82
Nobility of birth, 203, 213, 214
Non-exegetical works
audience, 20-21
Biblical Israel in, 59-60, 134
Chaldean in, 60